EISENHOWER VS. WARREN

ALSO BY JAMES F. SIMON

FDR and Chief Justice Hughes: The President,
the Supreme Court, and the Epic Battle Over the New Deal

Lincoln and Chief Justice Taney:
Slavery, Secession, and the President's War Powers

What Kind of Nation: Thomas Jefferson,
John Marshall, and the Epic Struggle to Create a United States

The Center Holds: The Power Struggle Inside the Rehnquist Court

The Antagonists: Hugo Black, Felix Frankfurter,
and Civil Liberties in Modern America

Independent Journey: The Life of William O. Douglas

The Judge

In His Own Image: The Supreme Court in Richard Nixon's America

EISENHOWER VS. WARREN

*The Battle for Civil Rights
and Liberties*

JAMES F. SIMON

LIVERIGHT PUBLISHING CORPORATION
A DIVISION OF W. W. NORTON & COMPANY
Independent Publishers Since 1923
NEW YORK   LONDON

For information about permission to reproduce selections from this book,
write to Permissions, Liveright Publishing Corporation, a division of
W. W. Norton & Company, Inc., 500 Fifth Avenue, New York, NY 10110

For information about special discounts for bulk purchases, please contact
W. W. Norton Special Sales at specialsales@wwnorton.com or 800-233-4830

Manufacturing by Quad Graphics Fairfield
Book design by Brian Mulligan
Production manager: Julia Druskin

ISBN 978-0-87140-755-9

Liveright Publishing Corporation, 500 Fifth Avenue, New York, N.Y. 10110
www.wwnorton.com

W. W. Norton & Company Ltd., 15 Carlisle Street, London W1D 3BS

1 2 3 4 5 6 7 8 9 0

To the memory of five exceptional teachers:

Margaret Sullivan and Nancy Vick,
McLean Junior High School, Fort Worth, Texas

Alexander M. Bickel, John Morton Blum, and Fred Rodell,
Yale University

You call Lincoln a radical, but every bit of reading I have done on his life convinces me that in many ways he was the greatest compromiser and the most astute master of expedience that we have known. I believe that the true radical is the fellow who is standing in the middle and battling both extremes.

—*President Dwight D. Eisenhower*
to Brigadier General Bradford G. Chynoweth[1]

Through politics, which has been defined as the art of the possible, progress could be made and most often was made by compromising and taking half a loaf where a whole loaf could not be obtained. The opposite is true so far as the judicial process was concerned. Through it, and particularly in the Supreme Court, the basic ingredient of decision is principle, and it should not be compromised and parceled out a little in one case, a little more in another, until eventually someone receives the full benefit. If the principle is sound and constitutional, it is the birthright of every American, not to be accorded begrudgingly or piecemeal or to special groups only, but to every one in its entirety whenever it is brought into play.

—*Chief Justice Earl Warren, recalling a conversation*
with retired President Eisenhower in which he distinguished the
obligations of the political and judicial branches of government[2]

[I]n the sixties, Eisenhower frequently remarked that his biggest mistake was "the appointment of that dumb son of a bitch Earl Warren."

—*Quoted in* Eisenhower: The President
by Stephen E. Ambrose[3]

Contents

PROLOGUE

FOR A PRESIDENT WHO WAS NOT A LAWYER, EISENHOWER had very firm ideas on the qualities he was looking for in a chief justice. His appointee must have a national reputation for honesty and fairness, possess wide experience in law and government, and be a statesman who could lead the court. When he announced his decision to appoint Governor Earl Warren of California to be Chief Justice of the United States on September 30, 1953, he praised Warren's character, his government experience, his moderate philosophy, and predicted that he would make "a great Chief Justice."[1]

Although the two men did not know each other well, the president and the new chief justice were photographed together in easy camaraderie shortly after Warren's appointment. Less than six months later, that camaraderie had evaporated, and so had their mutual respect.

The disintegration of their professional relationship began on the evening of February 8, 1954, at a White House stag dinner in which the chief justice, as the honored guest, was seated next to the president. Two months earlier, the court had heard oral arguments in *Brown v. Board of Education*, the legal challenge to public school segregation, and a decision was expected before the end of the judicial term. And yet the president seated John W. Davis, the attorney for South Carolina in the case, who had argued passionately against school desegregation, near Warren and told the chief justice what "a great man Mr. Davis was."[2] Later, Eisenhower compounded what Warren considered an unpardonable ethical lapse by taking him aside and assuring him that white southerners were not "bad people"[3] but only concerned that "their sweet little girls are not required to sit in school alongside some big overgrown Negroes."

Three months later, Warren announced the *Brown*[4] decision for a unanimous Supreme Court, declaring that the separation of public school students by race was unconstitutional. Within a few hours of the announcement of the *Brown* decision, the Voice of America had broadcast the news to foreign countries in thirty-five languages. The decision was widely acclaimed in the United States and later considered a catalyst for the modern civil rights movement in this country.

At his first press conference after the *Brown* decision was announced, Eisenhower's response was conspicuously brief. He said that the court's decision was now the law and should be obeyed. A year later, when the court handed down its implementation decision in *Brown*, ordering the dismantling of the segregated public school system in the South and border states "with all deliberate speed,"[5] the president's support remained minimal. The law should be obeyed, he said. But he also called for understanding of the white South where both custom and law had been turned upside down. Law alone, he said repeatedly, could not change people's hearts or minds.

Resistance to *Brown* in the Deep South quickly gained momentum. By legal maneuvering in court and violence and intimidation outside, the region effectively fought the court's *Brown* mandate throughout Eisenhower's presidency. Warren never forgave Eisenhower for his failure to put the prestige and moral force of the presidency behind the court's decision. Nor was he impressed when Eisenhower sent federal troops to Little Rock, Arkansas, in September 1957, to uphold the law. Warren thought that the president should have acted sooner to support *Brown* and to quell the violence that erupted when nine black teenagers attempted to integrate the city's Central High School.

A DECADE EARLIER, Eisenhower had earned his reputation as the superb military leader of Allied forces that defeated Germany in World War II. Although he had no combat experience before the war, he won the respect of field commanders and GIs alike for his uncanny ability to get the job done under the most excruciating pressure. As president, he also focused on accomplishing his objectives, which included averting violence in the Deep South after *Brown*. His "middle of the road" approach meant that he exhorted all Americans to uphold the law while counseling understanding of those in the Deep South who denounced the court's decision. That delicate balancing act required him to constantly preach respect for the law but, at the same time, show patience for those moderate leaders in the South who needed time to implement *Brown*.

In eliminating racial discrimination, Eisenhower's actions spoke louder than his words. He wielded his executive authority decisively to complete the desegregation of the armed forces. He also desegregated naval yards and public schools on military bases in the South, Veterans Administration hospitals, and public schools and restaurants in the District of Columbia. He appointed judges at all levels in the federal court system, including four Supreme Court justices after Warren, who supported the *Brown* decision. And he lobbied behind the scenes for the Civil Rights Acts of 1957 and 1960, the first civil rights legislation since Reconstruction.

Eisenhower never publicly criticized Warren's opinion for the court in *Brown*. But privately he complained that the court should have been more prudent and moved incrementally. During his second presidential term, when it was obvious that the *Brown* mandate was not being obeyed in the Deep South, Eisenhower cautioned his attorney general, William Rogers, to tone down a speech he had drafted that called for vigorous enforcement of the *Brown* decree. Complete desegregation of the public schools in the South, Eisenhower predicted, would take many years, perhaps decades, and it would be accomplished with persuasion and education, not solely by judicial mandate.

THE EISENHOWER-WARREN clash extended to the protection of civil liberties during the red-hunting McCarthy era. Eisenhower loathed the tactics of the reckless anti-Communist Wisconsin senator Joseph McCarthy, but never confronted him publicly. In a speech during his 1952 presidential campaign in Wisconsin, Eisenhower eliminated a paragraph in which he had defended General George C. Marshall, his mentor and boss during World War II, against McCarthy's baseless charges that Marshall was disloyal. After his election, Eisenhower adamantly refused to condemn McCarthy publicly, justifying his silence as a tactical decision to deprive the senator of the confrontation and publicity that he craved.

During Eisenhower's second presidential term, Chief Justice Warren often spoke for a court majority that upheld the constitutional rights of suspected Communists. Rabid anti-Communists in the Senate like Senator William Jenner of Indiana charged that the Warren Court rulings threatened national security and referred contemptuously to their "Red Monday" decisions. Eisenhower reacted angrily to many of those Warren Court decisions but confined his criticism to private conversations. When the president's criticism was reported in the press, he wrote the chief justice a brief letter saying that the press reports had exaggerated his reaction. Warren's reply was correct but frosty. Warren later recalled a conversation with Eisenhower in which the former president criticized "those Communist cases."[6]

How could two of the most revered American leaders of the twentieth century so profoundly disagree on their approach to the protection of basic civil rights and liberties? The lessons to be learned are as relevant and instructive today as they were more than fifty years ago.

EISENHOWER VS. WARREN

Chapter One

MAN OF
THE WEST

THE CALM, CONFIDENT FACE OF CALIFORNIA'S GOVER-
nor Earl Warren beamed from the cover of *Time* magazine on January
31, 1944. *Time* considered this "Man of the West"[1] the front-runner
for the Republican Party's vice-presidential nomination, presumably
on the ticket with New York governor Thomas E. Dewey in their party's challenge to President Franklin D. Roosevelt in November. *Life*
magazine went further, suggesting in a flattering story on Warren and
his large, photogenic family that the California governor might even
head his party's presidential ticket. Warren, fifty-two years old, had
become a star on the national political stage barely a year after he had
been elected to his first gubernatorial term.

The appeal of a Dewey-Warren ticket was obvious. Both men led
large states from opposite coasts with a treasure trove of electoral college votes. Both had earned reputations as fearless prosecutors who had
sent scores of corrupt officials, bootleggers, con men, and murderers to
prison. Both were dedicated family men without a scintilla of scandal
in their private lives. And they represented the moderate middle of
their party, not as liberal as the party's 1940 standard bearer, Wendell

Willkie, but more progressive than the leader of the conservative wing of the party, Ohio senator Robert A. Taft.

Warren offered a contrast in style and personality to Dewey. Whereas Dewey tirelessly promoted his image as an intrepid racket buster, Warren was more low-key, though he, too, cultivated reporters. Dewey was combative, while Warren seemed "to radiate goodness and warmth," impressing visitors with his "relaxed good nature" and "his evident simplicity."[2] *Time* reported that Warren's many admirers considered him not only to be "a perfect political candidate," but also the forerunner in U. S. politics to a new era of friendly men to succeed "the recent era of angry men."*

Nothing in Warren's speeches during his twenty-five years in public office could explain the adulation. He was neither scintillating in style nor original in policy. But his patient, indefatigable work ethic produced impressive results. In a mere seventy-one days of the state legislative session, Governor Warren had pushed through bills that reduced the state sales tax, increased old-age pensions, established a postwar reconstruction and reemployment commission, and earmarked $43 million of state funds for postwar development.

EARL WARREN'S FATHER, Methias "Matt" Warren, was an infant when his family emigrated to the United States in 1866 from southern Norway. Like many Scandinavian families in the mid-nineteenth century, the Warrens (anglicized from Varran) sought the open spaces of the upper Midwest that most resembled their native land. Matt's father, a small farmer in Norway, attempted to resume his occupation in rural Illinois and later in Eagle Grove, Iowa. The family grew—five boys and

---

* *Time*'s examples of "angry men" included Louisiana's late senator Huey Long and New York City's mayor Fiorello LaGuardia.

three girls—but the meager farm income could not support them. Matt and his older brother, Ole, therefore, were parceled out to neighboring farmers, earning their room and board by doing chores. After Matt completed the seventh grade, he and Ole moved to Chicago where Ole died of tuberculosis in his brother's arms. Penniless and alone, Matt vowed that he would never be broke again.

Earl Warren was born on March 19, 1891, on what was then called "Dingy Turner Street," in a poor neighborhood of Los Angeles. Methias had moved to Southern California from the Midwest a year earlier and begun working for the Southern Pacific as a repairman and car inspector. On his modest income he struggled to support his wife, Chrystal, a Swedish immigrant, their daughter, Ethel, four years old, and their infant son. Soon after Earl's birth, Methias went out on strike with other railroad workers in sympathy for the nationwide Pullman strike and, as a result, was blacklisted by the railroad's Los Angeles office. He moved his family to the dusty, desolate town of Sumner, California, outside of Bakersfield in the Joaquin Valley, where he again found employment with the Southern Pacific. Although the railroad was Methias's employer for thirty years, he told his son that the corporation did not respect its workers or treat them fairly. Earl, like his father, witnessed the railroad's indifference to workers' debilitating injuries and the instant dismissals of unneeded workers without warning or severance. The experience ingrained in both father and son an enduring suspicion of large corporations.

"Earl, saving is a habit like drinking, smoking, or spending," Methias Warren told his only son when he was growing up in the small town of Sumner.[3] "Always save some part of what you earn." Thrift was one of the important lessons that Earl Warren learned from his father, who was the greatest influence in his life. Methias also valued education, insisting that Earl graduate from high school in Bakersfield, when the children of most railroad workers had dropped out. Despite Methias's modest income, he saved enough to pay for his son's college and law school education at the Berkeley campus of the University of California.

The Warren family lived in a small row house across the street from the railroad yard in Sumner, a town of a few hundred people, a scattering of stores, saloons, gambling dens, and small hotels. The hotel patrons were usually itinerant railroad workers, known as "boomers," or French and Basque sheep herders who came to town to market their livestock in the winter. This rugged frontier town seemed especially ill-suited for the intense, teetotaling Methias Warren. Unlike the rootless boomers, he was a devoted family man who adhered to a strict moral code and believed in perpetual self-improvement. He took correspondence courses in accounting and mechanics and taught Earl to read and write before he was five years old.

When Earl was in elementary school, he earned money delivering baked goods in a covered wagon in the early morning hours and carrying blocks of ice to homes in the summer heat that soared above 100 degrees. Working for the railroad as a teenager, his favorite job was as a "caller,"[4] responsible for finding and rousing boomers to make sure they boarded departing trains for their next job. He searched for them in saloons and gambling dens, and, if unsuccessful, in their rooming houses and hotels. He proudly recalled that he never failed to find his man.

He also had fun, especially riding his burro, Jack, chasing jackrabbits, and trapping squirrels. His most exciting adventure occurred in April 1903, after he heard the news of a shootout between a notorious bandit named Jim McKinney and the Bakersfield marshal and his deputy, both of whom had been killed.* The boy rode his burro to the scene of the crime, a Chinese gambling house.† Later, when another deputy, not the bandit, was accused of the murder of the two lawmen, young Warren attended the trial, his dramatic introduction to

---

* The murdered deputy was Bert Tibbet, the father of Lawrence Tibbet, the famous Metropolitan Opera baritone.

† The Chinese population of Bakersfield was comprised of laborers who had been brought in to build and maintain the railroad.

his future career as a prosecutor. The defendant was found guilty and later slit his own throat in the local jail.

When the mesmerizing orator Russell Conwell delivered his inspirational "Acres of Diamonds" sermon in Bakersfield, young Warren listened intently and, decades later, recalled the details of the address. Greatness, said Conwell, was found in small deeds—providing better streets and sidewalks, schools and colleges, "more happiness and more civilization."[5] Highly moralistic in tone yet practical in advice, Conwell's lessons shaped Warren, who would later set his own moralistic, practical agenda as district attorney of Alameda County, attorney general and governor of California, and Chief Justice of the United States.

Warren was a good if uninspired student in high school, who in his graduating class "will" bequeathed "his ability to slide through, doing as little work as possible."[6] His most vivid memory from high school was not of a favorite teacher or class, but of his triumph in being reinstated after his principal suspended him shortly before graduation. He and two other seniors had been rehearsing for the senior play into the early morning hours, overslept, and missed the final graduation rehearsal. The principal suspended them for their truancy, but they appealed their suspensions to the school board and were allowed to graduate. It was not the last time that Earl Warren would take satisfaction in challenging authority that he considered unjust.

———

WARREN THOROUGHLY ENJOYED his six years at Berkeley, but by his own admission he was not a serious student. "I had no intention of failing," he wrote, "but neither did I have a burning desire for knowledge."[7] Shortly after arriving on campus, he joined the La Junta Club, a local fraternal organization, and spent his happiest hours talking, eating, playing cards, and drinking beer with his fraternity brothers. While at Berkeley, he grew to his adult height of over six feet tall and put on thirty pounds to weigh two hundred. He was an enthusiastic reader outside of class, and listed Kipling, Dickens, and the California author Jack London among his favorites. He and his fraternity brothers spent memorable evenings at the First and Last Chance Saloon, an Oakland waterfront bar frequented by London, where the author regaled them with tales of his adventures in the frozen North and the South Seas.

Although Warren was not active in campus politics, he took a particular interest in a moralistic, reform-minded young prosecutor named Hiram Johnson, who soon successfully ran for governor of California. As governor, Johnson instituted a series of progressive measures, making government more transparent and responsive to the voters and curbing the political and economic power of large corporations like the Southern Pacific. When Warren was elected governor more than three decades later, he hung only one photograph in his office, that of Hiram Johnson.

In Warren's senior year, he entered the law school at Boalt Hall but did not find the school's theoretical case method, patterned on Harvard's, stimulating. "This did not appear to me to be a practical approach to becoming a lawyer," he recalled.[8] To learn practical legal skills, he spent a few hours a day in a Berkeley law office, in violation of the law school's regulations. At the law firm, he served papers and "did anything of a nontechnical character that was asked of me."[9] Almost a half century later, Chief Justice Warren's judicial opinions reflected the practical approach that he had preferred as early as law school.

———

AFTER GRADUATION, Warren accepted a job in the law department of a small oil company in San Francisco. He remembered his boss, Edmund Tauske, as an irascible old man who never addressed him by name. Tauske ordered the young attorney around like a petty clerk, constantly criticizing his work and taking credit for anything Warren did that he found useful. Worst of all, he humiliated him by sending him downtown on personal errands, often to buy his favorite cigars. Warren left his job after a year, even though he had not found another. Before departing, he reprimanded his boss for running an office with "no human dignity."[10]

Shortly after leaving Tauske's firm, Warren was hired by the Oakland firm of Robinson and Robinson, where he kept the court calendar for the entire office, served as legman to the courthouse on minor matters, and researched cases for the senior partner.

After the United States entered World War I in April 1917, Warren volunteered for the army officers' corp, but was turned down twice, first due to the flood of applicants and later because of hemorrhoids and ether pneumonia. Finally he enlisted, rising to the rank of first lieutenant, and was sent as a bayonet instructor to Camp MacArthur in Waco, Texas, two days before the Armistice was signed.

He remained intensely patriotic throughout his life. In 1941, when he was fifty years old and the attorney general of California, he planned to accept a commission in the army after the Japanese bombed Pearl Harbor. He changed his mind only after being persuaded to run for governor. And in 1963, when he first resisted President Lyndon B. Johnson's entreaties to head the commission investigating the assassination of John F. Kennedy, LBJ successfully appealed to his patriotism. At Warren's request, he would be buried in Arlington Cemetery with full military honors.

Warren was still wearing his military uniform when he returned to California in January 1919. Thanks to the recommendations of two friends who had been elected to the state legislature, he was hired as clerk of the judiciary committee of the state assembly at six dollars a day. Though he held the job for only a few months of the 1919 legislative session, his most indelible memories were of corrupt legislators who lined their own pockets instead of doing the people's business. Some, he recalled, could be bought by lobbyists for "a steak, a potato, or a girl."[11] Others specialized in so-called cinch bills, in which they introduced legislation calculated to hurt vulnerable businessmen, then withdrew the bill at a price to the targeted victim.

The sobering experience did not deter him from public service. Indeed, that clerkship was the beginning of a career in government that spanned a half century. For the next five years, he worked as a deputy city attorney in Oakland and as assistant district attorney in the office of Ezra Decoto. During that time, he also met his future wife, an attractive young widow named Nina Meyers, a Swedish immigrant who was raising her son while managing a woman's specialty shop in Oakland. Though Warren worked long hours, he found time to court Nina, taking her to dinner and the theater on Saturday evenings. They were married in 1925 and raised a family of six children.

In Decoto's office, Warren became "a sort of Jack-of-all-trades"[12] who tried criminal cases, handled lawsuits against county officers, advised boards of education, and assisted the chief deputy in advising the Board of Supervisors. He worked day and night and, before long, became Decoto's indispensable top assistant. In 1925, when Decoto retired, Warren succeeded him. As district attorney of Alameda County for the next fourteen years, Warren was praised as "the most intelligent and politically independent district attorney in the United States" by Columbia University political scientist Raymond Moley, who was also a member of President Franklin D. Roosevelt's brain trust.[13]

DISTRICT ATTORNEY WARREN consciously modeled himself on his progressive hero, Hiram Johnson, constantly battling waste, crime, and corruption in government. Although he respected his predecessor, Warren made the DA's office more efficient, independent, and aggressive in the pursuit of law and order. Decoto had relied heavily on veteran deputies who were comfortable with the status quo. Warren hired young attorneys fresh out of law school or World War I veterans, demanding hard work and absolute loyalty. Whereas Decoto and his deputies maintained a private law practice, Warren forbid it to avoid any conflicts of interests. He kept a close eye on every facet of the office's business, meeting weekly for an hour with each department and with the entire staff on Saturday mornings. He tightened the schedule between arraignments and trial, then successfully prosecuted bunco artists, bootleggers, murderers, and corrupt officials. He also cultivated the press, sometimes inviting reporters or photographers to join him to make an arrest or take a hatchet to an illegal still.

Once he sniffed official corruption, he drove himself and his staff relentlessly until the schemes were fully exposed in court and the defendants convicted. One of his greatest triumphs came in 1930, when he warned Alameda County sheriff Burton Becker that he would face prosecution unless he stopped taking bribes for protecting bootleggers, brothel owners, and organized crime figures. "You take care of your business," Becker defiantly replied, "and I will take care of mine."[14] Warren responded, "That's exactly what I will do."

As promised, Warren brought charges against Becker, but the prosecution was complicated and prolonged. At the outset, the sheriff's grand jury presented a special challenge for Warren, since seven members, like the sheriff himself, belonged to the Ku Klux Klan. When Becker invoked the Fifth Amendment, pleading that his testimony might incriminate himself, Becker's fellow Klan members told Warren to prepare the indictment. Warren's staff looked in vain for more than a year for a key witness, an automobile dealer alleged to have collected payoffs for Becker. Finally, a reporter for the *San Francisco Examiner* told Warren that he knew where to find him. In exchange for the information, the DA agreed to take two of the newspaper's reporters with him for the arrest. On the evening before his scheduled testimony in court, the witness changed his mind and said he would not testify.

Warren gave him a choice: either testify or face charges of larceny. He testified. Becker was convicted of "willful and corrupt misconduct" and sent to San Quentin State Prison.

In 1936, Warren prosecuted his most celebrated and controversial case. It began with the brutal murder of George Alberts in his cabin on the freighter *Point Lobos,* docked on the Oakland waterfront. Alberts, the ship's chief engineer, had been a vocal opponent of unions and an outspoken anti-Communist, while many of the crew were members of a local union that was reputed to harbor Communists and other political radicals. At a news conference five months after the murder, Warren announced the arrest of four members of the union, linking the murder to labor unrest and to "a campaign of terrorism and sabotage for Communists to gain complete control of the waterfront unions."[15] After the defendants' indictments, Warren said the crime was a "paid assassin's job, and the basis of the plot was communistic."[16]

Labor protesters supporting the defendants picketed the courthouse during the trial as well as Warren's home. The DA was branded anti-union, though he had been sympathetic to workers since childhood and, as a teenager, had joined the musicians' union when he played clarinet in the town band. But he viewed the *Point Lobos* murder as a labor conspiracy inextricably linked to Communist influence in West Coast maritime unions. He prosecuted the defendants with single-minded determination.

In building the case for trial, Warren sometimes took unfair advantage of the defendants in ways that he, as the future chief justice, would have condemned. He approved of the secret and prolonged questioning of one of the defendants without counsel present, which resulted in a confession, later challenged as coerced. His deputies broke into a San Francisco hotel room to install a hidden microphone and used it to listen to conversations between one of the defendants and another union official. They also surreptitiously recorded the defendants' conversations while in custody. In the press, Warren pronounced the defendants guilty of murder before they had even been indicted.

None of these irregularities were unconstitutional at the time, though they were the subject of widespread criticism by defense attorneys and the labor movement on the West Coast. In addition to questionable prosecutorial conduct, Warren acted in other ways that were patently unfair to the defendants. In selecting a grand jury, he sought the recommendations of local bankers, lawyers, and other businessmen who were unlikely to be open-minded in a case involving violence and Communist influence in maritime labor unions. He also intervened personally in selecting the judge, Frank Ogden, who had worked for five years as his assistant in the DA's office before his judicial appointment, which was made with Warren's strong endorsement.

The jury deliberated less than five hours before convicting all four defendants of second-degree murder, and those convictions were upheld on appeal. In his memoirs, Warren maintained that there could be no doubt about the defendants' guilt. But in 1941, the state parole board, under pressure from Democratic governor Culbert Olson, paroled three of the convicted men. At the time, Olsen, a strong supporter of labor unions, viewed Warren, then the state's attorney general, as a potential political opponent. Warren lashed out at the pardons. "The murderers are free today, not because they are rehabilitated criminals but because they are politically powerful communistic radicals," he said. "Their parole is the culmination of a sinister program of subversive politics."[17]

IN FEBRUARY 1937, more than a year ahead of the election, Warren announced his candidacy for attorney general of California. He cross-filed on all three political lines—Republican, Democratic, and Progressive—and promised to impose even-handed justice on those who violated state laws with the same tenacity that had characterized his tenure as Alameda County's district attorney.

Shortly before the state primaries, Warren received the shocking news that his beloved father, Methias, had been murdered in the living room of his Bakersfield home, his skull crushed by a half-inch pipe. The intruder had apparently entered through the back door, which was open during the warm May evening. Only Methias's wallet was missing. Warren wept openly at a news conference after hearing the news and dispatched members of his staff to assist in the investigation. The murder was never solved. "My father's death must go down in history as one of the thousands of unsolved murder cases that plague our nation every year," Warren later wrote.[18] His speeches during his campaign were delivered in his familiar flat, controlled tone, though he might have used Methias's violent death to indulge in heated law-and-order rhetoric. He won an overwhelming victory in November.

On his first day in office, January 2, 1939, Attorney General Warren began to institute reforms similar to those that he had made as DA. He hired young, eager attorneys and discouraged the private practice of law. Under his tight management style, he supervised every aspect of the AG's office, and expanded its portfolio, targeting organized crime activities—gambling, bootlegging, and prostitution.

Barely six months after he assumed office, Warren dramatically demonstrated his resolve. With the cooperation of the Los Angeles district attorney and sheriff, Warren organized a flotilla of twenty boats and about three hundred officers to raid four offshore gambling ships floating a few miles off the Southern Californian coast. Three of the ships immediately capitulated, and their gambling proceeds and paraphernalia were confiscated. But the fourth ship, the *Rex*, owned by Antonio Stralla, a notorious underworld figure who had flouted the law for years, resisted. The *Rex*'s crew turned fire hoses on the flotilla while refusing officers' entry to the ship. An undaunted Warren, watching the confrontation through binoculars at a beach headquarters, ordered a blockade of the *Rex*, forbidding the ship's customers from leaving. Eventually the *Rex* surrendered and was towed to port, where its gambling devices and proceeds were seized.

Warren did not hesitate to use the power of his office to oppose those he perceived to be political radicals, like Professor Max Radin, an outspoken liberal on the Berkeley law faculty, who was nominated by Governor Olson to the California Supreme Court in June 1940. Radin, whose father was a rabbi in Poland, had immigrated with his family to the United States when he was four. Educated in New York public schools, he received his undergraduate degree from the City College of New York at the age of nineteen, a law degree from New York University, and a doctorate in classical languages from Columbia. He taught Latin in the New York public schools and lectured on Roman law at CCNY and Columbia before his appointment to the Berkeley law faculty. An extremely popular teacher at the law school, Radin's scholarship ranged widely, from Roman law and jurisprudence to the Bill of Rights and a layman's guide to law, *The Law and Mr. Smith*.

Warren did not challenge Radin's academic credentials or the quality of his publications. What roiled the attorney general was Radin's support for left-wing causes, especially his support for the *Point Lobos* defendants. Warren was also suspicious of Radin's other affiliations. He had been a close associate of his political archenemy, Governor Olson, and had aligned himself with the governor's liberal causes, including FDR's New Deal, organized labor, and civil liberties.*

The fate of Radin's nomination rested with the Commission on Judicial Qualifications, comprised of the chief justice of the California Supreme Court, the senior presiding judge of the California District

---

* In contrast to Olson, Attorney General Warren advocated expulsion of public school students who refused to salute the American flag, a requirement that was later declared unconstitutional by the Supreme Court. See *West Virginia State Board of Education v. Barnette*, 319 U.S. 624 (1943).

Courts of Appeal, and Warren, who as attorney general also served as the commission's secretary and presiding officer. Since Warren had been secretary of the commission, its practice had been to ask a committee of the California State Bar Association to submit a factual report on the nominee's qualifications. At the direction of the association's president, Gerald Hagar, a conservative Republican, the committee called witnesses, including Radin, on his alleged connections with the Communist Party and his support of the *Point Lobos* defendants. Radin denied that he had ever been a member of the Communist Party, but admitted that he believed that one of the *Point Lobos* defendants was innocent.

In its report, the bar association took no position on the nomination but recommended that the Commission on Judicial Qualifications make "the closest inspection and examination" of all the documents produced by its fact-finding committee.[19] On the same day that the bar association forwarded its report, the California Board of Governors, which had played no previous substantive role in judicial nominations, formulated two new principles to be applied to the Radin nomination: a nominee should not be confirmed if he had "given just ground to a substantial number of the public for believing that he is a member of, or in sympathy with, subversive front party organizations" and, secondly, that he had "given just cause for a substantial number of the public to believe that he is lacking in financial or intellectual integrity."[20]

Radin's nomination was defeated by a commission vote of 2–1, with Warren casting the decisive negative vote. After the failed Radin nomination, Warren refused to release copies of the evidence considered by the commission, nor would he disclose his vote or that of the other members. But one of Warren's closest friends, Robert Sproul, president of the University of California, wrote a memorandum to his files on a conversation that he had with Warren in December 1940 in which the attorney general "launched forth in a vigorous denunciation of

Professor Radin" who, he said, "constantly gives aid and comfort to Communists and other radicals."[21] Warren did not mention the Radin controversy in his memoirs.

Warren's serene public persona made him appear above partisan controversy. But behind that bland countenance was a shrewd, skillful political infighter, as Max Radin could attest.

AFTER THE BOMBING of Pearl Harbor, Warren attributed to Japanese Americans the same evil intent that he had previously reserved for Communists, other political radicals, and known organized crime figures. In January 1942, he declared that "the Japanese situation" in California "may well be the Achilles' heel of the entire civilian defense effort."[22] At first, he recommended that only the state's alien Japanese residents be evacuated. He quickly expanded the group to Japanese American citizens, but he did not make comparable demands on German American and Italian American citizens living in the state. When dealing with "the Caucasian race," he said, there were methods to test their loyalty. The Japanese were different. "If the Japs are released," he said, "no one will be able to tell a saboteur from any other Jap."[23]

Warren wholeheartedly supported the federal government's massive relocation program that uprooted more than 100,000 Japanese Americans from the West Coast to eastern California and six other states to live as prisoners in spare wooden barracks behind barbed wire. How could this future chief justice, later so sensitive to civil rights and liberties, enthusiastically implement a shameful, racist policy that swept away individual rights for tens of thousands of Japanese Americans?

In part, the explanation can be traced to Warren's upbringing in California. He adopted the prevailing nativist attitude toward outsiders, especially those of Japanese descent. By state law, they were excluded from trade unions, attended segregated schools, and lived in segregated neighborhoods. Hiram Johnson was openly hostile to Japanese Americans, as was Warren's literary hero, Jack London. After the United States declared war on Japan, General John DeWitt, the commanding officer for the Fourth Army with headquarters in San Francisco, put the issue bluntly: "The Japanese race is an enemy race."[24]

Warren certainly was not alone among high government officials supporting the internment of Japanese Americans. President Franklin D. Roosevelt issued the executive order that removed Japanese Americans from their West Coast homes, and Justices Hugo Black and William O. Douglas, both outspoken libertarians, joined a Supreme Court majority that declared the policy constitutional. But neither FDR nor the libertarian justices supported the removal of Japanese Americans from the West Coast with Warren's vehement conviction.*

Even before the United States had entered the war, Warren, as the state's attorney general, had made civil defense one of his top priorities. In August 1940, he lobbied vigorously for passage of the Uniform Sabotage Prevention Act, which penalized acts of sabotage in defense industries. After Pearl Harbor, Governor Olson, who had already attempted to preempt Warren on several civil defense issues, designated himself and other state officials as the central authority on civil defense policy. He conspicuously excluded Warren. Under the governor's plan, the state was divided into civil defense units under his authority, in which he replaced state law enforcement officers who reported to Warren with his own men. Warren felt "bedeviled" by Olson's partisan tactics.[25]

When Warren believed that someone in authority had treated him unfairly, he challenged his tormentor, whether it be his high school principal in Bakersfield or, in 1942, the governor of California. He announced that he would run against Olson in the 1942 gubernatorial

---

* In December 1944, after learning of the impending release of Japanese Americans from detention centers, Warren asked that the constitutional rights of those returning to California be protected. But he continued to defend the prior internment policy, finally expressing regret in his memoirs. (EWM, p. 149.)

election and filed for both the Republican and Democratic nominations. Presenting himself as the nonpartisan candidate, he campaigned under the banner, "Leadership, Not Politics."

Though he professed to be above politics, Warren proved to be an extraordinarily talented politician. He possessed a remarkable memory for names, which served as a valuable asset as he campaigned in town after town. He greeted everyone personally, shook their hands warmly, and asked about their families. That common touch endeared him to voters across the state. At the urging of his media advisers, Warren, who had assiduously protected his family from publicity, reluctantly agreed to have them photographed for a campaign mailer. The photo of the proud parents and their six attractive, smiling children linking arms projected the irresistible image of an all-American family. Three million copies of the photograph were mailed to California homes before the election. In November, Warren handily defeated the incumbent governor, winning 57 percent of the vote.

WARREN'S ELECTION AS governor represented the first major transition in his career. He had spent fourteen years as district attorney of Alameda County and four years as the state's attorney general, all devoted exclusively to law enforcement. As governor, he recognized that his policies must necessarily broaden far beyond issues of law and order. Cautious by temperament, Warren solicited views from advisers across the political spectrum.

He continued to rely on the support and advice of two wealthy Republican families, the Knowlands, publishers of the *Oakland Tribune*, and the Chandlers, publishers of the *Los Angeles Times*. But a relatively new adviser, Assistant Attorney General William Sweigert, played an increasingly influential role in molding Warren's thinking on public policy. Sweigert was a lifelong Democrat and passionate supporter of the New Deal. He and Warren discussed politics over weekly lunches and in frequent informal conversations. In the those early conversations in the AG's office, Sweigert remembered Warren as a fervent believer in states' rights who railed against the New Deal. By the time Warren had become a candidate for governor, however, he appeared more receptive to Sweigert's liberal views.

At the beginning of Warren's gubernatorial campaign, Sweigert wrote the candidate a memo that could have been cribbed from one of FDR's campaign speeches. Sweigert's memo began: "There is no place today for the so-called reactionary, the person who still thinks that government exists only to protect the power of a successful few against the demands of plain people for a greater measure of health, comfort and security in their daily lives. . . . [O]ur big country, our big projects, are, and always must be, the servants of our little people, our little families."[26] He then listed the basic needs of "the little people"—an opportunity to work under decent conditions, to own their own homes, to provide a good education for their children, and to have medical care for their families.

Warren kept Sweigert's memo in his desk drawer for many years, referred to it often, and incorporated many of the ideas expressed into his own policies as governor, beginning with his inaugural speech on January 4, 1943. Speaking under the capitol dome in Sacramento, Warren stressed the need to educate the young people of the state, deplored the miserable health conditions faced by arriving migrants, advocated an enlightened prison policy that would give returning inmates work upon reentry into society, and called for state pensions for the elderly based not "upon the requirement of pauperism" but rather "as a social right."[27]

As if to remind his audience that he had not forgotten his Republican roots, Warren also promised to lower taxes and manage the state's $60 million surplus prudently.

In his first year as governor, Warren was remarkably effective in delivering on his promises. He appointed a citizens' committee to study tax reform and acted on their recommendation to cut sales, income, and corporate taxes by 15 percent. But in the best progressive tradition, he refused to grant tax relief to special interests, such as the state's powerful banking industry whose lobbyists had sought to lower the industry's franchise tax. He balanced the state's budget, but still found additional money for the state universities and colleges, primary and secondary public schools, prison and juvenile correction facilities, and social welfare and state workers. At his request, the legislature approved a $25 million "war catastrophe fund" to rebuild the state should it be attacked. Surplus funds were also designated for postwar construction and unemployment relief for those who had worked in wartime industries. Other surplus money was used to retire the debt accumulated by his predecessor.

While adhering to conservative fiscal policies, Warren expanded the role of government to help "the little people" championed in Sweigert's memo. He appointed a nonpartisan committee to study pension reform. The committee's final report recommended more than a 20 percent increase in state pensions. With Governor Warren's strong support, the legislature passed a bill that made the average pension paid to seniors in California the highest in the nation.

Warren proved to be a savvy opportunist when he saw an opening to introduce one of his reform ideas: the reorganization of the state's prison system so that it would be immune to political influence. The opportunity presented itself after Warren's old friend, San Francisco police chief Charles Dullea, called the governor in late 1943 to alert him to a potentially embarrassing news report. Two inmates at Folsom prison had been leaving the prison every weekend, presumably as a result of well-placed bribes to prison authorities, to enjoy women and liquor in a San Francisco hotel. As Alameda County DA, Warren had prosecuted one of the inmates, Lloyd Sampsell, who had been known during his highly publicized trial as a "yacht bandit" for living on a luxury yacht and paying for his high life by robbing banks.

Sampsell's weekend escapades made a mockery of the prison system and, Police Chief Dullea feared, would create embarrassing publicity for the new governor. Warren's response surprised Dullea. "I urged him to arrest them the next time it happened and give the event the utmost publicity," Warren recalled.[28] "The arrest of Lloyd Sampsell during his illegal sojourn away from Folsom was the exact break I needed to do something about the prison system," he wrote.

In November 1943, Warren appointed a governor's investigating committee on penal affairs to report on what Warren knew was the sordid, politically corrupt prison system. Two months later, he received the committee's report recommending broad reforms. Warren summoned the legislature for a special session on prisons that produced a reform bill that insulated the prisons from politics. One of the key provisions of the new law was to create a nonpartisan director of corrections appointed by the governor with responsibility for the entire prison system.

Warren conducted a nationwide search to fill the position of California's first corrections chief, selecting Richard M. McGee, who was then serving as a high-level administrator to the governor of Washington state. In his interview with McGee, Warren told him, "I want you to know that as long as I am governor you will never be asked to do anything political, and if you do anything political with our prisons, I will fire you. How is that for an agreement between us?"[29] McGee replied with a smile, "That is good enough for me."

———

IN 1944, WARREN'S agenda combined social and economic reforms with conservative fiscal policies. His political appeal was not lost on the front-runner for the Republican presidential nomination, New York's Governor Dewey. But Warren, consumed with his new duties as governor, repeatedly denied interest in national office. Finally, he told Dewey he did not want the vice-presidential nomination. He agreed, however, to deliver the keynote address at the party's convention in Chicago.

His keynote address, delivered in the sweltering heat of Chicago Stadium, was at times highly partisan, quite different from his campaign speeches to California voters. States with Republican governors were responsible for much of America's war production, he boasted. "It is clear that Dr. Win the War* is a Republican."[30] He also credited Republican governors with progressive domestic policies that improved public education and health, and cared for neglected children, the aged, and "for the victims of economic misfortune." And he lambasted President Roosevelt's New Deal for centralizing power under one man and threatening basic American freedoms.[†] He further proved his party loyalty during the campaign, hosting the Republican vice presidential candidate, conservative Ohio senator John Bricker, an outspoken isolationist, who, according to Warren, had "lifted the candidacy of the Vice Presidency to a new level."[31]

———

ONLY WEEKS BEFORE the presidential election, Warren and Sweigert were having lunch at a private club in Sacramento when Warren, returning from the men's room, appeared pale and reported passing blood. He was hospitalized the same day and diagnosed with an infection in his right kidney. From his hospital bed, he made a final plea for the Republican ticket to defeat "the New Deal machine," which, he

---

* This was FDR's phrase used at a press conference in 1943 to announce that "Dr. New Deal," which, he said, had revived the nation's economic health, had been replaced by "Dr. Win the War" to defeat the Axis powers. (Simon, James F., *FDR and Chief Justice Hughes: The President, the Supreme Court, and the Epic Battle Over the New Deal* [2012], p. 399.)

† This was not the first time that Warren had publicly attacked the New Deal. In a speech supporting the 1936 Republican presidential candidate, Alfred "Alf" Landon, for example, Warren called the New Deal "a totalitarian state wherein men are but the pawns of a dictator." (*Oakland Tribune*, May 28, 1936.)

said, "is being held together today by the domination of one man."[32] He was too ill to speak into a microphone, so his comments were transcribed and read over the radio. But neither Warren nor any other Republican leader could stop FDR from easily winning reelection for a fourth term, defeating the Dewey-Bricker ticket by a thirteen-point margin.

Almost three weeks after the election, Warren, weak and ten pounds lighter, returned to his office for the first time since his hospitalization. While in the hospital, he had reflected on the problems faced by ordinary citizens coping with extraordinary medical bills. He recalled his father telling him of being penniless when his brother, Ole, had died in his arms from tuberculosis. He remembered that his ailing mother's poor health had required multiple operations costing thousands of dollars. And he considered his own experience as attorney general, living from paycheck to paycheck, when his own health insurance had almost been canceled because of a late payment.

Soon after his return to work, Warren discussed the issue of health care with Sweigert, who proposed a form of state-financed catastrophic health insurance. That was the impetus for Warren's most controversial initiative—to make California the first state in the nation to provide compulsory health insurance. That appeal to the needs of ordinary citizens foreshadowed his opinions as Chief Justice of the United States defending the constitutional rights of all Americans regardless of class or race.

Chapter Two

SUPREME
COMMANDER

A DENSE FOG HOVERED OVER LONDON ON JANUARY 15, 1944, forcing the aircraft carrying General Dwight D. Eisenhower, the Supreme Commander of Allied Expeditionary Forces, to make an unscheduled landing in Scotland. Eisenhower then boarded a private railway car, code-named Bayonet, for the trip to London, where he took charge of strategic planning for the Allies' cross-Channel invasion, code-named Overlord.

Ike, as Eisenhower was universally known, was chosen to lead Overlord in large part because of his superb organizational skills, demonstrated in the peacetime American army and honed under wartime pressure in North Africa, Sicily, and Italy. Perhaps more importantly, he had exhibited an extraordinary talent for forging consensus among strong-willed, often contentious American and British commanders. They liked him and valued his fairness in reaching critical decisions. He is "the best politician among the military men," said President Roosevelt.[1] "He is a natural leader who can convince other men to follow him."*

---

* Roosevelt thought that Army Chief of Staff George C. Marshall deserved the command, if he wanted it. When Marshall refused to state a preference, FDR chose Eisenhower.

D-Day was originally scheduled for early May, but Eisenhower postponed the invasion for a month so that the Allies could have the additional landing craft needed for such a massive invasion. On Sunday, June 4, the day before the scheduled invasion, Allied meteorologists forecast alarming weather conditions for the next day—low clouds, high winds, and formidable waves. If those conditions persisted, air support would be impossible, naval gunfire inefficient, and the navigation of the small boats difficult. Ike reluctantly delayed the invasion for a day.

While torrential rains and hurricane-force winds whipped outside, Eisenhower and his staff met at 3:30 a.m. the next morning at Allied naval headquarters. The meteorological staff reported that the same weather conditions prevailed on the Normandy coast and would have spelled disaster for an invading force. But then, Ike recalled, the meteorologists made an "astonishing declaration"—that relatively good weather was forecast for the next thirty-six hours.[2] It provided a narrow window of opportunity for the invasion, since the forecast was for more bad weather for at least two weeks afterward.

After soliciting the views of his commanders, Ike ruminated, rubbing his balding head. He then posed the critical question: "[H]ow long can you hang this operation on the end of a limb and let it hang there?"[3] And then, calmly, he answered it himself. "I'm quite positive we must give the order," he said. Troops were alerted to prepare for D-Day in the early morning hours of June 6.

That afternoon, Ike considered the terrible possibility that the invasion would fail. He wrote a note taking full responsibility and tucked it into his wallet. "Our landings in the Cherbourg-Havre area have failed to gain a satisfactory foothold and I have withdrawn the troops," he wrote. "My decision to attack at this time and place was based upon the best information available. The troops, the air, and the Navy did all that bravery and devotion to duty could do. If any blame or fault attaches to the attempt it is mine alone."[4]

In the final hours before the invasion, Eisenhower visited the camp of the U.S. 101st Airborne Division. "I found the men in fine fettle," he wrote, "many of them joshingly admonishing me that I had no cause for worry since the 101st was on the job."[5] He stayed with them until midnight, when the last man was airborne. He then returned to his camp in the woods outside Portsmouth where he smoked one Camel cigarette after another and waited for the first news of the invasion.

IN 1741, Hans Nicholas Eisenhauer sailed with his family from Rotterdam to Philadelphia on the *Europa* seeking, like so many other hopeful immigrants, religious freedom and economic prosperity. The Eisenhauers (name later anglicized) had been successful farmers in the Oldenwald region of Germany, south of Frankfurt, and devout Mennonites, a persecuted religious minority in their homeland. They settled in Pennsylvania's Susquehanna Valley, again prospered as farmers, and eventually joined the Brethren in Christ sect of the Mennonites, known as the River Brethren.

Ike's paternal grandfather, Jacob, with full black beard and a severe, commanding presence, became the patriarch of the sect. He preached to large audiences of the River Brethren in German and built a two story, nine-room brick house on his large farm in Elizabethville, north of Harrisburg, for his wife, Rebecca, and their fourteen children. In 1878, Jacob, lured by promises in railroad brochures of cheaper and more fertile land in the Midwest, sold his farm and persuaded three hundred River Brethren to join him and his family on a new adventure. They boarded a train at Harrisburg, filled fifteen cars with their freight, and rode for three days to reach their destination, Dickinson County, Kansas. Jacob purchased 160 acres of prime farmland outside of the town of Abilene, the county seat, added a dairy herd, and built a large house that also served as a meeting place for the River Brethren. Later, he bought more land, built a creamery, and established a bank in the nearby town of Hope. He prospered as never before, enabling him to offer a wedding present of 160 acres and $2,000 to each of his fourteen children.

Ike's father, David, who was Jacob and Rebecca's oldest son, hated farmwork as a boy and, despite pressure from his father, refused to become a farmer. Instead he enrolled at Lane University in Lecompton, Kansas, where he studied mechanics and Greek and fell in love with a bright, pretty young woman named Ida Stover a year his senior. The Stovers, like the Eisenhowers, had emigrated from Germany and were devout members of the River Brethren. At the age of twenty-one, Ida had used a small inheritance to buy a train ticket to Kansas from her native Virginia, paid her tuition to Lane to study music, and purchased an ebony piano, which became her prized possession for the rest of her long life. David and Ida were married on September 23, 1885, David's twenty-second birthday.

Ike was born on October 14, 1890, the third son of Ida and David, in a tiny rented house near the railroad tracks in Denison, Texas. David, having squandered his inheritance on a failed general store venture in Hope, Kansas, was scrubbing locomotives at ten dollars a week for the Missouri, Kansas and Texas Railroad. Jacob visited David and his family in Denison and was appalled by their desperate circumstances. He persuaded his son and his family to return to Abilene, Kansas, where David was hired as a refrigerator mechanic by his brother-in-law, who managed a new creamery in town. The family rented a small framed house without plumbing or electricity a few blocks from the creamery. David worked twelve hours a day, six days a week, but his meager salary (less than $50 a week) hardly covered necessities for his family.

In 1898, Jacob again came to David's rescue. David's younger brother, Abraham, had decided to sell his thriving veterinary practice and go west as a missionary. Jacob arranged for Abraham to sell his large two-story house set on a three-acre plot to David for $1,000. He then advanced his son the purchase price, though, as a precaution, he put the title in Ida's name. By then, there were five Eisenhower boys, so the extra space was easily filled by David, Ida, and their sons as well as Jacob, then a widower.

David, quick-tempered and brooding, remained a dour presence at home, leading the family in early morning bible reading and using a switch or leather harness to discipline his sons. Ida, warm, vivacious, and optimistic, was the emotional ballast for the family, dividing the chores among the boys, preparing their meals, supervising homework, and applauding their achievements in the classroom and on the ball fields. Ike remembered "[h]er serenity, her open smile, her gentleness with all and her tolerance of their ways, despite an inflexible loyalty to her religious convictions and her own strict pattern of personal conduct." Ike wrote that he and his brothers were "privileged to spend a boyhood in her company."[6]

Ike inherited his mother's infectious smile, fair good looks, and optimism, but not her strict code of conduct or religiosity. Before entering West Point, he played baseball for money under the pseudonym "Wilson" to avoid jeopardizing his amateur standing.[7] At West Point, he frequently made money playing poker. During his long, illustrious career, his private conversations with male friends and family members were generously sprinkled with profanity. And though he quoted passages from the Bible, he did not join a church or regularly attend Sunday services until he was elected president.

Ida's loving care not only gave her sons confidence, but imbued in each of them an ambition to succeed. Arthur, the oldest, quit high school but later served as executive vice president and director of the Commerce Trust, one of the largest banks west of the Mississippi. Edgar worked his way through the University of Michigan Law School and founded a successful law firm in Tacoma, Washington. Roy became a pharmacist, Earl an electrical engineer. Milton, the youngest surviving son, served as president of Kansas State, Pennsylvania State, and Johns Hopkins universities.* Dwight beat them all. After serving as Supreme Commander of Allied Expeditionary Forces during World War II, he was appointed president of Columbia University and later served as the thirty-fourth president of the United States.

Ike attended Abilene High School, but, like Earl Warren a half continent away in Bakersfield, was generally uninspired by his studies. He made an exception for the field of history, particularly military history dating back to ancient Carthage, Greece, and Rome. "Of course, I could read about scholars and philosophers, but they seldom loomed as large in my mind as warriors and monarchs," he recalled.[8] He gloried in the exploits of his heroes, from Hannibal and Caesar to George Washington. He particularly admired Washington's "stamina and patience in adversity, first, then his indomitable courage, daring, and capacity for self sacrifice"—the same qualities he extolled during his own military career.[9]

Quick-tempered like his father, if challenged, young Ike did not back down from a fight. But his intense competitive spirit was best demonstrated in organized sports, especially football (end) and baseball (center field). Though he was not a star athlete, he was elected the president of a volunteer athletic organization that scheduled games with other schools, raised money for sports equipment, and, when necessary, found free transportation (on freight trains) for out-of-town contests.

Growing up in Abilene, Ike expressed no interest in a military career. After high school graduation he worked at the town's Belle Springs Creamery to earn money for his older brother Edgar's tuition; Edgar had pledged to do the same for him. But one of Ike's high school friends, Everett "Swede" Hazlett, who had applied to the naval academy, convinced him that the service academies offered his best undergraduate option. The tuition-free education was obviously an

* Paul, born in 1894, died in infancy; Milton was born in 1899.

important factor, since his parents could not afford to send him or his brothers to college. In 1910, at the age of nineteen, he took the competitive exam for the military academies and placed second among eight applicants, assuring his admission to the U.S. Military Academy at West Point.

He graduated from West Point in 1915 (sixty-first in a class of 164). By his own admission, he spent more time at the poker table than in the library. He also took mischievous pleasure in flouting time-honored West Point traditions. After he and a classmate named Atkins had been found guilty of a minor rules infraction, they were ordered to the room of an upperclassman in "full dress coats." Ike and his colleague appeared in the upperclassman's room at the required hour in "full-dress coats" and otherwise stark naked. They saluted smartly and announced solemnly, "Sir, cadets Eisenhower and Atkins report as ordered."[10]

Ike's greatest disappointment at West Point had nothing to do with his unexceptional academic standing, but rather a knee injury that prevented the solidly built (5'11", 174 pounds) aspiring halfback from competing on Army's varsity football team. After his injury, he poured his considerable energies into coaching the academy's junior varsity football team.

AFTER GRADUATION, Second Lieutenant Eisenhower reported for duty to the 19th Infantry Regiment at Fort Sam Houston in San Antonio. The posting offered little to advance his career. He did, however, establish himself as an outstanding football coach for two local prep school teams, a reputation that led to coaching assignments at army posts for the next ten years. More importantly, he met and fell in love with Mary "Mamie" Doud, the pert, lively daughter of a wealthy Denver businessman and his wife who were vacationing in San Antonio the winter of 1915. Ike and Mamie were married in 1916 and their first son, Doud Dwight (called "Icky") was born a year later.*

After the United States declared war on Germany in 1917, Ike assumed that his regiment, the newly formed 57th, would see action on a battlefield in France. Instead, he was detached from the 57th and ordered to Fort Oglethorpe in Georgia to train newly commissioned reserve officers. For the next twenty years, he futilely sought the command of a combat unit. He steadily moved up through the ranks, nonetheless, because of the army's rigid promotion system based on seniority. Along the way, he impressed his superiors with his keen intelligence, extraordinary organizational skills, and intuitive leadership qualities.

Under the tutelage of General Fox Connor, for whom he served in Panama from 1922 to 1924, he deepened his study of military history, reading Clausewitz's *On War* three times, studying military leadership from Genghis Khan to Napoleon, as well as the fierce battles of the Civil War. After he received three years of superior efficiency ratings in Panama, Connor encouraged him to apply to the Command and General Staff School at Fort Leavenworth, Kansas. There, he finished first in his infantry class.

Following a three-year stint with the Battle Monuments Commission in Washington and Paris, Ike reported to the War Department in 1929 to serve as executive assistant to Major General George Van Horn Moseley, the principal military adviser to the assistant secretary of war. Ike's primary assignment was to draft an industrial mobilization plan. He admired Moseley's military skills and chose to ignore his boss's racist and anti-Semitic rantings. Moseley was impressed with Ike's work, as was his superior, Army Chief of Staff Douglas MacArthur. By 1932, at the age of forty-two, Ike had effectively become MacArthur's mili-

---

* In the great tragedy of their lives, Ike and Mamie's son Icky contracted scarlet fever in 1920 and died at the age of three. A second son, John, was born two years later.

tary secretary. He was awed by MacArthur's brilliance and remained loyal to him even after MacArthur's controversial handling of the so-called Bonus Army during the Great Depression.

In May 1932, thousands of desperate World War I veterans converged on the nation's capital to petition the president and Congress for immediate payment of the wartime bonuses that were due them in 1945. President Herbert Hoover and General MacArthur watched the Bonus Army with mounting concern. When the veterans refused to leave vacant government buildings on Pennsylvania Avenue, an ugly riot erupted. MacArthur sent heavy tanks and infantrymen, wearing gas masks and brandishing fixed bayonets, to battle the helpless veterans. The troops chased the veterans from the government buildings and set fire to their shantytown erected in southeast Washington.

Eisenhower drafted the report of the incident for MacArthur that commended "the exemplary conduct of the rank and file units" who frequently were compelled to act "under extreme provocation." The enlisted men "exhibited a patience, forbearance, and sympathetic though determined attitude that won the praise of every impartial observer," he concluded.[11] Newspaper photographers and newsreel cameramen on the scene told a different story, reinforcing the public's negative perception of heavily armed soldiers chasing defenseless, retreating veterans.

When FDR declared a bank moratorium shortly after his inauguration in January 1933, Eisenhower praised the new president's action. FDR's decision, Ike wrote in his diary, "shows that the Pres. is going to step out and take authority in his own hands. More power to him!"[12] Later that year he wrote that strong presidential leadership was necessary, even if individual liberties were subordinated. "I believe that individual right must be subordinated to public good, and that the public good can be served only by unanimous adherence to an authoritative plan." Reflecting on FDR's New Deal initiatives at the end of the president's first year in office, he wrote: "*The only chance* for success is *to follow where the Pres. Leads.* No matter what other scheme may be theoretically more applicable to our difficulties, the fact remains that this is the only one that can be tried during the next three years. Therefore unified support *must* be given."[13]

In the early years of the New Deal, Eisenhower continued to work for MacArthur in the War Department. MacArthur found Ike's administrative and writing skills indispensable, insisting that he accompany him to the Philippines in 1935 after he was appointed military adviser to Philippine president Manuel Quezon. Ike became MacArthur's chief of staff with overall responsibility for the office's day-to-day operations. During his Philippines tour, Eisenhower's admiration for MacArthur slowly dissipated, as his boss's arrogance, vanity, and manipulation of his staff became intolerable.

The final outrage for Eisenhower occurred in 1938, when he returned to the Philippines after a short business trip to the War Department to discover that MacArthur had reorganized his office and minimized his chief of staff's authority. In his diary, Ike seethed: "Why the man should so patently exhibit a jealousy of a subordinate is beyond me. But I must say it is almost incomprehensible that after 8 years of working for him, writing every word he publishes, keeping his secrets . . . he should suddenly turn on me, as he has all others who have ever been around him. He'd like to occupy a throne room surrounded by experts in flattery."[14]

At his own request, Eisenhower returned to the United States in December 1939, assigned to the 15th Infantry Division at Fort Lewis in Tacoma, Washington. He had, by then, compiled a superb eighteen-year record as a staff officer who mastered military procedure, produced lucid reports under pressure, and demonstrated an uncanny ability to implement his superiors' orders. Still, he was frustrated by his failure to command a combat unit. In September 1940, he wrote to his friend

Colonel George S. Patton, who commanded the 2nd Armored Brigade at Fort Benning, Georgia, that "I'm weary of desk duty . . . think I could do a damn good job of commanding a regiment."[15]

In the summer of 1941, Lieutenant General Walter Krueger, commander of the Third Army based in San Antonio, wrote Army Chief of Staff George C. Marshall requesting the appointment of a chief of staff "possessing broad vision, progressive ideas, a thorough grasp of the magnitude of the problems involved in handling an army, and lots of initiatives and resourcefulness."[16] He wanted Ike, and Marshall readily agreed to the appointment.

One week after the bombing of Pearl Harbor, Marshall ordered Eisenhower to fly to Washington to meet him in his office at the War Department. For twenty minutes, Marshall described in gruesome detail the vulnerability of the depleted Pacific fleet and predicted that the Japanese would soon attempt to overrun the Philippines. Aware that Eisenhower had spent three years in the Philippines, Marshall abruptly asked, "What should be our general line of action?"[17]

"Give me a few hours," Eisenhower replied.

Three hours later, he marched into Marshall's office prepared to defend his bleak conclusions. The people of China, the Philippines, and the Dutch East Indies, he told Marshall, will be watching the U.S.'s response to the Japanese attack on Pearl Harbor. "They may excuse failure, but they will not excuse abandonment," he said.[18] Using Australia as our base, he continued, the U.S. must take great risks to expand military operations to keep the vital South Asian sea corridor open. In this effort, he declared, "[W]e dare not fail."

Marshall listened impassively, then replied, "I agree with you."[19]

That day Marshall took the measure of Eisenhower and concluded that his strategic skills, toughness, and character merited a central leadership role in the Allies' formidable military challenge. Six months later, Marshall had catapulted Ike ahead of more than two hundred general officers with greater seniority to make him the commander of American forces in Europe.

―――――――

LATE IN THE afternoon of November 5, 1942, Eisenhower, who had the previous summer been appointed supreme commander of Allied forces for the invasion of North Africa, landed in a B-17 Flying Fortress on the tiny island of Gibraltar. The eight-hour flight from the United Kingdom had been a prolonged nightmare. To evade German fighter planes, his plane had flown only one hundred feet above the Atlantic through heavy rain and fog. Gibraltar, three square miles of solid limestone, was the temporary Allied headquarters for the invasion, since it was the only territory in Europe that remained under the control of the Western allies. Once Ike arrived at Gibraltar, he was taken to the headquarters of the Supreme Allied Command—a damp, dank cavernous office six hundred feet deep inside the rock—to await the first reports of the Allied invasion.

Shortly after 2 a.m. on November 8, Allied troops came ashore on the beaches of Morocco and Algeria with only minor mishaps and miscalculations. But once they had established beachheads, they encountered fierce, and unanticipated, resistance from French troops, especially at the ports of Algiers and Oran. A bruising three-day battle ensued, pitting the French infantry, navy, and air force against the invading Allied forces. The Allies eventually prevailed but at a high and unforeseen cost: three thousand Allied soldiers killed, wounded, or missing, more than a dozen Allied ships sunk or heavily damaged, and seventy planes shot down.

On November 13, Ike flew to Algiers to sign a cease-fire pact with Admiral Jean François Darlan, deputy head of France's Vichy regime and commander in chief of the French armed forces. Darlan was a short, portly, and thoroughly cynical opportunist who had been the principal architect of Vichy's military cooperation with the Third

Reich. In exchange for the cease-fire and enlistment of French troops in the Allied offensive, he insisted that the Vichy government in North Africa remain in power. That meant that the Allies must accept Vichy's fascist regulations, anti-Semitic restrictions, and its North African version of the SS.

Eisenhower did not hesitate to agree to Darlan's terms. His reasons for supporting the agreement were strictly military. He believed that the Allied forces could afford no further delay in their drive toward Tunisia. Otherwise, the Nazis, who had already begun moving troops, tanks, and aircraft into Tunisia (without opposition from the French army), would be entrenched for a long battle. The success of the invasion, already in jeopardy, would be further imperiled if the Allies were forced to occupy Morocco and Algeria surrounded by suspicious Arab tribes.

High officials and the press in London and Washington were appalled by the Allies' pact with the Vichy government. British foreign secretary Anthony Eden compared the agreement to Neville Chamberlain's ignominious 1938 pact with Hitler at Munich. London-based CBS correspondent Edward R. Murrow, in his daily broadcast to the United States, asked: "Are we fighting Nazis or sleeping with them?"[20] FDR, who had originally approved of the agreement, felt it necessary to respond to the unanticipated public anger. He issued a statement emphasizing that the Algiers agreement was temporary. Privately he cautioned Eisenhower: "It is impossible to keep a collaborator of Hitler [Darlan] and one whom we believe to be a fascist in civil power any longer than is absolutely necessary."[21]

Eisenhower was offended by the criticism of the Darlan deal. "I'm no reactionary!" he exclaimed. "Christ on the mountain! I'm idealistic as hell!"[22] But he never wavered in his judgment that facts on the ground dictated his pragmatic decision. Still, his vaunted political skills were not, in this instance, impressive. The Darlan pact effectively only applied to French troops in Morocco and Algeria, but not Tunisia where French soldiers stood aside while Germany poured in men and munitions. Nor did France's navy challenge the Nazis.

Although Ike alone was not to blame for the Allies's failure to anticipate French resistance to the invasion of North Africa, he was stuck with the result: slow progress and unexpected losses. The invasion plan, moreover, proved to be seriously flawed. The decision to land General Patton's troops in Morocco, a thousand miles west of Tunisia, guaranteed a long, laborious slog. The Oran and Algiers beaches were closer, but still more than four hundred miles of mud-rutted roads and rudimentary railroad tracks from the ultimate military prizes of the vital ports at Bizerte and Tunis in northern Tunisia. It would almost certainly have saved time and lives to have made Tunisia the initial target for the invasion.

Eisenhower's inauspicious combat debut in North Africa was not lost on the Allied high command. In late December, there was a subtle but critical change in the command structure. Ike remained supreme commander, but British combat veterans took over the day-to-day military operations. Though Ike was unhappy with the new command structure, it placed him in the position in which he excelled—coordinating the complicated plans among the advancing American and British troops. Once he was relieved of the pressure of overseeing daily military operations, he eagerly made repeated trips to the front, establishing a remarkable rapport with GIs that became a hallmark of his leadership throughout the war. His talent for writing clear, succinct reports, combined with his considerable charm, endeared him to his civilian bosses. Churchill loved Ike and trusted him implicitly, and the feeling was mutual. His relationship with FDR was edgier but grew closer as the campaign progressed.

Veteran German infantry and panzer divisions fought tenaciously, extending what Eisenhower and the other Allied commanders had originally predicted would be a quick, decisive victory into a vicious, six-month battle. The low point for the Allies was the great German counteroffensive known as the Battle of Kasserine Pass, which took place in mid-February 1943 in a strategic gap in Tunisia's Grand Dorsal mountain range. The American troops suffered more than five thousand casualties as well as the loss of hundreds of tanks and other equipment before reinforcements, under the skillful leadership of British general Sir Harold Alexander, finally repulsed the enemy.

IN THE MIDST of the fighting, Ike's intimate relationship with Mamie was sorely tested. The cause of the friction was a *Life* magazine article by photojournalist Margaret Bourke-White that described the dramatic rescue of a detachment of WACs whose troopship bound for North Africa had been torpedoed by a German submarine. Among the women rescued in lifeboats was "the irrepressible Kay Summersby, Eisenhower's pretty Irish driver."[23] Two photographs of "the beauteous Kay," a former model, accompanied the article.

In a letter to Mamie, Ike downplayed *Life*'s account of "my old London driver" and pooh-poohed the suggestion that the thirty-four-year-old Kay could be romantically linked to "an old duffer" like him (he was fifty-two).[24] He neglected to tell Mamie that Summersby had been sent to North Africa at his request. Once she arrived at Allied headquarters, Ike relaxed with her at a country cottage overlooking the Mediterranean, where they rode Arabian stallions together in the afternoon, shared cocktails and supper before returning to Algiers. Their companionship, which continued throughout the war, was an open secret among Ike's staff and officer friends and the subject of widespread speculation.

THE GERMANS FORMALLY surrendered in Tunis on May 13, 1943. Eisenhower refused to follow an old military custom of allowing the defeated enemy commander, General Jurgen von Arnim, to call on him as a matter of honor between professional soldiers. "For me World War II was far too personal a thing to entertain such feelings," he wrote.[25] The Allies were confronted by "a completely evil conspiracy" and only by "the utter destruction of the Axis was a decent world possible."

The lessons of the North African campaign were "dearly bought, but they were valuable," Eisenhower later wrote.[26] He was speaking of the need for Allied officers more experienced in combat and better-trained troops, but he could just as easily have been describing his own disappointing performance. Victory had come at a steep price: Allied casualties exceeded seventy thousand. The victory was due, in large part, to the phenomenal production of planes, tanks, and munitions by American factory workers that more than compensated for the GIs' weak combat performance. By February, the Allies had four times as many planes in North Africa as the Luftwaffe. By April, 1,400 tanks had been unloaded, more than fifteen times the number available to the Germans.

The Allied victory in North Africa, though unexpectedly prolonged and costly, had nonetheless begun to transform the callow American troops into a tough, formidable fighting force. And Eisenhower, who always learned from his mistakes, was now combat-tested, confident, and ready to command.

AT 3:35 A.M. on July 10, 1943, the first troops of the Allied invading force that would eventually number 500,000 went ashore on the beaches of Sicily. Thirteen divisions under the command of British general Sir Bernard Montgomery and American general George S. Patton established beachheads and moved virtually unopposed for several miles inland. Italian forces comprised the bulk of the estimated 300,000 enemy troops on the island and quickly capitulated, surrendering by the thousands. Eisenhower, who toured the beachheads two days after the landing, predicted that the Allies would conquer Sicily in two weeks. His inherent optimism caused him to underestimate the skill and tenacity of the experienced German panzer divisions that were entrenched in the higher mountainous terrain. It took six weeks to capture the island. Allied casualties numbered 20,000 to the Germans' 12,000. The victory felt hollow, since most of the German Army was evacuated before capture.

DURING THE SICILY campaign, Ike reluctantly reprimanded Patton, whom he considered the best combat commander in the American army, as a result of incidents that occurred during Patton's visits to two frontline hospitals. In the first incident, Patton accused a soldier of faking his injury, called him "a Goddamn coward," and slapped him twice.[27] A week later, he told another bedridden soldier that he was a malingering coward who deserved to be shot. He then pulled a pistol out of his holster as if he were going to do the job himself, before slapping the soldier so hard that his helmet liner fell to the ground.

After receiving a report of the incidents, Eisenhower wrote Patton a letter, which he said caused him the most anguish of his entire military career. "I assure you that conduct such as that described in the accompanying report will *not* be tolerated in this theater no matter who the offender may be."[28] He demanded that Patton apologize to the two soldiers as well as to the doctors and nurses in attendance. He later wrote that Patton was chastened and deeply grateful to him for giving him another chance. In Patton's own diary, however, he apologized grudgingly and complained that Ike did not defend him with sufficient vigor.

DURING THE SICILY campaign, the first Allied bombs were dropped on Rome, Mussolini was deposed, and the dictator's successor,

Marshal Pietro Badoglio, initiated secret discussions with the Allies for Italy's surrender. Ike, meanwhile, made final plans for the invasion of Italy. In early September, two veteran divisions of Field Marshal Bernard Montgomery's Eighth Army landed on the beaches at the toe of Italy's boot. Six days later, three divisions of General Mark Clark's Fifth Army came ashore on the beaches of Salerno, three hundred miles north of Montgomery's troops.

Montgomery's troops met little resistance, but the reception of Clark's troops at Salerno was harshly different. German mortars and artillery rained down on American troops from the low-level mountains above Salerno. The Americans were pinned down only a few hundred yards from the water. A day later, the Germans began a series of counterattacks, sending five divisions into the battle, attempting to exploit the gap between Montgomery's and Clark's forces. It appeared in those first harrowing days of the Germans' counterattack that the American troops might be annihilated or forced to be evacuated.

As in the North African campaign, Ike had planned badly, miscalculating the strength of Allied troops as well as the formidable power of the enemy. In hindsight, it was clear that Montgomery's experienced troops should have joined Clark's three divisions (one was a Texas national guard unit that had not seen combat) at Salerno. The Montgomery and Clark divisions combined were less than half the troop strength that had invaded Sicily. Ike's plan assumed that Clark's divisions would meet little resistance. With Italy's imminent surrender, he thought that the civilian population would welcome the Allies. He also did not expect the stiff challenge of multiple German divisions on the southern coast, but thought that they would be digging in for the inevitable battle for Rome.

Eisenhower believed that the successful military commander, in addition to exuding optimism, must be flexible if original battle plans failed. At Salerno, he realized that Clark's troops could not succeed without massive air and naval support. On his orders, Allied bombers dropped more than three thousand tons of bombs on the Germans daily. At the same time, the Allied fleet moved close to the shore and fired eleven thousand tons of shells in support of the troops on the beaches. Within a week, the crisis was over. Montgomery's troops linked up with Clark's, and the German divisions retreated. The Allies, at Ike's direction, trudged up the coast, captured Naples, then turned north. It would take another nine months of heavy fighting to conquer Rome.

AT APPROXIMATELY 6:30 A.M. on June 6, 1944, American General Omar Bradley's First Army troops landed at Normandy on Omaha and Utah beaches, while British and Canadian troops, under General Montgomery's command, waded ashore at Gold, Juno, and Sword an hour later (due to the tides). The Allied troops encountered little resistance at four of the five beaches.

Omaha, fifteen miles southeast of Utah, was the deadly exception. German defenses, contrary to Allied intelligence, were dug in and treacherous. Carefully laid mines permeated the wood pilings and iron barriers that were scattered across the beaches. Massive bunkers and pillboxes guarded the exits. Eighty-five German machine gun nests, more than those at all three beaches combined under Montgomery's command, mowed down the vulnerable infantry as they came ashore. By noon, the American assault troops were still pinned down barely one hundred yards from the Channel waters. But the beleaguered troops, with grit and courage, pushed forward. By nightfall, the beachhead was almost a mile deep along a four-mile front.

Eisenhower boarded the fast British minelayer H.M.S. *Apollo* after breakfast the next day, crossed the Channel, and met with Bradley at Omaha in late morning. He was satisfied, he wrote in his memoirs, that the troops "had finally dislodged the enemy and were proceeding swiftly inland."[29] He added, "[T]he resistance encountered on Omaha Beach was at about the level we had feared all along the line."

Ike's optimistic assessment benefited from his distant postwar perspective. In fact, much had gone wrong in the planning and execution of the Omaha Beach invasion. Allied intelligence had failed to notice that the German 352nd Infantry division, a veteran unit recently returned from the Russian front, had taken positions at Omaha. The invading troops also suffered unanticipated casualties because of inadequate naval bombardment in advance and the lack of air support due to low cloud cover. Lowering the Americans into assault craft twelve miles at sea (rather than the seven miles that was the common practice of the Royal Navy) avoided coastal shelling by the Germans, but virtually guaranteed that the men would be groggy when they landed at Omaha Beach after the three-hour voyage, ill prepared for the intense battle that awaited them.

The Allies suffered ten thousand casualties on D-Day, with the greatest number occurring at Omaha Beach. Still, the initial stage of Overlord was indisputably successful. Allied troops had consolidated a beachhead eight to twelve miles deep and fifty miles across the Normandy coast. By the first week in July, the Allies had landed more than a million men in Normandy, almost two hundred thousand vehicles, and a half-million tons of supplies. Allied aircraft and ships were unchallenged. Ike's worst fear, that Allied troops would be repulsed and forced to retreat across the Channel, was a fading memory.

Despite the success of the invasion, Eisenhower became increasingly impatient with Montgomery for holding his troops' beachhead positions instead of attacking the German troops entrenched at Caen. In a "Dear Monty" note, Ike urged him to "use all possible energy in a determined effort to prevent a stalemate."[30] But in a note to Churchill he was less diplomatic, pleading with the prime minister to "persuade

Monty to get off his bicycle and start moving."[31] Eisenhower's chief of staff, Lieutenant General Walter Bedell Smith, compared his boss to a nervous football coach pacing up and down the sidelines "exhorting everyone to aggressive action."[32]

Ike's fulminations notwithstanding, Montgomery's battle plan was working. His troops held their positions on the east coast of Normandy, drawing the preponderance of German troops. This allowed American Major General J. Lawton Collins's VII Corps troops to break away, capture Cherbourg, and prepare to breach the weaker western German defenses. Aware of Ike's impatience with Montgomery, General Sir Alan Brooke, chief of the imperial general staff, wrote, "It is clear that Ike is *quite* unsuited for the post of Supreme Commander as far as running the strategy of the war is concerned."[33] Even Bradley, Ike's close friend, was puzzled by his boss's anger at Montgomery, whose strategy, he later wrote, had been laid out in advance and proved effective.

On July 26, Montgomery's strategy was vindicated as Collins's troops broke through the western German line at Saint-Lô. In two days, the American troops had advanced thirty miles through crumbling enemy defenses. They were followed by Patton's Third Army, which exploited the gap in the German defense to race into Brittany virtually unopposed, then swung east into southern Normandy. In the next three days, Patton's troops advanced one hundred miles, penetrating deep toward the rear of the German Seventh Army and Fifth Panzer Army. At the same time, Canada's First Army attacked from the north with Patton's troops, now threatening to encircle the enemy forces.

On Hitler's orders, the Germans counterattacked, attempting to cut off Patton's armored columns. But American troops, supported by intense air bombardment, repulsed the enemy and very nearly trapped the entire German force. Although a substantial portion of the desperate enemy troops managed to forge a narrow corridor of escape across the Seine, their losses were devastating. Eisenhower later walked across the battlefield, "stepping on nothing but dead and decaying flesh." It was one of the war's greatest "killing grounds," he wrote, and "could only be described by Dante."[34]

The Allies were on the move and seemed unstoppable. Eisenhower wired Marshall on August 11 that once the retreating German troops were pushed out of northern France, he expected "things to move very rapidly."[35] It appeared that victory was imminent, possibly before the end of the year.*

On the evening of August 24, the church bells of Paris tolled the arrival of French General Jacques Leclerc's 2nd Armored Division on the outskirts of the city. The next day the French troops, supported by the U.S. 4th Division, entered Paris. The French Resistance leader, General Charles de Gaulle, wearing an unadorned khaki uniform, lit the flame at the tomb of the unknown at the Arc de Triomphe. With two million joyful Parisians lining the streets, he then walked with other leaders of the resistance down the Champs Élysées to the Place de la Concorde.

Eisenhower, demonstrating acute political judgment, waited until August 27 to enter Paris, so that de Gaulle could receive the full measure of adulation of the city's residents. He then paid a formal call on de Gaulle at the Palais de l'Élysée, aware of the symbolism of his action. "I did this very deliberatively as a kind of de facto recognition of him as the provisional President of France," he later wrote.[36] "He was very grateful—he never forgot it—looked upon it as a very definite recognition of his high position.†

---

* On August 15, the American Seventh Army and the First French Army successfully landed on the southern coast of France near Marseilles. Code-named Dragoon, the operation opened a second front in western Europe and provided a critical supply route for the final invasion of Germany.

† FDR, in contrast to Eisenhower, distrusted de Gaulle and refused to officially recognize him as the leader of the French resistance.

By the end of August, Allied forces had liberated most of France, Belgium, and Luxembourg. On September 1, Eisenhower assumed direct command of the ground war, a decision that General Brooke predicted would likely prolong the war three to six months.

Ike's great strength had been his extraordinary ability to organize a complex military operation and build consensus among brilliant, egotistical commanders like Montgomery and Patton. But Brooke doubted that he had the decisive instincts of a combat strategist.

Now Eisenhower was faced with a choice between competing strategic plans to end the war. Montgomery urged him to strike quickly north of the Ardennes, with troops led by Montgomery's 21st Army Group, cutting through the Ruhr toward the ultimate goal of capturing Berlin. Bradley, in charge of the Twelfth Army Group, was just as insistent that the major Allied thrust should come south of the Ardennes, spearheaded by Patton's Third Army driving toward Frankfurt. Ike rejected neither plan. Instead, he incorporated them into a larger, more deliberate, broad-based strategy in which six Allied armies would exert pressure across a 450-mile front, from Basel, Switzerland, to Antwerp, Belgium.

Eisenhower's compromise satisfied no one. Montgomery privately complained that Ike appeared "to have a curious idea that every army command must have an equal and fair share of the battle."[37] He predicted that Eisenhower's plan would lead to stalemate, just as a similar strategy had done in the First World War.* Patton called Eisenhower's decision "the most momentous error of the war."[38]

* Ike's plan was later defended by prominent military strategists and historians. "In both world wars there were countless examples of single thrusts, attracting the enemy's reserves and thus being brought to a halt," wrote Lord Carver, Britain's youngest brigadier in 1944 and future field marshal. The American historian Russell F. Weigley observed, "[T]he whole history of American strategy since U.S. Grant confirmed that the enemy can be hit with advantage at several places and thus forced to accentuate his weakness through dissipation." (Atkinson, Rick, *The Guns at Last Light* [2013], pp. 228, 229.)

Allied progress from mid-September to mid-December slowed to a crawl, while casualties mounted at an alarming rate. Patton's Third Army advanced less than twenty-five miles and suffered more than 53,000 casualties. The U.S. First Army lost more than 47,000 men killed, wounded, and missing. Ike's strategy, moreover, demanded a monumental logistical effort, transporting great quantities of food, fuel, and ammunition across muddy, sometimes impassable roads as winter approached. It also gave the German divisions, reeling and exhausted only a few months earlier, critical time to regroup across the Rhine.

ON DECEMBER 16, four German armies with 300,000 men and almost 1,500 tanks mounted a stunning counterattack through the Ardennes forest in snow, fog, and freezing cold, precipitating what became known as the Battle of the Bulge. Allied forces, spread especially thin in the Ardennes, suddenly had to defend an eighty-five-mile sector of the front. The initial German offensive was successful, forcing the surprised and outmanned Allied defenders to retreat. The bad weather became a valuable ally to the Germans, grounding the superior Allied air force in the initial phase of the battle.

Eisenhower, whose strategic proficiency had been so maligned by his own commanders, rose to the challenge with confidence, courage, and extraordinary skill. In an order to Allied troops, he wrote: "By rushing out from his fixed defenses, the enemy may give us the chance to turn his great gamble into his worst defeat. I call upon every man, of all the Allies, to rise now to new heights of courage, of resolution and of effort. Let everyone hold before him a single thought—to destroy the enemy on the ground, in the air, everywhere—destroy him!"[39]

In desperate need of additional troops, Eisenhower approved a directive that would have made black soldiers eligible for combat. After the War Department countermanded the directive, Ike renewed his effort to permit black soldiers to volunteer for combat. He complained to Marshall that more than 100,000 black Americans were performing "back-breaking manual work" on docks and roads and should be eligible to serve in battle.[40] Marshall authorized a modest black infantry unit, initially 2,500 (some of whom accepted a reduction in grade to qualify). Eventually, more than 4,500 black soldiers enlisted for combat duty.

Taking charge of battle strategy, Eisenhower acted decisively to shore up defenses on either side of the German breakthrough, narrowing the corridor of the invading enemy forces. Once the German advance had been contained, Ike ordered a massive counterattack by forces under Montgomery from the north and Patton from the south.

During the battle, in addition to fighting the enemy, Ike was forced to contend with his own obstreperous commanders. Bradley had angrily resigned after Ike announced that Montgomery would lead the troops in the north. Eisenhower calmly told his old West Point classmate, "Brad, I—not you—am responsible to the American people. Your resignation means absolutely nothing."[41] When Bradley persisted in his protest, Ike snapped, "Brad, those are my orders." Eisenhower's relations with the prickly Montgomery were also severely strained by this time. But he did not let his personal feelings interfere with his military judgment that Montgomery was an outstanding combat commander who should be given major responsibility.

By December 22, the threat of a German breakthrough had passed, though many weeks of intense fighting lay ahead. When the fog and clouds cleared on December 26, Allied planes bombarded the exposed German tanks and troops. Finally, the enemy armies began to retreat. But the Battle of the Bulge had inflicted enormous Allied casualties (more than 80,000 killed, wounded, captured, or missing), almost as great as those suffered by the German forces.

Eisenhower was selected as *Time* magazine's "Man of the Year" and appeared on the cover of the magazine's last issue of 1944. The supreme commander's leadership qualities and battlefield successes were described in admiring detail. But the celebration was premature. The year ended without the final Allied victory that Ike and other members of the high command had considered within their grasp in early fall. The original battle line of the Bulge was not restored until the last week in January, and the war continued for more than three months. German General Alfred Jodl formally surrendered to Eisenhower at Reims on May 7, 1945.

Chapter Three

"LOYALTY COMES FIRST"

IN 1946, WITH A WAR-WEARY NATION FINALLY AT PEACE, Earl Warren was so popular with California's voters that he not only won the Republican gubernatorial nomination for a second term but the state Democratic Party's as well. The booming postwar California economy helped burnish his image as a fiscally responsible administrator who could also provide new, valuable social services for the state's citizens. He increased spending for public health and mental health clinics, improved care at state hospitals and conditions in the state prison system, and designated funds for an additional state university campus at Santa Barbara. Without increasing taxes, he left the state with an unprecedented surplus of almost $150 million.

In November, he glided to an easy victory, becoming only the second chief executive in California's ninety-seven-year history to be reelected to a four-year term. On January 6, 1947, he took the oath of office in Sacramento, pledging to work "for the common good without regard to party, faction, or personality."[1]

As he had demonstrated during his first term, Warren's pledge of nonpartisanship went well beyond campaign rhetoric. His record defied orthodox political analysis. At the outset of his administration, his high-level appointments were drawn from the ranks of both major political parties. That initial gesture offended regulars of his Republican Party, but made him more popular with the vast majority of voters. His policies, like his appointments, could not be neatly categorized: he was a fiscal conservative who supported far-reaching social services. He was labeled a middle-of-the-road politician even as he continued to press the legislature to make California the first state in the union to provide prepaid health insurance.

Warren's personal style perfectly fit his nonpartisan image. Despite his intimidating frame (6'1", 215 pounds) his relaxed, avuncular manner and booming laugh immediately put visitors at ease. He had a standing order that his office door should remain open to all callers and regularly held informal, wide-ranging press conferences. He was a member of virtually every fraternal order chartered in the state, including the American Legion, Elks, Masons, and Native Sons of the Golden West. And whenever the handsome, wholesome Warren family was photographed, the governor's potential rivals had another reason to back away from a challenge.

Little wonder that as the 1948 presidential election approached, Warren's name was mentioned as a possible candidate for the Republican nomination should either of the front-runners, New York governor Dewey or Ohio senator Taft, falter. In a column headlined "WHAT ABOUT WARREN OF CALIFORNIA?" the *Los Angeles Times* political columnist Kyle Palmer also raised the name of General Dwight D. Eisenhower as a potential dark horse rival to Warren.[2] "It is undeniably true that Eisenhower looms as the most promising outside runner at this time," wrote Palmer. "And for this very reason he may appear less available when the convention ballots on a nominee than he does seven or eight months ahead of the event." Palmer cautioned Eisenhower supporters against a premature campaign. "[W]hen the general becomes a plain mister or, as the case may be, a university head, he may indulge a wish that his enthusiastic supporters had stepped on the brake instead of the accelerator back in November or December of 1947."

WARREN DID NOTHING to tamp down speculation about a potential presidential bid when he spent a week in Washington just five weeks after being sworn in for his second gubernatorial term. He privately weighed in on both international and domestic issues, according to *Boston Globe* columnist Doris Fleeson. The United States could not afford economic or political isolation, he said, if the world was to remain at peace in the postwar era. His national priorities would be to balance the budget and reduce the national debt, rather than reduce taxes. Fleeson concluded that "his cue is still to play his cards close to his chest."[3]

By the summer of 1947, there were widespread rumors that Warren would go to the Republican national convention as the "willing" favorite-son presidential candidate of the Far West.[4] In November, Warren made it official, announcing that he would seek the Republican nomination for president.

The California governor was "a picture book candidate," wrote *New York Herald Tribune* columnist Stephen White.[5] He radiated both geniality and strength as he parried questions from the national press corps in his Sacramento office. Since Warren was virtually unchallenged as a candidate of the West, he could afford to sidestep controversial national issues, and did so with aplomb. Warren, it was further noted, was an experienced organization man who had risen through the Republican ranks in his state. "The party likes a party man," White observed, rather than an outsider like General Eisenhower.

Only one organization, the Women's Political Study Club of California, openly and formally opposed Warren's candidacy. At its annual state convention, the delegates passed a resolution charging that "Governor Warren has only seen fit to give the Negro token and minor representation in state affairs during his administration."[6] The organization resolved to withdraw its long-standing support of the governor and pledged an all-out effort "to eradicate from high offices men who do not believe in an America for all Americans." Frustration with Warren was later repeatedly echoed in interviews with black Californians in the African-American newspaper, the *Chicago Defender.* "He's no good for Negroes," said one. "He interprets our race through a few pet-Negroes, for whom he will do some small favors, and that is the extent of his political dealings and thoughts of us," said another.[7]

By April 1948, with the Republican convention in Philadelphia only two months away, Warren came under increasing scrutiny. *Time* magazine reported that his admirers applauded him as "solid, patient, dependable, an able incorruptible administrator who has built up enormous public faith in his honesty and political integrity." His critics countered that "he is a confirmed fence-straddler who rides the donkey and the elephant at the same time, a phony liberal who proposes social reforms with one hand and fails to push them through with the other, a bullheaded, plodding mediocrity who never says or does anything out of the ordinary."[8]

National columnist Raymond Moley, an admirer of Warren since his days as Alameda County district attorney, observed that the California governor possessed a profound sense of the public interest, as distinguished from piecemeal concerns of the many special interests. *Washington Post* columnist Joseph Alsop wrote that Warren was a progressive Republican worried about the direction of his party and concluded that "[w]ise Republicans are likely to have reason to be grateful for such a champion."[9]

IN THE WAKE of Germany's surrender in May 1945, General Eisenhower became the heroic symbol of the Allied victory. He was feted and honored across Europe, from France (Grand Officer of the Legion of Honor) to the Netherlands (Knight Grand Cross of the Order of the Lion) to Norway (Grand Commander of the Order of Saint Olaf). In London's medieval Guildhall, he was presented the sword worn by the Duke of Wellington at Waterloo and delivered a speech that was both eloquent and humble. "Had I possessed the military skill of a Marlborough, the wisdom of Solomon, the understanding of Lincoln," he said, "I still would have been helpless without the loyalty, and vision, and generosity of thousands upon thousands of British and Americans."[10]

When Eisenhower returned to the United States, millions of New Yorkers cheered as he grinned and waved to the largest crowd in the city's history. In the nation's capital, speaking before a joint session of Congress, he received the longest ovation in congressional history. In his hometown of Abilene, Kansas, where crowds swelled to four times the town's population, reporters pressed Ike to declare if he would enter politics. He replied, "I'm a soldier, and I am positive that no one thinks of me as a politician. In the strongest language you can state that I have no political ambitions at all."[11]

He had made the same point—that he was a military man, not a politician—in a good-humored way to President Truman in Germany in July 1945. The president had told Eisenhower, "General, there is nothing that you may want that I won't try to help you get. That definitely and specifically includes the presidency in 1948."[12] Ike laughed and replied, "Mr. President, I don't know who will be your opponent for the presidency, but it will not be me."

Behind Ike's irresistible grin and relentless good humor was a man of strong opinions on the most controversial issues of the day. He had been appalled when he was told by Secretary of War Henry Stimson at Potsdam in July 1945 of the plan to drop an atomic bomb on Japan. "So I voiced to him [Stimson] my grave misgivings," he later wrote, "first on the basis of my belief that Japan was already defeated and that dropping the bomb was completely unnecessary, and secondly because

I thought that our country should avoid shocking world opinion by the use of a weapon whose employment was no longer mandatory as a measure to save American lives."[13]

Ever the optimist, even as tensions mounted with the Soviet Union over the governance of postwar Germany, Eisenhower believed that the United States and the Soviet Union could live in peaceful coexistence. On a visit to Moscow at Stalin's invitation in August 1945, he said at a news conference, "I see nothing in the future that would prevent Russia and the United States from being the closest of friends."[14]

After the euphoria of leading the Allies to victory in Europe, Eisenhower's postwar military career was, understandably, an anticlimax. He was first given the difficult task of commanding American troops in postwar Germany, where his restless soldiers' overwhelming desire was to come home. Upon his return to Washington in the fall, he was informed by President Truman that he would succeed Marshall as Army Chief of Staff. It was a natural progression in his illustrious military career but proved frustrating. Whereas his command of Allied forces during World War II required all of his extraordinary military skills, as army chief of staff he was bogged down with petty bureaucratic infighting among the services and the thankless task of overseeing the demobilization of the army in the postwar era.

Contemplating his postmilitary career, Eisenhower thought that he might accept the presidency of a small rural college. But in April 1946 he was presented with an unexpected option. Thomas J. Watson, a member of Columbia University's board of trustees, asked him to consider the presidency of the Ivy League university. Ike told him that he was speaking to the wrong Eisenhower; his brother Milton possessed the required scholarly depth and vast experience in academic administration. Undeterred, Watson told Ike that he, not Milton, was the choice of the trustees. He told Ike that the faculty would take care of academic affairs, and the trustees would do the fund-raising. Eisenhower would offer the university his enormous international stature and be free to lecture widely and write articles and books. The general listened attentively without making a commitment. Thirteen months later, Watson and Eisenhower had another conversation about the Columbia presidency. Watson, now speaking formally on behalf of his fellow trustees, emphasized the importance of the public service of the Columbia presidency and offered him the job. In June 1947 Eisenhower accepted, with his tenure to begin a year later.

Eisenhower's decision did not discourage Democratic and Republican leaders from courting him for their party's presidential nomination in 1948. Gallup and Roper polls showed that he was more popular than either President Truman or the leading Republican candidates, Dewey and Taft. But Ike refused even to say whether he was a Democrat or Republican, or if he would accept a draft at either party's presidential convention.

Finally, in January 1948, a week after New Hampshire Republicans had formally entered a slate of delegates pledged to Eisenhower in the state's March primaries, he wrote a letter to Leonard Finder, the publisher of the Manchester *Union Leader*, which had endorsed him for president, that appeared to take him out of the 1948 presidential race. "[L]ifelong professional soldiers, in the absence of some obvious and overriding reasons, should abstain from seeking political office," he wrote.[15] It was doubtful that he would find "obvious and overriding reasons" to change his mind in 1948, especially since he would surely face stiff opposition from either loyal Democratic supporters of President Truman or the two Republican front-runners, Dewey and Taft, who were unlikely to yield without a convention fight.

———

ON APRIL 3, 1948, a packed gallery greeted Eisenhower with spontaneous applause as he entered the Senate hearing room to testify before the Armed Services Committee. He was dressed in full military uniform, even though he was on terminal leave from the army.

"I am a brass hat and I say it with pride," he declared, as if anyone could forget his exemplary service as the Allies' supreme commander during World War II.[16] He had been asked to testify before the Senate committee about pending legislation providing for long-range military planning that included an immediate selective draft and universal military training.

Eisenhower, reading from notes but without a prepared text, strongly supported both measures. The legislation was necessary to preserve the democratic way of life and counter an ideology that "seeks to destroy democracy," he said.[17] He named no nation or ideology. But in the throes of the Cold War, everyone in the hearing room assumed that the target of his warning was the Soviet Union. "It is impossible to live isolated on an island of democracy in a sea of dictatorship," he asserted.

His testimony was less surefooted when he was asked about racial segregation in the armed forces. In response to a question by Senator Leverett Saltonstall (R-Mass.) about the army's racial policy, Eisenhower acknowledged that race prejudice was a fact of military life, as it was in the nation at large. After the Normandy invasion in the summer of 1944, he said, the Allied command became desperate for infantry replacements. Eisenhower recalled that he had approved the organization of black troops in segregated platoons to avoid racial friction. "I personally see no reason why he [the black soldier] should not be amalgamated to that extent," he told the committee.[18]

He foresaw problems if the postwar military racial policy went further. "In general, the Negro is less well educated than his brother citizen that is white," he testified, "and if you make a complete amalgamation, what you are going to have is in every company the Negro is going to be relegated to the minor jobs and is never going to get his promotions [e.g., to technical sergeant], because the competition is too tough." The problem will disappear, he said, "through education, through mutual respect." But, he added, "I do believe that if we attempt merely by passing a lot of laws to force someone to like someone else, we are just going to get into trouble."[19]

Even though he was expected to become president of Columbia in June, Eisenhower was still prominently mentioned as a potential presidential candidate. His every public statement, therefore, was tracked closely by the national media. His full-fledged support for military preparedness in his testimony before the Senate Armed Services Committee received extensive coverage. But his remarks on the military's racial policy were largely ignored. Leaders of the black community, however, took notice and soon registered their protest of his "jim crow" advocacy.[20] NAACP chapters from Connecticut to Virginia condemned Eisenhower's testimony.

His testimony was especially wrenching to Walter White, executive secretary of the NAACP, who recalled his conversations with Eisenhower during the war and in the United States upon Ike's return. Eisenhower appeared to White as "one who for both practical and idealistic reasons would never tolerate discrimination and segregation."[21] After the Normandy invasion, Eisenhower had written White that "Negro troops did their duty excellently under fire on Normandy's beaches in a zone of heavy combat and suffered substantial casualties. You may well be proud of [their] accomplishments."[22] But after Eisenhower's Senate committee testimony, White confessed that he had been naïve in paying tribute to Eisenhower in his newspaper column just a week before.

At the committee hearings, Eisenhower's sharp retort to Georgia senator Richard Russell's racist innuendo had gone virtually unnoticed in the press. Russell pointedly read into the record that black troops had higher crime and venereal disease rates than whites. Those damning statistics, Eisenhower replied, were the result of lower education standards among black soldiers and would change with greater educational opportunities.

Another segregationist Armed Services Committee member, Senator

Burnet Maybank (D-S.C.), claiming to be in "complete agreement" with Eisenhower's testimony on the military's racial policy, later introduced an amendment to the proposed legislation that would have assigned draftees to units composed of their own race. The *New York Herald Tribune* condemned Maybank's "pernicious" amendment, which failed, and attempted to explain the rationale behind Eisenhower's testimony. "What General Eisenhower argued against, "the *Herald Tribune*'s editorial observed, "was the idea that at a single blow, by one piece of legislation, this complex problem of the armed forces could be solved."[23]

New York City mayor William O'Dwyer, who would later join other prominent Democrats in a draft-Eisenhower movement, defended the general's testimony, placing it in the broader context of his World War II experience. He recalled an earlier Eisenhower speech in which the general had said, "The job of the army is to set up an efficient military machine. It isn't to carry out social reforms; nor is it the army's job to maintain an outmoded *status quo ante* of segregation."[24]

Eisenhower did not respond publicly to the furor created by his testimony.

But he privately wrote his approval of an explanation offered by a sympathetic correspondent, Rudolph Treuenfels, to a friend. "The only reason why he [Eisenhower] would counsel caution on the issue [of] desegregating the armed forces completely rather today than tomorrow," Treuenfels had written, "[was that] he realizes that the Army cannot succeed with the move unless backed by a more enlightened attitude throughout the Nation."[25]

––––––––––

BEFORE ASSUMING HIS new duties as president of Columbia, Eisenhower had one major piece of lucrative business to complete. He had signed a contract with Doubleday to write his wartime memoirs for $635,000 (more than $6 million in today's dollars). What made the deal particularly attractive was the Internal Revenue Service's benign interpretation of a lump sum advance by a one-time author. Had Eisenhower signed a traditional royalty contract with Doubleday or any other publisher, his advance would have been taxed as ordinary income at the rate of 82 percent. Since Eisenhower was paid in a single lump sum, however, his income was taxed as capital gains, not ordinary income, at the rate of 25 percent. This left the author with after-tax income of $476,250. The contract would make Eisenhower wealthy for the first time in his life.

In early February, Eisenhower had begun dictating his memoirs to three rotating secretaries for sixteen hours a day, seven days a week. Shortly after 7 a.m. every morning, for six weeks, he paced the four steps from the window of his office to his desk, then two steps from his desk to the door, and back again. Maps, personal letters, memoranda, documents, and books were assembled neatly on his desk for ready reference. In his rigorous daily routine, he not only dictated new chapters, but also revised earlier ones. His typists and editors were awed by his indefatigable energy, prodigious memory, and focus.

By early April, he had sent the final chapters of the memoirs to Kenneth McCormick, the editor in chief at Doubleday. Eisenhower had consciously modeled his memoir on that of Ulysses Grant, whose autobiography was considered one of the finest works of nonfiction in the English language. Though Eisenhower could not emulate Grant's spare, eloquent prose, his narrative was, nonetheless, a lucid, straightforward reminiscence devoid of both self-congratulations and score-settling.*

IN THE *New York Times Magazine* issue of April 18, 1948, Governor Warren defined "liberalism" as the belief "that the individual should

---

* More than 1,170,000 copies of *Crusade in Europe* were sold in the U.S.; the book was translated into twenty-two foreign languages. His royalties under a traditional publishing contract would have exceeded his one-time-payment contract.

be the all-important, precious object of consideration in every phrase of social relationship" and that "[c]ivil rights, representative government, and equality of opportunity are all part and parcel of the liberal tradition."[26] He noted that liberalism had been distorted and abused by Communists and Communist sympathizers who were interested neither in the freedom of the individual nor in liberal institutions. Instead of dividing political allegiances between liberals and conservatives, he suggested three groups: reactionary, progressive, and radical. He said that he was neither a reactionary who was indifferent to the welfare of others, nor a radical who wanted democratic institutions to fail. Instead, he firmly placed himself in the progressive tradition that sought to make government work every day to improve the lot of the individual.

Although Warren defined progressivism in platitudes, his version was rooted in practical, tangible results. Emulating his progressive hero Hiram Johnson, he had kept the public apprised of his policy agenda, which included taking on special interests, such as the banking lobby that had pressed for a tax break for the industry. He also successfully battled the oil-and-gas lobby over a 3 percent sales tax to fund new highway construction. Just as vigilantly, he continued to fight the American Medical Association, which opposed his plan for catastrophic state health insurance.

But Warren's progressivism went far beyond Johnson's pledge to make government transparent and to fight special interests. He implemented prison and pension reforms, education and highway improvements, and workmen's compensation. He persistently, though in vain, urged the state legislature to provide prepaid health insurance. Although he spoke of civil rights as a cornerstone of good government, he did not attack racial prejudice with the same vigor that he had pursued other policy initiatives. This could explain the resolution by the Women's Political Study Club of California to oppose his presidential candidacy.

On the eve of the 1948 Republican presidential convention, Warren appeared on the CBS television program "Presidential Timber," impressing the editors of *Time* as "the best campaigner yet on the newest communications medium to reach into the U.S. home. His big, square-cut Scandinavian face was etched handsomely on the screen," the editors observed.[27] "[H]e was relaxed, direct and confident." But at the convention, neither Warren's visceral appeal nor Taft's dogged opposition could derail the Dewey nomination. When the New York governor's nomination appeared inevitable, Warren called Dewey to pledge California's delegates to him.

At 2:30 a.m. on the day that Republican delegates were scheduled to choose a vice-presidential nominee, Warren was awakened by a phone call from Dewey asking him to come to his hotel headquarters. At their meeting, Dewey told Warren that he had polled Republican leaders from across the country, and all agreed that the California governor should be his running mate. If he accepted and the Republican ticket was elected, Dewey promised that he would give Warren important responsibilities in the new administration. Warren would have preferred to return to California to complete his gubernatorial term, but he knew that if he turned Dewey down a second time, he would forfeit any meaningful future role in the Republican Party. He accepted.

During the fall campaign, Warren, seated in his private railroad car, was the very picture of a happy, confident candidate. He chatted amiably with reporters, leisurely drank bourbon highballs before dinner, read Winston Churchill's *The Gathering Storm*, and was asleep before midnight. His fourteen-car "Vice Presidential Special" rolled down the eastern slopes of the Sierra Nevada Mountains toward Reno, one of the early stops on his thirty-one-day tour in which Warren planned to make twenty-five speeches and fifty-seven platform appearances in thirty of the forty-eight states.

He struck a congenial, nonconfrontational tone, speaking as if a Republican victory was inevitable, as every national poll confidently predicted. At every whistle-stop he appeared on the back platform smiling broadly, waving to the small crowds, leaning down to sign autographs, and shaking hands with well-wishers. He rarely abandoned his folksy, nonpartisan approach. "The vast majority of Americans know that good Americans are to be found in both parties," he said, and asked, almost reluctantly, if the time had not "come for better housekeeping methods that can only be supplied by new leadership and a new broom?"[28]

In Tulsa, he finally responded to President Truman's relentless attacks on the Dewey-Warren ticket by declaring that "the Democratic Party and its splinters, present to the people of the U.S. in this national campaign a sorry spectacle of warring factions, city machines, rebellious elements, pressure minorities, fellow travelers and left-wingers."*[29] For good measure, he accused the Truman administration of being soft on communism. But those attacks were aberrations from his usually soporific campaign speeches.

Behind the calm public facade, Warren was incensed by the treatment he received from his running mate. Dewey only spoke to him twice during the entire campaign. Worse, Dewey's strategists deployed speech writers to make sure that Warren said nothing that might contradict Dewey or stir controversy when it appeared that the Republican ticket was going to sail to an easy victory in November. "I'm so low in this campaign," Warren told Walter Jones, the editor of the *Sacramento Bee*, "I can't say what I want to say."[30] For a man of Warren's stature, accustomed to giving orders, it was not just demoralizing but humiliating.

Warren returned to California with noticeable relief and awaited the election returns. After Truman stunned the nation with his upset

---

* The "splinters" reference was to the rebellion of two groups of traditional Democrats: the segregationist Dixiecrat Party that nominated South Carolina governor Strom Thurmond as its presidential candidate, and the left-leaning Progressive Party's nominee, Henry Wallace, who had served in President Franklin D. Roosevelt's cabinet.

victory over Dewey, Warren said, "It feels as if a hundred pound sack had been taken off my back."[31]

———————

IN JUNE 1948, Ike and Mamie moved into a four-story palatial mansion at 60 Morningside Drive on New York City's Upper West Side, where Eisenhower's legendary predecessor, Columbia president Nicholas Murray Butler, had entertained British royalty, numerous heads of state, and scores of Nobel laureates. During Butler's presidency, dinner was served under crystal chandeliers at a dining table that comfortably seated thirty.

The Eisenhowers did not attempt to emulate Butler's grand style. They usually entertained informally, most often dinner and bridge with Ike's friends. Ike quickly converted the penthouse solarium into an art studio where he spent happy nocturnal hours painting in oils, a pastime that Churchill had urged upon him. He never took his paintings too seriously, calling them "daubs, born of my love of color and in my pleasure in experimenting."[32] But his "daubs" became a passionate hobby for the rest of his life.

Shortly after Republicans had nominated Dewey and Warren at their party's presidential convention, several hundred Eisenhower admirers gathered outside the new Columbia president's residence, chanting "We Like Ike." Ike waved to them from his balcony but made no comment.

With the Democratic convention less than two weeks away, pressure mounted on Eisenhower to say if he would accept a draft. Prominent party leaders sent telegrams to all 1,592 Democratic delegates inviting them to attend a caucus on July 10, just two days before the opening gavel in Philadelphia.* The purpose, the telegrams stated, was to "find the ablest and strongest man" available to lead the party.[33] It

* The list of signatories included Connecticut governor Chester Bowles, New York City mayor William O' Dwyer, Senator Lister Hill of Alabama, Minneapolis mayor Hubert Humphrey, and Congressman James Roosevelt of California.

was an obvious attempt to dump Truman, who immediately moved to squelch an incipient draft-Eisenhower movement. At the president's direction, Secretary of the Army Kenneth Royall spoke to Eisenhower by telephone, asking him to clarify his intentions. Finally, Ike put an end to speculation when he wrote leading Democrats supporting his candidacy, including Congressman James Roosevelt, declaring, "No matter under what terms, conditions, or premises a proposal might be couched, I would refuse to accept the nomination."[34]

Eisenhower moved the office of the Columbia president from his predecessor's isolated suite above the library rotunda (accessible by a single private elevator) to the first floor, where he hoped to meet faculty and students. At the same time, he brought in two career military men as administrators who assumed that their primary mission was to protect their boss from nettlesome faculty and students. Consequently, few members of the university community dropped in on their famous new president.

After the Soviet Union blockaded Berlin in June, Eisenhower came under pressure to keep Communist speakers off campus and to reject funding from governments behind the Iron Curtain. But he did not waver in his defense of academic freedom. He supported the invitation for the executive director of the American Communist Party to speak on campus. "I deem it not only unobjectionable but very wise to allow opposing systems to be presented by their proponents," he said.[35] He also defended the university's decision to fund an endowed chair by the Communist government of Poland to study that country's philology, language, and literature. "A great deal of the trouble in the world today is traceable to a lack of understanding of the culture of various countries," he said. "I intend to do all in my power to remedy the situation."[36]

At his formal installation as president of Columbia in October 1948, he received the greatest ovation of the day from the throng of more than twenty thousand that attended when he underscored his commitment to academic freedom: "Academic freedom is nothing more than the specific application of the freedoms inherent in the American way of life. There will be no administrative suppression or distortion of any subject that merits a place in this university's curriculum. The facts of Communism, for instance, shall be taught here—its ideological development, its political methods, its economic effects, its probable course in the future."[37]

In one of his most warmly received speeches to university students, Ike implored them to take a little time every day to have fun. The president set an example. He regularly attended the university's football games and sometimes slipped away from his office to watch the team's scrimmages under the watchful eye of Coach Lou Little, an old friend from Ike's coaching days. When he heard that Yale had made Little an offer, he personally persuaded him to stay at Columbia.

On Wednesday afternoons, Ike was driven to Blind Brook Country Club in Westchester County to play golf with William Robinson, publisher of the *New York Herald Tribune,* and other members of what became known as "the Gang." After Robinson had arranged for Ike's memoirs, *Crusade in Europe,* to be serialized in the *Herald Tribune,* he had escorted him to Georgia's Augusta National Golf Club for a vacation where he introduced him to the other members of the Gang. They were wealthy, successful businessmen and, with one exception, stalwart Republicans.* They became his closest friends, playing golf and bridge with him, talking politics, offering advice on his investments, and swapping jokes and aphorisms.† The Gang picked up all of

---

* Besides Robinson, they included Clifford Roberts, an investment banker, Robert Woodruff, chairman of the board of Coca-Cola, W. Alton "Pete" Jones, president of Cities Services Company (now Citgo), and Ellis Slater, president of Frankfort Distilleries. George Allen, a corporate lawyer and financier, was the only Democrat in the group.

† The only two professions in which amateurs excel, Ike told them, were prostitution and the military. (*New York Times,* November 16, 2014.)

Ike's expenses, built a cottage for him at Augusta, and stocked a nearby pond with bass for his private use.

On election night, Ike was joined at his Morningside Heights residence by Robinson, Roberts, and Allen for dinner and bridge. Roberts recalled that Ike was "just as disappointed as Robinson and I were" in Dewey's defeat and appeared to be "having second thoughts about his decision to stay clear of political involvement."[38]

———

BY 1949, the anti-Communist crusade had infected campuses and state legislatures across the country. At Columbia, Eisenhower had defended academic freedom, insisting that the university must remain a beacon of intellectual inquiry free from political orthodoxy. But on the West Coast, the University of California's board of regents, on which Governor Warren served as *ex officio* chairman, voted in late March 1949 to impose a loyalty oath on all university employees, including the faculty. Under the oath, employees were required to swear that they did not support "any party or organization that believes in, advocates, or teaches the overthrow of the United States Government by force or violence."*[39] Although Warren did not participate in the initial regents' vote, he eventually became embroiled in the university's heated oath controversy.

Pressure to require a loyalty oath at the University of California had been building since January 1949, when State Senator Jack Tenney, chairman of the legislature's Un-American Activities Committee, had introduced a bill to amend the state constitution to authorize the legislature, rather than the university's board of regents, to test the loyalty of university employees. While the Tenney bill was pending, the provost of UCLA approved invitations to two controversial speakers to the Los Angeles campus. The first invitation went to Harold Laski,

---

* University employees were already required to swear an oath of allegiance to the Constitution of the United States and the constitution of the state of California.

a member of the British Labour Party, who admitted that he was a socialist but denied that he was a Communist. The second invitation was extended to Professor Herbert J. Phillips, who had recently been dismissed from the faculty of the University of Washington because of his membership in the Communist Party. Phillips was asked to debate the question whether one who held membership in the Communist Party could be "an objective teacher and impartial researcher."[40]

The president of the University of California, Robert Sproul, proposed the loyalty oath at the university's board of regents' meeting on March 25, 1949. Sproul, an old friend of Warren's, who had nominated him for the presidency at the Republican convention the previous summer, was no anti-Communist crusader. His primary concern was that the state legislature might take authority for educational policy away from the university. The proposed oath was unanimously approved by the regents at their March meeting. The president told the board that the new oath would be in new faculty contracts for the 1949–50 academic year.

The university's faculty first learned of the oath in the *Faculty Bulletin* on May 9, 1949, but did not know the content of the oath until a month later. The faculty senate then voted to delete or revise the new oath and delegated the task to an advisory committee. The regents, in an attempt to avoid a confrontation with the faculty, met later in June and proposed revisions to the oath. But the revised oath still required that a faculty member swear, "I am not a member of the Communist Party." Sproul's office then issued contracts only to faculty members who had signed the oath. When the faculty senate next convened in September, a majority repudiated the oath and demanded that it be deleted from their contracts.

After the faculty senate's vote, Sproul changed his position, declaring that enforcement of the oath, even in its revised form, was "neither practical nor wise."[41] But now he faced ardent opposition from members of the regents, led by San Francisco attorney John Francis Neylan.

The attorney argued that the oath must be retained on two grounds: the university could not tolerate the employment of Communists, and the governance of the university must reside with the regents, not the faculty. The university senate, meanwhile, declared that the faculty was the ultimate authority on decisions "affecting the conditions crucial to the work of teaching and research," including qualification for membership on the university faculty.[42]

An embattled Sproul called Warren in late November, urging him to get involved in the regents' oath controversy. The governor received a similar request from Frank Kidner, an economics professor at Berkeley who had been an adviser to Warren during the 1948 presidential campaign and was an opponent of the oath.

On January 13, 1950, Warren attended his first regents meeting in which the oath was discussed. At a second meeting on February 24, 1950, a majority of the regents passed a resolution drafted by Neylan reaffirming the oath requirement and asserting the regents' authority to set conditions of employment for the university. Failure to sign the oath constituted severance of the nonsigner's connection with the university at the end of the academic year. The resolution passed by a vote of 12–6 with Warren's vote recorded in dissent.

"LOYALTY OATH OR NO JOB, CAL PROFESSORS ARE TOLD," read the banner headline on the front page of the *San Francisco Chronicle* the next morning.[43] "The Regents of the University of California, headed by Governor Earl Warren, laid down a flat policy yesterday to reluctant professors: Sign the anti-Communist oath or no job." The *Chronicle* article did not report the split among the regents over the resolution.

Warren waited three days before declaring publicly that he opposed the oath. In his public statement he said that the oath was ineffective since any Communist would sign it "and laugh about it."[44] He also contended that it was both unnecessary and unenforceable because the faculty was already required to support the U.S. Constitution.

At a regents' meeting on March 31, Warren elaborated on his reasons for opposing the oath. He began by pledging his continued opposition to Communists in California. "I have worked against the Communists and tried to thwart them in this State when my voice was like a voice in the wilderness, and I am not one whit less interested in trying to thwart them at the moment."[45] He then reiterated his loyalty to his alma mater where three of his children were enrolled and "God willing I will have two more in two or three years." He also defended the loyalty of the university's faculty. "I don't believe that it is soft on Communism and neither am I," he said. "The only thing the people of this State are interested in is our seeking to keep Communists out of the University and, believe me, I am interested in that too."

At a regents meeting on April 21, Warren supported a compromise resolution that passed 21–1. It provided for a prescribed form that the faculty signer was not a member of the Communist Party or other organization advocating the forcible overthrow of the government. Nonsigners were given the right to petition the president and the faculty committee on privilege and tenure, requesting a review of their cases to convince them that they were not members of the Communist Party. During their review, nonsigners could receive their salaries for the 1949–50 academic year. The only dissenter, Mario Giannini, resigned from the board, complaining that, as a result of the regents' compromise, "the flag would fly in the Kremlin."[46]

Neylan and other hard-liners on the board soon withdrew their support for the compromise, realizing that faculty members could refuse to sign the oath, receive a favorable review from the president and faculty committee, and still remain on the faculty. They were concerned, moreover, that the compromise undercut the board's ultimate authority to govern the university. At a board meeting on August 25, the regents voted 12–10 to dismiss thirty-one persons who had not signed the form and had been favorably reported on by the reviewing committee. Warren dissented.

A faculty group of nonsigners responded by declaring that any written statement requiring their political affiliation violated academic freedom. The nonsigners also prepared a legal challenge to the board's dismissals, which was ultimately successful.*

In late September, only weeks after an ugly regents-faculty showdown appeared inevitable, Warren called a special session of the legislature and attempted to wrest control of the oath controversy from the university and return it to the state legislature. On September 21, he proposed that the legislature require all state employees to sign an oath swearing that, as a condition of their employment, they did not support or belong to "any party or organization, political or otherwise, that now advocates the overthrow of the government of the United States or the State of California." In supporting the legislation, Warren said, "I approach this matter strictly as a matter of security for the state and the nation. Loyalty comes first—and hence this loyalty oath."[47] The bill, known as the Levering oath, named for its sponsor, passed overwhelmingly, and Warren signed the legislation on October 3, 1950.

Warren publicly professed uncertainty whether the proposed oath applied to the University of California. But on October 13, the state controller announced that University of California employees "must sign the new State loyalty oath or go without pay."[48]

Ironically, the legislation proposed by Warren in September 1950 was just as onerous as the oath sponsored more than a year and a half earlier by Senator Tenney who, not surprisingly, enthusiastically supported the governor's proposal. The governor's defenders later

---

* The California District Court of Appeals decided unanimously in favor of the petitioners, declaring that members of the faculty could not be subjected to a narrower test of loyalty than the constitutional oath prescribed. On appeal, the California Supreme Court ruled in favor of the faculty petitioners on different grounds: the regents' oath must be struck down, the court decided, because the faculty could only be required to sign an oath for all state employees.

explained that his motivation for proposing the legislation was to prevent the university from being singled out for an oath requirement. In his memoirs Warren did not offer any explanation for the legislation. Indeed, he did not even mention it.

From the outset, Warren's approach to the oath controversy was characterized by extreme caution. For the first year of the controversy, he took no public position on a loyalty oath, either the one proposed by Senator Tenney or that later introduced by Warren's close friend, University of California president Sproul. He waited until a meeting of the university's board of regents in February 1950 to record his opposition to the oath and another month before making his opposition public. In later meetings, he voted with Sproul and other members of the board who opposed an oath or, alternatively, favored a compromise that provided nonsigners with a hearing before they could be dismissed.

Part of the explanation for Warren's caution undoubtedly had to do with his political ambition. When the oath controversy first surfaced, Warren was considering a run for a third term as governor and, possibly, the presidency in 1952. His lieutenant governor, Goodwin J. "Goody" Knight, a vocal anti-Communist and supporter of the regents' oath, was considering a challenge to Warren for the Republican nomination for governor. And Congressman Richard M. Nixon, an ambitious young rising star in the Republican Party, was, like Knight, an outspoken anti-Communist and supporter of the regents' oath. By the fall of 1950, moreover, anti-Communist fervor in the United States was intense and pervasive. North Korea had invaded South Korea in June 1950, and the U.S. military defense of South Korea (under the auspices of the United Nations) was not going well. Warren had ample reasons to protect his right flank from charges that he was soft on communism.

The oath controversy forced Warren to defend two deeply held and potentially irreconcilable convictions. The first was his belief in the patriotism of the faculty of his beloved alma mater. At the same time he retained a visceral hatred for the Communist Party that dated back to his years as district attorney of Alameda County. His fear and loathing of communism remained unabated throughout his political career in California.*

In his memoirs, Warren never suggested that there was a conflict between his desire to defend the integrity of his alma mater's faculty and his determination to rid his state of Communists. His version of the oath controversy emphasized his outspoken and consistent opposition to the "hysteria about Communism" that was pervasive in the country at the height of the Cold War.[49] He blamed a small minority on the board of regents for instigating the oath controversy at the University of California. He wrote that he had played a major role in opposing the regents' loyalty oath from the beginning of the controversy, which was not true, and that his concern for academic freedom was an important reason for his opposition. But neither the internal record of the regents' deliberations nor Warren's public statements at the time support his later claim of outspoken support for academic freedom. If he had truly championed academic freedom throughout the controversy, as he later claimed, he would not have proposed and signed legislation imposing a state loyalty oath.

The only record of Warren's strong defense of academic freedom during the controversy was offered by Warren himself in his memoirs. He recalled a private conversation that he had with Norman Chandler, the publisher of the *Los Angeles Times*, at the annual retreat of members of the Bohemian Club of San Francisco. The conversation occurred, he wrote, after he heard that Chandler had ordered an editorial critical of Warren's opposition to the regents' loyalty oath. Warren

---

* While governor, Warren maintained a close working relationship with FBI director J. Edgar Hoover. He regularly asked the FBI to vet potential appointees to state office and once called on the bureau to check out a group requesting a meeting with him that he suspected of "Communist-infiltration." (Newton, Jim, *Justice for All: Earl Warren and the Nation He Made* [2006], p. 215.)

said that he convinced Chandler that the faculty's academic freedom was no less precious to them than the freedom of the press was to his newspaper.

In contrast to Warren, Eisenhower's defense of academic freedom was public and forceful, beginning with his inaugural address in October 1948. Eisenhower and Harvard's president, James Conant, were the first university presidents to publicly oppose faculty loyalty oaths. And after Senator Joseph McCarthy had accused Philip Jessup, a renowned professor of international law and diplomacy at Columbia, of "an unusual affinity for Communist causes," Eisenhower wrote Jessup a letter, placed in the public record, expressing his admiration for the professor's scholarship and deploring "the association of your name with the current loyalty investigation in the United States Senate."[50]

Eisenhower's defense of academic freedom, to be sure, had its limits. It was one thing for a faculty member to teach the tenets of communism; it was quite another to use the classroom for Communist indoctrination that would undermine democratic values. He vowed to dismiss any teacher "infiltrating our university with inimical philosophies."[51]

EISENHOWER'S EARLY TENURE in the Columbia presidency was a singular triumph.[52] He charmed faculty and students alike with his warmth and good humor. And, when he chose, he surprised them with his fine intellect. The entire university community applauded his vigorous defense of academic freedom. When he attended a black-tie dinner of the history faculty, he impressed the distinguished scholars with his knowledge of military history dating back to Thucydides and the Peloponnesian War.

He tackled tough administrative issues, including the university's precarious financial health, with straightforward determination. He set Columbia on a course of fiscal responsibility after a decade of budget deficits and a declining endowment. Although he had been promised by the university's trustees that he would have no role in fund-raising, he participated in an ambitious alumni campaign (goal: $210 million—more than $1.9 billion today) to replenish the university's coffers.

With flattery and cold, practical arguments, he persuaded Isidor Rabi, winner of the Nobel Prize in physics, to turn down an offer from Princeton's Institute for Advanced Study and stay at Columbia. Rabi's departure, Ike told the physicist, would have a devastating effect on the university, not only demoralizing the faculty but undermining Columbia's ability to attract brilliant graduate students.

He also successfully engaged in face-to-face negotiations with Michael Quill, the tough head of the Transport Workers Union of America, to reach a settlement with the university's maintenance workers. Ike offered the union workers what he considered to be a fair raise, but told Quill that, given the university's unstable financial condition, he could not offer another penny. "Look, General, I'm not going to have any trouble with you," Quill replied. "I've got more sense than to be taking on an opponent who is as popular as you seem to be in this city."[53]

After Truman's upset victory in the presidential election, Ike's attention started to wander from the Columbia campus. Certainly his political calculations changed. Instead of an anticipated two-term Dewey presidency (through 1956, when Ike would be sixty-six years old), the Republican presidential convention in 1952 suddenly appeared wide open.

Eisenhower had begun to tire of the day-to-day life of a university president. His top-down military command style did not suit the academic setting where the faculty, not the president, deans, and department chairmen, set policy. He expected decisions to be made quickly and implemented immediately. But the faculty insisted that every major change in policy and personnel be discussed thoroughly before any decisions could be made. He was forced to wade through a mountainous pile of white paper, a bureaucratic morass even worse than he endured during his military career.

Although he respected the scholars on Columbia's faculty, he stressed the need to teach the virtues of citizenship rather than pure academic subjects. He wanted to make the university's liberal education more relevant to the outside world. But his pet project, the "American Assembly," which brought businessmen, financiers, and professors together to discuss major issues of the day (e.g., tax policy), was greeted with disdain by the academic community.

Shortly after Truman's reelection, Eisenhower wrote both the president and Secretary of Defense James Forrestal that he was ready to take on an official assignment, in addition to the Columbia presidency. "I always stand ready to attempt the performance of any professional duty for which my constitutional superiors believe I might be specially suited," he wrote Truman.[54] He wrote to Forrestal "that I can scarcely think of any chore that I would refuse to do whenever people in responsible positions feel that I might be able to help."[55] Both Truman and Forrestal responded enthusiastically to Eisenhower's broad hints. In February 1949, Ike agreed to serve as informal chairman of the Joint Chiefs of Staff for three months. The Columbia trustees granted him a leave of absence.

His new job at the Pentagon proved to be extremely frustrating as he attempted to overcome bureaucratic infighting, especially the navy's resistance to unification of the services. His health began to suffer from the pressure at the Pentagon as well as the exhausting commute between New York and Washington. In March, he was diagnosed with a case of acute gastroenteritis and ordered to complete bed rest and a drastic reduction of his four-packs-a-day cigarette habit.

Truman offered Ike the use of the Little White House in Key West, where he stayed for three weeks and abruptly stopped smoking. He later said that the agony of having to count the number of cigarettes his physician allowed him to smoke every day was worse than just quitting. He was flown from Key West to Augusta for a month of painting, golf, fishing, and the companionship of the Gang. After an extended summer vacation of fishing and golf in Wisconsin and Colorado, he returned to the Columbia campus, but any enthusiasm for the university presidency had vanished.

Throughout his tenure at Columbia, Ike insisted that he had no political ambition. But his frequent speeches, often to wealthy, politically influential audiences, suggested that he was eager to share his views on major national issues. He still refused to say whether he was a Democrat or a Republican, but his positions frequently appeared to be aligned with his Republican friends in the Gang. In a speech delivered to a Chicago audience of prominent businessmen, publishers, and bankers, he warned of the dangers of big government and big labor, high taxes and creeping socialism.

In the summer of 1950, Eisenhower delivered two off-the-record speeches in which his anti-Communist rhetoric seemed calculated to appeal to his audience of California's business and political elite at San Francisco's Bohemian Club. Despite his public position against a loyalty oath at Columbia, he told one Bohemian Club audience, which included Congressman Richard Nixon, "that he did not see why anyone who refused to sign a loyalty oath should have the right to teach at a state university."[56]

In his speeches at the Bohemian Club, Eisenhower appeared to taunt Governor Warren, who was then deeply involved in the oath controversy at the University of California. Eisenhower, who, according to the columnist Drew Pearson, was a likely rival to Warren at the 1952 Republican convention, "took a crack at Governor Warren by saying that he didn't know of any loyalty oath that he wouldn't be willing to stand up and swear to."[57] Naturally, the columnist continued, the remark got back to Warren. "It is interesting," the governor commented, "that the general made his remark off-the-record so it would not be quoted in the East." Furthermore, continued Warren, "it happens that the university Ike heads has more Communists and Reds than any other in the country."

In other addresses, Eisenhower overtly tacked toward the center. In a speech to the American Bar Association, for example, he called for moderation, urging voluntary cooperation between labor and management to avoid debilitating strikes.

By the fall of 1950, there was renewed speculation that Eisenhower would become a candidate for the presidency. Truman continued to hope that Eisenhower would run for office as a Democrat, sending word through George Allen that he could have the Democratic nomination for senator from New York. No thank you, Ike promptly replied. Later, Governor Dewey told Ike that he was a public resource and must answer the call to political service, presumably as a Republican. Ike demurred.

On Friday, October 13, 1950, Dewey called Ike to inform him of his scheduled appearance on *Meet the Press* two days later in which, he said, he planned to endorse Eisenhower for the 1952 Republican presidential nomination. If asked about Dewey's endorsement, Ike said that he would have "no comment."[58]

The next day Eisenhower issued an official statement saying that his job at Columbia remained challenging. But he also said that he was complimented by the endorsement of the governor of a great state that he was "qualified to fill the most important post in our country."[59] Governor Warren, who harbored his own presidential ambitions, translated Dewey's endorsement into practical political language: "When Tom Dewey announced that General Eisenhower was his candidate," he recalled, "I felt rather sure that Ike would be in the race."[60]

Chapter Four

EYES ON THE
WHITE HOUSE

BY THE FALL OF 1950, THE PROMISE OF AN ENDURING world order, ostensibly secured by the Allied victory in World War II, had been shattered. In China, Mao Tse-tung's Communist forces had routed the Nationalist army of General Chiang Kai-shek. Communist North Korea's army had launched a surprise attack on South Korea. The Soviet Union had detonated its first atomic bomb, while eighty Soviet armored divisions were deployed ominously throughout Eastern Europe. Residents of West Berlin were isolated by a Russian blockade, dependent on an American airlift for food and other necessities.

The United States had begun to revive the prostrate Western European economies through the Marshall Plan, the massive, multimillion-dollar aid program. But a military antidote to the Soviet threat was still in the planning stages. Secretary of State Dean Acheson had skillfully negotiated the terms of the North Atlantic Treaty Organization with America's allies, pledging the United States, Canada, and Western European nations to a collective security pact. In the fall of 1950, however, NATO was little more than an organizational shell, with no leader and only twelve Allied divisions in Europe, hardly a deterrent to the Red Army's threat.

President Truman wanted Eisenhower to head NATO and first broached the subject to Ike in a telephone conversation in late October 1950. He expected to make the offer official in December and attempted to reach Eisenhower by phone while Ike and Mamie were en route to Denver for a Christmas vacation with Mamie's family. Their train had stopped in rural Ohio so that Eisenhower could deliver a speech at Heidelberg College, fulfilling a promise to a Columbia dean who was a Heidelberg alumnus. After his speech, Ike returned the president's call from a freight office of a railroad yard in Bucyrus, Ohio. Truman did not mince words. The members of NATO had unanimously requested Eisenhower to command the alliance forces. Eisenhower, the career military man, took Truman's request as an order. "I had been a soldier all my life and by law was still an active soldier and I would report at any time he said," he told the president.[1]

For Eisenhower, the assignment to lead NATO was both timely and welcome. His tenure as Columbia's president had become a burden.* Building an Allied force in Western Europe to insure the peace, a peace he had fought so valiantly for in World War II, was virtually an obligation.

On January 6, 1951, Eisenhower, in uniform for the first time in more than two years, made an exploratory trip to Europe, visiting every Western European nation in the new alliance. Returning to Washington at the end of the month, he addressed a joint session of Congress, exhorting the lawmakers to give bipartisan support to NATO. After his speech, he arranged for a private meeting at the Pentagon with Senator Robert Taft, the conservative Republican leader of the isolationist wing of his party. He was determined to persuade Taft, who had voted against the NATO treaty, of the necessity of the alliance.

Before his meeting with Taft, Eisenhower called two staff members

---

* After accepting the NATO assignment, Eisenhower offered to resign from the Columbia presidency, but the university's trustees insisted on placing him on indefinite leave.

into his office, and together they drafted a statement that Eisenhower planned to issue that evening. The statement assumed that Taft would endorse NATO, guaranteeing the bipartisanship that Eisenhower sought, and agree that the alliance should become an integral part of U.S. foreign policy. In return for that assurance, Eisenhower's draft statement eliminated him from consideration for any future political office. That assurance, Ike reasoned, would be incentive enough for Taft, the front-runner for the Republican presidential nomination in 1952, to support NATO. Eisenhower's statement would effectively eliminate Taft's most serious potential challenger for the nomination.

After Taft sat down in Ike's Pentagon office, the general posed one crucial question: "Would you, and your associates in the Congress, agree that collective security is necessary for us in Western Europe—and will you support this idea as a bi-partisan policy?"[2] He explained to Taft that if his answer was "yes," then "I would be completely happy in the new job and would spend my next years attempting to fulfill the great responsibility given me." If, however, Taft refused to give his unqualified support to NATO, the success of the alliance would be in jeopardy. As a result, Eisenhower said, he would probably return to the United States. Eisenhower's return to the U.S., both men knew, would mean that Taft might well face a formidable challenger for the Republican nomination.

Taft said that he did not know how many U.S. divisions he would support. Ike pressed him for a direct answer to his question. He was not interested in debating the number of American divisions assigned to NATO, but only in the senator's commitment to the military alliance. Taft refused to make that commitment.

After Taft left, Eisenhower called his assistants into his office, took the drafted statement from his pocket, and tore it up in front of them. The announcement, now in tatters, had been calculated to end all speculation about his becoming a candidate for the presidency. "Having been called back to military duty," he had written, "I want to announce that my name may not be used by anyone as a candidate for President—and if they do I will repudiate such efforts."[3] Eisenhower later recalled that the Taft meeting had disappointed him in two ways. "First, now I could not feel the unity of our government behind me, and, second, I had lost the chance to settle the political question once and for all."[4]

EISENHOWER REALIZED THAT forging consensus among Allies during World War II was a relatively easy task compared to the challenge he faced with NATO. In war, necessity was a powerful incentive to induce cooperation. In peacetime, each Allied nation could find multiple excuses to shift the heavy burdens of responsibility to others. In 1951, only Belgium among all Western European nations required military service, which Ike considered important to handle the highly sophisticated weaponry. But no nation joined Belgium in requiring a draft, and Belgium eventually dropped its own. The capacity of each nation, moreover, differed dramatically. Tiny Luxembourg could not be expected to produce modern jet fighters, nor Holland or Belgium to contribute to the Atlantic fleet. There was the temptation among the weaker members of the alliance to let the United States, the only superpower in the alliance and only member with a nuclear deterrent, to assume the entire burden of defense. But Ike put a stop to that talk. "We cannot be a modern Rome guarding the far frontiers with our legions," he said.[5]

Despite the obstacles, Eisenhower was determined that every member assume responsibility for the collective defense. It was not just a matter of equitable sharing of the burden. He believed that active participation by all Western European nations would promote self-confidence while they continued to recover from the devastation of World War II.

He was not only the Supreme Commander of NATO, but also the organization's chief cheerleader, a talent to which he brought enthusiasm and a keen understanding of the need to build morale among its members. In this task, he could be tough on reluctant allies. He told the Dutch that their government was not "showing a sense of urgency, readiness to sacrifice, and determination to pull its full share of the load," and wondered out loud why a country of ten million people could not provide a five-division army.[6]

On the seventh anniversary of D-Day, he delivered a radio address from Normandy to all of Western Europe reminding them that "never again must there be a campaign of liberation fought on these shores."[7] Less than a month later, he gave a major speech to the English-Speaking Union in London, warning that "this project faces the deadly danger of procrastination, timid measures, slow steps and cautious stages." But together, the members of NATO could not only build adequate security for the post–World War II era, but "continue the march of human betterment that has characterized Western civilization." Churchill, who was too deaf to hear the speech but read it, told Ike that "I am sure this is one of the greatest speeches delivered by any American in my lifetime."[8]

While applying pressure and charm in equal measure, Eisenhower never doubted that NATO would succeed. "The defensive forces that existed at the start could not match, or even scratch those of the Communist bloc nations," he conceded. "But the knowledge that a unified, progressive effort to mobilize and generate strength was under way had an almost electrifying effect on European thinking."[9]

––––––––

NATO PROVIDED IKE and Mamie with a stately villa, the former residence of the Emperor Napoleon III, about ten miles west of Paris. When he was not conferring with leaders in the capitals of NATO countries, Ike entertained a steady stream of visitors—generals, diplomats, and politicians, including an ambitious young senator from California, Richard M. Nixon, who recalled his discussion with Ike on the threat of the Communist conspiracy in the United States and abroad. But most frequently, Eisenhower hosted members of the Gang, who joined him for golf (a course was on the premises), bridge, raucous jokes, and political talk. The question uppermost in every visitor's mind: Would Eisenhower become a candidate for president in 1952?

Massachusetts senator Henry Cabot Lodge delivered an urgent directive to Ike at his NATO office on September 4, 1951, imploring him to run for president as a Republican. He must become a candidate, Lodge said, to save the nation from the "paternalism" of a burgeoning federal bureaucracy, and the Republican Party from extinction. If the Republicans did not break the twenty-year Democratic monopoly of the presidency, he warned, it could be the elimination of the two-party system. "You are the only one who can be elected by the Republicans to the Presidency," he said. "You must permit the use of your name in the upcoming primaries."[10]

One of the Gang, Bill Robinson, the editor of the *New York Herald Tribune*, pressed the issue with a front-page editorial in his newspaper on October 25, 1951, endorsing Eisenhower for the Republican nomination for president. "At rare intervals in the life of a free people the man and occasion meet," Robinson wrote.[11] Eisenhower possessed "the vision of the statesman, the skill of the diplomat, the supreme organizing talent of the administrator, and the human sympathies of the representative of the people." Although Eisenhower had not yet declared publicly that he was a Republican, Robinson had no doubt. Eisenhower "is a Republican by temper and disposition," he wrote, and "by every avowal of faith and solemn declaration."*

It is unlikely that Robinson would have written the editorial with-

---

* Privately, Eisenhower had assured Robinson and other friends that he was resolutely opposed to the Democrats' domestic policies, which he characterized as a "planned economy, the 'hand out' state, and the trend toward centralization of economic and political power in the hands of Washington bureaucrats." (Ambrose, Stephen E., *Eisenhower*, Vol. 1, *Soldier, General of the Army, President-Elect* [1983], p. 511.)

out Eisenhower's knowledge. The next day, however, he wrote Ike a letter of apology, hoping that his editorial "did not cause you too much displeasure or irritation."[12] He added that he considered the editorial necessary to slow Taft's momentum, and that the response had been "terrific."

Eisenhower replied that he was neither displeased nor irritated by the editorial. To the contrary, he was "highly complimented" and hopeful that the newspaper's endorsement might encourage a true grassroots movement for his nomination.[13] Ike's positive, though noncommittal, response suggested that he was still conflicted about a decision whether to seek the presidency or not. He was flattered by the attention but not yet certain that he wanted to fight for the presidential nomination. As a career military man, he was accustomed to following orders. In the political context, he wanted voters, through a grassroots movement, to effectively order him to run. There was, moreover, a calculated shrewdness to Ike's indecision. "The seeker is never so popular as the sought," he told Robinson. "People want what they can't get."[14]

Meanwhile, a powerful group of East Coast Republicans were working feverishly behind the scenes to promote Eisenhower's candidacy. They were led by New York Governor Dewey, Senator Lodge, and General Lucius D. Clay, a trusted friend of Eisenhower who had been his military deputy in postwar Germany and was then chairman and CEO of the Continental Can Company. The group included Herbert Brownell, Jr., who had managed Dewey's presidential campaigns, Russell Sprague, the GOP national committeeman for New York, and Harold Talbott, a New York businessman who had been the principal fund-raiser for Dewey's campaigns.

Clay served as liaison between the group and Eisenhower. The Clay-Eisenhower secret correspondence could have been lifted from the pages of a taut espionage novel. It was replete with code names

(Dewey was "Our Friend," Taft was "G"), stealth couriers (their letters were hand delivered by TWA pilots on the Paris-New York route), and surrogate signatures (Clay's secretary, Eisenhower's aide).[15]

Clay's job was delicate—to persuade Ike to publicly declare his candidacy without pushing him so hard that he make an irrevocable decision to remain at NATO. The correspondence, therefore, took the form of a subtle verbal minuet. Clay wrote Eisenhower, for example, that two reliable sources had reported to him that Truman would not run for reelection if Ike ran. But (Truman) "will run if [Taft] does, and in my opinion would beat [Taft] to a frazzle. The result would be four more years of the very bad government we have today, and it could even mean the downfall in the country of the two-party system."[16]

Ike replied, "I am *now* on a job assigned to me as a duty. This makes it impossible for me to be in the position (no matter how remotely or indirectly) of seeking another post." Nonetheless, he added encouragingly, "You need not worry that I shall ever disregard Our Friend."[17]

When Eisenhower returned to Washington in November and met with Clay in his suite at the Statler, he was no closer to a decision. "The sum and substance of our talk," Clay recalled, "was that I could say [when Clay returned to New York] that I had reason to believe that if the movement generated enough public support, that we *might* have a candidate. It wasn't a green light, but it wasn't a red light either. And in my own mind I thought he would run—although he hadn't said that."[18]

Truman, meanwhile, renewed his offer, first made in 1945, that he would step aside if Eisenhower would accept the Democratic nomination for president. "If I do what I want to do I'll go back to Missouri and *maybe* run for the Senate," he wrote Eisenhower in December.[19] "If you decide to finish the European job (and I don't know who else can) I must keep the isolationists out of the White House. I wish you would let me know what you intend to do."

Ike politely demurred. He, too, would like to retire from public life, he replied. "But just as you have decided that circumstances may not permit you to do exactly as you please so I've found that fervent desire may sometimes have to give way to conviction of duty."[20] He would not seek the presidency, he told the president, and added, disingenuously, that "the possibility that I will ever be drawn into political activity is so remote as to be negligible."

Clay knew that Ike could not procrastinate much longer and still have a chance of stopping Taft. He boldly took matters into his own hands. On January 4, 1952, without Eisenhower's approval, he authorized Senator Lodge to enter Ike in the New Hampshire Republican primary to be held in early March. Two days later, Lodge met with reporters and declared that Eisenhower would accept the Republican nomination if it were offered. "I know I will not be repudiated," he said.[21]

Clay and Lodge had pushed Eisenhower one step closer to a decision. On January 7, 1952, Ike issued a formal statement at his NATO headquarters, saying that Lodge's announcement "gives an accurate account of the general tenor of my political convictions and of my voting record."[22] But he immediately placed conditions on his still unannounced candidacy. "Under no circumstances will I ask for relief from this assignment in order to seek nomination for political office, and I shall not participate in . . . preconvention activities."

If Eisenhower's statement lacked clarity and firm conviction, it, nonetheless, satisfied Truman that Ike would become the Republican presidential nominee. With the threat of an isolationist president (Taft) eliminated, he could retire to Missouri. After Eisenhower's announcement, the president praised the NATO commander. "I think he [Eisenhower] is one of the great men produced by World War II [and] I don't want to stand in his way at all," he said at a press conference.* "If he wants to get out and have all the mud and rotten eggs thrown at him, that's his business."[23]

Former president Herbert Hoover did not share Truman's enthusiasm for an Eisenhower candidacy. A Taft supporter, Hoover issued a statement, signed by sixteen prominent Republicans (including Taft), declaring that "American troops should be brought home."[24] In Hoover's view, the United States should become the "Gibraltar of freedom."

Hoover's statement incensed Eisenhower, goading him further to challenge Taft for the Republican nomination. He thought the idea that the United States could effectively fight aggression from our shores was pure foolishness. Hoover and Taft were prophets of "the false doctrine of isolationism," Ike wrote Clay. Taking the Gibraltar analogy seriously for a moment, he added, that fortress "could be reduced to nothing by a few modern guns posted in the hills and concentrating their fire on it."[25]

Every signal from Ike strongly suggested that he was running, but he continued to withhold a public declaration of his candidacy. He awaited a dramatic demonstration of support from ordinary voters that it was his duty to run. That demonstration occurred at midnight on February 8, 1952, at a rally at Madison Square Garden, staged by Governor Dewey's team. More than 30,000 supporters chanted "We Like Ike" and waved "I Like Ike" banners until dawn. The event was filmed by financier Floyd Odlum and his wife, the celebrated aviator Jacqueline Cochran, who immediately flew to Paris with the film to

---

* Ike did not have a similarly high opinion of Truman. He complained privately that Truman and his military advisers were indecisive in responding to North Korean aggression. "[P]oor HST [is] a fine man who, in the middle of a stormy lake, knows nothing of swimming. . . . If his wisdom could only equal his good intent." (DDE diary, November 6, 1950, DDEP.) After Truman submitted his annual budget with a $14 billion deficit to Congress in late January 1952, Eisenhower devoted eight pages in his diary to a blistering criticism of what he considered the administration's profligate spending. (DDE diary, January 22, 1952, DDEP.)

show Ike. After Ike and Mamie watched the film, visibly moved, Ike instructed Cochran to "tell Bill Robinson that I am going to run."[26]

———————

THE CALIFORNIA GUBERNATORIAL race in the fall of 1950 attracted national interest not only as a result of the two outsized personalities involved but also because the winner might well become his party's candidate for the presidency. Governor Earl Warren, seeking an unprecedented third term, faced Democrat James Roosevelt, FDR's colorful, audacious oldest son. Jimmy, as he was known, displayed his father's charm and a resonant voice strikingly similar to FDR's. He was also a Marine veteran who had seen combat in the Pacific in World War II and an accomplished public speaker who was prepared to carry on his father's New Deal legacy.

If Jimmy Roosevelt won, which every pundit conceded was highly unlikely, he could well catapult himself into consideration for the Democratic presidential nomination, if not in 1952, then four years later. But Roosevelt's immediate challenge was formidable. His opponent, wrote columnist Drew Pearson, was "about the toughest man to run against in the entire United States of America."[27] Warren was enormously popular with Democrats as well as Republicans, nullifying any advantage that Roosevelt might expect to enjoy because of the lopsided advantage of registered Democrats in the state.

Warren's record over eight years was the envy of governors across the nation. He had satisfied his Republican constituents with conservative, pay-as-you-go fiscal policies, consistently balancing the annual state budgets. But he could also be mistaken for a liberal Democrat with his sweeping programs to improve the lives of ordinary Californians. "I believe that most Californians want our State to be as liberal as our finances will permit," he said.[28]

During his two terms, Warren had added 20,000 classrooms and at least that many teachers to meet the needs of a student population that had grown by 500,000 in a decade. He improved health care centers that served more than 10,000 patients. The state's pensions were the most generous in the country. Jobs had increased by 1.45 million. More than 4,000 miles of new highway had been constructed, and more than 625,000 new homes had been built, a fourth of all new homes built in America.

At the outset of his campaign, Warren presented himself as the nonpartisan, hard-working governor whose record provided the state's voters with multiple reasons to elect him to a third term. In his first campaign radio address, he told listeners that he would continue to work on state problems, "beholden to no one but you who elected me."[29] He was their governor—experienced, competent, trustworthy.

Roosevelt came out swinging. He attacked Warren's vaunted "nonpartisanship," depicting him as "the agile political trapeze performer who floats through the air with the greatest of ease, first as a Republican, then as a nonpartisan in the hopes that he will please."[30] He accused Warren of controlling a Republican machine that was beholden to a raft of special interests, all the while fleecing the unsuspecting public. It was time, Roosevelt proclaimed, "to repudiate the crafty operations of Warren and his Republican machine."[31]

Warren had planned an above-the-fray campaign, but Roosevelt's broadsides quickly changed his mind. Warren as a crafty, machine-driven politician? He had built his reputation as a model progressive, insisting on transparency in government and beholden to *no* special interests.

Warren slowly warmed to the attack, speaking of unnamed candidates "who promised everything under the sun and a reduction of taxes at the same time."[32] He called such promises "magic" conjured "either by beginners or charlatans." His opponent bore "the distinction of being the first candidate for governor of California to reveal on the official ballot that he has no occupation." When Roosevelt attacked Warren's public education policies, the governor retorted that "James

Roosevelt has never been in a public school in his life, except to make a political speech."[33] After Eleanor Roosevelt came to the state to boost her son's sagging campaign, Warren said that he would not challenge the former First Lady. "I don't like to argue with a mother about her boy," he archly told reporters.[34]

In the last week of the campaign, Warren dismissed Roosevelt's charge that he was antilabor, challenging him to name a state with better labor laws concerning collective bargaining, workmen's compensation, industrial safety, social security, and old-age assistance. "My father worked with his hands as a mechanic," he told the Sailors' Union of the Pacific.[35] "Both he and I have worked twelve hours a day, six days a week, at twenty-five cents an hour. I know what better wages mean to a home. I know what better hours mean to a family."

Warren trounced Roosevelt in the election, winning by more than one million votes, the largest majority in California history. The *New York Times* called the vote "beyond the greatest expectations of most Republican leaders" and reported that the sheer size of Warren's victory had stimulated "talk of Mr. Warren as a serious contender for the Republican nomination in 1952."[36]

THE OTHER BIG winner in California's election in November 1950 was Congressman Richard Nixon, who defeated his liberal opponent, Congresswoman Helen Gahagan Douglas, by 700,000 votes to win a seat in the U.S. Senate. Nixon had run a nasty, no-holds-barred campaign against Douglas, distributing a pink flyer accusing Douglas of Communist sympathies. And if anyone missed the point, Nixon said his opponent was "pink right down to her underwear."[37] He had employed the same tactic in his congressional race four years earlier against liberal five-term Congressman Jerry Voorhis, linking him, inaccurately, with an organization that was reputedly influenced by Communists. In both campaigns, Nixon was guided by Murray

Chotiner, a tough, cigar-smoking criminal defense lawyer, who, like the candidate himself, was focused on winning with little regard for the means used to achieve their goal.

Warren and Nixon were strikingly different politicians. Warren made nonpartisanship the centerpiece of his politics. As governor, he appointed Democrats as well as Republicans to high office. His policies cut across party lines. He rarely attacked a political opponent. Jimmy Roosevelt was the exception, and Warren's attacks only came after Roosevelt had blasted him with a battery of incendiary, baseless charges.

Nixon, in contrast, did not hesitate to savage his opponents, treating them as ideological enemies to be destroyed. Though attempting to present himself as a moderate Republican, he attracted Democratic votes primarily as a result of withering attacks on his opponents. Once in Congress, he did not hew to a strictly conservative Republican agenda. He was deeply interested in international affairs, for example, distancing himself from the isolationist wing of his party led by Senator Taft. But he chose to make his political reputation as an anti-Communist, endearing him to the conservative Republican base. Exhibiting both skill and guile as a member of the House Un-American Activities Committee, he captured national headlines with his aggressive interrogation of the former State Department executive Alger Hiss, then president of the Carnegie Endowment for International Peace, who was accused of passing classified documents to the Soviet Union.*

Nixon and Warren did not like each other. After the 1950 election, their animosity could be attributed, in part, to professional rivalry, each aspiring to be the acknowledged political leader of the second most populous state in the union. But their hostility ran deeper. Warren disdained Nixon's bare-knuckle tactics. Nixon resented Warren's

---

* Hiss was later convicted of perjury.

sanctimonious public persona, and that resentment was both per-sonal and long-standing. It began when Nixon first ran for Congress in 1946. Despite repeated pleas for support from the popular gover-nor, Warren refused to endorse Nixon (or any other candidate). As Nixon's embittered supporters saw it, Warren was happy to receive endorsements from other politicians, but gave nothing in return. Four years later, Nixon's strategists again sought Warren's endorsement and assigned aides to stalk his opponent, Congresswoman Douglas, repeat-edly asking her at public events who she was going to vote for in the gubernatorial election. Finally, toward the end of the campaign, an exasperated Douglas said that she would vote for Roosevelt. Asked to comment, Warren said, "In view of her statement . . . I might ask her how she expects I will vote when I mark my ballot for United States senator on Tuesday."[38] That was hardly the forthright endorsement that Nixon sought. Warren's backhanded endorsement would soon be returned in kind by Nixon after Warren announced that he would seek the Republican nomination for the presidency in 1952.

ON NOVEMBER 14, 1951, Warren declared that he was a candidate for the Republican presidential nomination, warning that his party could not run "solely on the mistakes of the present twenty-year admin-istration," but must present a constructive program for the nation.[39] In an editorial, the New York Times welcomed Warren's candidacy, describing him as an internationalist in foreign policy and progressive in domestic policy—"a liberal Republican of foremost rank."[40] A Gal-lup poll indicated that voters favored Warren in a presidential election over Truman by 55 to 33 percent. With Taft as the favorite of the con-servative wing of the party, Warren was seen as a formidable candidate who could rally moderate delegates opposed to the Ohio senator.

Taft replied cheerily to Warren's announced candidacy. "The more, the merrier," he said.[41] But then he made a telling Freudian slip. "I certainly have the most kindly feeling toward General—that is, Governor Warren," he said. "Mr. Taft thus appeared to betray the fact that another possible Republican nominee, General Eisenhower, was much on his mind," the *Times* reported.

In fact, General Eisenhower was very much on Warren's mind as well. He knew that Taft would come to the party's convention with a strong contingent of delegates, especially from the South and Midwest. He also expected that Eisenhower, as yet an unannounced candidate, would attract a very large block of delegates with Governor Dewey's strong backing. Warren's best chance for the nomination lay in a convention deadlock between Taft and Eisenhower. He assumed that the seventy votes of the California delegation would be pledged to him and planned to enter the primaries in Oregon and Wisconsin, where he hoped to pick up additional delegates. If he came to the convention with at least seventy-five delegates pledged to him, he could present himself as an attractive alternative to Eisenhower among moderate Republicans, should the general's drive for the nomination falter.

In his effort to show political strength outside of California, Warren cleared his calendar from Thursday through Sunday to campaign in Wisconsin. In February, deep snow prevented him from keeping to his campaign calendar in the rural areas of the state, but he gamely made dozens of appearances, particularly in the urban areas of Milwaukee and Madison, where his message of social progress resonated. He favored collective bargaining and social security, which, he said, had been advocated by the Republican party for years.

He tread cautiously when discussing the subject of civil liberties. In Wisconsin, he distanced himself from Senator McCarthy, the state's Communist-hunting junior senator, condemning "blanket indictments against groups without naming them or substantiating them by substantial evidence."[42] But he did not criticize McCarthy by name or engage him in debate. He said that it was inappropriate for him to get involved in another state's politics.

Warren did surprisingly well in Wisconsin, polling more than 260,000 votes, but was a distant second to Taft. He carried two congressional districts in Milwaukee and the district that included Madison. As a result of the election, six Wisconsin delegates were pledged to him.

When Warren raised the issue of civil rights, which was not often, he spoke in vague generalities. In a Lincoln Day speech, he noted that "some of the inequalities of his [Lincoln's] day still existed and that the freedom of opportunity he strove for was not yet a reality."*[43] He insisted that there should be "but one law for all men."

Such noble talk without specific action continued to frustrate black voters, as it had when Warren had considered running for president in 1948. He was mute on controversial national issues important to black communities, such as the filibuster, the procedural tool wielded so effectively by southern segregationists in Congress to block civil rights bills. Walter White, executive secretary of the NAACP, wrote a column with the headline "WARREN PRESIDENTIAL HOPEFUL, DODGES CHANCE TO HIT FILIBUSTER."[44] White, who had deplored Eisenhower's Senate committee testimony on African Americans in the military in 1948, complained that Warren did not return three telephone calls or offer to send a letter or telegram opposing the filibuster.

At a meeting of NAACP representatives from six southern states in April 1952, the delegates gave both Warren and Eisenhower low marks on civil rights. "Gov. Earl Warren has given lip service to civil rights but has failed to deliver in his home state of California," the representatives declared.†[45] "General of the Army Eisenhower is on record in

* Warren's Lincoln Day speech was delivered in Boston to the oldest Republican club in the state. He was not on the ballot in Massachusetts but hoped to impress moderate Republicans in the East, should Eisenhower fail to get the nomination.
† Warren supported a bill for a state Fair Employment Practices Commission (FEPC), but was unable to persuade the state legislature to pass it.

defense of segregation in the army," they asserted. "He has not publicly disavowed his testimony in 1948 before the Senate Armed Services Committee in support of dualism in the army."

Warren responded to criticism of his civil rights record from the black community in an exclusive interview with the *Pittsburgh Courier*, the largest newspaper with a predominantly black readership in the country. He insisted on "one law for all men" and supported "a sweeping civil rights program, beginning with a Fair Employment Practices Act."[46] Eisenhower made no such public statement on civil rights. Privately, he told General Clay that he did not consider race relations or labor relations to be issues. "And I don't believe the problems arising within either of them can be ended by punitive law or a statement made in a press conference," he wrote.[47]

———

WARREN'S EARLY CAMPAIGN for the presidency began with enthusiasm, but was not without its difficulties. Shortly after the announcement of his candidacy, Warren underwent surgery for abdominal cancer. The press was not told about the illness but informed that the governor's appendix had been removed. After the surgery, Warren's doctors assured him privately that there was no malignancy left in his system, but he was advised to modify his schedule while he recuperated. Taft supporters circulated the rumor that Warren was terminally ill. Warren later recalled that former President Hoover, an ardent Taft supporter, gave his own dramatic spin to the rumor at a dinner for several dozen national leaders of the Republican party. "You don't have to be concerned about Warren," Hoover reputedly said.[48] "I know the doctors who operated on him. They opened him up, took a look, and sewed him up again."

By midwinter, Warren had fully recovered from the surgery. But as a candidate, he had a much more serious problem. Eisenhower was now a declared candidate for the Republican presidential nomination, and a well-oiled political machine, led by Governor Dewey and General Clay, was moving into high gear on his behalf. In early March, Ike won the New Hampshire primary handily, taking 50.4 percent of the vote to Taft's 38.7 percent. In the Minnesota primary a week later, he received 108,692 write-in votes to 129,706 for the state's former governor, Harold Stassen, who was on the ballot. In Oregon, where both Warren and Eisenhower were on the ballot, Ike crushed the California governor, winning by a margin of 2½ to 1.

In early June, Warren faced an unexpected challenge in the California primary for control of the state delegation from conservative Congressman Thomas Werdel, who accused Warren of "Trumanistic idolatry." Werdel's challenge forced Warren to engage in a modest campaign, and he easily won the primary and control of the delegation.

But the more serious threat to Warren's control of California's delegation came from Senator Nixon. Nixon had never been an enthusiastic Warren supporter. After Warren had announced his candidacy, Nixon acknowledged that Warren could beat Truman in a general election, but added that he was no better than a dark horse for the Republican nomination, far behind the leading contenders, Eisenhower and Taft. In private, Nixon made no secret of his support for Eisenhower, who had impressed him in their meeting at NATO headquarters in the fall of 1951. "I don't believe that any of us should have any illusions on the possibilities of Warren being selected for the top spot," he wrote one delegate confidentially.[49]

At Nixon's request, Warren had earlier appointed him and a half dozen of his supporters to the California delegation. He had also agreed to have Nixon's campaign aide, Murray Chotiner, manage a section of the train that was bound for the convention in Chicago. Warren understood that Chotiner would have nothing to do with political matters, but merely handle logistics for the trip.*

---

* In Chicago, Warren was surprised when Chotiner, his "manager" on the train, greeted him at the door of Eisenhower's suite. (EWM, p. 252.)

Prior to the Republican convention, Nixon sent out 23,000 cards from his senate office to California Republicans asking them to name their favorite candidate for president, should Warren's bid fail. A majority of respondents favored Eisenhower and, though Nixon had promised that the results would be kept secret, he shared them with *Los Angeles Times* columnist Kyle Palmer. Palmer told Warren, who reacted angrily, telling the newspaper columnist that Nixon's poll was inconsistent with the oath all delegates had taken to support him at the convention.

Unknown to Warren or Eisenhower, top Eisenhower strategists Senator Lodge and Governor Dewey had begun to court Nixon. They did not know Warren's intentions beyond the first ballot and worried that the state's senior U.S. senator, William Knowland, a Taft supporter, would deliver a block of delegates to Taft on the second ballot. They thought that Nixon's strong support for Eisenhower in the California delegation could fend off a movement among the delegates to support Taft. Nixon, moreover, could provide an attractive balance on an Eisenhower ticket as the party's vice presidential candidate. He was young (thirty-nine years old; Ike was sixty-one), vigorous, a tough campaigner, and ardent anti-Communist, and he represented a populous state three thousand miles away from the eastern Republican establishment of Dewey, Clay, and Lodge.

In April, Lodge had approached Nixon on the Senate floor and asked if he would be interested in the vice presidency. "Who wouldn't?" Nixon replied.[50] Lodge reported the conversation to Dewey, who then invited Nixon to be the principal speaker at the annual GOP fundraising dinner in New York City on May 8. In Nixon's speech, delivered without notes, he urged Republicans to nominate a candidate who could appeal to Democrats and independents. After the speech, Dewey invited Nixon to his suite and repeated Lodge's suggestion that he might join Eisenhower on the Republican ticket as the party's vice presidential candidate. Nixon said that he would be honored.

In late June, Nixon was the only member of the California delegation who did not board the eighteen-car Warren Special in Sacramento that was bound for the Republican convention in Chicago. When he finally boarded the train the night before its arrival in Chicago, Nixon told his supporters that Warren's candidacy was a lost cause, and that the delegation could only make a crucial difference if it supported Eisenhower. Nixon loyalists, in turn, held caucuses with other members of the delegation, urging them to vote for Eisenhower on the first ballot. Some who were importuned by the Nixon delegates came to Warren and asked his advice. He told them "that the delegation was not a front for anyone, and that no matter what happened it was obligated to vote for me on the first ballot at least."[51]

ON APRIL 1, Eisenhower wrote Truman requesting that he be relieved of his NATO command on June 1. "Your resignation makes me rather sad" Truman replied. "I hope you will be happy in your new role."[52] On June 1, Eisenhower paid a farewell call on the president at the White House. After giving Truman an upbeat progress report on NATO, he complained of the scurrilous campaign that the Taft forces were waging against him. They had circulated rumors that Ike was having a secret and continuing love affair with his World War II companion Kay Summersby, that Mamie was an alcoholic, that he was Jewish, and that he secretly caroused with his "Communist drinking buddy," Marshal Zhukov, the Soviet general who was Ike's military counterpart in Berlin at the end of World War II. A bemused Truman replied, "If that's all it is, Ike, then you can just figure you're lucky."[53]

Three days after his meeting with Truman, Eisenhower officially opened his campaign in his hometown of Abilene. The plan was for Eisenhower to attend the dedication of his boyhood home, lay the cornerstone for the Eisenhower museum, and deliver a nationally televised address to an overflow crowd of 30,000 supporters in the town's high school football stadium. Torrential rains spoiled the climactic event. Ike read haltingly from a prepared text to a half-empty stadium. He did not look presidential in a dripping poncho with wind sweeping over the few remaining hairs on his head. The speech was cliche-ridden—complaints of big government, high taxes, and inflation—and delivered in a mechanical manner.

In New York City, Dewey, Clay, and Brownell watched Eisenhower's dismal performance on television. They realized that Ike was not the polished candidate he needed to be to win the nomination. In the weeks ahead, they advised Ike to speak, whenever possible, in informal, unscripted settings where his warm personality and facile mind could best be displayed.

At a press conference the next day, Ike's performance was much improved. His answers were crisp and to the point. "He is direct," wrote the *New York Times*'s James Reston. "He speaks in sentences and avoids intellectual detours."[54] Eisenhower told reporters that he had no magic formula to end the Korean War but, if elected, would work for a "decent armistice." He would try to lift artificial government controls on the economy and rely on a free marketplace. Though he supported civil rights, he thought the responsibility should be left to the individual states. And he opposed a federal Fair Employment Practices Commission that could require contractors with the federal government to practice nondiscrimination in hiring and promotion. Repeatedly, he ducked the question of whether he would support the reelection of Wisconsin's Senator McCarthy, but he emphatically opposed "any kind of Communistic, subversive or pinkish influence" in government.

Dewey, Clay, and Lodge were pleased. Ike had subtly positioned himself to attract undeclared delegates who were being heavily lobbied by the Taft forces. He had embraced orthodox Republican positions—small government, low taxes, outspoken anticommunism—without the rigidity associated with Taft. His states-rights positions on civil rights, moreover, could attract votes from southern delegations where Taft remained strong.

Two days later, he began the critical task of meeting state delegations. In one-on-one meetings, he applied his legendary charm—the firm handshake, direct eye contact, that grin, and a few informal, just-folks comments that enthralled.

When the Republican National Convention convened in Chicago on July 6, Taft claimed 525 delegates, less than 100 votes shy of the 604 votes needed for the nomination. Eisenhower trailed Taft by about twenty-five votes. The crucial struggle between Taft and Eisenhower centered on the contested delegations from Georgia, Louisiana, and Texas, which represented another seventy votes. The credentials committee, controlled by the Taft forces, voted to seat the Taft delegates in the three southern states, bringing the Ohio senator close to the magic number of 604. The Eisenhower forces challenged the credential committee's decision.

Brownell, Eisenhower's chief strategist at the convention, proposed a "Fair Play" amendment that would force a floor vote on the seating of any contested delegation. If Taft won that floor vote, he was assured of virtually all of the votes from the contested delegations. If the Eisenhower forces deprived Taft of those contested votes, the momentum would shift to Eisenhower.

With the stakes so high, Taft and Eisenhower supporters fought tenaciously for the vote of the California delegation over the Fair Play amendment. Taft supporter Senator Knowland urged the delegates to split their vote on the amendment, a tactic that would have blunted the strong pro-Eisenhower sentiment in the delegation. Nixon, in an impassioned speech to the delegates, portrayed the Fair Play amendment as a moral issue and urged them to vote as a unit to support it. Warren opposed the split vote favored by Knowland and requested that the resolution be supported or defeated by a majority of delegates.

The delegation then voted overwhelmingly to support the resolution. In a floor vote, the resolution was narrowly approved, which was viewed as a critical victory for Eisenhower.

One day before balloting on the presidential nomination, Taft approached Warren and offered him the cabinet position of his choice if he released the California delegation pledged to him on the first ballot in favor of the Ohio senator. "No, Senator," Warren replied firmly, "we will go ahead as promised."[55]

Even if Warren had not been so adamant in preserving the California delegation's votes for himself on the first ballot, he would not have been enticed by Taft's offer. Warren's core positions—for social progress at home and international cooperation abroad—were antithetical to Taft's. Also, the rough tactics by the Taft forces during the primaries had alienated him. His sense of propriety had been offended by Taft's staff after he had won six delegates in the Wisconsin primary. "The Taft people were so angry at the result that they banished my six delegates and would not even make hotel reservations for them at the convention," he recalled.[56] Taft forces, who dominated the seating arrangements at the convention, compounded the insult when they seated Warren's wife and three daughters in the last row in the farthest corner of the auditorium.

Warren's moderate views were naturally more compatible with Eisenhower's than Taft's. In Chicago, Warren and Eisenhower also established a personal rapport. When Warren paid a courtesy call on Eisenhower at his suite in the Blackstone Hotel, Ike greeted him warmly. The two men then sat down alone for a discussion that lasted for almost an hour. Afterward, when they met the press, Warren said, "I know enough about him [Eisenhower] to know he is a great American." Eisenhower told reporters that he liked the governor because they shared middle-of-the-road views. "Neither Warren nor I is going to get involved with a lot of pinkos," Eisenhower said, "but we're not going to get dragged back by a lot of old reactionaries either."[57]

After the California delegation had voted in favor of the Fair Play amendment, Warren could have further ingratiated himself with Eisenhower if he had released the California delegation, which overwhelmingly favored Eisenhower over Taft, on the first ballot. He refused, adhering to his original plan to have the state delegation vote for him. This allowed the Minnesota delegation, originally pledged to their favorite son, former governor Stassen, to switch to Ike and put him over the top on the first ballot. His nomination in place, Ike's respect for Warren was not diminished.

Ike was strangely detached through the tension-filled convention, leaving Brownell, Dewey, and Lodge to make the strategic and tactical decisions that led to his nomination. His aloofness was also apparent when Brownell raised the discussion of his vice-presidential running mate. "Well, I thought that was up to the convention," Eisenhower told his incredulous advisers.[58] "I didn't realize it was up to me to decide." Brownell, Clay, and Dewey wanted Nixon, and they had no trouble persuading Ike.*

If Eisenhower had not firmly grasped the intricacies of political strategy, he retained his sure instincts for building coalitions that he had honed to perfection during World War II. He made an unprecedented call to his defeated rival, Senator Taft, and asked if he might meet with him in the senator's suite at the Hilton, across the street from Eisenhower's headquarters. Surprised but not displeased, Taft told Eisenhower to come over. It took twenty minutes for Eisenhower to wade through throngs of reporters and well-wishers before he arrived at Taft's ninth-floor suite. Ike told Taft that he did not want to discuss policy but only expressed his desire to work with him toward a

---

* Shortly before the balloting for vice president, Warren was invited by Brownell to sit down with a group of prominent Republicans ostensibly to select a vice-presidential candidate. He had read earlier reports that Nixon had already been selected. "Believing that it was already a *fait accompli*, I declined," he wrote. (EWM, p. 254.)

Republican victory in November. It was an offer that Taft, if not many of his embittered supporters, readily accepted.[*]

In his acceptance speech, Eisenhower drew upon the imagery of his wartime memoirs. "I know something of the solemn responsibility of leading a crusade," he told the delegates. "I accept your summons. I will lead this crusade."[59]

AFTER THE CONVENTION, Ike and Mamie flew to Denver where Ike set up campaign headquarters in the Brown Palace Hotel. Two days later, he left the city for an extended vacation sixty miles northwest of Denver at the 1,900-acre cattle ranch of Aksel Nielsen, a close friend of Mamie's family. It was one of Ike's favorite vacation spots, where he could indulge his recreational pleasures of fly-fishing for trout, painting, and cooking steaks on an outdoor grill. He welcomed a host of visitors, including politicians and members of the Gang. After the Democrats nominated Illinois governor Adlai Stevenson as their presidential candidate, Ike and George Allen, a Gang member and seasoned political insider, listened intently to Stevenson's acceptance speech. Both were impressed with his style and polish. "He's too accomplished an orator," said Allen. "He will be easy to beat."[60]

While on vacation, Eisenhower severed his relations with Truman over what appeared to be an inadvertent White House miscommunication. Shortly after the Democratic convention, Truman had invited both presidential candidates to the White House for a briefing on foreign policy. The president asked General Omar Bradley, the chairman of the Joint Chiefs of Staff, to extend the invitation to Eisenhower. Apparently, Bradley failed to do so. As a result, only Stevenson came

---

[*] Two months later, Taft met Eisenhower for breakfast at Ike's Morningside Heights residence. Afterward, Taft enthusiastically endorsed Eisenhower and told reporters that he and Ike agreed on domestic policy and that their disagreement on foreign policy was only a matter of degree.

to the White House for the briefing. Despite Truman's apology and renewed invitation to Eisenhower, Ike fumed in a press statement that the president was playing politics with the vital subject of national defense. Actually, it was Ike who was playing politics. Bradley's miscue provided Ike, who had been a key adviser to Truman as Army Chief of Staff and NATO Supreme Commander, with the opening he needed to break away from the administration's foreign policy.

Eisenhower also attempted to distance himself from the Republicans' most zealous anti-Communists, Senators William Jenner of Indiana and Joseph McCarthy of Wisconsin. Both had singled out General Marshall, Ike's old boss and mentor, as an ominous player in a widespread Communist conspiracy. Jenner accused Marshall of being "a front man for traitors" and "a living lie" while McCarthy accused him of being a "part of a conspiracy so immense as to dwarf any previous such venture in the history of man."[61] Eisenhower had been alerted before his first postconvention press conference that he would be asked about the charges against Marshall.

"General, what do you think of those people who call General Marshall a living lie?" asked Murray Kempton, a reporter for *The New Yorker*.[62] Visibly angry, Eisenhower, who was sitting behind a desk, pushed his chair back, came to his feet, and wagged a finger at Kempton. "There was never a more patriotic, loyal citizen than he [Marshall]," he said. "I have no patience with anyone who attacks him."

Eisenhower prepared for his presidential campaign with the intense focus that had characterized his preparation for crucial battles during World War II. It would be a top-down operation, with Ike making the big decisions and leaving the day-to-day logistics to his staff. He would celebrate his sixty-second birthday in October and made a realistic calculation of just how much energy he needed to expend to win. He would rest until Labor Day, he decided, then undertake a rigorous seven-day-a week schedule for eight weeks, crisscrossing the country by plane, train, and automobile until election day. He purposely included stops throughout the South, which had been solidly Democratic since Reconstruction. He wanted to signal his intention to represent every section of the country, but the decision was also personal. "I had lived for years among the Southern people and liked them," he said.[63]

––––––––––

EISENHOWER KICKED OFF his campaign in Atlanta, where he received an enthusiastic introduction from Georgia's Democratic governor, Herman Talmadge, a zealous segregationist, who welcomed him as a friend of the South. In his speech before a cheering audience of 35,000 in the heart of the Georgia capital, Ike struck hard and often at what he termed "the mess" in Washington. The problem, he said, was "the inevitable and sure-fire result of an Administration by too many men who are too small for their jobs, too big for their breeches, and too long in power."[64] To cries of "Yahoo" and "Pour it on," he said that the problem "was not a one-agency mess, or a one-bureau mess, or a one-department mess. It is a top-to-bottom mess." He promised, if elected, to replace "the whitewash brush" with a "scoop-shovel" to throw the rascals out of office.

Ike's charges of waste and corruption in official Washington were met with loud applause and waves of Confederate flags by large, enthusiastic crowds throughout his two-day, six-city aerial tour in four Southern states. At each stop, he told large crowds that "the mess" in Washington "is taken out of your hide in higher taxes."[65] He praised only one federal institution in Washington, the U.S. Supreme Court, for a decision handed down the previous term declaring that President Truman had exceeded his constitutional authority in seizing the nation's steel mills during a labor strike. "Luckily," Eisenhower told the crowd in Birmingham, "we had a Supreme Court that tackled them [the Truman administration] on the five-yard line before they really got going."*[66]

Crowds totaling 100,000 over two days responded with whoops of delight and rebel yells to his down-to-earth rhetorical thrusts at the Truman administration. But they were silent when he dealt briefly and gingerly with the controversial subject of civil rights, telling white southerners in Tampa and Little Rock that they were in danger of losing their own rights unless they were willing to protect the rights of their neighbors "whatever the color of their skin."[67]

Throughout the campaign, Eisenhower carefully balanced his civil rights positions. He appealed to southern whites with his states' rights views and refusal to endorse a federal Fair Employment Practices Commission. But he told a black congressional candidate, Lawrence Payne, in a question-and-answer session with Republican office seekers in Cleveland that "if I do not protect and support your rights, I will lose my own." In response to Payne's question about segregation in the nation's capital, he declared, "I believe we should eliminate every vestige of segregation in the District of Columbia."[68] When he campaigned in Texas and Louisiana, he insisted that two black reporters and a black member of his staff be assigned to desegregated quarters on the train. And in the final week of the campaign, when his election was all but assured, he promised a crowd in Harlem that in an Eisenhower administration there would be no discrimination "wherever I can help it." When the federal government had responsibility, he said, there would be no discrimination in private or public life based on color, creed or religion—"never."[69]

Eisenhower's civil liberties positions, like those on civil rights, were carefully calibrated so that he did not offend constituencies he needed

---

* Eisenhower's reference was to the court decision in *Youngstown Sheet & Tube Co. v. Sawyer* 343 U.S. 579 (1952), in which a six-member majority declared that the president did not have the executive power under Article 2 of the Constitution to close the steel mills.

for a resounding victory at the polls. His desire to distance himself from the reckless Communist hunters, Senators Jenner and McCarthy, for example, was severely tested when he campaigned in their home states of Indiana and Wisconsin. In Indianapolis, he delivered a major address at Butler University, aware that Senator Jenner was scheduled to introduce him. Should he appear on stage with the man who had called General Marshall "a living lie"?

On the advice of Dewey, Clay, and Brownell, Eisenhower agreed to share the platform with Jenner. He roused the audience in the conservative heartland by telling them that he considered his decision to run for president his patriotic duty to free the country from "the prey of fear-mongers, quack doctors, and bare-faced looters."[70] Each attack on the Truman administration elicited rapturous applause from the audience and drew an exultant Jenner to his side, triumphantly raising his and Ike's arms together in a gesture of victory. At the end of his speech, Eisenhower asked support for the entire Republican ticket, but did not mention Jenner by name. Afterward, he whispered a command to Congressman Charles Halleck, "Charlie, get me out of here."[71] Later, he recalled, "I felt dirty at the touch of the man [Jenner]."[72]

He faced a similar problem later in the campaign when he made a whistle-stop tour of Senator McCarthy's home state of Wisconsin. In a major speech he prepared to give in Milwaukee, he inserted a paragraph intended to stand up to McCarthy's smear of General Marshall. "I know that charges of disloyalty have, in the past, been leveled at General George C. Marshall," he wrote.[73] "I know him as a man and a soldier, dedicated with singular selflessness and the profoundest patriotism to the service of America. And this episode is a sobering lesson in the way freedom must *not* defend itself."

But Wisconsin's Republican governor Walter Kohler, Jr., read Ike's prepared remarks and urged him to delete the paragraph on Marshall. Besides jeopardizing the governor's chances for reelection, Kohler argued, Ike's reference to Marshall could jeopardize Eisenhower's chances in the state. Eisenhower also met with McCarthy, who advised him that his defense of Marshall should be made before another audience. Eisenhower not only deleted the paragraph, but emulated McCarthy in his charges that the Truman administration had been infiltrated by Communists who were responsible for the loss of China and the "surrender of whole nations" in Eastern Europe.*[74]

EISENHOWER'S ATTACKS ON the Truman Administration were aggressive and, as his Milwaukee speech demonstrated, sometimes demagogic. But charges by his running mate Senator Nixon descended to an edgier, darker place. Nixon accused Truman, Secretary of State Acheson, and Governor Stevenson of being "traitors to the high principles in which a majority of the nation's Democrats believe."[75] He referred to Stevenson as a "waltzing mouse" and a graduate of Acheson's "Cowardly College of Communist Containment." An Eisenhower administration, he promised, would clean out the crooks, incompetents, and Communist coddlers in Washington.

The Eisenhower/Nixon campaign was moving efficiently forward when, on September 18, the *New York Post* reported an $18,000 secret slush fund for Nixon, paid for by the senator's wealthy supporters. Suddenly, Eisenhower's and Nixon's attacks on corruption in the Truman administration looked hypocritical. When the story broke, Eisenhower was on a whistle-stop campaign in the Midwest, aboard the "Look Ahead, Neighbor Special." He was putting the final touches on a speech in Omaha in which he promised America "what everybody wants—an honest deal."[76]

After news of Nixon's fund made headlines across the country, Eisenhower's closest advisers, Dewey, Clay, Brownell, and Ike's brother

---

* In his memoirs, Eisenhower regretted that he had made the deletion. Later in his campaign, in a speech in Newark, he said that he considered Marshall a great American.

Milton, wanted Nixon to resign from the ticket. Though Ike was inclined to agree with them, he would not be rushed. Pencil and paper in hand, he retired to a corner of his private railroad car and wrote Nixon a personal note ordering him to provide a thorough accounting of the fund. The letter was never sent. Later, speaking to reporters, he expressed grave concern over the reported fund. He knew Nixon only slightly, he said, and did not think he would be involved in anything unethical or illegal. But Nixon must prove it. How could the Republicans wage a great crusade against the corruption in Washington, he asked, "if we ourselves aren't as clean as a hound's tooth?"[77]

Nixon was furious at Eisenhower. Why hadn't he, at least, heard Nixon's side of the story before issuing his "clean as a hound's tooth" challenge? Without waiting for Ike to defend him, Nixon went on the attack. The slush-fund story was a Communist conspiracy to ruin him, he said. "But the more they smear me the more I'm going to expose the Communists and the crooks and those that defend them until they throw them all out of Washington."[78] Insiders in the Nixon campaign did not suspect that Communists leaked the story, but, rather, disgruntled supporters of Earl Warren who were still angry over Nixon's efforts to undermine Warren at the Republican convention.

In fact, there was nothing illegal or unethical about the fund. It was used largely to pay office expenses not covered by Nixon's Senate allowance, which was not uncommon. Later in the campaign it was revealed that Stevenson had a similar fund.

But the story would not go away. The *New York Herald Tribune* and the *Washington Post*, both strong supporters of Eisenhower, called for Nixon's resignation. Eisenhower expectantly waited for Nixon to submit his resignation. Ike and his advisers, meanwhile, agreed on a plan: the Republican National Committee would pay $75,000 for a half-hour nationally televised address by Nixon in which he would provide a thorough explanation of the fund and offer to resign, if he had not already done so before the telecast.

Eisenhower waited four days before placing a telephone call to Nixon, who was campaigning in Portland, Oregon. He told Nixon that he had not made a decision on whether he should stay on the ticket and waited for Nixon's offer to resign. Nixon refused, determined that Eisenhower would have to ask for his resignation. Neither man spoke for almost a minute. Ike then said that he did not want to condemn an innocent man and advised Nixon to lay out his case in the national telecast.

Would Eisenhower support him? Nixon asked. That really depended on Nixon, he replied. After the telecast, Nixon persisted, would Ike endorse him? Eisenhower made no commitment, but further aggravated Nixon by saying that he would need a few days after the telecast to make that decision.

"The great trouble here is the indecision," Nixon said.[79] Still, Eisenhower would not be pressed for a decision. "There comes a time in matters like this," an exasperated Nixon added, "when you've either got to shit or get off the pot."

"Well, go on television and good luck," Eisenhower replied.[80]

That tense telephone conversation infuriated both men. Eisenhower had never been talked to in such common gutter language by a subordinate during his entire military career, even by the famously combative George Patton. Nixon, who nursed a chronic paranoia, read Ike's indecision as a sign of disloyalty and, he suspected, a clumsy attempt to ruin his political career. Their personal relationship, which had begun coolly at the Republican convention, turned frigid.

When Nixon delivered his famous "Checkers" speech on national television, he retaliated for what he considered Ike's shoddy treatment.*

---

* After recounting his humble upbringing and modest lifestyle, Nixon told the television audience that an admirer in Texas had given his two young daughters a cocker spaniel puppy named Checkers and "the kids love the dog and I just want to say right now, that regardless of what they say about it, we're going to keep it." (*New York Times*, September 24, 1952.)

After pleading his case in emotional, often maudlin terms, he took the decision of whether he should stay on the ticket out of Eisenhower's hands. He told viewers to send their opinions to the Republican National Committee, not Eisenhower, and that he would abide by the RNC's decision. If that act of insubordination wasn't enough, he demanded that Stevenson and his running mate, Senator John Sparkman of Alabama, make a full financial accounting, as he had done. Eisenhower, who was watching the telecast and taking notes in the manager's office in the Cleveland Public Auditorium, pressed down so hard on his pencil that the lead broke on his yellow pad. He knew that Nixon's demand would mean that he, too, would have to make his income a matter of public record, including the favorable tax treatment he received for *Crusade in Europe.**

Just like that, Nixon had turned the tables on Eisenhower, and Ike was angry. He refused to allow Nixon to control the issue. He immediately went before the crowd in the Cleveland Public Auditorium and congratulated Nixon on a fine performance, but, conspicuously, did not commit to keeping him on the ticket. He cabled Nixon to meet him in West Virginia the next day. When Ike met Nixon's plane, he exclaimed, "You're my boy!"[81] The patronizing remark, with no accompanying endorsement, let Nixon know who was in charge.

The response to Nixon's telecast was overwhelmingly positive, and Eisenhower made the now easy decision to keep him on the ticket.

———————

ALL MAJOR POLLS pointed to a Republican victory. Ike, nonetheless, kept to a frenetic, exhausting schedule, covering four thousand miles and visiting twelve states in one two-week period. No town was

———————

* Eisenhower was fortunate that he was not asked about the many gifts and trips that the Gang, many of whom had important dealings with the federal government, had lavished on him for years.

too small for his attention. One day in Iowa, his train started in Davenport, then proceeded to Wilton Junction, West Liberty, Iowa City, Marengo, Brooklyn, Grinnell, and Newton. The train stopped for approximately seven minutes at each stop. He and Mamie appeared on the rear platform and waved happily to the assembled crowd. Ike would be introduced, say how pleased he was to be in Wilton Junction or Marengo or Newton, endorse the local Republican candidate, give a short talk attacking the incompetence or corruption in Washington, smile exultantly, and wave goodbye.

As Truman had recognized as early as 1945, no presidential candidate could compete with the charismatic Eisenhower. He was the nation's greatest military hero of World War II. He stood for honesty, decency, and patriotism and promised the voters a brighter future under his leadership.

Though Eisenhower did not appear to need much help from other prominent Republican politicians, he asked those, like Governor Earl Warren, for advice. The two men met several times after the Republican convention and, in one notable conversation, Warren told Ike that he had nothing to worry about in California from a rumored write-in candidacy of General Douglas MacArthur. No one knew California politics better than Warren, who predicted, accurately, that Eisenhower would comfortably carry his state.* In addition to campaigning with Eisenhower in California, Oregon, and Washington, Warren stumped for him in several Plains and upper midwestern states. He assured voters in South Dakota that Eisenhower supported water and soil conservation and those in Minnesota that the party's presidential candidate was a friend of unions.

Eisenhower campaigned in forty-seven states (skipping only Mississippi), traveled more than 50,000 miles, visited 232 towns and cities, and appeared headed for certain victory. His coup de grace was delivered on October 24 in a nationally televised speech in Detroit's

---

* Eisenhower won 56.8 percent of the five million votes cast in California.

Masonic Temple, where he promised to go to Korea if elected president. U.S. troops had been fighting a bloody war in Korea for more than two years, and there appeared to be no end in sight. Who better than the Allied Supreme Commander in WW II to deal with the quagmire in Korea? Ike's poll numbers, already high, spiked with this pledge.

Eisenhower won thirty-nine of the forty-eight states, including four states of the once solidly Democratic South (Florida, Louisiana, Texas, and Virginia), capturing 442 electoral votes to Stevenson's 89. He won 55 percent of the vote, the greatest majority since FDR's reelection in 1936.

———————

ONCE THE EUPHORIA of victory had passed, Ike settled down to the hard task of governing.

For his cabinet, he chose Brownell to be his attorney general, New York attorney John Foster Dulles as secretary of state, and General Motors CEO Charles Wilson as secretary of defense.

In early December, during Eisenhower's cabinet selection, Warren received a telephone call from the president-elect. "Governor," Eisenhower said, "I am back here [in Washington, D.C.] and I want to tell you I won't have a place for you in it [the cabinet]."[82] He told Warren that he had considered him to be attorney general but chose Brownell for his political as well as his legal advice. Warren replied that Brownell would make a "splendid" attorney general. Eisenhower then said, "But I want you to know that I intend to offer you the first vacancy on the Supreme Court."*[83]

———————

* Eisenhower's version of the offer is slightly different from Warren's. In Ike's memoirs, he recalled that the telephone conversation between him and Warren occurred several months later and, though he made no commitment, he told Warren that he was inclined to appoint him to the first court vacancy. (DDEMC, p. 228.)

Chapter Five

"TO MY MIND, HE IS A STATESMAN"

In 1950, at the age of seventy, James F. Byrnes, former seven-term Democratic congressman from South Carolina, U.S.
senator, associate justice of the Supreme Court, director of war mobilization, and secretary of state, emerged from political retirement to
successfully run for governor of his state. Byrnes's primary motivation
for extending his political career was to preserve public school segregation in South Carolina.

When Byrnes took his oath as governor in 1951, segregation in
the public schools in his state faced a serious legal challenge. In a suit
brought by the NAACP, the organization's chief counsel, Thurgood
Marshall, argued before a three-judge federal district court in Charleston that the segregated public schools in rural Clarendon County,
South Carolina, violated the Equal Protection Clause of the Fourteenth
Amendment. The South Carolina case was one of five law suits brought
by the NAACP challenging the constitutionality of segregated schools
in four states and the District of Columbia (under the Due Process
Clause of the Fifth Amendment).[*][1]

* The other cases were brought in Delaware, Kansas, Virginia, and the District
of Columbia, but all twenty-one states with segregated public schools would be

In June 1951, the district court panel that heard the South Carolina case split 2–1, upholding the state's right to separate public school children in Clarendon County on the basis of race. But the majority also ordered the state to expend the necessary funds to make black schools equal to white schools in the predominantly black county. This was a daunting task since the facilities, curriculum, and teachers' salaries in the county's black schools lagged woefully behind those of the white schools. Most of the sixty-one black schools in the county were housed in ramshackle shanties, many without heat or electricity. The total value of the black schools attended by 6,531 pupils was listed at $194,575. The value of the twelve white schools in the county attended by 2,375 students was listed at $673,850.

Byrnes hailed the decision upholding segregated schools in the county. At the same time, the governor, who had built a reputation over four decades as a shrewd, pragmatic politician, immediately proposed to the state legislature a $75 million bond issue for improvements in the public schools with most of the expenditure to be earmarked for black schools. The legislature approved the bond issue, which was paid for with a 3 percent sales tax.

After the NAACP appealed the district court decision to the U.S. Supreme Court, Byrnes hired his good friend, the prominent New York attorney John W. Davis, to argue South Carolina's case before the court. Davis, former solicitor general of the United States, president of the American Bar Association, and Democratic candidate for president in 1924, was considered one of the greatest advocates ever to appear before the court.

And if the state lost its appeal? Byrnes proposed an amendment to the state constitution that would permit the legislature to close the public schools and lease them to private groups in order to maintain

bound by a ruling of the U.S. Supreme Court if, as expected, the court agreed to hear the appeals.

segregation. The amendment passed by a 2–1 margin in a referendum held shortly before Davis was scheduled to argue South Carolina's case before the Supreme Court. "South Carolina will not, now nor for some years to come, mix white and colored children in our schools," Byrnes declared.[2] "If the Court changes what is now the law of the land [so that we cannot] maintain segregation . . . we will abandon the public school system. To do that would be choosing the lesser of two great evils."

———————

THE ISSUE OF race was on Governor Byrnes's mind in February 1952, five months before Democratic delegates were to meet to select the party's presidential candidate. In an address to the Georgia legislature, he charged that black politicians in recent years had wielded the balance of power in the elections in the big cities in the North. As a result, he said, the national Democratic Party had rejected the states'-rights doctrine espoused by the South and treated the region as a "step-child."* He declared that the South's dissident Democrats must "stand up and fight for their political independence."[3] Recalling the words of Thomas Jefferson that "there were times when a political revolution was desirable," he said that "he [Jefferson] was right."

A month after Illinois governor Adlai Stevenson was nominated as the Democrats' presidential candidate, Byrnes announced that he would vote for Eisenhower. He said that Eisenhower offered the best hope to stop the war in Korea. A big factor in his decision to abandon the Democratic ticket, he added, was Stevenson's support for a federal Fair Employment Practices Commission. He also condemned Stevenson for favoring changes in Senate rules that would limit debate. The

* Byrnes had bolted the Democratic Party in 1948 over the issue of race, supporting the third-party candidacy of South Carolina's Governor Strom Thurmond, an ardent segregationist who had run for president on the Dixiecrat Party ticket.

proposed changes were seen as a direct threat to the filibuster, which had been used effectively for years by southern congressmen to block civil rights legislation.

Two weeks later, Eisenhower received a hero's welcome from 35,000 South Carolinians, including Governor Byrnes, on the lawn of the state capital building in Columbia. Eisenhower thanked his "close and long-time friend, your distinguished governor, Jimmy Byrnes,"[4] then lashed out at the Truman administration for corruption and inflation at home and a muddled foreign policy that produced the stalemate in Korea.[5] His attacks were frequently interrupted by loud cheers. But a silence "as still as the starless night" fell over the crowd when Eisenhower spoke of his intention to make equality of opportunity a living fact for every American.[6]

A MONTH AFTER Eisenhower's election, the nine justices of the U.S. Supreme Court, led by Chief Justice Fred Vinson, heard three days of arguments in the five cases brought by the NAACP challenging public school segregation.[7] The cases had been placed on the court docket collectively under the name of the Kansas case, *Brown v. Board of Education of Topeka*. In the press, the arguments were billed as the most momentous constitutional challenge to racial discrimination since the *Dred Scott* decision in 1857 in which the court declared that black Americans, whether slave or free, had no cognizable constitutional rights.

On the first day of arguments, all three hundred seats in the elegant courtroom were taken, many by African Americans, and a waiting line stretched out the doors through the long marble corridor and down the front steps of the Supreme Court building. Although the Kansas case was argued first, it was the second case, the challenge to the segregated public schools in Clarendon County, South Carolina, that generated the most public attention. It promised to produce a brilliant courtroom drama, pitting the two most celebrated attorneys in the nation against each other.

Arguing for the NAACP was forty-four-year-old Thurgood Marshall, who, with persistence and extraordinary skill, had devised and implemented the successful litigation strategy that had struck down racial barriers on railroads, reduced voter discrimination, and desegregated graduate schools in the South. He was opposed by John W. Davis, seventy-nine years old, urbane, confident, and immaculate in morning attire, who had argued more cases before the court (140) than any lawyer in the institution's history. In the previous term Davis had achieved one of his greatest victories, convincing a court majority that President Truman had exceeded his constitutional authority in seizing the nation's steel mills.

Marshall opened his argument boldly by declaring that "slavery is perpetuated" when black children were forced by law to attend separate schools from whites. Drawing on the testimony of prominent sociologists at the district court trial in Charleston, Marshall contended that there was no discernible difference between the ability of black and white children to learn. But studies by the sociologists showed that the impact of segregation on the minds of black children was to make them feel that they were of an inferior race. That feeling of inferiority was a far more serious burden on black children, Marshall argued, than their schools' inferior physical facilities, teaching standards, and curriculum. "The humiliation the children go through will affect their minds as long as they live," he said. "I believe that there is a body of law [under the Fourteenth Amendment] that holds that distinctions on the basis of race are odious and invidious."

Justice Felix Frankfurter interrupted Marshall's argument to express his concern that a ruling striking down segregated schools in the South might be evaded, undermining the court's authority. Marshall said that the court could allow local school boards great flexibility in implementing a desegregation decree, even drawing new boundary lines that put large numbers of one race disproportionately in a public school.

Frankfurter exploded. "You mean we might have gerrymandering?"* He added angrily that "nothing would be worse for this Court than to make abstract statements against segregation and then have them defeated by tricks." He also challenged Marshall's contention that there were ample judicial precedents to strike down public school segregation. He noted that there was a "long line of decisions" by state courts and the Supreme Court upholding segregated schools, a legal history "almost more impressive than any one single decision" that could be cited on the other side.

Now was the time, Marshall responded, for the court to overturn the judicial precedents that had upheld school segregation. For too many decades, he asserted, judicially sanctioned segregation had erected "roadblocks" in the minds of black children, resulting in their progressing more slowly in their studies than white children.

Addressing the concern implicit in Frankfurter's questions, Marshall sought to assure the justice and his brethren that a desegregation ruling would be accepted in the South as had other recent court decisions eliminating racial barriers. School segregation was not "any more ingrained in the South than segregation in transportation," he said, and "the Court upset that." In the South "white and colored kids walk down the road together on their way to school, separate and go to separate schools, and then play together." Local schools would have discretion in adjusting to the new conditions, he said, perhaps two months in one school, six months in another. The "rank and file of people in the South," he predicted, would accept the court's decision.

When it was Davis's turn to address the justices, he spoke in a conversational tone that, nonetheless, resonated throughout the chamber.

---

* The term "gerrymandering" referred to the redrawing of district lines by state legislatures to exclude or diminish the votes of a particular group, often racial minorities.

The thrust of his argument, laid out early in clear, precise phrases, was that school segregation was a matter of public policy for state legislatures and local school boards to devise. If there were a constitutional issue for the court to decide, which he doubted, then it was to uphold the court's 1896 decision in *Plessy v. Ferguson* that declared separate but equal public facilities to be constitutional. The court's *Plessy* decision, he contended, reflected the intention of the framers of the Fourteenth Amendment. In 1866, when the amendment was proposed, Congress did not view the Constitution as a bar to segregation, he maintained. As proof he noted that in that same year Congress enacted a school segregation law for the District of Columbia. He cited a vast body of court rulings and legislation that had supported the constitutionality of school segregation over a period of ninety years.

Davis pointed with pride to the recent efforts in South Carolina to improve black schools. "[U]nder the leadership of the present governor [Byrnes], there has been a surge for educational reform and improvement that I suspect has not been equaled in any other state," he said. "It includes a 75 million dollar bond issue to improve Negro schools." If the court ignored this tangible progress, he suggested that dire consequences might follow. Black students outnumbered whites in Clarendon County by 10–1, he said. The consequences of combining the two school systems, he said, "cannot be contemplated with entire equanimity."

Davis built his argument to a climax with a series of rhetorical questions:

"What is the great national policy underlying this whole question?" he asked.

"Is it not the fact that the very strength and fiber of our federal system is local self-government in those matters for which local action is competent?

"Is it not of all the activities of government one which more nearly approaches the hearts and minds of people: the question of the education of their young?

"Is it not the height of wisdom that the manner in which that shall be conducted should be left to those most immediately affected and the wishes of the parents—both white and colored—be ascertained before forcing children into contacts that may be unwelcome?

"I respectfully submit to the Court that there is no reason assigned here why this Court or any other should reverse the findings of 90 years."

At one point during the oral arguments Frankfurter had cautioned the public not to read too much into his and his colleagues' questions. Their interrogation of attorneys did not necessarily reflect their views on the cases, he said, but were merely efforts to educate themselves about the complex legal issues being argued. Despite that disclaimer, the justices' many probing questions appeared to reflect their anxiety in contemplating a broad desegregation ruling that would uproot both custom and law in the South.

One of the court's keenest observers, John W. Davis, ignored Frankfurter's admonition. After the completion of the oral arguments, Davis predicted that the court would rule 5–4 or 6–3 in favor of upholding school segregation.

The justices met in conference to discuss the five segregation cases on December 13, 1952, two days after the final arguments had concluded. Although the justices' deliberations are unrecorded and held in secret, memoranda from individual justices and other sources have suggested that the justices were deeply divided on the issue. One inside source, Associate Justice William O. Douglas, corroborated Davis's prediction on the split among the justices. A memorandum from Douglas to his files recorded the initial breakdown among the justices as 5–4 to uphold segregation. According to Douglas's memorandum, four justices—Hugo Black, Harold Burton, Sherman Minton, and Douglas—supported the NAACP's argument that segregation in the public schools was unconstitutional. "Vinson was of the opinion that the *Plessy* case was right and that segregation was constitutional," Douglas wrote.[8] "Reed followed the view of Vinson and [Tom] Clark was inclined that way." According to the Douglas memo, "Frankfurter and [Robert] Jackson viewed the problem with great alarm and thought that the Court should not decide the question if it was possible to avoid it."*

Commentators were also split on the issue. After a visit to South Carolina the week following the court's arguments, columnist Raymond Moley reported that the recently built black schools in the state were more modern and physically better than the white schools. Still, Moley wrote, there had been no unrest among the white parents about these improvements. "The new building will go on until the goal of equality is reached," he wrote approvingly, and suggested that this result would comport with the court majority's wishes, based on the justices' questioning at the oral arguments.[9]

But Eleanor Roosevelt questioned whether separate facilities for

---

* There are good reasons to question the accuracy of Douglas's memorandum. It was not written immediately after the justices' conference in December 1952, but seventeen months later, after a unanimous court had declared school segregation unconstitutional. It was not uncommon, moreover, for Douglas and his chief nemesis on the court, Frankfurter, to write memoranda to their files or to sympathetic colleagues, reporting the positions of their colleagues as they would have liked history to record them. Frankfurter, who did not speak to Douglas for years, often assigned to Douglas, and his close ally on the court, Black, the most cynical motives in arriving at their judicial decisions. (See Simon, James F., *The Antagonists: Hugo Black, Felix Frankfurter and Civil Liberties in Modern America* [1989], pp. 120–9, 187–92.) Similarly, the accuracy of Douglas's recollections of the justices' positions in *Brown* in December 1952 has been challenged by scholars. (See Tushnet, Mark, with Katya Lezin, "What Really Happened in *Brown v. Board of Education*," 91 *Columbia Law Review* 1867 [1991]; see also, Hutchinson, Dennis J., "Unanimity and Desegregation: Decisionmaking in the Supreme Court, 1948–1958," 68 *Georgetown Law Journal* 1 [1979].)

blacks could ever be equal. "It has always seemed to me that there could be separate facilities, and technically they might offer the same opportunities for both Colored and White," she wrote.[10] "But the mere fact of segregation, which is not a voluntary act but an imposed one, makes equality impossible."

———————

DURING EISENHOWER'S PRESIDENTIAL campaign, he had actively courted leaders from the segregated South. His forays into the South had paid handsome political dividends. He carried four southern states, the best showing of a Republican presidential candidate in that section of the nation since Reconstruction. His strong support for state ownership of the oil-rich offshore tidelands undoubtedly attracted voters in Louisiana and Texas. But southern leaders from states without tidelands, such as Senator Harry Byrd of Virginia and Governor Byrnes of South Carolina, also supported Ike, calculating that he was more likely to protect their states' interests than the Democrats' Stevenson.

Eisenhower's states'-rights perspective was evident in the federal-state tidelands dispute and underscored by his opposition to a federal Fair Employment Practices Commission. His rapport with southern audiences was obvious in their enthusiastic responses to his attacks on the Truman administration. That rapport vanished only when he called for one law for all Americans, regardless of race. He was conspicuously more outspoken about civil rights in his speeches in the North, promising audiences in Ohio, New Jersey, and New York that he would use his presidential authority to break down racial barriers controlled by the federal government, including the District of Columbia.

Would President Eisenhower make good on his campaign promise to enforce civil rights? His answer was contained in his first State of the Union address, delivered to Congress on February 2, 1953. "I propose to use whatever authority exists in the office of the President to end segregation in the District of Columbia, including the Federal Government, and any segregation in the Armed Forces," he said.[11]

Eisenhower had proved to be a masterful executive as Supreme Commander of Allied Forces in Europe during World War II. He made the tough decisions but knew instinctively when and to whom he could delegate the critical tasks of implementation. The man primarily responsible for enforcing the new president's civil rights mandate was his attorney general, Herbert Brownell, Jr.

Brownell, forty-eight years old, was born in Peru, Nebraska, one of seven children of a political science professor at the University of Nebraska and his wife. He graduated Phi Beta Kappa from the University of Nebraska and received a scholarship to Yale Law School, where he edited the law review and graduated with honors. A partner in the prestigious New York City law firm of Lord, Day, and Lord, he was best known as the Republican Party's most skilled political strategist, first for Dewey and later for Eisenhower. His allegiance to the moderate wing of the Republican Party was unwavering. While working for Governor Dewey, he fought successfully for New York's Fair Employment Practices Commission. Slightly built with thinning brown hair, he often slumped deep in his chair at strategy sessions, spoke softly, and made his points succinctly. Ike valued no one's opinion more than Brownell's.

After Eisenhower's State of the Union address, Brownell moved aggressively to fulfill the president's promise to desegregate the District of Columbia. In March, the attorney general asked the Supreme Court to uphold two post–Civil War congressional statutes forbidding restaurants in the District of Columbia to refuse service to blacks. In his *amicus* (friend of the court) brief for the Eisenhower administration, Brownell urged the court to overturn a federal appeals court decision that had found the statutes invalid. The appellate court decision was clearly "erroneous," Brownell asserted, since there was a long, unbroken line of Supreme Court decisions upholding Congress's authority to make laws governing the District of Columbia. He quoted the passage from Eisenhower's State of the Union address promising to end segregation in the District of Columbia and suggested a much broader application of the president's mandate. "It is the established policy of the United States that its employees shall be hired, and shall work together, without regard to any differences of race or color," he wrote.[12]

Shortly after Brownell had filed the administration's brief, Eisenhower was asked at a press conference if anything had been done to end segregation in the military. At first, he responded vaguely that he would look into the matter. But then he added that he didn't see how any American could justify discrimination in the expenditure of federal funds "on legal, logical, or moral grounds."[13] Any benefits to be derived from federal money should all be shared, he said, "regardless of such inconsequential factors as race or religion."

Within days, the White House announced that segregation would end in schools operated by the army with federal funds for children of army personnel.[14] The announcement said further that the army was negotiating with local authorities in an effort to achieve "integration" of schools at those army posts in states with a policy of segregation. Secretary of the Army Robert Stevens then issued his own statement announcing that, beginning in the fall, all schools owned and operated entirely by the army would be integrated.[*15]

On June 8, 1953, the U.S. Supreme Court, without dissent, reversed the appellate court and upheld the 1873 law that required restaurants in the District of Columbia to serve black customers.[16]

---

* After Harlem congressman Adam Clayton Powell, Jr., complained to Eisenhower that three members of his administration—Secretary of the Navy Robert Anderson, Secretary of Health, Education and Welfare Oveta Culp Hobby, and Vice Admiral Joel Boone—were undermining his desegregation policy, the president made inquiries and assured Powell that all three administration members were pursuing "the purpose of eliminating segregation in federal controlled and supported institutions." (*Washington Post*, June 11, 1953.)

Attorney General Brownell said that the court's ruling represented "a significant forward step toward accomplishment of President Eisenhower's anti-segregation program."[17] Eisenhower himself listed the court's decision as one of the most important early achievements of his administration, an example of his middle way "which avoids extremes in purpose and in action."[18]

Without fanfare, Eisenhower had, in the first months of his administration, begun to make good on his campaign promise to end segregation in the District of Columbia and the military.* His "middle way" appeared to be leaning heavily in the direction of enforcing the civil rights of all Americans.[19]

ALTHOUGH EACH JUSTICE had discussed his views on the school segregation cases at the December 1952 conference, no vote was taken. The failure to vote was not an oversight, but rather a conscious effort by several members of the court, including Chief Justice Vinson, to delay a final judgment on such a momentous issue for the court and the nation while the justices were so divided. Although Frankfurter's position at that conference has been the subject of debate, his role in urging the justices to delay a final decision cannot be doubted. At the December conference, he had proposed that all five cases be set down for reargument and that the incoming Eisenhower administration, which would be responsible for enforcing any court decision, be invited to submit a brief and

---

* President Truman signed an executive order on July 26, 1948, desegregating the military services, but military leaders, including General Omar Bradley, chairman of the Joint Chiefs of Staff, and Secretary of the Army Kenneth Royall, resisted implementing the order. The navy and the Marine Corps did not alter their racial policies, and the air force implemented only a limited program of compliance. In 1953, at the time of Eisenhower's presidential inauguration, progress in desegregating the military was slow and uneven.

participate in the second oral argument. The purpose, he said, was for the new administration to present its ideas on possible implementation procedures, should the court issue a desegregation order. He proposed that March might be a suitable time for reargument.

But the justices were no closer to a decision in March 1953 than they had been three months earlier, even as to whether to ask for reargument in the cases. Finally, in late May, Frankfurter circulated a memorandum to his colleagues suggesting a reargument and attaching a series of questions for the attorneys to answer. The questions were framed in such a way as to hide their essential purpose to delay a final decision, he wrote. They were drafted to "look in opposite directions," he continued, so that each side might be encouraged. "I know not how others feel, but for me the ultimate crucial factor in the problem presented by these cases is psychological—the adjustment of men's minds and actions to the unfamiliar and the unpleasant...."[20]

The five questions that Frankfurter attached had been drafted by him and his law clerk, Alexander Bickel. The first question asked if there was evidence that the framers of the Fourteenth Amendment and the states that ratified it intended to abolish segregation in the public schools. Second, if there was no such evidence, would it, nonetheless, have been contemplated by the framers that future congresses might abolish segregation, and that the court, in light of future conditions, could construe the amendment to abolish segregation? Third, even if the attorneys could not answer the second question authoritatively, was it within the court's power to abolish segregation in the public schools? Fourth, if the court decided to abolish segregation, would the decree necessarily order the immediate desegregation of public schools or, alternatively, could there be a gradual adjustment to eliminate segregation? Finally, if the court ordered desegregation, should it formulate a detailed decree, appoint a special master to hear evidence and make recommendations, or remand the cases to the lower courts to provide directions as to how the decree should be implemented?

With minor changes, the questions were approved by a majority of Frankfurter's colleagues, and the date for reargument was set for the next court term. Attorney General Brownell was invited to submit a brief and take part in the oral argument, an invitation that had not been extended to his predecessor when the cases had originally been argued.

DESPITE SOUTH CAROLINA governor Byrnes's endorsement of Eisenhower and speeches on his behalf, Ike failed to carry the state of South Carolina. Byrnes, nevertheless, stayed in close touch with the new president. At Byrnes's request, the two men met for lunch at the White House on July 20, 1953 to discuss the school segregation cases.

On August 14, 1953, Eisenhower wrote Governor Byrnes that "[since] our recent lunch together at which we discussed the pending 'School Segregation' case, it has scarcely been absent from my mind."[21] The lunch had taken place to discuss, according to Eisenhower's diary, "the possibility of a Supreme Court ruling that would abolish segregation in public schools of the country."[22] Byrnes had stressed that a Court decision overturning the *Plessy* decision would result in states abolishing the public school system throughout the South, an action that he had already promised to take in South Carolina. White southerners could tolerate interaction with adult African Americans, Byrnes told Eisenhower, but they were violently opposed to mixing the races in the public schools. Anticipating that the president's position on the school segregation cases might be influenced by a large black vote, Byrnes produced a document analyzing the 1952 election. On the basis of the analysis, he predicted that blacks would continue to vote as a bloc for Democrats.

Eisenhower responded cautiously to Byrnes's arguments. "I told him that while I was not going to give in advance my attitude toward a

Supreme Court opinion I had not even seen and so could not know in what terms it would be couched," he wrote in his diary, "my convictions would not be formed by political expediency."[23] He believed that the best result would be achieved by cooperation between the federal government and the states, he told Byrnes, not by a federal law that imposed a solution on the states. He doubted that coercion by the federal government would be effective and agreed with Byrnes that improvement in race relations required local support. "Consequently, I believe that Federal law imposed upon our states in such a way as to bring about a conflict of the police powers of the states and of the nation would set back the cause of progress in race relations for a long, long time," he told Byrnes.

But the president drew a distinction between action by the federal government totally within its control and that which required cooperation between the federal and state governments. "I feel that my oath of office, as well as my own convictions, requires me to eliminate discrimination within the definite areas of federal responsibility," he told Byrnes.[24]

"You can do no less," Byrnes replied.[25]

In his August 14 letter to Byrnes, Eisenhower reminded the governor of their July luncheon conversation and agreement that in a field completely under the control of the federal government his presidential oath of office, as well as his convictions, "requires me to eliminate discrimination within the definite areas of Federal responsibility."[26] There was one area of federal responsibility, he continued, "where my efforts may run counter to customs in some states." It involved the "nondiscrimination" clauses in federal contracts. "I do believe that states should cooperate in, and never impede, the enforcement of Federal regulations *where the Federal government has clear and exclusive responsibility in the case,*" he wrote. The emphasis was Eisenhower's.

In raising the issue of federal responsibility with Byrnes, Eisenhower had a particular subject in mind—federal nondiscrimination contracts at the Navy Yard in Charleston, South Carolina. "I feel that if there should be any trouble at the Yard in enforcing the nondiscrimination regulations, you as Governor could instantly announce that, since this is clearly a Federal matter, beyond State jurisdiction, compliance should be complete and cheerful," he wrote.[27] "I sincerely believe that such cooperation would reassure those who seem to feel that the only alternative to stringent Federal action is no action as all." He assured Byrnes that he was respectful of other officials' constitutional responsibilities and that all, he assumed, wanted to make progress toward the elimination of "those things that all of us would class as unjust and unfair." In this category, he continued, "there clearly falls, to my mind, the right to equal consideration in Federal employment, regardless of race or color." He closed with the request that Byrnes communicate with his fellow governors "who feel generally as you do in these matters."

Eisenhower's letter in response to his luncheon conversation with Byrnes was a vivid example of his forcefulness when he was confident of his constitutional authority as president. Choosing his words carefully, he skillfully asserted federal control of contracts at military facilities in the segregated South, including Charleston's Navy Yard. But in his letter as well as his earlier luncheon conversation with Byrnes, he also expressed his reluctance to impose federal authority on the states where that authority was not clear cut.

Byrnes responded to the president's letter by assuring him that "I as Governor certainly would assert no right to interfere with any operations at the Charleston Navy Yard."[28] He had already asked for full compliance with the federal nondiscrimination order, he wrote. But he quickly drew a distinction between compliance with the nondiscrimination federal contracts at the Navy Yard and a court decree to desegregate the public schools in South Carolina. "Unlike the public school situation, no man is compelled to work at the Navy Yard," he wrote.

The day after Eisenhower wrote Byrnes cordially demanding the governor's cooperation in the enforcement of federal nondiscrimination contracts at the Charleston Navy Yard, he formally appointed Vice President Nixon to be the chairman of the newly created President's Committee on Governmental Contracts. The purpose of the committee was to enforce the "principles of equality that we [as a Nation] preach," the president wrote Nixon.[29] "On no level of our national existence can inequality be justified," he continued. "Within the Federal government itself, however, tolerance of inequality would be odious."

Governor Byrnes was extremely unhappy when he read reports in the press of the establishment of the president's committee. "I think you and I would agree its aim or purpose is the same as the FEPC legislation which in recent years has been considered and rejected by Congress," he wrote Eisenhower.[30] He pointed out that Eisenhower had steadfastly opposed a federal FEPC during his presidential campaign. Once in office, he admitted, a presidential candidate could change his views. But he wanted the president to know that his endorsement of Eisenhower during the campaign was partially predicated on Eisenhower's opposition to a federal FEPC. If the president's views had changed, Byrnes would have much preferred that he advocate legislation rather than issue an executive order, which, he was convinced, could not be effectively enforced.

Eisenhower sent Nixon a copy of Byrnes's letter and told the vice president that he had had a long telephone conversation with the South Carolina governor about the new committee's purpose. He iterated his view that the federal government had a duty "to insure equality in all areas in which it has complete and unquestioned jurisdiction."[31] But he also agreed with Byrnes that "a so-called federal FEPC law" would be ineffective and "undoubtedly by creating antagonisms, set back the cause of progress by a good many years." He predicted that there would probably be a constitutional challenge to such federal legislation by some states as a violation of their reserve powers, resulting in "confusion and misunderstanding," and "thus increasing prejudices."

As the deadline approached for Attorney General Brownell to file the administration's brief in the school segregation cases, Eisenhower expressed concern about answering the court's question on the purpose of the Fourteenth Amendment. "It appears that the Supreme Court desires both a memorandum of fact as well as an opinion concerning the intent of the fourteenth amendment," he wrote in a memorandum to his files on August 19, 1953.[32] "It seems to me that the rendering of 'opinion' by the Attorney General on this kind of question would constitute an invasion of the duties, responsibilities and authority of the Supreme Court." The court, he continued, "cannot possibly abdicate; consequently it cannot delegate its responsibility and it would be futile for the Attorney General to attempt to sit as a Court and reach a conclusion as to the true meaning of the fourteenth amendment."

Eisenhower called Brownell to discuss his objections. Brownell told the president that the administration could not evade its responsibility to respond to the court's questions in the school segregation cases. The Attorney General said that the justices would undoubtedly ask, "Is school segregation constitutional?" What was Brownell's response to that question, Eisenhower asked. "I answered that in my professional opinion public school segregation was unconstitutional and that the old *Plessy* case had been wrongly decided." Eisenhower replied that if that was Brownell's professional opinion, he "should so state, if the Court asked the question."[33]

Eisenhower appeared ambivalent in his approach to the school segregation cases, in contrast to his enthusiastic endorsement of his administration's legal role in support of desegregating restaurants in the District of Columbia. His apprehension was evident in his objection to the administration's taking a position on the purpose of the Fourteenth Amendment. It was further demonstrated in his detached acceptance of Brownell's legal opinion on the unconstitutionality of

Plessy. He trusted Brownell's professional judgment but did not express any enthusiasm, indeed, any opinion on the issue. This was a strangely detached Eisenhower, the same president who repeatedly had vowed to enforce nondiscriminatory federal laws. His evident detachment may have concealed a deep anxiety, expressed in his conversations with Byrnes, that an eventual court desegregation decree would result in a political and constitutional clash between the president and recalcitrant southern states.

BY THE TIME Governor Warren celebrated his sixty-second birthday in March 1953, he had begun to think anew about his future. Still vigorous, he did not want to retire. In fact, retirement was not a realistic option, since his government pension would amount to only $900 a month, hardly sufficient to support his wife and growing family, including four children then in college. He could run for a fourth term as governor in 1954, but he had nothing to prove, having already compiled a remarkable record of accomplishment over his ten years in office. Besides, there were widely circulating reports that conservative Lieutenant Governor Knight planned to challenge him for the Republican nomination, a prospective fight that promised to be both nasty and debilitating. Over his years as governor, Warren had received lucrative offers to enter the private sector after retirement, but he had no interest. He could also join a private law firm, but working for fees after more than thirty years of public service held no appeal.

President-elect Eisenhower had told Warren that he intended to appoint him to the first Supreme Court vacancy, but Warren knew that such commitments were not binding. And a vacancy might not occur for many years; the oldest justice, Frankfurter, was only sixty-nine years old. It was not uncommon for the life-tenured justices to serve into their seventies and eighties and, in rare cases, into their nineties. Justice Oliver Wendell Holmes, Jr., retired at the age of ninety.

In late May, Attorney General Brownell raised another possibility with Warren. The administration was having difficulty filling the position of Solicitor General of the United States, the government's chief advocate in cases argued before the Supreme Court. Would Warren consider accepting the appointment? The position interested Warren for a number of reasons. He could again return to the courtroom where he had made his reputation as an outstanding prosecutor. As California's attorney general, he had represented his state's legal interests in both civil and criminal cases, including twenty-five arguments before the Supreme Court. As SG, he could continue his government service but on a larger national scale. There was an additional incentive: the office of solicitor general was viewed as a stepping-stone to the court. Justice Jackson, for example, had served as FDR's solicitor general before his appointment to the court.

Warren told Brownell that he would seriously consider the SG position. The two men devised a coded telegraphic message in which Warren would signal his willingness to take the job, if offered, and Brownell, with Eisenhower's approval, would extend the formal offer. Meanwhile, Warren flew to London with his family where the governor, at Eisenhower's invitation, served as a member of the official U.S. delegation (led by General George C. Marshall) to the coronation of Queen Elizabeth II. Later, Warren and his family toured the Scandinavian countries and made a special visit to the farm and home where his mother was born in the Swedish province of Hälsingland.

During the summer, Warren made two important decisions. He would not run for a fourth term as governor, and planned to announce his decision publicly upon his return to California in early September. He also wired Brownell that he would accept an offer from the administration to be solicitor general. Brownell promptly sent a return telegram in their agreed-upon code that the job was his.

On September 3, Warren announced that he would not seek a fourth gubernatorial term. He then focused on his new duties as Solicitor General of the United States. For the first time in his life, Warren prepared for a job and a home with his family outside the state of California.

Five days later, Chief Justice Vinson died of a heart attack in the middle of the night. His death had come without warning. He was only sixty-three years old and in apparent good health. Vinson was mourned as a kindly man and dedicated public servant who had been elected U.S. senator from Kentucky and served as President Truman's secretary of the treasury before being named chief justice. But his seven years as chief justice had not been happy or productive. His colleagues liked him but considered him intellectually shallow. And he was no leader, as the court's frustratingly inconsequential deliberations in the school segregation cases had demonstrated. With the pending *Brown* reargument on his mind, Justice Frankfurter remarked to a former clerk that Vinson's death had been "the first indication I have ever had that there is a God."[34]

Speculation about Vinson's successor began immediately, and Warren's name was prominently mentioned. To Warren, the appointment as chief justice was enormously attractive. He had become accustomed to leadership—as Alameda County district attorney, state attorney general, and governor. To serve as the Chief Justice of the United States would be the crowning achievement of an extraordinary career of public service.

Warren's memory of the telephone conversation in which President-elect Eisenhower expressed his intention to name him to the first court vacancy included Eisenhower's "personal commitment" to the appointment.[35] Of course, Warren conceded that Eisenhower might not honor that commitment. The president could also elevate a sitting member of the court to the chief justiceship. In that case, Warren would be content with an appointment as an associate justice. But he coveted the top role now that it was suddenly and unexpectedly available.

Although Eisenhower did not think he owed Warren anything, in fact the California governor had given Eisenhower's candidacy significant boosts both at the Republican convention and during the campaign.[36] Warren had undermined his own presidential ambitions when he supported the vote of the California delegation for the Fair Play amendment, which led to Eisenhower's nomination on the first ballot. He closed ranks with other Republican leaders around the party's vice presidential candidate, Richard Nixon, after his "Checkers" speech, though he personally loathed Nixon. And in the general election he campaigned enthusiastically for Eisenhower in California and other states.

After the announcement of Vinson's death, Warren went to extreme measures to avoid the press. He arranged with a friend, Edwin Carty, who was Ventura County supervisor and former state fish-and-game commissioner, to take their sons with them on a deer hunt. They chose their favorite deer-hunting area on Santa Rosa Island, one of the channel islands off the southern shore of California about forty miles from Santa Barbara. There was no telephone on the island. Communication with the mainland was through a ship-to-shore radio used primarily by coastal vessels and local fishermen.

———

AFTER ATTENDING VINSON'S funeral, Eisenhower began to think seriously about the appointment of a new chief justice. He knew that he must make the decision in a matter of weeks, since he had been advised by Brownell and members of the court that it was vital to have the court at full strength for the beginning of the 1953 term in which the school segregation cases were to be reargued. For a man with no training in law or the history of the court, Eisenhower held strong opinions on the qualities he was looking for in a chief justice. He wrote his brother Milton that he sought "a man (a) of known and recognized integrity, (b) of wide experience in government, (c) of competence in the law, (d) of national stature in reputation so as to be useful in my effort to restore the Court to the high position of prestige it once enjoyed."[37] He added, as an explanation for his remark about the court's low prestige, that "[t]his prestige, I think, was lost in the appointment of such men as [Frank] Murphy and [Wiley] Rutledge, and a few others." Justices Murphy and Rutledge were FDR appointees. In later correspondence he expanded his category of Justices who had lowered the prestige of the court to appointees during the New Deal (FDR) and Fair Deal (Truman) without mentioning specific names.

Eisenhower was besieged with friendly advice on the appointment. Young B. Smith, former dean and Kent Professor of Law at Columbia, wrote that he was gratified by reports that Eisenhower would not make a political appointment but fill Vinson's position with an experienced and able jurist. He recommended Chief Justice Arthur Vanderbilt of the New Jersey Supreme Court, a Columbia law graduate, and "an able and experienced jurist with administrative ability."[38]

The president responded that Vanderbilt was, indeed, on his list of candidates.* He told Smith further that the reports were correct that he did not intend to make an appointment motivated by politics. But he added, "This does not mean that a political figure cannot be, with propriety, considered for the post. Certainly both [William Howard] Taft and [Charles Evans] Hughes were of this category."[39] Taft had been elected president and Hughes had served two terms as governor of New York.

Eisenhower's brother Edgar, a successful lawyer in Tacoma, Washington, was eager to share his opinions on men the president should consider for chief justice. His short list of candidates included Vanderbilt and others who were outstanding lawyers, judges, and scholars. But he impressed upon the president that he should not appoint a politi-

---

* Early in Eisenhower's search, according to his memoirs, he asked his secretary of state, John Foster Dulles, if he would consider the appointment. Dulles declined, saying that he preferred his cabinet position. (DDEMC, p. 227.)

cian. "I have such a low regard for the legal ability of most politicians, including governors, that I naturally strike them off any list of judicial appointments."[40]

The president's response to his brother Edgar was swift and challenging. He pointed out that four respected chief justices—John Marshall, William Howard Taft, Charles Evans Hughes, and Harlan Fiske Stone—did not have extensive judicial experience before their appointments.* "I cite these things just to suggest that a Governor with a *good* legal background just might be about the best type we could find—provided of course, that he had a successful record of administration and experience and was nationally known as a man of integrity and fairness."[41] In this letter to Edgar Eisenhower, dated September 22, 1953, the president had accurately described the qualities of Governor Earl Warren of California.

Three days after the president had written Edgar, Warren received a ship-to-shore message from Attorney General Brownell asking him to call him in Washington. Warren requested a small airplane to pick him up on Santa Rosa Island and take him to the mainland. He called Brownell from Santa Barbara. The attorney general asked Warren if he could fly to California to meet with him two days later, September 25. They agreed to an 8 a.m. meeting at McClellan Air Force Base at Sacramento. At their early morning meeting, Warren recalled that Brownell told him that the president was considering him for an appointment to the Supreme Court and wanted to know if Warren would accept.[42] He did not specify whether the appointment was to be as an associate justice or chief justice. Warren said he would accept a court appointment if it was offered. Brownell's ver-

---

* Ike was inaccurate. Hughes had previous judicial experience, having served for six years as an associate justice of the Supreme Court before resigning in 1916 to accept the Republican Party's nomination for president. He lost narrowly to the incumbent, President Woodrow Wilson. Stone had served as an associate justice for sixteen years before his appointment as chief justice.

sion of their meeting was somewhat different.[43] He recalled that he and Warren discussed the governor's political views and that he was satisfied that Warren shared Eisenhower's nondoctrinaire, middle-of-the-road Republican values. According to Brownell, he asked Warren if, given his lack of judicial experience, he would be willing to serve as chief justice. Warren said yes. Brownell returned to Washington highly impressed with the governor. "I think we've got the top man," he told the president.[44]

Warren heard nothing more for three days. But the Washington press corps was widely reporting that Eisenhower would appoint Warren to be chief justice. On Wednesday, September 30, Warren received a call from Brownell saying that his appointment as chief justice was to be announced at the president's press conference later that day. At his press conference, Eisenhower, almost casually, confirmed "something that is by no means news any more." He intended to appoint Warren as chief justice. He told reporters that he was impressed with the governor's honesty, experience in law and government, and moderate philosophy and predicted that he would make "a great Chief Justice."[45] He also said that Warren would receive a recess appointment, since Congress was adjourned, so that he could preside at the opening of the new court term the following Monday.

In a private letter to his brother Edgar, the president was more candid and outspoken in his praise of Warren. He reacted angrily to Edgar's prediction (made shortly before the announcement) that Warren's appointment "would be a tragedy."[46] The president wrote, "What you consider to be a tragedy, I consider to be a very splendid and promising development."[47] Based on his conversations with Warren and a study of his record, he had concluded: "Here is a man of national stature (and I ask you when we have had any man of national stature appointed to the Supreme Court), of unimpeachable integrity, of middle-of-the-road views, and with a splendid record during his years in active law work." He added one more important attribute. "To my mind, he is a statesman," he wrote. "We have too few of these."

In his diary, Eisenhower provided further reasons for appointing Warren. He had eliminated well-qualified judges who were over the age of sixty-four; he wanted a chief justice who would serve many years and create an enduring legacy. He had rejected the choice of a prominent Republican politician like Governor Dewey, who had also been mentioned as a candidate and was closely associated with Eisenhower's nomination and election. In contrast to Dewey, no one, in Eisenhower's view, could consider the Warren appointment as the payment of a political debt. He noted that Warren had not consented to turn over any of his own delegates at the Republican convention to ensure Eisenhower's nomination. "Dewey is so political in his whole outlook that I could scarcely imagine him as a Federal judge," he wrote.[48] "Earl Warren, on the contrary, is very deliberate and judicial in his whole approach to almost any question."

He predicted that the Senate would promptly confirm Warren's permanent appointment in January. "If the Republicans as a body should try to repudiate him," he wrote in his diary, "I shall leave the Republican Party and try to organize an intelligent group of Independents, no matter how small."[49]

On October 5, 1953, Eisenhower attended the brief, dignified ceremony in the courtroom of the Supreme Court in which Warren was sworn in as chief justice. Shortly after noon, the clerk of the court read aloud the commission of the president that began, "Know ye, That reposing special trust and confidence in the wisdom, uprightness and learning of Earl Warren of California, I do appoint him Chief Justice of the United States."[50]

WARREN'S CHALLENGE IN his new position was formidable. He had not practiced law in a decade and had no judicial experience. When he had practiced law, as Alameda County's district attorney and

California's attorney general, his focus was on state law. As chief justice, his primary legal references would be federal statutes, Supreme Court precedents, and the U.S. Constitution. Still, he considered his practical legal skills, even if somewhat rusty, to be excellent. He was, moreover, confident in his leadership qualities, including his ability to bring strong-minded, independent men together to work toward a common purpose.

On his first day at the Supreme Court, Warren exhibited his sure political instincts, calling first on the senior associate justice, Hugo Black. After introducing himself to the justice, his clerks, and personal staff, Warren fell into a warm, informal conversation with Black. With admirable humility, he asked Black to preside at the early judicial conferences until he could settle into his new job. He also asked the senior justice to introduce him to the other members of the court. In each chamber, Warren displayed the same unpretentious intelligence and plainspoken congeniality that had endeared him to California voters. Black, in correspondence with his sons, recorded his favorable first impression of the new chief justice. "I am by no means sure that an intelligent man with practical, hard common sense and integrity like he has is not as good a type to select as could be found in the country," he wrote.[51]

Eisenhower never mentioned the school segregation cases in his discussions of Warren, either in his public statements or private correspondence and diary entries. But the cases, which were scheduled to be reargued in early December, were the central topic of his dinner conversation with Governor Byrnes on November 16 as well as many of his conversations with Attorney General Brownell. Mindful of Byrnes's threat to close the public schools in South Carolina, Eisenhower asked Brownell, "What would happen if states would abandon public education?"[52] The attorney general, who was scheduled to meet with Byrnes the day after the governor's November 16 dinner with the president, told Eisenhower that he would attempt to convince Byrnes that a desegregation decision would take years, perhaps a decade or more to fully implement.

With the rearguments only weeks away, the press was rife with speculation on the much anticipated brief from the attorney general. "Brownell must know the perils of his decision," wrote the *Washington Post*'s Chalmers Roberts.[53] "American prestige abroad has been damaged because of the racial problem," he wrote. "Brownell knows President Eisenhower is keenly aware of this. He also knows the President favors States' rights more than any other Chief Executive in modern times."

On November 27, Brownell submitted the Justice Department's 188-page brief to the court, asserting that the Supreme Court had both the authority and duty to order an end to racial segregation in the public schools. The brief found the history of the Fourteenth Amendment "inconclusive" on the issue, but nonetheless argued that the framers understood that the amendment established the broad constitutional principle of full and complete equality of all persons under the law and forbade legal distinctions on the basis of race or color. The amendment, it concluded, "compels a state to grant the benefits of public education to all its people equally without regard to differences of race or color."[54] But it also recommended that a court decree abolishing school segregation permit a reasonable length of time for the integration of the white and black school systems.

Georgia's Governor Herman Talmadge denounced the Justice Department's brief as "wholly political," adding that "radical elements are vying with each other to see who can plunge the dagger deepest in the back of the South."[55] Talmadge announced his support for a pending measure in the Georgia legislature that would convert the state's public schools into private schools to avoid a dreaded court desegregation decree.

Eisenhower wrote Governor Byrnes shortly after Brownell's brief was filed, seeking to assure him that he understood the "very serious problems that you have to face—regardless of the exact character of the court decision in the pending cases."[56] He then distanced himself from his attorney general's brief. He told Byrnes that he had delegated to Brownell full responsibility for his administration's response to the court's questions. "He [Brownell] and I agreed that his brief would reflect the convictions of the Department of Justice as to the *legal aspects* of the case," he wrote. No political consideration was given any weight, he wrote Byrnes, and "no matter what his [Brownell's] legal conclusion might be, the principle of local operation and authority would be emphasized to the maximum degree consistent with his legal opinions."

Again, Eisenhower's ambivalence toward the school segregation cases was evident, as it had been in his conversations and exchange of letters with Byrnes over the summer. He believed in justice for all, regardless of race or color. But he also believed in states' rights, and he was hard-pressed to reconcile these conflicting values in the cases pending before the court. In closing his letter to Byrnes, the president wrote, "Whatever the outcome, I hope most fervently that all of us may work together so as to insure the steadiness of progress toward justice for all in the United States."[57]

———

AT THE STROKE of noon on December 7, 1953, the new chief justice and his eight associates stepped through the red velour draperies that hang behind the long mahogany bench of the U.S. Supreme Court. Once settled in the center chair, Warren broke into a quick smile as he looked at his wife, Nina, who was seated in the gallery nearest the bench. Despite the chief justice's pleasant demeanor, there was an air of tense expectation in the courtroom. The justices prepared to hear three more days of arguments and finally decide the question whether segregated public schools violated the Constitution.

The NAACP's Thurgood Marshall returned to the lectern and

again charged that the defenders of school segregation were asking for "an inherent determination that the people who were formerly in slavery . . . shall be kept as near that state as possible." It was time for the court to "make clear that that is not what our Constitution stands for."[58]

Marshall was challenged repeatedly by Justices Frankfurter and Jackson when he attempted to bolster his argument with references to a post–Civil War civil rights statute and to prior court decisions on racial classifications. They interrupted him often and admonished him for taking up the court's valuable time with irrelevant citations. None were central to the key question that the court had asked the attorneys to address at the reargument—Is it within the judicial power of the court under the Fourteenth Amendment to abolish segregation in the public schools?

Warren interrupted Marshall only once during his argument. "I would like to have you discuss the question of power because I believe that is the question the Court asked you to discuss."

"The power?" asked Marshall.

"Yes, the power," Warren replied.

Warren had cut to the core of the constitutional challenge. Did the Fourteenth Amendment alone, as interpreted by the justices, give the court authority to outlaw public school segregation? Neither post–Civil War statutes nor court precedents would decide the issue. Nor would a study of the history of the Fourteenth Amendment to determine the intent of the framers on the issue. The attorney general's brief had found that history "inconclusive." And, unknown to Marshall and the other attorneys in the case, so had independent research by Justice Douglas and Justice Frankfurter's law clerk, Alexander Bickel.

At the age of eighty, John W. Davis was making his last appearance before the court. His rhetorical gifts remained intact. The Supreme Court, he reminded the justices, had ruled not once but seven times over the years that the *Plessy* doctrine of separate but equal was constitutional. "Somewhere, some time, to every principle there comes a moment of repose when it has been so often announced, so confidently relied upon, so long continued, that it passes the limits of judicial discretion and disturbance."

He warned of the problems awaiting black and white children in Clarendon County should the court order desegregation. Noting the ratio of ten black children for every white child in the county, he doubted that a classroom of twenty-seven black children and three white children would eliminate the psychological burdens of blacks suffered in segregated schools, as claimed by Marshall. Nor, he suggested, would it prevent the three white children in a classroom "from getting a distorted idea of racial relations."

At the end of his argument, an emotional Davis pleaded with the justices to uphold the principle of states' rights and recognize the good intentions and progress of his client, South Carolina, to make black and white schools equal. "Here is equal education, not promised, not prophesied, but present. Shall it be thrown away on some fancied question of racial prestige?"

During the three days of oral arguments, Warren had said very little and given no indication of his views on the cases. When the justices met in conference to discuss the cases on Saturday, December 12, Warren immediately set the agenda, suggesting that the justices discuss the cases informally without taking any votes. His intention was to eliminate the possibility of polarization among the brethren at the outset, a problem that had plagued the justices when Chief Justice Vinson presided after oral arguments a year earlier. Warren planned to keep the discussion going for as long as was necessary until, he hoped, a consensus could be reached.

As soon as he spoke on the merits of the cases, it was clear that Warren held strong, unequivocal views on how the cases should be decided. "I can't escape the feeling," he began, "that no matter how much the Court wants to avoid it, it must decide the issue of whether segregation is allowable in the public schools."[59] He acknowledged that there were legitimate concerns about reversing *Plessy* and its progeny. "But the more I've read and heard and thought, the more I've come to conclude that the basis of segregation and 'separate but equal' rests upon a concept of the inherent inferiority of the colored race. I don't see how *Plessy* and the cases following it can be sustained on any other theory. If we are to sustain segregation, we also must do it upon that basis."

The new chief justice had thrown down the gauntlet to the other justices. If you vote to sustain the constitutionality of public school segregation, you must acknowledge that forced separation of the races is based on the theory that the black race is inferior. And then he emphatically rejected that theory. "I don't see how in this day and age we can set any group apart from the rest and say that they are not entitled to exactly the same treatment as all others. To do so would be contrary to the Thirteenth, Fourteenth, and Fifteenth Amendments. They were intended to make the slaves equal with all others. Personally, I can't see how today we can justify segregation based solely on race."[60]

Warren had not only introduced himself as the new, decisive leader of the court, he had signaled to his brethren that there were now almost certainly five votes, a majority, to declare public school segregation unconstitutional.* In both style and substance, the new chief was strikingly different from his predecessor. He demonstrated confidence in his ability to lead, whereas Vinson had appeared unsure of himself and created unease among the brethren when he argued without much conviction or force that the court should uphold *Plessy*'s separate-but-equal doctrine.

Once Warren had announced his position, rooted in morality as much as constitutional law, that it was wrong to separate groups according to race, he approached the implementation of an anticipated desegregation decree with his politician's pragmatic sense of what was

---

* Warren probably knew that Black, Burton, Douglas, and Minton had strongly favored a desegregation ruling at the justices' first conference on *Brown* and were unlikely to change their votes.

possible. "It would be unfortunate," he said, "if we had to take precip-
itous action that would inflame more than necessary."[61] He was not
especially concerned with an order to desegregate schools in Kansas
and Delaware where the ethnic makeup of the population was not so
different from California's. "But it's not the same in the Deep South,"
he continued. "It will take all the wisdom of this Court to dispose of
the matter with a minimum of emotion and strife. How we do it is
important." He concluded by saying that "my instincts and feeling lead
me to say that, in these cases, we should abolish the practice of segregation in the public schools—but in a tolerant way."[62]

By tradition, Justice Black, the senior associate justice, would have
spoken after the chief justice. Black was absent from the conference
because his sister-in-law was near death in Alabama. He left word that
his position on the cases had not changed—public school segregation
was unconstitutional.

Justice Stanley Reed spoke after Warren and was forced to confront
the chief justice's premise: that a vote to uphold school segregation could
only be justified on the racial theory that black students were inferior.
Reed, a Kentucky native, dismissed "the argument that the Negro is an
inferior race."[63] He conceded that "there is no inferior race, though they
may be handicapped by lack of opportunity." He nonetheless strongly
urged the court to follow the *Plessy* precedent. But even as he defended
Plessy, he recognized that "this is a dynamic Constitution and what was
correct in *Plessy* might not be correct now." Reed, the most adamant
supporter of *Plessy* at the justices' first conference, thus gave Warren a
glimmer of hope that he might be persuaded to join the majority.

Justice Clark, a Texan, had agreed with Reed and Vinson at the justices' conference a year earlier to uphold *Plessy*. He told Warren and the
other justices that he felt he understood the race problem in the segregated
South. He was, nevertheless, now willing to support a desegregation decision, but "it must be done carefully or it will do more harm than good."[64]
He could join the majority if there was "no fiat" and the judicial remedy

could be adjusted to local conditions. Warren, of course, had already expressed his sensitivity to the problems of a desegregation decree in the Deep South. Clark appeared to be a sixth vote for the majority.

Justice Jackson, who had been unwilling to overrule *Plessy* at the first *Brown* conference, also appeared to change his position, though more subtly than Clark. He was dismissive of the NAACP's sociological arguments and, as a matter of constitutional law, still thought *Plessy* should be upheld. He declared that the desegregation issue was largely "a question of politics and, as a political decision, I can go along with it."[65] His remarks suggested that he might support the majority but file a concurrence, disagreeing with the reasoning of the court's opinion and, therefore, detracting from its impact.

Justice Frankfurter spoke somewhat ambiguously about the constitutional foundation for a desegregation ruling. As he had pointed out in both oral arguments, there was ample support in court precedent to uphold *Plessy*. But he had been a powerful advocate for the cause of racial justice his entire adult life. He was a founding member of the NAACP and had hired the court's first black law clerk, William Coleman. He continued to struggle to find a constitutional justification for a desegregation decree, but was searching for a rationale to support the chief justice.

At the end of the conference, a firm court majority was committed to a decision to declare public school segregation unconstitutional. Justices Black, Burton, Douglas, and Minton held to their original position in support of a desegregation decree. Warren, without doubt, and Clark, more tentatively, were ready to join them. Frankfurter and Jackson, two of the most formidable intellects on the court, appeared to be leaning toward joining the majority, but still would have to be persuaded by a carefully crafted opinion. And Reed continued to oppose overruling *Plessy* but was willing to keep an open mind.

Warren suggested that the justices meet informally during the next two months, over lunch and in chambers, to further discuss the cases. He still had work to do.

Chapter Six

A LIST OF 205 COMMUNISTS

WHEN PRESIDENT-ELECT EISENHOWER FLEW TO KOREA in early December 1952 to fulfill his campaign pledge, there could be no doubt of his serious purpose. He discussed military strategy with senior commanders at the front and ate K rations with troops from the 1st Battalion of the 15th Infantry. Bundled in a heavy pile jacket, fur-lined hat, and thermal boots, he peered through binoculars to witness an artillery duel. And he squeezed behind the pilot of a tiny propeller reconnaissance plane to observe the desolate, snow-covered mountainous terrain below and the entrenched defensive positions of the North Korean and Chinese soldiers.

Eisenhower ignored the bellicose talk of victory from Mark Clark, commander in chief of the United Nations Forces, and South Korean President Dr. Syngman Rhee. Both vowed to drive the enemy troops across the Yalu River into China. Ike feared that such an all-out attack could turn the conflict into a global war. But he also concluded that U.N. forces (90 percent comprised of U.S. troops) could not stand forever on a static front and suffer mounting casualties. "Small attacks on small hills would not end the war," he wrote.[1] And he knew that the American public's support for the war was waning.

THE WAR HAD begun on the night of June 25, 1950, when ten divisions of the Communist North Korean People's Army, backed by a phalanx of Russian T-34 tanks, crossed the 38th parallel, stunning the South Korean forces defending the border between the two countries. With lightning speed, the North Korean army smashed through the South Korean defenses. Within days, the South Korean capital of Seoul had fallen, and the panicked South Korean army had abandoned their weapons and were in headlong retreat.

President Truman correctly assumed that Kim Il Sung, the North Korean dictator, had been encouraged by the Soviet Union and Communist China to invade the south, presumably to unite the Korean peninsula under Kim's Communist regime. The Soviet Union and China had calculated that the U.S. would not intervene. But even though South Korea was of little strategic value to the United States, Truman vowed to fight the Communist aggressors. "It looks like World War III is here," he wrote in his diary.[2] "I hope not—but we must meet whatever comes—and we will."

On June 29, General Douglas MacArthur, the brilliant, egomaniacal leader of U.S. forces in the Pacific during World War II, flew from his headquarters in Tokyo, where he then served as viceroy of postwar Japan, to Suwon, a small airfield twenty miles south of Seoul. He was appalled by the sight of the retreating South Korean army. Throughout his celebrated career, MacArthur, then seventy years old, had wrenched victory from certain defeat, and the debacle-in-progress in Korea appeared perfectly suited to his grandiose ambitions.

At first, the U.S. troops sent from Japan performed miserably. Most of them were occupation soldiers who, as their field commander Major General William Dean ruefully remarked, were used to being "fat and happy in occupation billets, complete with Japanese girl friends, plenty of beer, and servants to shine their boots."[3] By August, however, MacArthur's assumption of command appeared to have worked a minor military miracle. Fresh, combat-trained U.S. troops landed at the southern tip of the Korean Peninsula and, supported by new tank-killing American arms and the U.S. air force, halted the North Korean army's drive to the sea. In late August, MacArthur ordered a daring amphibious landing at the western port of Inchon where 13,000 U.S. Marines poured ashore and overwhelmed the thin line of enemy resistance. U.N. troops recaptured Seoul and drove the retreating enemy forces across the 38th parallel. MacArthur, once again the hero, was emboldened to press his advantage and ordered troops across the 38th parallel in pursuit of the North Korean army.

In late October Truman scheduled a meeting with MacArthur at Wake Island to discuss military strategy. MacArthur had always considered civilian supervision, including that of the president of the United States, to be a nuisance and in no way binding on his military judgment. For his part, Truman found MacArthur insufferably arrogant. He had earlier written about his MacArthur problem: "And what to do with Mr. Prima Donna, Brass Hat, Five Star MacArthur. He's worse than the Cabots and the Lodges—they at least talked with one another before they told God what to do. Mac tells God right off."[4]

MacArthur arrived first and met the president's plane in his signature open shirt and rumpled field hat. Though Truman was angered by the general's casual attire, he quickly calmed down, and the two men had a respectful, if somewhat strained, discussion of the war. Truman expressed his concern about reports that the Chinese would not stand aside if the U.N. forces threatened the sovereignty of North Korea. MacArthur assured him that victory was imminent and predicted that enemy resistance would end by Thanksgiving. He belittled the suggestion that the Chinese would intervene. At most, 50,000 or 60,000 troops might cross the Yalu, he said, but, if they moved farther south, "there would be a great slaughter."[5]

In late November, 260,000 Chinese troops crossed the Yalu River and attacked the outnumbered U.N. forces, delivering a devastating blow and forcing a bitter winter retreat. MacArthur's reaction was to demand that the war be expanded. He requested that additional troops from the defeated army of Nationalist Chinese General Chiang Kai-shek be flown in from the island of Formosa and suggested the use of atomic bombs. But the Truman administration was moving in the opposite direction, planning to announce in the spring of 1951 that it would seek a cease-fire as a first step toward an armistice with the enemy. In a thinly veiled effort to undercut the administration's initiative, MacArthur publicly taunted the Chinese's "exaggerated and vaunted military power."[6] Finally, on April 11, 1951, Truman had had enough and fired MacArthur.

Americans were outraged. The Gallup poll reported that 69 percent of those interviewed supported MacArthur and only 29 percent backed the president. Eight days after his dismissal, MacArthur walked down the aisle of the House of Representatives to address a joint session of Congress. He wore a short army jacket; his back was straight, his face somber. The packed galleries, together with members of Congress, rose as one, wildly applauding the legendary military leader. For the next thirty-four minutes the general addressed the crowd "with neither rancor nor bitterness in the fading twilight of life, with but one purpose in mind: To serve my country."[7] He was interrupted thirty times with applause during his speech.

The speech was a masterpiece of political theater. "Why, my soldiers asked of me, surrender military advantages to an enemy in the field?"[8] He paused, then said sadly, "I could not answer." He ended with the refrain from an old barracks ballad that had been popular when he had joined the army as a young West Point graduate: "[O]ld soldiers never die; they just fade away. And like the old soldier of that ballad, I now close my military career and just fade away, an old soldier who tried to do his duty as God gave him the light to see that duty. Good-by."

But, of course, MacArthur did not intend to fade away but, rather, ride a tide of public emotion, perhaps to the White House. Seven million people turned out for the parade in his honor in New York City, exceeding the multitudes that had previously welcomed General Eisenhower. Recordings of "Old Soldiers Never Die" topped the charts of the hit parade. Stores selling MacArthur buttons, pennants, and corncob pipes left over from the brief MacArthur-for-President boomlet in 1948 did a bonanza business.

After a week, MacArthur emerged from self-imposed seclusion in his suite at the Waldorf Astoria to announce a "crusade." He made impassioned speeches across the country, from the West Coast to Massachusetts, denouncing the Truman administration's foreign policy as the "appeasement of Communism."[9] Returning to Washington to appear before a joint Senate Committee investigating his dismissal, he again attacked the administration.

By late May, MacArthur's outrage and patriotic rhetoric had worn thin, and his approval ratings began to sink. Meanwhile, the administration launched an effective counteroffensive spearheaded by appearances of the Joint Chiefs of Staff before the Senate committee investigating MacArthur's dismissal. To a man, they testified that MacArthur had repeatedly and publicly challenged the Korean polices of the administration, flagrantly violating a basic principle of the Constitution—that military leaders were subordinate to the democratically elected civilian government.

In Korea, there was still no progress toward an armistice. For the next eighteen months, negotiations went nowhere, and the opposing armies fought a vicious war of attrition. American troops would take an unnamed hill near the 38th parallel, only to lose it a few days later. "[T]he idea of this war as an endless one is almost universally accepted here," reported journalist E. J. Kahn, Jr., from the front.[10] When Eisenhower's plane left Seoul on December 5, 1952, the border between

North and South Korea stood roughly where it had been before the North Korean army's invasion.

———————

EISENHOWER'S OBSERVATIONS AND conversations with American commanders in Korea had convinced him that the best option for the United States was a negotiated peace. But how was he to succeed when all previous efforts had failed? Ike began to lay the foundation for renewed negotiations during his return trip. "We face an enemy," he announced at Pearl Harbor, "whom we cannot hope to impress by words, however eloquent, but only by deeds—executed under circumstances of our own choosing."[11] He anticipated that the threat of escalation of the war, delivered by the victorious Supreme Commander of Allied Forces during World War II, would be taken seriously by the Chinese.

Eisenhower was prepared to back his threat with the full arsenal that the U.S. military possessed, including nuclear weapons. Only days after North Korean forces had crossed the 38th parallel in June 1950, Ike had written in his diary that the United States must take a firm stand against Communist aggression or "we'll have a dozen Koreas soon."[12] It was imperative that the U.S. "be prepared for whatever may happen, even if it finally came to the use of an A-bomb (which God forbid)."

Throughout his military career, Eisenhower had advocated the use of maximum force to defeat the enemy. At Normandy and the Battle of the Bulge he threw every available military resource at the Nazis. It was not surprising, therefore, that Ike raised the possibility of the use of nuclear weapons in the Korean war only three weeks after his presidential inauguration.

The discussion occurred at a National Security Council meeting on February 11, 1953, following a report from General Clark warning of a buildup of Chinese troops around Kaesong, the ancient Korean capital, apparently in preparation for a massive offensive. Eisenhower, according to the official NSC note taker, "expressed the view that we should consider the use of tactical nuclear weapons on the Kaesong area, which provided a good target for this type of weapon."[13] It was not clear whether Eisenhower was advocating use of nuclear weapons or merely raising the issue for discussion.

Secretary of State John Foster Dulles, supported by the president's suggestion that the U.S. might use nuclear weapons, declared that atomic bombs ought to be an integral part of the nation's arsenal. But Omar Bradley, the chairman of the Joint Chiefs of Staff, discouraged talk of the nuclear option, saying that it was "unwise to broach the subject yet of the possible use of atomic weapons."[14]

Eisenhower appeared to agree with Bradley, steering the discussion away from the use of nuclear weapons. He nonetheless considered raising the nuclear option with U.S. allies Great Britain and France, whose governments, he knew, opposed it. He suggested that it might serve as a negotiating chip to induce them to provide three or four more divisions in Korea to drive back the Communists. He then closed off further discussion, ruling out immediate talks with our allies "of military plans or weapons of attack."[15]

Eisenhower's willingness to consider the use of nuclear weapons contrasted with his position only eight years earlier when he had told Secretary of War Henry Stimson that he opposed dropping an atomic bomb on Japan. In 1945, when Ike had voiced his objections to Stimson, he thought that the Allied victory against Japan was imminent and could be achieved without the bomb. He also was hopeful then that the U.S. and the Soviet Union could peacefully coexist in the postwar era. By 1953, however, cooperation with Moscow no longer appeared to be a realistic option. The Soviet Union had exploded an atomic bomb and subjugated the nations of Eastern Europe with the fist of the Red Army. In Asia, Mao's Communist government was firmly in control and, with Communist North Korea, was threatening to conquer South Korea. Under these ominous circumstances, Eisenhower did not hesitate to consider the use of nuclear weapons in the fight against Communist aggression.

During the first month of his presidency, Eisenhower expressed increasing frustration at the lack of progress in the long-stalemated Korean negotiations. He sent a discreet message to the Chinese at the stalled armistice talks in Panmunjom, North Korea, that unless satisfactory diplomatic progress was made, the United States "intended to move decisively without inhibition in our use of weapons, and would no longer be responsible for confining hostilities to the Korean Peninsula."[16] He added, "We would not be limited by any world-wide gentleman's agreement."

At the same time, Eisenhower conspicuously bolstered U.S. forces and weapons in Asia. An additional Marine division was sent to Korea while air force squadrons there were reequipped with Saber jets. Atomic weapons were dispatched to Okinawa.

In late February, on instructions from the White House, General Clark offered to exchange sick and wounded prisoners with the Chinese and North Koreans in accordance with Article 109 of the Geneva Conventions. A similar offer had previously been rejected. In March, the commanders of both the North Korean and Chinese armies not only replied positively to Clark's offer, but suggested full-fledged peace negotiations, which had been suspended for the previous six months. Two days later, China's foreign minister Chou En-lai added his support to the negotiations, recommending a broader exchange to include the return of all prisoners who wished to be repatriated.

Eisenhower quickly accepted the offer at his press conference on April 2. "We should take at face value every offer that is made to us, until it is proved not to be worthy of being taken," he said. The quick exchange of sick and wounded soldiers "would be a clear indication that deeds, rather than words, are now coming into fashion."[17]

At a National Security Council meeting a week later, Secretary of State Dulles argued that the Chinese offer to negotiate should be rejected. "It was now quite possible to secure a much more satisfactory settlement in Korea than a mere armistice at the 38th parallel," said Dulles.[18] The long-term goal for the U.S. should be the reunification of Korea, he contended, and predicted that any armistice at the 38th parallel would ultimately have to be broken.

Eisenhower abruptly cut off Dulles. "It will be impossible to call off the armistice and go to war again," he said.[19] "The American people will never stand for such a move." When Secretary of Defense Wilson supported Dulles, the president lost patience. He had already pledged the nation's good faith in the exchange of sick and wounded prisoners, he said, and there would be no reneging on that pledge.

Operation Little Switch began two weeks later with the first exchange of prisoners. Within days plenary sessions between the U.S. and Communist negotiators resumed in Panmunjom.

In June, the final obstacle to the armistice was not posed by the Communist negotiators but by our ally, South Korea's president, Syngman Rhee. Like Secretary Dulles, Rhee held out hope for a military victory and reunification of the two Korean nations under his rule. During the final stages of the armistice negotiation, Rhee defiantly ordered the gates of South Korean stockades opened, leading to the unauthorized escape of 25,000 North Korean and Chinese prisoners. Rhee also threatened to withdraw South Korean forces from the U.N. command.

Eisenhower promptly issued an ultimatum to the South Korean president. Should Rhee carry out his threat to withdraw South Korean troops from the U.N. command, the United States would withdraw all troops from Korea and cease military and financial aid to Rhee's government. Rhee reluctantly capitulated. On July 27, 1953, the armistice was officially signed at Panmunjom, ending the war in which more than 142,000 Americans were killed, wounded, or reported missing.

Eisenhower announced the armistice to the American people in a brief, sober address. The cost of repelling Communist aggression in Korea had been high, he conceded, incalculably high for those thousands of American families who had lost loved ones in the war. "We have won an armistice on a single battleground," he concluded, "not peace in the world."[20]

The American public reacted to the armistice with relief more than exaltation. There were no victory parades and no breast-beating editorials of triumph. Conservative Republicans, however, loudly protested. Republican majority leader Senator William Knowland of California denied that Eisenhower had achieved "peace with honor" and predicted that "we will inevitably lose the balance of Asia."[21]

Despite criticism of the armistice from Knowland and other conservative Republicans, Eisenhower was satisfied that he had achieved his primary goal of repelling Communist aggression. He was determined that U.N. forces not be defeated, but he never envisioned the total victory and reunification of Korea by force that Rhee and conservative Republicans demanded. The armistice comported with the pragmatic, middle-of-the-road philosophy that he had extolled in his presidential campaign and later emphasized in his consideration of high-level appointments such as that of Chief Justice Earl Warren.

———————

DURING EISENHOWER'S FIRST year in office, Senator Joseph McCarthy, the junior senator from Wisconsin, reached the pinnacle of his popularity. Millions of Americans were mesmerized by his increasingly wild accusations that Communists were directing U.S. foreign policy in the State Department. And neither President Eisenhower nor the congressional leadership of his party were willing to publicly challenge him.

McCarthy's rise to immense political power had begun modestly enough. One of nine children, he had grown up on his family's farm in an Irish settlement in northern Wisconsin. Joe was an awkward, shy, and sulky boy who was often teased. "Don't you mind," his mother Bridget told him.[22] "You be somebody. You get ahead." Cutting corners wherever possible, he barely managed to graduate from Marquette University. Outside the classroom, he demonstrated a fierce, blinding drive. In the boxing ring, he always attacked, though often bloodied from an opponent's punishing blows, hoping to land a knockout punch. In poker, he had the "guts of a burglar," remembered one friend.[23] "He was brutal. He'd take all the fun out of the game, because he took it so seriously." After Pearl Harbor, McCarthy enlisted in the Marines and gave himself the name "Tail-gunner Joe," though he served mostly behind a desk as an intelligence officer doing paperwork for a squadron of pilots.[24]

For the first four years of his senatorial term, McCarthy labored in obscurity, always looking for his main chance. It finally came in the winter of 1950, shortly after the former State Department executive Alger Hiss had been convicted of perjury, and the British government announced that Dr. Klaus Fuchs, a high-level scientist who had done atomic research in the United States and Great Britain, confessed that he had systematically passed atomic secrets to Soviet agents.

McCarthy wasted no time in exploiting the issue of Communist infiltration into the highest echelons of the U.S. government. His attack began in a Lincoln Day speech, on February 9, 1950, to the Ohio County Women's Republican Club in Wheeling, West Virginia, when he announced that he had a list of 205 Communists who were shaping policy in the State Department. The accusation moved over the Associated Press wire that night, and by the next day reporters were clamoring for the names on the list. From Wheeling, McCarthy flew west, stopping at Denver, where he told reporters at an airport news conference that his list was in a pocket of his suit that he had left on the plane. By the time McCarthy reached Reno, Nevada, his list had been reduced to fifty-seven names and later dropped to four. He never produced any list.

With unscrupulous zeal, McCarthy fed on Americans' pervasive anxiety during the Korean War. He achieved both notoriety and power, hurling accusation after bold accusation of Communist infiltration in the Truman administration based on virtually nothing more than innuendo and swagger. Though McCarthy was not America's first anti-Communist crusader, his demagoguery ushered in a new era of paranoia with its own label: McCarthyism.

McCarthy's virulent anticommunism seeped into the popular culture. Mike Hammer, author Mickey Spillane's hero in his runaway best seller *One Lonely Night,* boasted: "I killed more people tonight than I have fingers on my hands. I shot them in cold blood and enjoyed every minute of it. . . . They were Commies, Lee. They were red sons-of-bitches who should have died long ago. . . . They never thought that there were people like me in this country. They figured us all to be soft as horse manure and just as stupid."[25]

McCarthyism also cast a pervasive pall on free expression in the United States. Monogram Pictures canceled a movie about Henry Wadsworth Longfellow. Hiawatha, the studio explained, had tried to stop wars between the Indian tribes, and the public might construe the movie as propaganda for the Communist "peace offensive." College president Harold Taylor of Sarah Lawrence offered a mocking definition of the patriotic American: "One who tells all his secrets without being asked, believes we should go to war with Russia, holds no political view without prior consultation with his employer, does not ask for an increase in salary or wages and is in favor of peace, universal military training, brotherhood and baseball."[26]

EISENHOWER HAD FIRST experienced the force of McCarthy's political power during his 1952 presidential campaign, when he reluctantly deleted a paragraph in a scheduled speech in Milwaukee that forthrightly defended his mentor, General George C. Marshall, whom

McCarthy had accused of being a traitor. Better to delete the paragraph, he was advised, than to offend McCarthy and possibly lose crucial votes in the state. It was a deletion that Ike would always regret.

Eisenhower detested McCarthy but, as president, he steadfastly refused to criticize him in public. "Senator McCarthy is, of course, so anxious for the headlines that he is prepared to go to any extreme in order to secure some mention of his name in public," he wrote in his diary. "I really believe that nothing will be so effective in combating his particular kind of trouble-making as to ignore him. This he cannot stand."[27] The president blamed the press, which demanded that he rebuke McCarthy, for keeping the senator in the headlines by reporting every baseless charge.

Eisenhower, in addition to depriving McCarthy of more headlines, had a practical reason for avoiding a confrontation. Republicans controlled the Senate by a single vote. If the president alienated the Wisconsin senator, he could instantly lose his majority on any key bill. It was common knowledge that McCarthy wielded substantial influence over more than a half-dozen like-minded senators on the right wing of his party.

McCarthy tested Eisenhower's oath of public silence almost immediately. Two days after his inauguration, the new president sent the name of Walter Bedell Smith, his trusted wartime chief of staff, to be undersecretary of state, the highest subcabinet appointment. Smith had served in the Truman administration as ambassador to the Soviet Union and CIA director. Eisenhower assumed that confirmation by the Senate would be a mere formality. But he received word that McCarthy had put a hold on the appointment. The senator accused Smith of being a possible Communist sympathizer since, as ambassador to the Soviet Union, he had defended John Patton Davies, a career diplomat at the embassy, against McCarthy's charges of disloyalty. This was the new president's rude introduction to McCarthyism, and he was furious. To consider Smith a security risk was preposterous. He called Senator Robert Taft and demanded that Smith's name be taken off hold and confirmed, and it was.

Soon afterward, McCarthy told Eisenhower that he would oppose his appointment of Dr. James B. Conant, the distinguished president of Harvard, to be U.S. high commissioner to Germany. Conant had once said there were no Communists on the Harvard faculty, an obvious sign to McCarthy that Conant was a fellow traveler. Eisenhower sent Vice President Nixon as his emissary to persuade McCarthy to relent in his opposition. Although McCarthy refused to drop his opposition to Conant's appointment, he promised the president in a letter that he would not "make a row" over the nomination.[28] Conant was confirmed.

McCarthy's most protracted battle over an Eisenhower appointment came a few weeks later when the president sent the name of Charles "Chip" Bohlen, a career foreign service officer who had served in the American embassy in Moscow, to be U.S. ambassador to the Soviet Union. Fluent in Russian and an expert on Soviet affairs, Bohlen had accompanied President Roosevelt to the Yalta conference in 1945, serving as both interpreter and adviser. That proximity to FDR and Bohlen's refusal to disavow the Yalta accords were sufficient grounds for McCarthy to suspect Bohlen of Communist sympathies. He went to the floor of the Senate to inform his colleagues that Bohlen had been "at Roosevelt's left hand" at Yalta and warned of his "ugly record of betrayal."[29]

Eisenhower was astonished and infuriated by McCarthy's charges. He had become friends with Bohlen when the diplomat, who was fluent in French, had served in the U.S. embassy in Paris while Ike was the head of NATO. They had dined and played golf together. In addition to rejecting McCarthy's charges of disloyalty, Eisenhower dismissed rumors circulating in official Washington corridors that Bohlen was not a proper "family man," a euphemism in the fifties for being homosexual. Without mentioning McCarthy, the president strongly defended Bohlen at his press conference in late March. "I have known Mr. Bohlen for some years," he told reporters.[30] "I have listened to his philosophy. So far as I can see, he is the best-qualified man for that post that I could find. That is the reason his name was sent to the Senate and the reason it stays there."

One day after Eisenhower's press conference, the Senate confirmed the Bohlen nomination by a vote of 74–13. Eleven of the "no" votes were Republican senators, including McCarthy. The president wrote in his diary that he was surprised by the "no" votes of Republican Senators John Bricker of Ohio and Barry Goldwater of Arizona but dismissed the other nine Republicans as "the most stubborn and essentially small-minded examples of the extreme isolationist group in the party."[31] He considered Bricker and Goldwater "a bit more intelligent than the others, who sought to defend their position with the most specious kind of excuse and misleading kind of argument."

Nothing slowed McCarthy down in his hunt for Communists and fellow travelers. As chairman of the Senate's Government Operations Committee, McCarthy was authorized to investigate government subversion and prepared to purge the State Department's Voice of America's 189 overseas libraries of pro-Communist authors. McCarthy's chief counsel, twenty-six-year-old Roy Cohn, and his friend G. David Schine, heir to a chain of luxury hotels, soon were perusing the stacks of the VOA libraries in Europe. As a result, McCarthy charged that his committee had identified more than 30,000 books by 418 suspect writers, including W. H. Auden, Edna Ferber, John Dewey, Arthur Schlesinger, Jr., and the detective writer, Dashiell Hammett, that should be removed from VOA library shelves. The *New York Times* lashed out at the committee's investigation as "a public carnival for television and newspaper audiences."[32]

Eisenhower was asked repeatedly in his press conferences whether McCarthy's committee investigation was helping in the fight against Communists. At first, he expressed ignorance of the committee's work but, when pressed, he offered a separation-of-powers rationale for keeping his distance. "[I]t would be extremely dangerous to try to limit the power of Congress to investigate," he said.[33] Asked about McCarthy's methods, he added, "I think it would be completely inappropriate for me to comment specifically on individuals in Congress and their methods, because presumably the Congress approves these, or they wouldn't go on."

Finally, on June 14, 1953, the president publicly condemned the threat of widespread censorship posed by McCarthy's investigation. The occasion was Eisenhower's commencement address at Dartmouth College. On the dais, he sat next to another honorary-degree recipient, John McCloy, the former high commissioner of Germany. McCloy told Eisenhower that books were being burned in Voice of America libraries at the instigation of McCarthy. The president questioned McCloy more closely about the book burning, then quietly ruminated on what he had been told. When he stood up to address the graduates, he set aside his prepared text and spoke extemporaneously. "Don't join the book burners," he warned.[34] "Don't think you are going to conceal faults by concealing evidence that they ever existed. Don't be afraid to go in your library and read every book, as long as that document does not offend your own sense of decency. That should be the only censorship." And then he asked, "How will we defeat communism unless we know what it is?"

Eisenhower's denunciation of censorship at Dartmouth was reminiscent of his stalwart defense of academic freedom at his induction as president of Columbia almost five years earlier. At both events, he made an unequivocal commitment to freedom of speech. His address at Columbia served as a vigorous rebuttal to the anti-Communist fervor that was then sweeping the country.

Eisenhower's remarks at Dartmouth were widely interpreted in the national press as a condemnation of McCarthy. But no sooner had the president's speech made headlines than he awkwardly backpedaled, denying that he had targeted the Wisconsin senator. At his press conference three days after his Dartmouth speech, he was asked by United Press International's Merriman Smith if his speech should be interpreted as a criticism of McCarthy. "Now, Merriman, you have been around me long enough to know I never talk personalities," Eisenhower replied.[35] While he reiterated his opposition to the suppression of ideas, he said that pure Communist propaganda had no place in VOA libraries.

With smug satisfaction, McCarthy told reporters that Eisenhower's Dartmouth speech could not have been about him, since he had burned no books. And he praised Eisenhower's press conference statement as "commendable," because the president's "no book burning" stand at Dartmouth did not apply to books in which Communists openly appealed for people to join them.[36]

ON JUNE 19, 1953, Eisenhower refused to stay the executions of Julius Rosenberg and his wife, Ethel, who had been convicted of conspiracy to pass atomic secrets to the Soviet Union. In a statement from the White House, the president said that the Rosenbergs "have received the benefit of every safeguard which American justice can provide."[37] The couple were electrocuted shortly before sunset.

The Rosenbergs had gone to trial on espionage charges in a federal district courtroom in lower Manhattan in 1951, at the height of anti-Communist hysteria in the United States, stoked by McCarthyism and the stalemated war in Korea. Both Julius Rosenberg and Ethel Rosenberg's brother, David Greenglass, had been members of the Communist Party in the thirties. Questioned by then Assistant U.S. Attorney Roy Cohn, Greenglass testified at the Rosenbergs' trial that he had passed drawings and other classified materials to Julius when Greenglass, as a sergeant in the army during World War II, had been assigned to the atomic weapons laboratory at Los Alamos. Greenglass also testified that he had seen his sister, Ethel, type his notes. Both Julius and

Ethel were convicted and sentenced to death by the presiding federal judge, Irving Kaufman.

At the Rosenbergs' sentencing, Judge Kaufman told the couple that he considered their crime worse than murder. By putting the atomic bomb in the hands of Russia, he said, they had caused the Communist aggression in Korea. "[B]y your betrayal you undoubtedly have altered the course of history to the disadvantage of our country."[38]

After Eisenhower's inauguration, the new president was deluged with letters and telegrams pleading for the Rosenbergs' lives. From the Vatican, the Pope asked that the president grant clemency. From the U.S. embassy in Paris, Ambassador Douglas Dillon cabled Eisenhower that the Rosenbergs' execution would have a deleterious effect on European public opinion. He told the president that there were legitimate reasons for doubting the Rosenbergs' guilt. Even those who believed they were guilty thought their execution was "completely unjustified from moral standpoint and due only to political climate peculiar to the United States."[39] Referring to the disastrous impression on Europeans left by McCarthy's investigators, Cohn and Schine, Dillon warned that virtually all Europeans would regard the Rosenbergs' executions as another example of the craven appeasement of Senator McCarthy.

Throughout the final months of the Rosenbergs' lives, Eisenhower did not waver in his belief that the Rosenbergs were guilty and should die for their treasonous acts. In response to a plea for clemency from Columbia University professor Clyde Miller, Eisenhower wrote that Communist leaders believed "that free governments—and especially the American government—are notoriously weak and fearful and that consequently subversive and other kind of activity can be conducted against them with no real fear of dire punishment."[40] The Rosenbergs, he argued, had "exposed to greater danger of death literally millions of our citizens."

Eisenhower was troubled that a woman, Ethel Rosenberg, who was the mother of two small children, would be executed. But he was convinced that she was "the strong and recalcitrant character; the man [Julius] is the weak one," he wrote his son, John, only days before the couple's execution.[41] "She has obviously been the leader in everything they did in the spy ring."

Decades after the Rosenbergs' executions, Soviet intelligence cables and archives confirmed that Julius Rosenberg was a spy. But contrary to Eisenhower's conviction that Ethel was the leader of the spy ring, there was no evidence that she was a major participant, though she was aware of her husband's activities. David Greenglass, who had pleaded guilty and received a fifteen-year sentence in exchange for testifying against the Rosenbergs, admitted before his death in 2014 that he had lied when he had sworn that he saw Ethel type his notes. More than fifty years after the Rosenbergs' trial, he told *New York Times* reporter Sam Roberts that he had given key testimony incriminating his sister to save his wife from prosecution.

EISENHOWER'S VIGILANT anticommunism was reflected in both his foreign and domestic policies. He pushed hard for an armistice in Korea, but was determined to roll back Communist aggression. At home, he worked closely with Attorney General Brownell to develop stringent procedures to root out Communists in the federal government. And he brooked no compromise in punishing Americans convicted of spying for the Soviet Union, as demonstrated by his rejection of clemency pleas for the Rosenbergs.

At the same time, he deplored McCarthy's reckless search for suspected Communists and fellow travelers. In a memorandum to Attorney General Brownell dated November 4, 1953, Eisenhower distinguished Communists from left-leaning Americans who may have been sympathetic to the Soviet Union before the Berlin blockade in 1948. "The Communists are a class set apart by themselves," he wrote Brownell.[42] "Indeed, I think they are such liars and cheats that even when they apparently recant and later testify against someone else for his Communist convictions, my first reaction is to believe that the accused person must be a patriot or he wouldn't have incurred the enmity of such people. So even when these 'reformed' Communists have proved useful in helping us track down some of their old associates, I certainly look for corroborating evidence before I feel too easy in my mind about it."

Eisenhower requested that Brownell develop a legal rationale to separate Communists from those who were "inclined toward leftish thinking," particularly in expressing sympathy for the Soviet Union before 1948.[43] An American could be excused for statements or actions favorable to the Soviet Union even in the early years of the Cold War, the president reasoned, but if he continued his support after the Berlin blockade, he "is either very stupid or very dangerous."

McCarthy was not interested in such fine distinctions. His bludgeoning tactics seemed only to make him more popular. According to a Gallup poll taken at the end of 1953, 50 percent of Americans approved of his investigations. Emboldened by his poll numbers, he selected his biggest target yet: the U.S. Army. In late January 1954, he accused the army of coddling Communists. His prime suspect was Dr. Irving Peress, a dentist who had been called to duty at Camp Kilmer, New Jersey, under the doctor's draft law. Peress was a member of the American Labor Party, a Trotskyite group on the attorney general's subversive list, and had refused to sign a loyalty oath. He was, nonetheless, inducted at the rank of captain, promoted to major (as required by the Doctor's Draft statute), and granted an honorable discharge.

McCarthy subpoenaed Peress to testify the day before his discharge, but the dentist invoked his constitutional privilege against self-incrimination. An irate McCarthy then subpoenaed Brigadier General Ralph Zwicker, the commanding officer at Camp Kilmer. Zwicker had been wounded at Normandy on D-Day and decorated for heroism, but his outstanding war record did not shield him from McCarthy's merciless interrogation. The senator repeatedly asked Zwicker who had promoted Peress. When the general persisted in saying he that he knew nothing about the promotion, McCarthy, in a rage, said that Zwicker did not "have the brains of a five-year-old" and was a disgrace to his uniform.[44]

McCarthy had finally gone too far. The American Legion and Veterans of Foreign Wars publicly condemned his insulting interrogation of Zwicker. On the Senate floor, Republican Senator Ralph Flanders of Vermont held McCarthy up to rare, scathing ridicule. "He [McCarthy] dons his war paint. He goes into his war dance. He emits war whoops. He goes forth to battle and proudly returns with the scalp of a pink dentist."[45] That evening CBS's Edward R. Murrow, after showing clips of McCarthy's committee interrogations on his *See It Now* telecast, told viewers that "[t]he line between investigation and persecution is a very fine one and the junior senator from Wisconsin has stepped over it repeatedly."[46] McCarthy's poll numbers began to drop.

McCarthy had attacked Eisenhower's revered U.S. Army and singled out a decorated D-Day veteran, and still the president refused to publicly condemn him. Indirectly, however, Eisenhower signaled that he deplored McCarthy's methods. His press secretary, James Hagerty, announced that the president wholeheartedly approved of Secretary of the Army Robert Stevens's press statement to "never accede to the abuse of Army personnel [or to] them being brow-beaten or humiliated." Ike sent Senator Flanders a note shortly after his attack on McCarthy, writing that "I think America needs to hear more Republican voices like yours."[47] He then invited CBS's Murrow to the White House after his criticism of McCarthy on *See It Now*.

The president also worked to erect procedural roadblocks to frustrate and ultimately undermine McCarthy's investigation. He persuaded Republican Senator Everett Dirksen of Illinois, a member of McCarthy's committee and the de facto Republican Senate leader after Taft's death from cancer in July 1953, to change committee rules so that a majority vote would be required to issue subpoenas. The procedural move eliminated McCarthy's solitary, bullying interrogations of witnesses like General Zwicker. More importantly, Ike asked Attorney General Brownell to provide legal precedent for his anticipated expansive use of the constitutional doctrine of executive privilege, justifying the president's refusal to allow McCarthy to subpoena official records or force testimony of members of the executive branch. Without that subpoena authority, McCarthy's power, built on high-profile targets and headlines, would be sapped.

By early March, the army was preparing an aggressive counterattack against McCarthy, whose committee had scheduled televised hearings in April promising to uncover Communists in their ranks. In late January, army general counsel John Adams had told Attorney General Brownell and other high-ranking members of the Eisenhower administration that McCarthy and his committee counsel, Roy Cohn, had sought favors for G. David Schine, who had been drafted into the army in November. (Schine was the young man who, with Cohn, had romped through Europe in search of subversive books in VOA libraries.) Adams's office documented sixty-five phone calls and nineteen meetings between army personnel and McCarthy committee representatives discussing special requests for Schine, including relief from KP duty, extra time off, and special visitor privileges. Schine received fifteen passes between early November 1953 and January 1954, while most inductees received three. On March 11, the army submitted an official complaint to McCarthy's committee charging that McCarthy and Cohn had repeatedly exerted pressure on army personnel to give Schine preferential treatment.

After McCarthy announced that he would participate as a committee member in what became known as the Army-McCarthy hearings, Eisenhower discussed with his staff whether he should comment publicly on the propriety of McCarthy's serving on the committee that was judging him. "I'm going to say that he can't sit as judge," the president declared emphatically.[48] "I've made up my mind you can't do business with Joe, and to hell with any attempt to compromise." At his morning press conference, however, he spoke more obliquely, telling reporters "that in America, if a man is a party to a dispute, directly or indirectly, he does not sit in judgment on his own case."[49]

The hearings were nationally televised for two months, beginning on April 22. McCarthy was at his most obstreperous, disrupting the proceedings with repeated shouts of "point of order," regularly followed by ad hominem accusations. His objections were usually made over trivial issues and often backfired, making him look ridiculous. With Cohn on the witness stand, for example, the army's shrewd, courtroom-savvy lawyer, Joseph Welch, asked his witness about a cropped photo of a smiling Army Secretary Stevens and Private Schine. The original photo showed Stevens smiling at General Omar Bradley (omitted from the displayed photo), not Schine. Who had cropped the photo? Welsh asked. When Cohn was evasive, Welsh impishly said, "Surely, Mr. Cohn, you don't suggest it was done by a pixie?"[50]

"Point of order, Mr. Chairman," McCarthy interrupted. "Will Mr. Welch please tell the committee what a pixie is?"

Welch paused for effect, then turned toward McCarthy. "Senator, a pixie is a very close relation to a fairy."[51] The rejoinder brought unwelcome attention to gossip of a homosexual relationship between Cohn and Schine.

Welch's response elicited howls of laughter in the committee room.

McCarthy, the brawler, was not done. He attempted to put Welch on the defensive by attacking Fred Fisher, one of the young associates in Welch's Boston law firm who had helped Welch for a short time to prepare for the hearings. Fisher, while a student at Harvard Law School, had briefly been a member of the National Lawyers Guild, an organization that had represented clients accused of Communist affiliations.

Welch had anticipated and dreaded McCarthy's attack. He shook his head and spoke with barely disguised disgust. "Until this moment, Senator, I think I never really gauged your cruelty, or your recklessness."[52] He then explained that Fisher had been a member of the National Lawyers Guild for a few months while a student at Harvard and was at the time of the hearings the secretary of the Young Republicans in Newton, Massachusetts. "Little did I dream you could be so reckless and so cruel as to do an injury to that lad," Welch continued. When McCarthy persisted, Welsh cut him off. "You've done enough," he said, staring coldly at McCarthy. "Have you no sense of decency, sir, at long last?"

A desperate McCarthy reverted to puerile name-calling, referring to "the complete phony Mr.Welch."[53] But Welch would not be intimidated, or yield the floor. He declared that he would not discuss the matter further and asked the committee chairman to call the next witness.

The audience was silent for a moment, and then began to clap. McCarthy stared blankly ahead. For all intents and purposes, his reign of terror was over.

After the hearings concluded, Eisenhower invited Welch to the White House to congratulate him on his presentation of the army's case. Welch told the president that the only good to come out of the hearings was that the country was given the opportunity to see McCarthy in action, his irresponsible charges and ugly gutter tactics televised to millions of Americans in their living rooms.

Six months after the Army-McCarthy hearings adjourned, the Senate officially censured the Wisconsin senator. McCarthy, already a heavy drinker, became an alcoholic and died of cirrhosis of the liver in 1957 at the age of forty-eight.

HOW IMPORTANT WAS Eisenhower to McCarthy's political demise? He certainly worked effectively behind the scenes to undercut the senator's authority, especially in his expansive use of the executive-privilege doctrine, which blocked McCarthy's demands to subpoena documents and interrogate witnesses from the executive branch. That was an example of Eisenhower's subtle leadership qualities in what Princeton political science professor Fred I. Greenstein called his "hidden-hand presidency."*

But Eisenhower's refusal to publicly rebuke McCarthy at the height of the senator's powers frustrated many in the press as well as some of the president's closest advisers, including his brother Milton. He was not just the nation's favorite war hero and popular president, but also the leader of the world's greatest constitutional democracy. If Eisenhower had openly denounced McCarthy and his reckless methods, he might have prevented the trampling of the civil liberties of the many Americans whose reputations, livelihoods, and lives were ruined by the senator.

Eisenhower did not think so. He insisted that his public silence was exactly the antidote needed to hasten McCarthy's downfall. It robbed McCarthy of publicity, the necessary oxygen for his power. In Eisenhower's view, it also underscored a cardinal principle of his leadership style that had served him so well in war and peace. He avoided public criticism of any individual, saving his candid critiques for private meetings. In a letter to his businessman friend, Paul Helms, he insisted that there was nothing "namby-pamby" or "Pollyanna-ish" about his method. "It is just sheer common sense," he said. "A leader's job is to get others to go along with him in the promotion of something. To do this he needs their good will. To destroy good will, it is only necessary to criticize publicly."[54]

*Historian David A. Nichols in his book *Ike and McCarthy: Dwight Eisenhower's Secret Campaign Against Joseph McCarthy* (2017) has presented extensive new documentary evidence to demonstrate the critical role that Eisenhower's "hidden hand" played in undermining McCarthy's power.

Chapter Seven

"THIS IS A DAY
THAT WILL LIVE
IN GLORY"

BY LATE DECEMBER 1953, THE SENATE STILL HAD NOT formally confirmed Earl Warren as Chief Justice of the United States. In fact, Republican Senator William Langer of North Dakota, the irascible chairman of the Senate Judiciary Committee, had undertaken a search for reasons to turn down the president's nominee. Langer, an ardent isolationist opposed to the military draft, the United Nations, and the Marshall Plan, was naturally suspicious of the internationalist wing of his party represented by Eisenhower and Warren. He began to collect letters and witnesses opposed to Warren, producing a poisonous swill of wild, unsubstantiated accusations that, among other things, charged that the chief justice–designate was a closet Marxist who, as governor, had led a corrupt administration that permitted organized crime to establish national headquarters in California.

Warren, meanwhile, went about the serious business of building consensus among his new judicial colleagues to rule in *Brown v. Board of Education* that segregated public schools were unconstitutional. At the justices' conference on December 12, 1953, following oral argument in *Brown*, Warren had introduced himself as a very different chief justice from his predecessor, Fred Vinson. In contrast to the vacillating

Vinson, Warren had declared that the justices must decide the core constitutional issue. He then claimed the moral high ground, asserting that to oppose public school desegregation was to give implicit credence to the racist theory that black Americans were inferior. But he also discussed the practical problems inherent in implementing a desegregation order, especially in the states of the Deep South.

After the judicial conference, Warren's first tactical decision was to bypass further discussion of the merits of the court's decision. He knew that a court majority was prepared to declare public school segregation unconstitutional. Further debate among his brethren could only be divisive. Instead, he urged his colleagues to concentrate on the difficult challenge of crafting a decree that would assure compliance, especially in the southern states where the court's decision was likely to provoke the greatest resistance.

Warren's plan risked alienating at least one justice, Stanley Reed of Kentucky, whose position at the *Brown* conference indicated that he believed the separate-but-equal doctrine of *Plessy v. Ferguson* was still good law.[1]

Reed was a genteel southerner, educated at Yale and the Columbia Law School, who had been considered a moderately liberal state representative in the Kentucky legislature. President Roosevelt had been impressed with Reed's work in the Hoover administration as counsel to the Reconstruction Finance Corporation, charged with attempting to keep banks and businesses open during the worst period of the Great Depression. FDR appointed him solicitor general with the unenviable task of persuading a conservative Supreme Court majority that New Deal legislation was constitutional. Roosevelt rewarded Reed for his workmanlike advocacy with his second appointment to the court. Hugo Black, FDR's loyal lieutenant in the Senate, had been his first court appointee.

Shortly after the justices' conference in December, the chief justice embarked on a subtle diplomatic mission to win Reed's vote. Warren invited Reed to join him for frequent lunches, most often with Justices Harold Burton and Sherman Minton, stalwart members of the majority in favor of overturning *Plessy*. Burton and Minton were genial midwesterners and warm friends of Reed. Equally important, they did not intimidate, unlike their more intellectually gifted colleagues Black, Douglas, Frankfurter, and Jackson. At the informal lunches, Warren played the gracious host, always an attentive listener who exuded good will.

Reed was not the chief justice's only challenge. Even if he were able to convince Reed to join the majority on the merits, he still needed to find common ground among the justices on the critical implementation decree. Tom Clark of Texas had been a shaky "yes" vote at the *Brown* conference and expressed anxiety about a court order that could breed unrest in the southern states. Warren also had to satisfy Justices Frankfurter and Jackson, both brilliant and prickly, who would demand that their philosophical commitment to judicial restraint be addressed.

Warren began to court Frankfurter at the same time that Frankfurter, who savored court intrigue, was happily wooing the new chief justice. They met in chambers to discuss the segregation cases and, at Frankfurter's invitation, at his home where he promised to offer "the stimulating accompaniment of a bourbon highball."[2]

Warren and Frankfurter were improbable partners in the court's historic deliberations. Warren, the big, bluff, no-frills politician from Bakersfield, California, appeared to have little in common with the intense, intellectual Frankfurter, the diminutive (5'5") Jew who had immigrated to the United States with his family from Vienna in 1894. Young Felix was twelve years old when his family settled in a cold-water flat on New York's Lower East Side, and he did not speak a word of English. But he soon mastered the new language, read voraciously at the Cooper Union library, and graduated with superb grades from the City College of New York and the Harvard Law School. Though a brilliant student, he was no ivory-tower academic. He demonstrated an extraordinary gift for making friends and giving advice to men in high office, including three presidents—Theodore Roosevelt, Woodrow Wilson, and Franklin D. Roosevelt. The only Jew on the Harvard Law School faculty, he championed liberal, often unpopular causes. He wrote a celebrated article in the *Atlantic Monthly*, citing multiple irregularities in the convictions of two Italian-born anarchists, Nicola Sacco and Bartolomeo Vanzetti, who had been sentenced to death for the robbery and murder of a paymaster and his guard at a shoe factory in South Braintree, Massachusetts. He was a founding member of the NAACP and the American Civil Liberties Union. And he pressed for social and economic reform, successfully arguing before the Supreme Court that state legislation providing minimum wages and maximum hours was constitutional.

When Frankfurter was appointed to the Supreme Court in 1939 by FDR, it was generally assumed by legal academics and the press that he would lead the liberal wing of the court. Once on the court, however, Frankfurter counseled judicial restraint, the school of legal thought that urged the justices to defer whenever possible to the elected branches of government. As a result, Hugo Black, the former populist Democratic senator from Alabama, became the liberal leader of the court and outspoken protector of civil rights and liberties.

In January 1954, despite the vast differences between Frankfurter and Warren in background, temperament, and intellect, the two justices shared an overriding goal in *Brown:* to unite the justices on an implementation decree that would adhere to constitutional principle but also provide realistic guidelines to dismantle the wide range of segregated public school systems.

Working toward their common goal, Frankfurter drafted a five-page memorandum that was circulated to his colleagues on January 15, one day before Warren had scheduled another conference to discuss *Brown.* In his memo, Frankfurter cautioned that a court decision declaring segregated facilities unconstitutional was "not a wand by which these transformations can be accomplished."[3] Such a declaration, with nothing more, would be "the most prolific breeder of litigation and chaos." When the wrong is "deeply rooted state policy," he continued, the court must uproot it 'with all deliberate speed.' " He emphasized that the court must anticipate that the "pace and scope" of desegregation would differ, depending on local conditions. For that reason, he suggested that the court delegate the difficult task of implementation to federal district courts or to a special master.

In both tone and content, Frankfurter's memo reflected the views expressed by Warren at the court's *Brown* conference in December. It was important, the new chief had stressed, that a court desegregation decree be sensitive to local conditions, particularly in the Deep South. That cautious approach revealed Warren's acute pragmatic assessment, honed over a lifetime in professional politics. It also was calculated to appeal to all of his new colleagues, not just those like Clark, from segregated states, but also others, like Frankfurter and Jackson, who were concerned that the justices could do irreparable harm to the court's authority and prestige by issuing an ultimatum demanding immediate compliance.

At the conference held the day after the justices had received Frankfurter's memo, Warren arranged for a special luncheon treat— roast duck and pheasant, courtesy of bird-hunting friends of the chief justice. Once the discussion began, Warren reiterated a major point made in Frankfurter's memo. The court should issue a flexible decree, he said, that "will permit different handling in different places."[4] He also stressed a second point made in Frankfurter's memo—that the court should be as little involved in administration as possible. He recommended that district courts enforce the decree, but added that "we ought not turn them loose without guidance of what paths are open to them."

There was general agreement around the conference table on Warren's two major points—that the decree must show flexibility, and that the court should delegate implementation. The most outspoken advocate for both positions was Justice Black. "Leave it to the district courts," Black said, "let them work it out."[5] Reed added that implementation should not be "a rush job," the first indication that the single holdout against a desegregation decree might be persuaded to join a majority opinion. Jackson was still not convinced that a court decision outlawing school segregation was based on sound constitutional law or history. "If what we're doing is to uproot social policy, what business is it of ours?" he asked. He suggested that his colleagues schedule reargument for the next term focused on the remedy.

Black spoke last and urged caution. "Let it [the decree] simmer," he said. "Let it take time."[6] In the Deep South, he said, "any man who would come in [supporting the court's decision] would be dead politically forever." In his home state of Alabama, he continued, "most liberals are praying for delay." He warned his brethren that enforcement would give rise to a "storm over this Court."

WHILE WARREN WAS immersed in the court's deliberations in *Brown*, he received an invitation to dine at the White House with President Eisenhower and a select group of prominent men in government and the private sector. Ike considered his stag dinners an opportunity to exchange candid views on pressing issues of the day in a relaxed atmosphere encouraged by good food, wine, and cigars.

But Warren was not just another prominent government official on the president's guest list. As chief justice, he was leading deliberations in the school segregation cases. The court's decision in those cases, both Warren and Eisenhower knew, could profoundly change the constitutional, political, and social fabric of the nation. Warren realized that it would be difficult to decline the invitation of the president who had appointed him. Besides, he was still the acting chief justice and could not take his formal confirmation for granted. He was grateful to the president for his appointment and valued his continued support. He accepted the invitation.

Warren arrived with the other guests at the White House on the evening of February 8. He knew immediately upon sitting down to dinner next to the president that he should not have been there. Not far from him sat attorney John W. Davis, who had argued the *Brown* case in December for his client, the state of South Carolina. To make matters worse, Warren recalled, "the President went to considerable links to tell me what a great man Mr. Davis was."[7] Warren's discomfort intensified when he realized that Davis's opponent in *Brown*, Thurgood Marshall, was not at the dinner. The chief justice considered it inappropriate for Eisenhower to have invited him to such a dinner. To have seated him within earshot of one of the attorneys in a pending case before the court, and then to have effusively praised that attorney, was unconscionable.

Eisenhower never acknowledged that his invitation to Warren or Davis was a mistake. He apparently saw nothing wrong with inviting Warren to one of his informal stag dinners. And Davis was not only a longtime Eisenhower friend but a valued adviser to the new president. The president considered him a great lawyer and said so in his correspondence. Had Davis not been eighty years old, Eisenhower would seriously have considered appointing him chief justice. Early in his first presidential term, Eisenhower solicited Davis's advice on a constitutional issue unrelated to *Brown*. He asked Davis if he should actively oppose a constitutional amendment, sponsored by Ohio senator John Bricker, that would have required Senate approval of any international treaty before it could be enforceable in the United States. Davis advised the president to vigorously oppose the amendment as a usurpation of the president's constitutional authority in foreign affairs, advice that Eisenhower followed.[8] With the president's forceful though indirect opposition, the amendment was defeated.

After the dinner, the president and his guests moved to another room for coffee and cigars. Eisenhower took Warren by the arm and pointedly commented on the problem faced by the southern states in the school segregation cases. "These are not bad people," he told Warren, referring to white parents in the Deep South.[9] "All they are concerned about is to see that their sweet little girls are not required to sit in school alongside some big overgrown Negroes."*

Eisenhower's racist remark could just as easily have been uttered by South Carolina governor Jimmy Byrnes or his state's attorney in *Brown*, John W. Davis, who was also a committed segregationist. Byrnes had told Eisenhower during their luncheon conversation the previous summer that white southerners could tolerate mixing with black adults but were "frightened at putting the children together."[10] Davis, in his oral argument before the court in *Brown*, had warned of dire consequences should the court force integration of black and white children in the public schools in the segregated South.

Eisenhower did not mention this conversation with Warren in his memoirs, diaries, or private correspondence. William Ewald, Jr., who assisted Eisenhower with his memoirs, denied that the president had invited Warren to the White House to influence the court's decision in *Brown*. He suggested that "in a moment of thoughtless candor" Eisenhower shared with the chief justice the southern whites' fear of race mixing.[11] Attorney General Herbert Brownell, Jr., also defended the president's remark, writing in his memoirs that Eisenhower was expressing "his personal sympathy for the mothers of young white children in the South who had been reared in a segregated society and feared the unknown—the arrival of a time when the public schools would be desegregated."[12]

---

* Eisenhower's phrase was "some big black bucks," according to Professor Bernard Schwartz, a Warren confidant, not the sanitized version reported in the chief justice's memoirs. (Schwartz, *Super Chief, Earl Warren and His Supreme Court—A Judicial Biography* [1983], p. 113.)

Eisenhower's racist comment to Warren, in addition to expressing sympathy for white southern parents, may have drawn on his experiences in Abilene and the military. After all, he had attended segregated public schools in Abilene and made a military career in a segregated army. In Eisenhower's private conversations with his friends and colleagues, it would have been surprising if there had not been an occasional racial slur. Whatever Eisenhower's personal views on race, Brownell and Ewald emphasized, they did not interfere with his civil rights policies as president. At the time of his February stag dinner, Eisenhower had already made impressive strides in fully desegregating the military, veterans hospitals, and public accommodations in the District of Columbia. It was "unthinkable," said Ewald, that Eisenhower used his February stag dinner to lobby against desegregation.[13]

A WEEK LATER, Warren confronted yet another problem in his efforts to lead the justices toward a unanimous decision in *Brown*. Justice Jackson wrote a long, provocative memo to his colleagues on February 15 that raised multiple problems for the chief justice. Jackson was not just a formidable advocate but also a temperamental, unpredictable member of the court.

Jackson had been such a superb advocate as Roosevelt's solicitor general (after Stanley Reed had been appointed to the court) that the great justice Louis Brandeis had said that he should have been appointed SG for life. Roosevelt later appointed Jackson his attorney general before naming him to the Supreme Court in 1941. He quickly became the court's most eloquent opinion writer. But the mercurial Jackson also developed a blood feud with his colleague Hugo Black that played out in headlines across the country in 1946. Jackson, then on leave from the court to serve as a prosecutor at the Nuremberg trials, threatened to resign from the court if rumors were true that Truman planned to appoint Black to be chief justice to fill the vacancy left by the death of Harlan Fiske Stone. Truman passed over Black to appoint his secretary of the treasury, Fred Vinson.

In Jackson's February memo on *Brown* to his judicial colleagues, he slashed away at the conventional judicial rationale for overturning *Plessy*. No matter how wrong or harmful segregation was to African Americans, Jackson wrote, a desegregation ruling could not be justified on the basis of the text or history of the Equal Protection Clause of the Fourteenth Amendment. In the absence of federal statutes, he insisted that the issue of segregation had been left to the states. And the court, as John W. Davis argued, had repeatedly found state laws enforcing segregation to be constitutional. Jackson dismissed as irrelevant Thurgood Marshall's argument that sociological and psychological studies demonstrated that segregation produced a feeling of inferiority among black children. However painful segregation was for them, Jackson did not think "we should import into the concept of equal protection of the law these elusive psychological and subjective factors."[14]

Having listed the obstacles the justices faced, Jackson nonetheless indicated that he would support a court decision striking down school segregation. His position was not based on judicial precedent or constitutional history, but, rather, on the progress that African Americans had made since the Fourteenth Amendment was ratified. Black Americans had made "one of the swiftest and most dramatic advances in the history of man," he wrote.[15] "That Negro segregation in the schools has outlived whatever original justification it may have had and is no longer wise or fair public policy is a conclusion congenial to my background and social and political views." He concluded that the only legitimate ground for a desegregation decision was that the "Negro" population, not the Constitution, had changed. Black, no less than white Americans, were entitled to a public education, "a right more than a duty to be performed not merely for one's own advantage but for the security and stability of the nation."

Although Jackson's memo offered many stimulating thoughts for his colleagues to consider, it did not suggest that he would readily sign on to a majority opinion. He had raised too many issues that he was likely to articulate in a concurrence.

During the court's February recess, Justice Reed began to draft a dissenting opinion in the school segregation cases. In his draft, he argued that every court precedent on school segregation stood for the proposition that a good-faith, realistic effort to provide separate and substantially equal facilities for black public-school children would be constitutional. He asked his law clerks to provide details of the holdings in three court decisions to bolster his argument.

The earliest precedent on Reed's list was a 1938 decision, *Missouri ex rel. Gaines v. Canada,* in which the court ruled that Missouri had violated the Equal Protection Clause by its refusal to admit a prospective black law student to the segregated state law school, but, instead, offered to pay his tuition to a desegregated law school in another state. Chief Justice Charles Evans Hughes's majority opinion concluded that Missouri was obligated to furnish the black law student "within its borders facilities for legal education substantially equal to those which the State then offered for persons of the white race."[16]

Reed also requested materials on two more recent precedents, *Sweatt v. Painter* and *McLaurin v. Oklahoma,* both decided in 1950. In *Sweatt,* a unanimous court held that Texas had not provided equal facilities for a black mail carrier from Houston who was tutored by three part-time faculty members of the University of Texas law school in three small basement rooms of an office building eight blocks from the law school.[17] Sweatt's education did not satisfy *Plessy*'s separate-but-equal doctrine, Chief Justice Vinson wrote for a unanimous court. Not only was Sweatt denied access to the spacious facilities, vast library, and large faculty at the main campus, but he was deprived of the association of 85 percent of the population of the state, including most of the lawyers, witnesses, jurors, and judges who would be critical to his future practice.

In *McLaurin*, again a unanimous court ruled that Oklahoma had violated the Equal Protection Clause by forcing a black graduate student at the state university to sit at a table outside the classroom, customized for his special status as black with a rope and a sign "For colored only."[18] He also was required to eat and study alone. Chief Justice Vinson's opinion for the court found that the restrictions impaired McLaurin's "ability to study, to engage in discussions and exchange views with other students and, in general, to learn his profession."

Reed had joined the court's opinions in both *Sweatt* and *McLaurin*, but, nonetheless, thought it possible to satisfy the *Plessy* doctrine, as John W. Davis had argued in *Brown*.

MARCH WAS A MORE encouraging month for Warren. On March 1 he was confirmed without dissent by the Senate as chief justice. A few days later, James Reston, the influential columnist of the *New York Times*, wrote that Warren's colleagues gave him high marks for his leadership in their judicial conferences. According to Reston's sources, Warren had shown "an ability to concentrate on the concrete; a capacity to do his homework; a sensible, friendly manner, wholly devoid of pretense, and a self command and natural dignity so useful in presiding over the court."[19]

Warren's reputation for evenhandedness was underscored during his first term as chief justice. He had certainly demonstrated his liberal sensibilities in his resolute determination to strike down school segregation in *Brown*. But during his first term, he also cast the decisive fifth vote in *Irvine v. California* for a majority opinion written by Jackson that overlooked invasive police methods to uphold a conviction for bookmaking.[20] The case arose after police officers secretly entered the defendant's house and installed a hidden microphone in his bedroom. Officers at a nearby listening post recorded incriminating conversations that helped convict the defendant for gambling. Despite the fact that the police misconduct was illegally obtained under state law, the majority ruled that it did not violate the U.S. Constitution.

In a second case that belied Warren's libertarian credentials, the chief justice joined a six-man majority that encouraged the scourge of McCarthyism. In *Barsky v. Board of Regents*, the court upheld the six-month suspension of the medical license of a prominent physician because he had been convicted of a misdemeanor for failing to produce papers of the Joint Anti-Fascist Refugee Committee before the House Un-American Activities Committee.[21] In dissent, Justice Frankfurter wrote that the court majority had sanctioned the "destruction of a man's professional life on grounds having no possible relation to fitness, intellectual or moral, to pursue his profession."

In late March, Warren called for a formal vote in *Brown*. Eight justices voted to declare public school segregation unconstitutional. Reed was the only dissenter. The justices also decided that the majority opinion would be limited to constitutional principle. They would schedule reargument during the next term on the difficult issue of implementation, as Jackson had suggested in his February memo. Warren, as chief justice and a member of the majority, was entitled to assign the majority opinion. He was encouraged by his colleagues to assign the opinion to himself, which he did.

On March 30, Justice Jackson, only sixty-two years old and in apparent robust health, suffered a serious heart attack. The attack made it doubtful that Jackson could fully participate in the court's business for the remainder of the term, including final deliberations in the *Brown* decision. And even if he could, it was highly unlikely that he would have the strength to write a concurring opinion in *Brown*.

By mid-April, Warren had outlined his thoughts in pencil on a yellow legal pad for his *Brown* opinion. He would use language that an ordinary American could understand. His opinion would not be heavily laden with complicated legalese or a litany of court precedents. He would be unemotional and nonaccusatory, so that white southerners, in particular, would have no reason to read his opinion as an indictment of their history or culture. And he hoped to speak directly to the American people, more as a statesman than judge, fully aware that the court was opening a new and critical chapter in the nation's troubled history of race relations.

Warren took a break from his work on *Brown*, asking his chauffeur, who was black, to drive him to some of the Civil War sites in nearby Virginia. After a day of touring, Warren checked into a hotel and assumed that his driver would find his own accommodations. The next morning, when his chauffeur greeted him at his car, Warren realized that his driver, slightly disheveled, had slept in the vehicle. "Have you slept here all night?" Warren asked.[22]

"Well, Mr. Chief Justice," the driver replied nervously, "I just couldn't find a place."

It suddenly struck Warren that no hotel rooms were available to him in the segregated town, not even for the driver of the Chief Justice of the United States. Warren, ashamed and embarrassed, asked his driver to return immediately to the nation's capital.

When Warren met with his three law clerks in his chambers to discuss his lead *Brown* opinion striking down school segregation in four states, he already had a firm idea of the structure and even some specific phrases he intended to use. He met alone with Earl Pollock, a Northwestern Law School graduate, who was assigned the difficult task of translating the chief justice's thoughts into a coherent draft declaring school segregation unconstitutional in the states of Delaware, Kansas, South Carolina, and Virginia. A second clerk, William Oliver, was given primary responsibility for the draft in the case involving school segregation in the District of Columbia. The third clerk, Richard Flynn, assisted on both opinions, supplying footnotes to support Warren's conclusions.

By early May, Warren had reviewed his clerks' drafts and made the two *Brown* opinions his own. His lead opinion declaring school segregation in the states unconstitutional was only eleven pages long, extraordinarily short for a landmark court opinion.[23] At the outset, the chief justice rejected claims from both sides that the history of the Fourteenth Amendment provided the constitutional answer in the state school segregation cases. At best, the amendment's history was inconclusive, he wrote. This was not surprising, he noted, because public school education for whites was rudimentary in 1868, when the amendment was ratified, and virtually nonexistent for blacks. In fact, the overwhelming number of school-age children of both races were illiterate.

Warren spent little time on court precedents, as he had noted in his original outline. He cited *Gaines*, *Sweatt*, and *McLaurin*, all graduate-school cases striking down segregation policies, but observed that in none of the decisions had the court directly overruled *Plessy*'s separate but equal doctrine. In *Brown*, unlike those decisions, the states claimed that they had made good-faith efforts to equalize the schools, at least in terms of tangible factors such as facilities, curricula, and teachers' salaries. But the court could not rely on tangible factors alone, Warren wrote, and returned to the court's *Sweatt* and *McLauren* decisions to make his point. In *Sweatt*, the court had struck down the dual system of educating law students, in part because segregation deprived the black law student of the opportunity to associate with the state's overwhelmingly white population, including the lawyers, jurors, and judges central to his future practice. And in *McLaurin*, the court again relied on intangible factors, such as the black graduate student's lack of opportunity to study and exchange views with white students in order to learn his profession. Warren concluded that the court in *Brown* must look broadly to both tangible and intangible factors to determine the effect of segregation on public education.

"In approaching this problem, we cannot turn the clock back to 1868 when the [Fourteenth] amendment was adopted, or even to 1896 when *Plessy* was written," Warren wrote. "We must consider public education in the light of its full development and its present place in American life throughout the Nation." In 1954, he asserted, education was not only a critically important function of state and local governments, but also the very foundation of good citizenship.

He then posed the crucial constitutional question before the court. "Does segregation of children in public schools solely on the basis of race, even though the physical facilities and other 'tangible' factors may be equal, deprive the children of the minority group of equal educational opportunities?" His answer: "We believe that it does." Intangible factors, which the court had considered important in the graduate school cases of *Sweatt* and *McLaurin*, were even more critical to the education of primary- and secondary-school students. "To separate them from others of similar age and qualifications solely because of their race generates a feeling of inferiority as to their status in the community that may affect their hearts and minds in a way unlikely ever to be undone," he wrote.

Segregation by race also affected the motivation of a black child to learn, Warren continued. "Whatever may have been the extent of psychological knowledge at the time of *Plessy*, this finding is amply supported by modern authority," he wrote. "Any language in *Plessy* contrary to this finding is rejected." Finally, Warren declared that "in the field of public education the doctrine of 'separate but equal' has no place. Separate educational facilities are inherently unequal."

The chief justice had expeditiously accomplished the task he had originally outlined on his yellow legal pad. He had dismantled fifty-eight years of constitutional law with only the sparest references to judicial precedent. In citing the court's most recent desegregation decisions, *Sweatt* and *McLaurin*, he insisted that the high bar set in those cases to uphold *Plessy*, which included intangible factors, could not be satisfied in primary and secondary schools. His indignation at the racism implicit in school segregation was evident when he wrote of the inferiority felt by black students that could forever affect "their hearts and minds." While firmly condemning segregation, he carefully avoided blaming the states that had perpetuated the system. And he spoke in plain, simple English, readily understood by the average American.

In just six paragraphs, Warren's second opinion found that racial segregation in the District of Columbia public schools violated the Due Process Clause of the Fifth Amendment, which applied to the federal government. The concepts of equal protection and due process both stemmed from "our American ideal of fairness," he wrote, and were not mutually exclusive.[24] "In view of our decision that the Constitution prohibits the states from maintaining racially segregated public schools, it would be unthinkable that the same Constitution would impose a lesser duty on the Federal Government," he concluded.

Warren's lead opinion striking down public school segregation in the states contained language that could appeal to his two most likely critics on the court, Justices Reed and Jackson. Reed had joined the court's opinions in *Sweatt* and *McLaurin*, so Warren held out some hope that his colleague might be persuaded by his contention that the intangible factors emphasized in those precedents doomed the state segregated systems at the primary and secondary public school levels. But Reed had given no indication in the justices' *Brown* conferences or lunches with Warren and other colleagues that he considered the *Plessy* doctrine undermined by *Sweatt* and *McLaurin*.

For Jackson, Warren's emphasis on the critical role of public education in 1954 and its contribution to citizenship echoed thoughts expressed in Jackson's February memo. And Jackson had insisted that the court could find no support for its decision in the history of the

Fourteenth Amendment, a concession made by the chief justice in his draft opinion. The chief justice also included the justices' intention to schedule reargument during the next term on the issue of the implementation decree, a suggestion made by Jackson in his memo. But Warren also relied on psychological studies, cited in a footnote, that Jackson had rejected as irrelevant.

Once he had completed his drafts, Warren called on Reed in his chambers. The chief justice had encouraged dialogue with Reed throughout the winter and spring. He had shared lunch with Reed at least twenty times since the justices had first discussed *Brown* in conference. Warren put the question to Reed gently, but directly. "Stan, you're all by yourself in this now," he said.[25] "You've got to decide whether it's really the best thing for the country."

Warren knew that he was unlikely to persuade Reed that *Plessy*, as a matter of law, should be reversed. But appealing to Reed's patriotism was a different matter. "I think he [Reed] was really troubled by the possible consequences of his position," said Reed's clerk, George Mickum, who was in the room when Warren visited Reed in his chambers.[26] "Because he was a Southerner, even a lone dissent by him would give a lot of people a lot of grist for making trouble. For the good of the country, he put aside his own basis for dissent." Reed agreed to join Warren's opinion after receiving the chief justice's assurance that the implementation decision would call for the gradual dismantling of segregated public schools in the South.

Warren personally delivered a copy of his draft opinions to Jackson in his hospital room. After Warren left, Jackson asked his clerk, Barrett Prettyman, Jr., to read them. Prettyman retreated to the hall, read the drafts, and returned to give Jackson his assessment. The clerk told his boss that he wished that there had been more law in the lead opinion dealing with the states but that he found nothing "glaringly unacceptable."[27] Prettyman marveled at the chief justice's talent for writing an opinion that could appeal to even his most independent colleague. "He

[Warren] had come from political life and had a keen sense of what you could say in this opinion without getting everybody's back up," Prettyman said.

When Warren returned to Jackson's hospital room later in the day, Jackson told him that he would join both opinions. He suggested only two minor insertions in the lead opinion. He urged Warren to issue a broader condemnation of segregation. Warren politely declined, explaining that he wanted the opinion to be as narrowly circumscribed as possible. But he readily accepted Jackson's second suggestion—to include a sentence noting the professional success of black Americans in many fields. It was an observation that Jackson had emphasized in his February memo.

Warren's achievement was remarkable. A year earlier, the justices had been hopelessly split and dispirited after the first *Brown* argument. The man called upon to heal the court's wounds had never been a judge in his thirty-four years of public service. But Warren had proved to be the consummate politician as governor of California, and he applied the same skills as chief justice. He probed tirelessly for common ground. And though he did not possess the extraordinary intellect of a Hugo Black or Felix Frankfurter, he offered qualities more valuable in his new leadership role: an open, unpretentious manner, a quiet dignity, and a palpable sense of fairness. Ultimately, all of his colleagues proudly supported his *Brown* opinions.

ON MONDAY MORNING, May 17, Warren made another visit to Jackson's hospital room, this time to deliver printed copies of his desegregation opinions. He informed Jackson that the court's decision in *Brown* would be announced and that he would read his opinions aloud after the justices formally convened in the courtroom at noon. To Warren's surprise and chagrin, Jackson, looking weak and pale, said that he intended to join his colleagues for the announcement. Later that morning, Jackson entered the Supreme Court building by a side entrance and was taken to his chambers in the justices' private elevator.

At noon, the nine justices entered the ornate courtroom and took their seats. Warren, in his large black robe, sat in the center chair, serene in contrast to the tense atmosphere in the courtroom. His wife, Nina, and their daughter, Virginia, sat in the visitor's gallery, as did Attorney General Brownell, who had been tipped off by Warren to the court's auspicious announcement. By custom, the chief justice began the proceedings by welcoming newly admitted members of the Supreme Court bar. Warren smiled warmly at each admitted lawyer, including David Acheson, who had been introduced by his famous father, the former secretary of state. After the bar admissions, Justices Clark and Douglas announced the court's decisions in three minor cases.

At 12:52, Warren, in a firm, steady voice, said, "I have for announcement the judgment and opinion of the Court in No.1—*Oliver Brown et. al. v. Board of Education of Topeka.*[28] Reporters in the basement press room scrambled up the marble stairs to enter the courtroom. The Associated Press put the first bulletin over the wire: "Chief Justice Warren today began reading the Supreme Court's decision in the public school segregation cases. The court's ruling could not be determined immediately."[29] Through the first two-thirds of the *Brown* opinion, Warren had not indicated the result.

The tension in the courtroom mounted. Finally, the chief justice asked the crucial question: Does the segregation of children in public schools solely on the basis of race deprive them of equal educational opportunities? "We believe it does," he answered. Instantly newsrooms across the country hummed with the nervous excitement of a historic story. But Warren still had one more piece of stunning news to announce. When he said that the decision was unanimous, a tremor of emotion swept through the courtroom that even Warren had not anticipated.

As Warren read the final words of the court's decision, tears could be seen in Stanley Reed's eyes. Later, Reed was asked by one of his clerks to name the most important decision during his fifteen years on the court. *Brown* he said, without hesitation. And, he added, "if it was not the most important decision in the history of the Court, it was very close.[30]

"Dear Chief: This is a day that will live in glory," Frankfurter wrote Warren on the day of the *Brown* decision.[31] "It's also a great day in the history of the court, and not in the least for the course of deliberation which brought about the result. I congratulate you."

Within hours of the announcement of the *Brown* decision, the Voice of America had broadcast the news to foreign countries in thirty-five languages. Former secretary of state Acheson called the decision "great and statesmanlike." *Brown* was widely viewed as a triumph for democracy at the height of the Cold War.

Time magazine lauded *Brown* as the court's most important landmark decision. "In its 164 years the court had erected many a landmark of U.S. history," *Time* declared.[32] "None of them except the Dred Scott case (reversed by the Civil War) was more important than the school segregation issue. None of them directly and intimately affected so many families."

The *New York Times* columnist James Reston, however, faulted Warren's reliance on social science in *Brown*, a criticism that was to be repeated in legal journals. "Relying more on the social scientists than on legal precedents—a procedure often in controversy in the past—the Court insisted on equality of the mind and heart rather than on equal school facilities. . . . The Court's opinion read more like an expert paper on sociology than a Supreme Court opinion."[33]

A hopeful Thurgood Marshall predicted, "Once the decision is made public in the South as well as the North, the people will get together for the first time and work this thing out."[34]

Leading southern politicians were not reassuring. Governor Talmadge of Georgia was blunt and combative, denouncing the decision as "a mere scrap of paper" that "had blatantly ignored all law and precedent."[35] South Carolina governor Byrnes was "shocked" that the court had overruled *Plessy* but, nonetheless, counseled restraint in the southern states.[36]

Black communities across the county were euphoric. "It would be impossible for a white person to understand what happened within black breasts on that Monday," wrote author Louis Lomax.[37] "An ardent segregationist has called it 'Black Monday.' He was so right, but for reasons other than the ones he advances. That was the day we won; the day we took the white man's laws and won our case before an all-white Supreme Court with a Negro lawyer, Thurgood Marshall, as our chief counsel. And we were proud."

EISENHOWER PREPARED HIS response to the *Brown* decision for his press conference on May 19. It was brief and stiff, almost as if he were reading from a cue card. "The Supreme Court has spoken, and I am sworn to uphold the constitutional process in the country," he told reporters two days after the court's decision.[38] "And I will obey." He did not elaborate.

This was the same president who, at his first State of the Union address in February 1953, had vowed to eliminate racial discrimination in the nation's capital and in the armed forces. Eisenhower, moreover, had praised the Supreme Court's *Thompson* decision that had struck down racial discrimination in public accommodations in the nation's capital only eleven months before *Brown*.

Although Eisenhower had distanced himself from full-fledged support for his attorney general's brief in *Brown* calling for the reversal of *Plessy v. Ferguson*, that legal position was an integral part of the administration's brief that was submitted to the court. At the second oral argument in *Brown*, Assistant Attorney General J. Lee Rankin, representing the Eisenhower administration, contended that public school segregation was unconstitutional.

Why was Eisenhower's response to *Brown* so pallid compared to his public pronouncements and those of his Justice Department condemning racial discrimination? The most frequently offered explanation was that the president was committed to the concept of separation of powers between the executive and judicial branches of the federal government. He believed that the court's role was to interpret the laws and the executive's was to make sure the laws were faithfully executed, as he promised at his May 19 press conference.

But in practice Eisenhower never acted as if his concept of the separation between the branches was so rigid. The court had requested a brief from the Eisenhower administration in *Brown*, and Attorney General Brownell readily complied, submitting a forceful brief calling for the reversal of *Plessy*. Eisenhower, moreover, showed no reluctance in praising court decisions he approved of, such as *Thompson* and earlier, during his presidential campaign, the court's ruling in the steel seizure case. Nor did he adhere to an inflexible separation-of-powers stance when his own constitutional powers were threatened by Congress. He fought vigorously to defeat the Bricker Amendment, which he believed gave Congress the power to undermine his authority as commander in chief.

Eisenhower's minimalist response to *Brown* has also been explained as his refusal, as president, to make moral judgments. But his insistence that the federal government end segregation wherever it had the authority to do so was an implicit moral judgment.

The most plausible explanation for Eisenhower's formalistic response to *Brown* is his fear of the consequences of the decision in the Deep South. He continued to worry that the southern states would shut down public schools and pass legislation to finance private schools, a threat South Carolina governor Byrnes had expressed in his private conversations with the president. The day after the *Brown* decision was announced, Eisenhower told aides that such action by the southern states "would not only handicap Negro children but would work to the detriment of the so-called 'poor whites' in the South."[39] The president appeared to consciously insulate himself from the court's ruling. At the same time, he remained sensitive to the states' rights arguments raised by Byrnes and John W. Davis—that the problem of segregation in the public schools in the South should be solved gradually and at the local level.

Had Eisenhower been privy to the court's deliberations in *Brown*, he would have known that his appointee, Chief Justice Earl Warren, had shared his concern about the reaction to *Brown* in the southern states. At the first *Brown* conference in which he presided, Warren had expressed his apprehension about implementation of the court's desegregation order, especially in the Deep South. He said that the justices must be sensitive to the consequences of their decision in that region of the country. It was a concern shared by every member of the court, particularly the three justices from segregated states. That anxiety led the justices to request reargument during the next term on the issue of implementation. The request for reargument was clearly articulated by Warren in his *Brown* opinion.

Eisenhower, in his private correspondence, acknowledged that the court's implementation decision would be crucial to the success of the order to desegregate public schools in the South. "The segregation issue will, I think, become acute or tend to die out according to the character of the procedure orders that the Court will probably issue this winter," Eisenhower wrote his childhood friend, Everett "Swede" Hazlett, before the court had heard reargument on the issue of implementation in *Brown*.[40] "My own guess is that they will be very moderate and accord a maximum of initiative to local courts."

During his presidency and in his retirement, Eisenhower never communicated directly to Warren that he supported *Brown*. His only public praise for the court's decision came in his memoirs, published in

1963, in which he wrote that "there can be no question that the judgment of the Court [in *Brown*] was right."[41]

Eisenhower's measured public response after Warren had announced the *Brown* decision left Warren with the indelible impression that the president disapproved of the court's ruling. In his memoirs, Warren wrote of his dismay at the president's stag dinner when Ike praised John W. Davis and commented on white southerner parents' fear of their daughters going to school with overgrown black boys. He also did not hide his resentment "that no word of support for the [*Brown*] decision emanated from the White House."[42] Warren suggested that a strong endorsement of the decision by the very popular president could have lent critical political support for the decision. He observed sardonically in his memoirs that "the fatherly President Dwight Eisenhower was widely quoted as having said his appointment of me as Chief Justice 'was the biggest damn fool thing I ever did.' "[43]

Eisenhower and Warren's relationship noticeably cooled after Warren's announcement of the *Brown* decision in May 1954. There were polite, dutiful exchanges between the men in person and in their correspondence, but little warmth expressed. Ironically, Warren had demonstrated in the court's deliberations in *Brown* the very qualities that Eisenhower had praised when he nominated him to be chief justice. Warren's new judicial colleagues were immediately impressed with his extraordinary capacity for quiet leadership. They also appreciated his pragmatic instincts that cautioned against a judicial decision demanding immediate implementation of the desegregation order in the South. To his brethren, to the overwhelming majority of Americans, and to millions of people around the world, Earl Warren epitomized the statesmanship that Eisenhower had said was the crucial credential he possessed when he appointed him to be Chief Justice of the United States.

Chapter Eight

"WITH ALL DELIBERATE SPEED"

WARREN AND FRANKFURTER WROTE TO EACH OTHER frequently during the justices' summer recess in 1954, eagerly exchanging news on the public's reaction to the court's school desegregation decision. Both were heartened by the initial muted response from the some of the South's most influential politicians including Governor Byrnes of South Carolina. Byrnes had joined other southern governors in expressing shock and dismay over the *Brown* decision, but he tempered his reaction by counseling calm among his fellow southerners, in contrast to his pre-*Brown* statements of defiance.

Byrnes "was certainly conciliatory," Warren wrote Frankfurter, "but I cannot escape the thought that he would have been much more helpful, had he been as restrained in recent years."[1] Frankfurter replied, "I quite agree with you that Jimmie Byrnes has shown more good sense after the event than before it."[2] He added that "one had a right to expect more reticence from so sensible a fellow as Jimmie." Frankfurter was, nonetheless, encouraged by a telephone conversation during the summer that he had with Byrnes. "I have hopes that the sobriety of thought that he showed in his talk with me," he wrote Warren, "will continue to guide him in what is ahead of us."

Warren had the opportunity to gauge southern reaction to *Brown* in late September when he made his first public address in the South since the decision. The occasion was the commemoration of the two hundredth anniversary of the birth of Chief Justice John Marshall at the College of William & Mary in Williamsburg, Virginia. The chief justice, flanked by three of his judicial colleagues (Burton, Clark, and Frankfurter), addressed an audience of three thousand, including law students, faculty, and delegates from more than one hundred colleges and universities.

Without mentioning *Brown* by name, Warren declared that "the most sacred of the duties of a government is to do equal and impartial justice for all its citizens."[3] The country's "passion for justice," he said, had often required that it "wipe some things from the slate and start again." Among the "mistakes" to be erased, he continued, was the use of the government for "selfish and even oppressive ends." He noted that in the United States "waves of passion, prejudice and even hatreds have on occasion swept over us and almost engulfed us," but that the nation had "never failed in our climb toward the pinnacle of true justice."

The audience applauded Warren's address respectfully. But conspicuously absent from the dais were Virginia governor Thomas Stanley and the state's attorney general, J. Lindsay Almond, Jr., who was scheduled to represent the state in the *Brown* reargument before the court. Their absence was widely interpreted as an expression of displeasure with the court's school desegregation ruling. Governor Stanley sent word that his presence was required at a sale of cattle on his farm rather than on the dais with the Chief Justice of the United States, who received an honorary degree.

Governor Stanley had originally said that *Brown* called for "cool heads, calm study, and sound judgment" and promised to consult leaders of both races in the state.[4] By late September, however, the governor's attitude toward *Brown* had hardened into outright hostility; he vowed to fight any order to immediately desegregate the Virginia public schools by every available legal means.

Shortly before the opening of the new court term in early October, Warren noted the ominous change in attitude in the South toward *Brown*. He sent Frankfurter an article reporting the proposed disbarment of two attorneys for seeking to register black children in a segregated school. "I call your attention to the statement of Jimmy Byrnes concerning the isolated instances in the border states and inviting 'far more serious ones' in the deep south," he wrote.[5] Given the likely political exploitation of the *Brown* decision in the South, both Warren and Frankfurter thought it prudent to postpone reargument on the terms of the implementation decree until after the congressional midterm elections in November.

ON OCTOBER 9, less than a week after the court had begun its new term, Justice Robert Jackson died of a second heart attack. He was remembered for the vigor, incisiveness, and clarity of his judicial opinions. Warren and his brethren, in addition to mourning their colleague's death, were forced to contemplate their impending decision on *Brown*'s implementation decree without knowing who would take Jackson's place. Warren concluded that reargument on implementation of *Brown* would necessarily have to be delayed until the spring; the court would need to be at full strength for so momentous a decision.

Who would succeed Justice Jackson? Would Eisenhower possibly complicate matters for the Warren Court in *Brown* by appointing a white southerner who supported segregation? On November 8 the president gave his answer, nominating New York's John Marshall Harlan II, the grandson of the lone dissenter in *Plessy v. Ferguson*. The nominee's grandfather, the first Justice Harlan, had made constitutional history with his rousing dissent in *Plessy* declaring, "Our Constitution is color-blind, and neither knows nor tolerates classes among citizens."[6]

The symbolism of Eisenhower's nomination of Justice Harlan's grandson to the court was not missed by southern senators. Their opposition to the nominee was acknowledged by the chairman of the Judiciary Committee, who announced that Harlan's confirmation hearings would be delayed. No date for the hearings was set.

If Eisenhower intended to send a loaded message to segregationists with his nomination of Harlan, he did not say so publicly, in his private correspondence, or in his diary. In fact, the Harlan nomination was not Eisenhower's idea, but that of Attorney General Brownell, who was a longtime personal friend of Harlan. They had first met when both men worked as young lawyers in one of Wall Street's most prominent law firms, whose partners had included former secretary of state Elihu Root and New York governor Thomas E. Dewey. Eisenhower, on the recommendation of Brownell, had appointed Harlan to the U.S. Court of Appeals, Second Circuit, earlier in the year. At the time Brownell privately hoped that Harlan would later be named to the Supreme Court.

White southerner politicians excepted, Eisenhower's choice of Harlan was widely praised and highly meritorious. A graduate of Princeton and a Rhodes Scholar at Oxford, Harlan received his law degree from New York Law School before embarking on a successful legal career as a trial lawyer for private, mostly wealthy, corporate clients. Throughout his career, Harlan remained supremely aloof from the causes he represented—except in the courtroom. There he left no argument untouched, no judicial precedent unstudied. As with most great trial lawyers, Harlan owed his success to two rather unspectacular traits: thorough preparation and impeccable organization of his case. In his brief tenure on the federal appellate court, he quickly established his reputation as a lawyer's judge, fastidious in his study and articulation of the relevant law.

———————

AFTER WARREN HAD announced in *Brown* that the court would hear reargument on the implementation decree, Eisenhower was bombarded by his southern friends with pleas that the Justice Department refuse to participate in what would be known as *Brown II*. South Carolina governor Byrnes was especially active in the effort, but the president was also lobbied by governors Allan Shivers of Texas and Robert Kennon of Louisiana; all three governors were Democrats who had supported Eisenhower in his 1952 presidential campaign. They predicted that public schools in the South would shut down rather than follow a court order to desegregate and counseled the president to keep the executive branch of the federal government out of what they viewed as the inevitable battle between the southern states and the court.

In his *Brown* opinion, the chief justice had invited the Justice Department to submit a brief for the *Brown* reargument, an invitation that Attorney General Brownell was eager to accept. Brownell readily supported the position of his new solicitor general, Simon Sobeloff, who believed that the Justice Department should file a strong brief on the question of relief. But Brownell knew that he could not file such a brief if the president did not support it. And Eisenhower's strained endorsement of the court's decision in *Brown* cast doubt on his willingness to support the Justice Department's participation in the *Brown* reargument, much less sign off on an outspoken government brief advocating relief. Brownell, therefore, cautioned Sobeloff, who had been active in civil rights litigation in his home state of Maryland, that the Justice Department could not accept the court's invitation to participate without the president's approval. Sobeloff, nonetheless, worked on the Justice Department brief, having argued in a memorandum to Brownell during the summer that "the Supreme Court is

entitled to as much help as it can get in the difficult matter of formu-
lating the decrees to implement the decision we ourselves urged upon
the Court."[7]

Even though Eisenhower withheld his strong public endorsement
of *Brown*, there is no written evidence that he disapproved of the decision. He did not criticize the court's decision in public, in his private
correspondence, or in his diary entries. Nor did he hint at any animosity toward Warren. In a letter to his old Abilene friend, Swede Hazlett,
in October 1954, he predicted that the court in *Brown II* would "be
very moderate and accord a maximum of initiative to local courts,"
a pragmatic approach that comported with his own moderation in
dealing with difficult policy issues.[8] Implicit in such an approach
was his concern for states' rights and local governance. In the same
letter he also took the opportunity to challenge Hazlett's suggestion
that his appointment of Warren as chief justice was political. "It was
most emphatically not," Eisenhower wrote. The chief justice, in addition to demonstrating personal leadership, "must be a statesman and,
in my opinion (since I have my share of egotism), I could not do my
duty unless I appointed a man whose philosophy of government was
somewhat along the lines of my own." The president's description of
the qualities that had led him to appoint Warren appeared to remain
intact almost five months after the chief justice had announced the
court's *Brown* decision.

In a letter to his brother Edgar, two weeks later, Eisenhower wrote
that "the meaning of the Constitution is what the Supreme Court says
it is."[9] He admitted that he had disagreed with some Supreme Court
decisions, including unnamed decisions involving interstate commerce.
But he expressed no disagreement with the *Brown* decision.

During the fall, Solicitor General Sobeloff continued to work on the
Justice Department's brief for *Brown II* and on November 8 met with
Brownell to review his draft. The attorney general was satisfied with
the brief, which called for federal district courts to require desegrega-

The Warren family in 1894, the year Earl's father, Methias (top right), found work as a repairman and car inspector for the Southern Pacific Railroad in Bakersfield, California. From left, Methias's wife, Chrystal; Earl, age three; and Ethel, age seven. *(U.S. Supreme Court Archives)*

The Eisenhower family in 1902. Front: David, Milton, and Ida; back: Dwight, Edgar, Arthur, Earl, and Roy. Ida, warm, vivacious, and optimistic, was the emotional ballast for the family. *(Dwight D. Eisenhower Presidential Library & Museum)*

District Attorney Earl Warren (left) and deputies destroying a still during Prohibition. Warren relentlessly prosecuted bootleggers, bunco artists, murderers, and corrupt officials to earn the reputation as one of the most politically independent and respected district attorneys in the country. *(U.S. Supreme Court Archives)*

Major Eisenhower (right) accompanies his superior, General Douglas MacArthur, the army's chief of staff, to supervise the rout of World War I veterans, known as the Bonus Army, from downtown Washington in July 1932. Eisenhower later drafted the official report that commended "the exemplary conduct" of the army's troops. *(Getty/Bettmann)*

General Eisenhower visits troops of the 101st Airborne Division on the eve of D-Day, June 5, 1944. He stayed with the troops until the last man was airborne at midnight. *(Dwight D. Eisenhower Presidential Library & Museum)*

Governor Earl Warren on his campaign train surrounded by his family when he ran as the Republican candidate for vice president in 1948. Privately, Warren bristled under the tight control of strategists for the party's presidential nominee, Governor Thomas E. Dewey of New York. Democratic president Harry S. Truman defeated the Dewey-Warren ticket in a stunning upset. *(U.S. Supreme Court Archives)*

Senator Joseph McCarthy (R-Wis.) testifying before the Senate Foreign Relations Committee in March 1950. McCarthy wielded extraordinary political power with his unsubstantiated charges of subversion in the federal government. Eisenhower loathed McCarthy but, as president, refused to publicly condemn him, believing that depriving the senator of the publicity he craved was the best antidote to his demagoguery. *(U.S. Information Agency, courtesy of the Dwight D. Eisenhower Presidential Library & Museum)*

General Eisenhower, the Republican candidate for president in 1952, campaigning in California with Governor Warren. Eisenhower insisted in his memoirs that he owed Warren no political debt but, nonetheless, appointed him in 1953 to fill the first Supreme Court vacancy during his presidency, replacing Chief Justice Fred Vinson. *(U.S. Supreme Court Archives)*

President Eisenhower and his wife, Mamie, with Chief Justice Warren and his wife, Nina, shortly after Warren was sworn in at the Supreme Court on October 5, 1953. In announcing the Warren appointment, Eisenhower predicted that he would be "a great chief justice." The initially warm Eisenhower-Warren relationship disintegrated into mutual suspicion and harsh recriminations.
(Photograph by Harris & Ewing, Collection of the Supreme Court of the United States)

The justices of the U.S. Supreme Court meet with President Eisenhower and administration officials at the White House in November 1953, six months before they would rule in *Brown v. Board of Education*. Front row: William O. Douglas, Stanley F. Reed, Chief Justice Warren, President Eisenhower, Hugo Black, Felix Frankfurter. Back row: third from left, Robert H. Jackson, Tom C. Clark, Sherman Minton, Harold H. Burton, unknown, Attorney General Herbert Brownell, Jr.
(National Park Service, courtesy of the Dwight D. Eisenhower Presidential Library & Museum)

The victorious lead attorney for the NAACP, Thurgood Marshall (center), with his deputies, George Hayes (left) and James Nabrit, Jr. (right), on the steps of the U.S. Supreme Court after the Warren Court had announced on May 17, 1954, in *Brown* that public school segregation by race was unconstitutional. *(AP Photo)*

Soldiers of the 101st Airborne Division escorting nine black students into Central High School, Little Rock, Arkansas, on September 25, 1957. President Eisenhower had ordered the federal troops to Little Rock to enforce a federal court decree to desegregate the high school in compliance with *Brown* after he had failed to persuade Arkansas governor Orval E. Faubus to obey the law. Eisenhower insisted that he was upholding the rule of law, not endorsing the court's *Brown* decision, a position that angered Chief Justice Warren. *(National Archives)*

"IMPEACH EARL WARREN" billboards were erected throughout the Deep South in the early 1960s. The chief justice was vilified for the court's desegregation rulings as well as for decisions upholding the constitutional rights of suspected subversives. *(Bob Fitch Photography Archive, Department of Special Collections, Stanford University Library)*

President Eisenhower greeting President-elect John F. Kennedy on the steps of the White House after the Massachusetts senator's election in 1960. Eisenhower resented Kennedy's attacks on his administration during the presidential campaign but later became a valued counselor to the young president during the Cuban missile crisis in 1962. *(National Park Service, courtesy of the Dwight D. Eisenhower Presidential Library & Museum)*

Chief Justice Warren with members of the Warren Commission presenting their report to President Lyndon B. Johnson in September 1964. The commission concluded that Lee Harvey Oswald had acted alone in the assassination of President Kennedy. Despite the controversy over the commission's findings, Warren never wavered in his belief that Oswald was the lone assassin. *(National Archives)*

Chief Justice Warren, President Richard Nixon, and Warren's successor, Chief Justice Warren E. Burger, on the steps of the Supreme Court, June 23, 1969, after the president had spoken at the ceremony in which Burger was sworn in. Warren despised Nixon and feared that the new chief justice and other Nixon appointees would overrule major Warren Court decisions that had expanded the constitutional rights of criminal defendants. *(AP Photo)*

tion plans from local school districts within ninety days of the implementation decree. Brownell delegated to Sobeloff the delicate task of
persuading the president to approve the brief. Less than two weeks
later, on Saturday morning, November 20, Eisenhower met with Sobeloff and other Justice Department attorneys to discuss the brief. The
president then spent approximately a half hour alone reviewing the
brief and making several revealing handwritten revisions.

Eisenhower changed the last word in this key sentence: "Racial segregation in public schools is unconstitutional and will have to be terminated as quickly as possible."[10] He substituted the word "feasible"
for "possible" at the end of the sentence in an apparent effort to make
the implementation standard more flexible. In the margin of the brief,
the president also wrote that "the Court's finding that segregation is
a denial of constitutional rights is recognition of the importance of
emotional [factors]; it is recognition that the impact upon the emotions of children can so affect their entire lives as to preclude their full
enjoyment of constitutional rights." The president's addition implicitly validated one of the most controversial points made in Warren's
opinion—that psychological factors affected the ability of black students to learn in segregated schools.* Eisenhower added another sentence that demonstrated his sensitivity to the difficulties faced by white
southerners asked to change both their customs and the law. "In similar fashion," he wrote, "emotions are involved in the alterations that
must now take place in [illegible] during the years that not only had
the sanction of Supreme Court decisions but have been fervently supported by great numbers of people as both legal and moral."[11]

After Eisenhower made several other minor changes, he approved

* The final Justice Department draft submitted to the court added the words
"psychological and" before "emotional" in the sentence revised by Eisenhower.
(Kramer, Victor H., "President Eisenhower's Handwritten Changes in the Brief in
the School Segregation Cases: Minding the Whys and Wherefores," 9 *Minnesota
Law Review* 223 [1992], p. 228.)

the brief. The essential substance and forceful language in Sobeloff's brief, which strongly supported court-ordered desegregation, survived the president's scrutiny. The brief filed by the Justice Department stated: "Racial segregation in public schools is unconstitutional and will have to be terminated as quickly as feasible, regardless of how much it may be favored by some people in the community. There can be no 'local' option on that question, which has now been finally settled by the tribunal empowered under the Constitution to decide it."[12]

Eisenhower was "entirely satisfied" with Sobeloff's brief, Brownell later recalled, a tribute to the solicitor general's diplomacy as well as his advocacy.[13] But the president must also be given credit. He signed off on Sobeloff's brief knowing that it would be condemned by his political friends in the South. As president, he still hoped to keep the conversation open with southern leaders to avoid massive resistance to the court's decree.

WHILE SOBELOFF WAS deeply engaged in drafting the Justice Department's brief, a fierce debate was taking place at the NAACP over the timeline for implementation that its brief should recommend to the court. Dr. Kenneth Clark, the sociologist who had testified on the psychological harm to black students in segregated schools, urged Thurgood Marshall to demand immediate implementation of the desegregation order. He was supported by one of Marshall's chief deputies, Spottswood Robinson III, who had argued the Virginia case for the organization. On the other side was another valued Marshall adviser, William Coleman, an honors graduate of Harvard Law School and former clerk to Justice Frankfurter. Coleman cautioned that such a demand could irritate the court. "We would be much better off under a decree which would permit the States to file for Court approval plans which would permit . . . gradual effective transition," he wrote Marshall.[14]

Marshall was uncertain whether to take the aggressive approach recommended by Clark and Robinson or the more moderate, gradualist position favored by Coleman. Ultimately, Marshall's brief, submitted to the court in November, came closer to the Clark-Robinson position, calling for immediate desegregation but also suggesting some flexibility, recommending that "the outer limit" for compliance be September 1956.[15]

Meanwhile, three parties in *Brown*—Kansas, Delaware, and the District of Columbia—assured the court in their briefs that they had already begun the process of desegregation without any goading from the justices. But no such assurance was given in the briefs from the two southern states that were parties to the suit, South Carolina and Virginia, or the *amicus* briefs submitted by six other southern and border states with segregated public schools. To the contrary, their briefs showed both frustration and anger at the court's edict and hinted at the likelihood of defiance among the white residents of their states should the court order immediate desegregation.

South Carolina's brief urged the court to show "a decent respect" for the sovereignty of the states.[16] Any attempt by the court to set up "criteria of desegregation," the brief continued, would be an invasion of the state's prerogative. Virginia's brief stated that white Virginians "feel a sense of bewilderment that traditions and systems that have operated with judicial approval since 1870, and, in fact, since 1619, can be so readily swept away."[17] The brief also included the text of a resolution passed two months after *Brown* by the Board of Supervisors of Prince Edward County, the Virginia county challenged in the school segregation cases, stating that it was "unalterably opposed to the operation of nonsegregated public schools in the commonwealth of Virginia" and pledged to use its "power, authority and efforts to insure a continuation of a segregated system." Florida's *amicus* brief reminded the justices that the state's public school segregation laws had been "rigidly" enforced for the previous sixty-nine years. "[A]n immediate inrush of turbulent ideas," the brief suggested, might cause "a tornado which would devastate the entire school system."[18]

Months before the court had scheduled the reargument in *Brown*, southern governors vowed to fight *any* desegregation order. Governor Byrnes of South Carolina publicly called on his state legislature to preserve school segregation by placing control of public schools in the hands of local boards and to end compulsory school attendance laws. When Byrnes made his request of the legislature, his state, as well as Georgia and Mississippi, had already taken steps toward turning the schools over to private ownership as a last resort to preserve segregation. Georgia governor Marvin Griffin was even more defiant. "[B]oth the white and colored races have been living in peace and harmony here in Georgia," Griffin declared, adding that "we want to keep it that way."[19]

MIDWAY THROUGH HIS first presidential term, Eisenhower continued to adhere to his campaign pledge to govern as a middle-of-the-road, nonideological leader. He believed in a smaller federal government, lower taxes, and a balanced budget, all staples of economic conservatism identified with the Republican Party. But he also supported social security, unemployment insurance, and trade unions, political centerpieces of the New and Fair Deals of the Roosevelt and Truman administrations. He deplored the reactionaries in his own party whom he characterized as "the isolationists, the high tariff people, the union busters, and the anti-social security people" in a letter to Bill Robinson.[20] He was equally dismissive of those he characterized as "left-wingers," the extreme liberals in the Democratic Party "who believe that the Federal government should enter into every phase and facet of our individual lives . . . who knowingly or unknowingly, are trying to put us on the path toward socialism."[21]

Eisenhower spoke admiringly of President Abraham Lincoln as

a great compromiser, challenging the characterization of Lincoln as a "radical Republican" by Ike's old military friend, retired Brigadier General B. G. Chynoweth. In his response to Chynoweth, Eisenhower wrote, "[E]very bit of reading I have done on [Lincoln's] life convinces me that in many ways he was the greatest compromiser and the most astute master of expediency that we have known."[22] He added, "I believe the true radical is the fellow who is standing in the middle and battling both extremes."

Eisenhower stacked his cabinet with successful businessmen such as Charles Wilson, his secretary of defense, who had been the head of General Motors, and George Humphrey, secretary of the treasury, who had served as president of a multinational conglomerate involved in iron and steel production. He worried that the financial sacrifice was too great to attract more business leaders from the private sector, leaving, by default, important government positions to "business failures, college professors, and New Deal lawyers."[23] But the president also counted among his closest advisers moderates like Attorney General Brownell and his brother Milton Eisenhower, a prominent academic who was then president of Pennsylvania State University and had held high-level positions in the Roosevelt and Truman administrations.

In the fall of 1954, Eisenhower was immensely popular, his approval ratings consistently topping 60 percent. His calm, reassuring public demeanor appeared well suited to the mood of the nation. The United States was at peace and, after Joseph Stalin's death in 1953, new leadership in the Soviet Union raised the possibility of a thaw in the Cold War. At home, America's middle class was growing, and so were the mushrooming miles of suburbs. The new age of television not only inspired a culinary phenomenon, the TV dinner, but also reordered Americans' domestic routines. The water commissioner of Toledo, puzzled that water consumption rose dramatically during certain three minute periods, finally hit upon the explanation: residents were flushing their toilets during television commercials. The tumultuous Army-

McCarthy hearings were over, and Americans had happily returned to weekly episodes of "I Love Lucy."

But there were disquieting signs in the economy. Agricultural prices were dropping, and the textile and auto industries were laying off workers. Mounting unemployment figures coincided with the fall congressional elections. Suddenly, the Republicans' congressional majority was in jeopardy.

Nervous party leaders urged Eisenhower to campaign for vulnerable congressional Republicans. Responding to one such plea from New York governor Thomas Dewey, Eisenhower agreed with Dewey that he would face severe difficulties in working with a Congress controlled by Democrats. But then he ticked off his reasons for refusing to campaign for fellow Republicans. "I believe the American people like to feel that their President is not as completely partisan as is a candidate," he wrote. In addition, he continued, "History proves that no President, regardless of his popularity, can pass that popularity on to a Party or to an individual."[24] He also worried about conserving his energy. "[A]fter all, I am 64 years old," he wrote. "The presidency is a job that would tax the intellectual and physical energies of a far younger man."

Republicans lost control of both houses of Congress in the November elections, causing party leaders to lean more heavily than ever on Eisenhower to ensure their political future. The party appeared likely to face defeat in the next presidential election if Eisenhower did not run for a second term. Ike's old friend and adviser Lucius Clay went further, telling the president that only he could assure a reformed and revitalized Republican Party. Reflecting on this conversation with Clay in his diary, Ike agreed that "the Republican party must be known as a progressive organization or it is sunk" and must ignore or repudiate the "the dyed-in-the-wool reactionary fringe."[25]

But Eisenhower was unwilling to accept the next step in Clay's syllogism: only his reelection, Clay had argued, could save the moderate wing of the Republican Party. Ike doubted that any man was indispensable to the party's future.[26] But he also questioned whether he, starting a second term at the age of sixty-six, would have the physical and intellectual vitality to deal with the complex problems of the modern presidency. It would be better for the party and the nation, he maintained, to have a younger man in the White House. He also raised a pragmatic consideration: historically, lame-duck presidents lose their power to get things done the instant they take their second oath of office.

Eisenhower reiterated his opposition to seeking a second term in a letter to Hazlett in early December. "[T]he only thing that could possibly make me change my mind would be an unforeseen national emergency that might possibly convince me that it was my duty to stay on."[27] But he bristled when Senate Republican leader Knowland suggested in a television interview on *Meet the Press* in January 1955 that Republicans should not draft a reluctant Eisenhower for a second term and stressed that no man was indispensable to the party. Ike commented that in Knowland's case there seems to be no final answer to the question "How stupid can you get?"[28] He then restated that "[i]f I feel, in 1956, that there is no patriotic compulsion on me to run (war or imminent war), I shall not do so. But it will be my decision and no action of the Republican Party will have the slightest effect."

At the time of his *Meet the Press* interview, Knowland was considered a dark horse candidate for the Republican nomination. The Republican most frequently mentioned as the party's presidential nominee in 1956, should Eisenhower refuse to run, was Chief Justice Earl Warren.

CHIEF JUSTICE WARREN'S record during his first two years in office, like President Eisenhower's, was that of a moderate, nonideological leader. His *Brown* opinion, supported by both the liberal and

conservative wings of the court, was replete with the language of compromise. It delayed action on implementation, confined the impact
of the desegregation ruling to public schools, avoided emotional language, refused to stigmatize segregationists, and invited the southern
states in the case (South Carolina and Virginia) to participate in the
formulation of a remedy. In forging consensus, Warren had worked
closely with Frankfurter, who was the court's leading proponent of
judicial restraint.

Warren's willingness to compromise in *Brown* was reminiscent of
his years as California's governor who was so adept at finding common
ground among Republicans and Democrats. His early voting pattern
on the court also suggested the influence of his previous experience
as a county prosecutor in California. In his first two court terms, the
chief justice consistently supported the government in criminal law
and procedure cases. His prosecutorial perspective was demonstrated
in his decisive fifth vote in *Irvine v. California*.[29] In *Irvine*, the court
majority found no constitutional violation in the case of a California
man convicted of bookmaking despite the fact that the incriminating
evidence was supplied by secretly installed police wiretaps in the defendant's home without his knowledge or a warrant.

Warren's well-documented anticommunism throughout his career
in California appeared to influence his early votes on the court when
civil liberties claims were raised by defendants accused of disloyalty.
He had voted with the court majority that sustained the suspension of
the medical license of a prominent New York physician who refused to
provide information to the House Un-American Activities Committee about a suspected subversive organization. And he wrote the opinion for the court that sidestepped the constitutional issue raised by Dr.
John Peters, a senior professor at the Yale University Medical School,
who had been dismissed from his job as a special consultant to a federal
agency because the government's Loyalty Review Board concluded that

there was "reasonable doubt" of his loyalty. Dr. Peters claimed that the denial of his opportunity to confront and cross-examine his accusers violated his constitutional right to due process. Warren based his opinion for the court in the Peters case on procedural grounds, writing, in the best tradition of judicial restraint, that "this Court has declined to anticipate a question of constitutional law in advance of the necessity of deciding it."[30]

If Chief Justice Warren's nonideological approach to the law in his early judicial tenure had its roots in his political career, so too did his strong moral sensibility demonstrated in his *Brown* opinion. As governor, he was outraged that most Californians could not afford adequate health care, which motivated him to push for government-sponsored medical insurance. That his drive was long and ultimately futile did not diminish Warren's fervor or conviction that the state's failure to provide health insurance for its poor and middle-class citizens was wrong. Warren's *Brown* opinion was similarly infused with an unmistakable moral tone: segregation was not just unconstitutional but wrong.

———

BOTH WARREN AND Eisenhower waited impatiently for the Senate to confirm the president's nomination of John Marshall Harlan II to fill the vacancy on the court left by Justice Jackson's death. Harlan's appointment languished in the Senate Judiciary Committee for months, due primarily to opposition from southern senators. Finally, the nomination was confirmed by the Senate on March 16, 1955; nine senators from the South voted against the confirmation.

Eisenhower wrote Harlan a brief letter of congratulations after the Senate vote, expressing his confidence that he would serve with "wisdom, ability, and high distinction."[31] He also told Harlan that he regretted that "you were subject to the harassment and delay that was involved in the confirmation of your appointment. I assure you, however, that as I have grown wiser, I hope, in the ways of political life, such things tend to bother me less—or perhaps I merely become inured to them."

With the Warren Court finally at full strength, the *Brown* reargument was placed on the court's docket for April 11.

————

THE COURT SCHEDULED seventeen hours for the reargument in *Brown,* spread over four days during the second week in April. The extended time was necessary to allow arguments, in addition to the parties to the lawsuits, by those states that had submitted *amicus* briefs as well as the Justice Department. Capacity crowds, equally divided between white and black onlookers, filled the courtroom each day of the reargument. Every three minutes during the reargument a new batch of schoolchildren was ushered through maroon velvet curtains to take their seats at the back of the courtroom. The atmosphere in the courtroom was suffused with taut excitement. And yet there was a quiet dignity that pervaded the proceedings, dominated by the large presence of Chief Justice Warren.

The most charismatic participant in the *Brown I* argument, John W. Davis, the attorney for the state of South Carolina, was absent from the courtroom. He had died at his South Carolina vacation home at the age of eighty-one a few weeks prior to the reargument. In fact, he had bowed out of the case shortly after the court announced its decision in *Brown I*. "We have met the enemy and we are theirs," he had written Charleston, South Carolina, attorney Robert Figg, who worked with Davis on the case.[32] "I have no stomach for personal participation in the Court's effort to frame a decree." He declined a fee of $25,000 from South Carolina, his way of reciprocating for the hospitality that he had enjoyed for many years from the people of the state. Instead, he accepted a sterling silver tea service.

The urbane Davis had been replaced by S. Emory Rogers, a blunt, combative lawyer from the small town of Summerton in Clarendon County, South Carolina. Rogers, scion of the plantation aristocracy in the rural county, attempted to explain to the court the racial facts of life in his county.[33] He described the "terrific problems" facing his county where the small number of white families living on the large estates had been asked by the court to send their children to public schools with an overwhelming majority of poor blacks. Referring to Warren's opinion in *Brown I* that the court could not turn the clock back to 1868 (when the Fourteenth Amendment was ratified) or 1896 (when *Plessy* was decided), Rogers countered, "I do not believe that in a biracial society we can push the clock forward abruptly to 2015 or 2045." It would take many years before the public schools in Clarendon County could be desegregated, he told the justices, and advised them to send the case back to the county "without instructions."

Warren interrupted, asking Rogers to clarify what he meant by a decree "without instructions." Was his recommendation based on the assumption that the county school district would "immediately undertake to conform to the opinion of this Court of last year?"

"Mr. Chief Justice," replied Rogers, "to say we will conform depends on the decree handed down. I am frank to tell you right now in our district I do not think that we will send—the white people of the district will send their children to the Negro schools. It would be unfair to tell the Court that we are going to do that.... But I do think that something can be worked out. We hope so."

Rogers's audacious offer "to work something out" with the Supreme Court of the United States severely challenged the outward calm of the chief justice.[34] "It is not a question of attitude," Warren replied curtly. "It is a question of conforming to the decree. Is there any basis upon which we can assume that there will be an immediate attempt to comply with the decree of this Court, whatever it may be?"

Rogers refused to give the chief justice the assurance he was seeking—that the school district would comply with a decree issued by the court, even if the specific order was left to a district court.

Warren stared down at the attorney. "But you are not willing to say here that there would be an honest attempt to conform to this decree, if we did leave it to the district court?"

"No, I am not," replied Rogers, poking his forefinger toward Warren. "Let us get the word 'honest' out of there."

"No, leave it in," snapped Warren, his face flushed.

"No," Rogers said, "because I would have to tell you that right now we would not conform—we would not send our white children to the Negro schools."

Warren appeared so disturbed by Rogers's defiance that Virginia attorney general Almond, who was in the courtroom during the tense exchange, thought the chief justice might charge Rogers with contempt of court. But he did not.

"Thank you," Warren said, signaling to Rogers that his time for argument had expired.

When Almond addressed the court on behalf of Virginia, he was more respectful than Rogers but no less discouraging when asked about the state's willingness to accept a court decree ordering immediate desegregation. He told the justices that "forthwith enforcement of integration would be pre-emptive of the rights of a sovereign people" and asserted that the public schools of his state "might have to close" if an abrupt end to segregation were ordered. He predicted that "enforced integration of the races" would not occur in Virginia's Prince Edward County "in the lifetime of those of us hale and hearty here."

John Ben Shepperd, attorney general of Texas, one of the six states submitting an *amicus* brief, declared that "Texas loves its Negro people," but, nonetheless, admonished the justices that any attempt of immediate desegregation would be "rash, imprudent and unrealistic." And the attorney for North Carolina, another southern state that had submitted an *amicus* brief, warned that a court order requiring immediate desegregation might provoke "racial tension and animosities unparalleled since those terrible days that gave rise to the original Ku Klux Klan."

U.S. Solicitor General Sobeloff, representing the Eisenhower administration, treaded carefully as he attempted to steer a moderate course. He suggested that the court not issue an immediate order to desegregate, but that the states and local communities receive a reasonable time to integrate their public schools. But he said that a "reasonable time" was not an invitation for officials to "drag their feet," and that "discretion must not be used to accomplish frustration." He reiterated the plan recommended in the Justice Department's brief: that the cases be remanded to the appropriate federal district courts with instructions to local authorities to submit within ninety days a plan to end segregation "as soon as feasible."

Sobeloff's argument for a "reasonable time" to implement the court's desegregation decree, with built-in time limits for the submission of local plans, sharply contrasted in both tenor and substance with the proposals urged by lawyers from the southern states. They called for "gradual" desegregation, but their generous time frames for implementation ranged from five to ninety years. And the southern attorneys' unmistakable undercurrent of dread and loathing at the prospect of the mixing of the races in their states' public classrooms strongly suggested the possibility of massive resistance to the court's ruling.

If the Justice Department's recommendation was offered as a good faith, middle-of-the-road proposal, it nonetheless fell far short of the NAACP's expectations. At the reargument, Spottswood Robinson III, again arguing the Virginia case for the organization, asserted that desegregation should begin when public schools opened in the fall. The rights involved were those of children, he said, "and if they are ever going to be satisfied, they must be satisfied while they are still children."

Thurgood Marshall was even bolder. Once he stood at the podium, his earlier reservations in demanding immediate desegregation had vanished. There can be no middle ground on constitutional rights, he told the justices. The idea that constitutional rights can be postponed was unheard of "until Negroes are involved." The Constitution does not recognize a "local option on the Fourteenth Amendment in the question of rights," he asserted, refusing to grant any special consideration to southern counties where segregation had been entrenched for centuries. If the court left the timing and substance of the plans to the district courts, he predicted that "the Negro in this country would be in a horrible shape. He, as a matter of fact, would be as bad, if not worse, off than under the 'separate but equal doctrine.'"

ON APRIL 14, shortly after the court had heard the final reargument in *Brown*, Justice Frankfurter sent a memorandum to his colleagues laying out his views on an implementation decree.[35] The court must exercise caution and not function as a "super-school board," he wrote. He then posed two possible approaches. The first would be a narrow "bare bones" decree permanently barring segregation in the school districts challenged in the cases before the court. Alternatively, Frankfurter suggested, the court's decree might be drafted in more general language that would allow the district courts to take into account local attitudes in devising a desegregation plan.[35] It would also provide a set of guidelines for the lower courts "and yet not serve as the mere imposition of a distant will."

When Chief Justice Warren convened the justices' conference on Saturday, April 16, to discuss the implementation decision, he and his brethren possessed, in addition to Frankfurter's memo, a lengthy advisory report that Warren had requested the previous summer from six law clerks.[36] His charge to the clerks was to provide their thoughts on how the court could best accomplish desegregation. The clerks concluded, as had Frankfurter, that the court's decree should be simple and remand the cases to the district courts with guidelines for execution. They differed, however, on the timeline for desegregation. One clerk opposed a decree allowing a "gradual" approach to desegregation, arguing that such an order would "greatly weaken the Court's moral position."[37] But the other five clerks concluded that a court decree ordering immediate desegregation was "impractical" and likely to be ignored by the most recalcitrant school districts in the South. They offered a number of suggestions, ranging from leaving the timing entirely to the district courts to a process allowing up to twelve years for the full integration of the school districts.

Warren opened the justices' conference by conceding that he had not reached any firm conclusion on the court's implementation decision and was willing to extend the discussions for as long as was needed. Though he did not say it, implicit in the chief justice's openended schedule for discussion was his unspoken goal of a unanimous court decision. At the outset, he emphasized that he believed the justices should give district courts great flexibility in overseeing the desegregation process, a position supported by Frankfurter's memo as well as five of the six clerks who had sent him their advisory report. He suggested a court opinion rather than a decree that would allow lower-court judges to decide if specific segregation plans from school districts should be required and whether to set deadlines for the completion of the desegregation process. He, like Frankfurter, did not want the court to function as a "super-school board." He also agreed with Frankfurter that the court should provide broad guidelines for the lower courts that, Warren suggested, might take into consideration financial problems and the conditions of local schools. So long as school districts were acting in good faith and progress was being made toward desegregation, Warren concluded, the court should give district courts "as much latitude as we can but also as much support as we can."[38]

Hugo Black, as the senior associate justice, spoke after Warren and presented a starkly pessimistic perspective on the future of enforced school desegregation in the Deep South. Recalling his upbringing in rural Alabama, he described the negative attitude of southern whites toward the authority of the federal government, especially on the question of race. "The South would never be a willing party to Negroes and whites going to school together," he said.[39] "There's no more chance of enforcing school integration in the deep South than Prohibition in New York City," he continued. The court should "say and do as little as possible," he advised, warning against issuing an order it could not enforce. The best the court could hope for was "glacial movement" toward desegregation. "It is futile to think that in these cases we can settle segregation in the South," he concluded.

Only a single sentence in Black's otherwise dark assessment offered the chief justice any encouragement: "If humanly possible," Black said, "I will do everything possible to achieve a unanimous result."

Warren's prospects for forging a consensus brightened after Black had spoken. The two other justices from segregated states, Clark of Texas and Reed of Kentucky, offered more sanguine assessments of the likelihood that a court decision could effect meaningful desegregation in the South. Clark did not think an enforcement order would be "too much trouble in Texas."[40] And Reed, the last justice to have signed on to Warren's *Brown I* opinion, expressed his "firm belief" that a significant group of white southerners in the South would be "willing to give sympathetic consideration" to the enforcement problem. Once the desegregation process began, he thought that the pace would move more quickly.

In a tribute to Warren's leadership, Frankfurter welcomed the "candid relaxed way" in which the justices were discussing the profoundly difficult issue of implementing *Brown I*.[41] He predicted that desegregation would begin in the border states and spread gradually to the Deep South. It was important, he said, that the court demonstrate a sympathy for the problems involved in the South, an attitude he had expressed in private correspondence with Warren. The decision, he stressed, should serve as a valuable reminder that the court represented the entire United States, including the Deep South.

Several justices emphasized the importance of a unanimous decision. The newest member of the court, Associate Justice Harlan, joined his brethren in requesting that the chief justice draft an opinion for the court.

Within a week, Warren had written a first draft, which remained largely unchanged after his colleagues had reviewed it. His final opinion, announced on May 31, 1955, was just seven paragraphs and covered the main points he had made in conference. Without mentioning the words "segregation" or "desegregation" in his opinion, he acknowledged "the complexities arising from the transition to a system of public education freed of racial discrimination." He gave district courts broad supervisory authority and assigned primary responsibility for implementation to local school districts. The court anticipated that the defendant school districts would "make a prompt and reasonable start toward full compliance" with the court's original desegregation ruling of May 17, 1954. Without setting a timetable, Warren wrote that the court expected a good-faith effort to achieve desegregation "as soon as practicable."[42] At the end of his opinion, Warren remanded the cases to the district courts to see that the public schools be desegregated "with all deliberate speed."*[43]

It was not the decision that had been pressed upon the court by the NAACP's Thurgood Marshall, who had argued that the court should

---

* The phrase "with all deliberate speed" was used in Frankfurter's memorandum of January 1954 in anticipation of the court's deliberations in *Brown II* on an implementation decree. Frankfurter had borrowed the phrase from the 1911 court opinion written by Justice Oliver Wendell Holmes, Jr., in a controversy over the public debt owed to the state of Virginia by West Virginia. The phrase had first been used in the school segregation cases by Justice Department attorney Philip Elman, a former Frankfurter clerk, in the department's brief submitted before the first *Brown* argument in December 1952.

set a deadline requiring fully integrated public schools no later than September, 1956. The "all deliberate speed" phrase in Warren's opinion set no quantifiable limit on the desegregation process, offering school districts maximum flexibility in complying with the court's order. The court did not even impose the stricture on local school districts that had been recommended in the Justice Department brief—the submission of a desegregation plan to the district court within ninety days.

The Warren opinion in *Brown II* came closest to responding to the arguments made by the attorneys for the southern states that urged a gradual process of desegregation with no time limit. But whereas Warren's opinion was written in a spirit of hopeful reconciliation with the segregated South, the vehemence with which the attorneys from the southern states had argued that immediate desegregation was impossible suggested that they had no expectation that desegregation would take place in the Deep South in the foreseeable future.

———

THE DAY THAT *Brown II* was decided, Virginia attorney general Almond's prediction of his state's resistance to desegregation proved grimly prophetic. The school board of Prince Edward County, the Virginia district that Almond had represented before the court, voted to cease funding its public schools. Two days later a state judge ruled that bond money for school construction could not be spent on any desegregated school. And the state's leading newspaper, the *Richmond News Leader*, carried an editorial charging that *Brown II* was not law and urging the South to see that " 'that as soon as practical' means not at all."[44]

Georgia governor Marvin Griffin, who had successfully campaigned on a pledge of maintaining segregated schools "come hell or high water," ignored the court's decision, declaring "we will continue to run our schools as we always have."[45]

But the editorial response to the court's decision in leading newspapers in other southern states was positive, an encouraging reaction that

Warren and Frankfurter had anticipated among moderate leaders in the South. "The Supreme Court recognized that the process of desegregation in public schools will not come easily," the *Miami* [Florida] *Herald* editorialized.[46] "In its wisdom it has directed a course of gradual compliance, thereby giving the South the opportunity to adjust itself to the court's history-making decision of May 17, 1954." The *Louisville* [Kentucky] *Courier Journal* urged a good-faith effort to comply with the court's "all deliberate speed" mandate. "Any effort by segregationists to maintain the status quo through delay will be the product of passion rather than wisdom."[47] The *Raleigh* [North Carolina] *News and Observer* reported that the court "has gone about as far as any Southerner could have expected," recognizing that local conditions must be taken into account by supervising federal district courts.[48]

Meanwhile, Thurgood Marshall concluded that the court's decision, even without the specific desegregation deadline he had advocated, could still serve as an effective legal instrument to force integration of public schools in rebellious southern states. "The more I think about it, I think it's a damned good decision," he told his good friend, Carl Murphy, president of Baltimore's *Afro-American* newspaper.[49] Armed with the *Brown II* decision, Marshall was prepared to take any southern state to court that failed to follow the court's directive to dismantle its segregated schools. "Virginia we're going to bust wide open!" he exclaimed.

"I don't see any reason why, if we beat Virginia and Carolina, the rest of them aren't going to wake up," Murphy responded.[50]

"You're damned right they are," said Marshall. "You can say all you want but those white crackers are going to get tired of having Negro lawyers beating 'em every day in court."

————

ATTORNEY GENERAL BROWNELL telephoned Eisenhower shortly after *Brown II* was announced to tell him that the justices had done "almost exactly" as the president had hoped: they had produced a moderate decision that left enforcement of public school desegregation to the district courts.[51] The president had predicted that the court would demonstrate just that spirit of moderation in a letter to his friend Swede Hazlett in October 1954, seven months before the court's decision.

Although the court delivered a decision that met Eisenhower's limited, pragmatic expectations, the president conspicuously ignored the ruling. No public statement was issued from the White House, although the New York Times reported that "[o]fficials in the Eisenhower Administration generally were gratified by the court's ruling."[52]

Three days later, Eisenhower extolled individual liberty, but confined his remarks to the victims of Nazi tyranny. The occasion was a ceremony in the Rose Garden with a group of leaders of the United Jewish Appeal who honored Eisenhower's humanitarian service as Supreme Allied Commander during World War II. The president asserted that the Allied forces had represented "what we would call the heart of freedom, the belief that all people are entitled to life, liberty and the pursuit of happiness—that where these are denied one man, they are threatened for all."[53]

A day after the Rose Garden ceremony, Eisenhower wrote a long letter to Swede Hazlett discussing domestic legislation (tax reduction, pay and reform of the postal services, a new farm program), foreign policy, and his reluctance to run for a second presidential term. He did not mention Brown II.[54]

In a pre–press conference briefing on June 8, Eisenhower appeared to take little notice of the court's decision. The notes taken at the briefing by his personal secretary, Ann Whitman, gave only the slightest attention to Brown II. She typed: "Segregation ruling—going back to the states. [Jerry] Persons (the president's longtime aide), said a number of very complimentary editorials had been written about it."[55] Whitman's notes are more extensive under the heading "On segregation," with separate subsections for federal and local programs. "In federal programs," she wrote, "no place for segregation; have largely eradicated it there—historic progress in veterans hospitals, armed forces, civilian employment, District of Columbia theaters and restaurants." In the second subsection, listed as "predominantly local affairs," Whitman wrote: "federal approach should be by example and persuasion; exceptional progress here also in past two years."*

At his press conference on June 8, the president called reporters' attention to the invitation by the Soviet Union to West German chancellor Conrad Adenauer as well as to the robust U.S. employment figures for the month of May.[56] He did not say a word about *Brown II*.

———

WHILE THE PRESIDENT was studiously inattentive to *Brown II*, resistance to the court's decision in the Deep South began to gain momentum. Four states—Georgia, Louisiana, Mississippi, and South Carolina—adopted rigidly intransigent attitudes toward the court's decision. Their officials prepared programs to abolish public education, to make segregated schools a matter of public welfare under the state police powers, or, in some instances, to cut off tax funds where desegregation was attempted. In Virginia, Governor Stanley announced that his state would continue to maintain segregated public schools for the next school year. Alabama's state senate unanimously passed a bill aimed at continuing school segregation, then considered a resolution calling for the impeachment of the justices of the U.S. Supreme Court.

* A *Washington Post* editorial, published in late April, underscored the president's view of the administration's accomplishments in eliminating segregation in the District of Columbia, complementing "the broader stimulus of the Administration on a national scale in reducing the cancer of racism." Referring to the *Post*'s earlier criticism of the administration's civil rights policies, the editorial stated: "Now we are happy to acknowledge that it has become one of the the strongest features of the Eisenhower Administration—and the community and the country are healthier for it." (*Washington Post*, April 22, 1955.)

The *Richmond News Leader* summed up the growing opposition in the South to the court's *Brown* decisions: "In May of 1954, that inept fraternity of politicians and professors known as the United States Supreme Court chose to throw away the established law. These nine men repudiated the Constitution, spit upon the Tenth Amendment, and rewrote the fundamental law of this land to suit their own gauzy concepts of sociology. If it be said now that the South is flouting the law, let it be said to the high court, *You taught us how.*"[57]

Crosses were burned in front of the Washington residences of Chief Justice Warren and several other Supreme Court justices. Early one Sunday morning, Attorney General Brownell discovered that kerosene had been dumped on the ground under the bedrooms where his children slept. Afterward, the FBI provided protection at Brownell's residence and accompanied his children to school and to their social activities.

WHY DID EISENHOWER make such a concerted effort to put distance between himself and the court's *Brown II* decision? One reason, Attorney General Brownell suggested, was that both Eisenhower and Brownell were disappointed that the court's decision had not included the ninety-day deadline recommended by the Justice Department. Had the court set a specific deadline for desegregation plans, Brownell wrote in his memoirs, the Justice Department would have had the authority to "step in as soon as a [district] court approved the plan to enforce desegregation."[58] But Brownell added that the president was "relieved" that the federal government was not asked by the court to "immediately take over the question of enforcement."

It seems highly unlikely that the president would later have been willing to instruct Justice Department attorneys to go to court to force school integration in the Deep South. Such an aggressive enforcement strategy would have invited confrontation between the Eisenhower administration and the southern states, a confrontation that the president gave every indication he wanted to avoid.

Brownell offered a second reason for Eisenhower's refusal to support *Brown II*.[59] The president was intent, said Brownell, to retain the trust of all Americans, including those in the Deep South. Only by keeping the dialogue open, he believed, could he persuade the contending sides to come together when the inevitable showdown over enforcement occurred. This attitude was consistent with Eisenhower's long-held belief that the nation's race problems could best be solved by education and persuasion, not laws, a position he first stated publicly in his testimony before the Senate Armed Services Committee in 1948.

Despite his conspicuous silence on *Brown II*, Eisenhower justifiably took credit for desegregating the military, schools on military bases, civilian labor on naval bases, and veterans hospitals. He also publicly supported the desegregation of public accommodations in the District of Columbia after the Supreme Court's *Thompson* decision in 1953. And after the court's *Brown I* decision, in *Bolling v. Sharp*, the case that had challenged school segregation in the nation's capital, he called for the desegregation of the public schools in the District of Columbia. In his actions, Eisenhower, in addition to using persuasion, was willing to invoke federal authority, including two Supreme Court decisions, to accomplish his goals.

When the president refused to openly endorse the court's decision in *Brown II* to desegregate public schools in the South, he missed a critical opportunity to persuade law-abiding white southerners that the court's decision was constitutional and its implementation feasible. This was the position of his Justice Department's brief that he read, edited, and approved in November 1954.

In the summer of 1955, the president's approval rating rose to an astonishing 79 percent. James Reston, writing in the *New York Times*, declared that "the popularity of President Eisenhower has got beyond the bounds of reasonable calculation and will have to be put down as a national phenomenon, like baseball."[60] Had this extraordinarily popular president exercised leadership and put the prestige of his office behind *Brown II*, he would undoubtedly have lost the support of the most defiant white citizens in the Deep South. But he also would have reinforced the authority of the court as the nation's ultimate interpreter of the meaning of the Constitution and mitigated the reaction to *Brown II* in the Deep South. Instead, he left the Warren Court, moderate white southern leaders, and hundreds of thousands of black school children isolated and vulnerable to the rising storm of resistance from hard-core segregationists.

Chapter Nine

DOUBLE-CROSSING IKE

"No man has ever reached his 70th year in the White House," Eisenhower wrote Swede Hazlett in early June 1955, again raising his concerns about his age and the physical and mental stamina required for a second presidential term.[1] He continued to insist that, barring a national or international crisis, he would not run for reelection. "[I]f I should come to feel any weakening of my own resolution in this whole affair," he continued, "I may get you on the phone. You are one of the very few who has seemed, from the beginning, to have been on *my* side in such matters."

When Eisenhower spoke to Republican politicians in San Francisco later in the month, however, he talked "like a man who was going to run for re-election." At least that was the clear impression left with a handful of California political leaders who had joined the president for breakfast. Nine days later, after Ike held his seventy-second presidential press conference, the *New York Times* led with the headline "EISENHOWER, IN GAY MOOD, ACTS JUST LIKE A CANDIDATE."[2] The president brushed aside all talk about a second term, exchanging good-natured banter with reporters. But "all the time he was talking," the *Times* reported, "he acted very much like a man who was enjoying his job and who was ready to take on another four-year term."

Eisenhower looked forward to a Geneva summit meeting in July with leaders of the Soviet Union, Great Britain, and France, the first Big Four conference in a decade. "Personally, I do not expect any spectacular results from the forthcoming 'Big Four' Conference," he wrote Hazlett.[3] "Nevertheless, I should think that Foster [Secretary of State John Foster Dulles] and I should be able to detect whether the Soviets really intend to introduce a tactical change that could mean, for the next few years at least, some real easing of tensions."

In Geneva, little progress was made on the major agenda items—disarmament, European security, and German reunification. But Eisenhower did not expect major breakthroughs on such complicated issues. The conference, nonetheless, was a major success for Ike. He readily joined in the conference's spirit of informal collegiality, hosting a long, private luncheon with his old wartime Soviet friend, Marshal Zhukov.

Later, at the Palais des Nations, Eisenhower stunned the Soviet delegation with an "Open Skies" proposal to open the airspace above the United States and the Soviet Union to mutual inspection flights by each country. Speaking without notes and looking directly at the Soviet representatives, he said that his proposal would give each nation "a complete blueprint of our military establishments from beginning to end, from one end of our countries to the other."[4] His proposal would reduce "the possibility of great surprise attack, thus lessening danger and relaxing tension." It would be a serious step, he concluded, toward "a sound peace with security, justice, well being, and freedom for the people of the world."

The French and British delegations enthusiastically supported Ike's proposal, and Nicolai Bulganin, the chairman of the Soviet Council of Ministers, said that it had merit. But Nikita Khrushchev, First Secretary of the Communist Party, quickly rejected it. In a private conversation with Khrushchev, Eisenhower tried to persuade him of the merits of his proposal. Khrushchev not only resisted the president's overture, but later denounced his proposal as an American plot to spy on the Soviet Union.

In the West, Eisenhower's proposal made him, once again, an international hero. France's *Le Monde* declared that the American president "has emerged as the type of leader that humanity needs today."[5] At home, his approval ratings spiked upward.

After his triumphant return to Washington, fifty-four Republican members of the House of Representatives implored Eisenhower to seek a second presidential term. Ike gave an amiable, indecipherable answer. In mid-August, he flew to Denver for a long summer vacation. He appeared in great spirits, rising early, spending a couple of hours on official business, playing golf at the Cherry Hills Country Club, fly-fishing, and painting at his easel. In the evenings, he grilled trout or steak for close friends and family at the home of his mother-in-law, Elvira Doud, then played bridge or billiards, and retired early. The subject of the 1956 presidential election came up repeatedly in conversation, but, despite the urging of friends that he run, Ike demurred. He told his brother Milton that he wanted to "retain as long as possible a position of flexibility," but, barring an unforeseen crisis, he would not run for a second term.[6]

On the morning of September 23, Eisenhower arose at 5 a.m., cooked breakfast for house guests, then drove to his office at Lowry Air Force Base to answer correspondence before heading with his friend George Allen to Cherry Hills for a late morning round of golf. Twice during the round, he had to return to the clubhouse to take calls from Secretary of State Dulles, which an annoyed Ike considered unnecessary. After eating a hamburger smothered with raw onions for lunch, he returned to the course for more golf. Complaining of indigestion, which he attributed to the onions he had eaten at lunch, he left before completing his afternoon round. He went to bed at 10 p.m. but woke up three and half hours later with a severe chest pain. He thought the pain was nothing more than indigestion, and asked Mamie for a dose of milk of magnesia.

Concerned that her husband's pain was more serious than indigestion, Mamie called his longtime personal physician, Major General Howard Snyder, who had accompanied the president to Denver and was staying at Lowry Air Force Base. Dr. Snyder, seventy-five years old, was a career army doctor who had trained as a surgeon and had been Eisenhower's personal physician since 1945. Ike's close friends Lucius Clay, Cliff Roberts, and Bill Robinson considered Snyder long past his professional prime and for years had urged Eisenhower to switch to a younger, more proficient physician. But the president refused to fire Snyder, his frequent bridge and golfing partner, whom he considered one of his closest friends.

Snyder arrived at the Doud home shortly before 3 a.m. After examining Eisenhower, he concluded that the president was suffering from acute indigestion and gave him painkillers, including two doses of morphine. Shortly after noon, a member of the White House press office met with reporters and told them that Dr. Snyder had diagnosed the president's pain as indigestion. By 1:15 p.m. Snyder had changed his diagnosis, concluding that Eisenhower's symptoms suggested that he might have suffered a heart attack. He called Denver's Ftizsimmons Army Hospital and ordered equipment to be brought to the Doud home so that the president could be given an electrocardiogram. At 2 p.m., it was announced that the cardiograph disclosed a coronary thrombosis condition.*

Eisenhower was immediately moved to the army hospital, where he

---

* Dr. Snyder went to elaborate lengths to hide the fact that he had initially misdiagnosed the president's serious condition. He later insisted that he had known from his first examination that the president had suffered a heart attack, His misdiagnosis and cover-up were documented by Clarence G. Lasby in his book, *Eisenhower's Heart Attack: How Ike Beat Heart Disease and Held on to the Presidency* (1997).

was placed in an oxygen tent. Cliff Roberts arranged for Dr. Paul Dudley White, the nation's preeminent heart specialist, to fly from Boston to take charge of the president's care. Meeting the press shortly after examining Eisenhower, Dr. White told reporters that the president had suffered a "moderate" heart attack and expressed confidence that his patient could make a complete recovery.

Ike exceeded White's most optimistic prediction, making a remarkable recovery. On his sixty-fifth birthday, October 14, he was photographed in a wheelchair on the hospital roof with the embroidered words on his shirt pocket: MUCH BETTER THANKS. Less than a month later, he returned to Washington and was disappointed that his doctors forbid him to stand up in his bubble-top limousine to wave to the thousands of well-wishers along the route from the airport to the White House. "I expect to be back at my accustomed duties," he told reporters, "although they say I must ease into them and not bulldoze my way into them."[7]

AFTER DEMOCRATS GAINED seats in Congress in the midterm elections, solidifying their majority, speculation intensified in the press on the question of whether Eisenhower was able and willing to seek a second presidential term. The *Times* columnist James Reston reported that momentum was building in the Republican Party to draft either Eisenhower or Chief Justice Warren for the 1956 Republican presidential nomination. The prevailing sentiment among party insiders, Reston reported, was "Eisenhower if possible, or Warren without his consent if necessary."[8]

Eisenhower remained silent on the issue. Warren, whose candidacy had persistently been a subject of speculation, had attempted to put a stop to such talk seven months earlier with a statement that he issued from the court. When he had accepted the position of chief justice, he said in the statement, "it was with the fixed purpose of leaving politics permanently for service on the court. That is still my purpose. It is irrevocable. I will not change it under any circumstances or conditions."[9] Relieved by the chief's statement, Justice Frankfurter had written Warren that he never doubted his "exclusive dedication" to the court "which you now have so definitively and so finally expressed even for the most cynically minded."[10]

Eisenhower's heart attack revived talk of Warren's candidacy, though the *Times*'s Reston reported that Warren had convinced most of his supporters that he could not be talked into it, "even by President Eisenhower."[11] Warren said that he had never been happier in his life, according to Reston. More importantly, he would consider himself unfaithful to his responsibilities as chief justice if he allowed the court to become involved in politics. Warren's supporters were undeterred, Reston reported, and prepared to turn to a more aggressive strategy. They no longer would try to persuade him that it was his duty to run, but, rather, work to draft him without his consent. If successful, Reston wrote, they would confront him "with the hard decision of turning down the party he has been identified with all his life."

Although Eisenhower said nothing publicly, he had his own ideas about his successor, should he choose not to run. When his press secretary, James Hagerty, asked about Warren as a presidential candidate, the president snapped, "Not a chance."[12] He expected Warren to complete his public career as chief justice and added, "I do not think I would approve of a Chief Justice stepping down from the bench to run for office."

When rumors of a Warren candidacy continued to circulate in January 1956, Eisenhower expressed his disapproval at a press conference. After a reporter asked if the chief justice's return to politics would set a bad precedent, Ike replied, "The second I was nominated by the Republican Party, I resigned from the Army. Now, I just don't believe we ought to cross over, we oughtn't to get the military and the civil powers tangled up. We shouldn't get too great a confusion between politics and the Supreme Court."[13]

Warren was annoyed by the president's advice to him offered at his press conference and expressed his displeasure to Eisenhower's press secretary at a party. After Hagerty told Eisenhower of his conversation with Warren, the president returned to the subject of a possible Warren candidacy in his diary and offered a slightly revised version of what he had said at his press conference. If the chief justice was interested in the nomination, Eisenhower wrote, he should resign from the Supreme Court.[14]

Eisenhower suspected that Warren was complicit in perpetuating rumors of his availability as a presidential candidate. His suspicions said more about Ike's growing interest in running for a second presidential term than it did about Warren's plans. Indeed, Warren had become increasingly exasperated if anyone attempted to persuade him to leave the court for the presidency. Professor Jerome Cohen, one of Warren's law clerks for the 1955 court term, which ran from October 1955 to June 1956, recalled the chief justice's irritation when the subject of his candidacy was raised. Cohen had been asked by William Timbers, general counsel to the Securities and Exchange Commission, to arrange a luncheon with the chief justice at Washington's Capitol Hill Club to be hosted by Timbers and attended by Attorney General Brownell. The purpose was to persuade Warren to become a Republican presidential candidate if Eisenhower did not run. When Cohen told Warren of the proposed luncheon, the chief justice was "furious," emphatically telling his clerk that "he was not going to get involved in politics."[15]

In informal conversations, Ike rejected one potential Republican presidential nominee after another. He dismissed Warren as someone who took too long to make decisions to be a good president. He ruled out Vice President Nixon, also mentioned as a potential candidate, as too inexperienced, and California's Senator Knowland as "impossible." He thought former Governor Dewey or Attorney General Brownell could be good presidents but would split the party. He rated both Secretary of the Treasury Humphrey and his own brother Milton as excellent potential presidents but concluded that neither could get the nomination. As to the most likely Democratic presidential nominees, Adlai Stevenson, former New York governor Averell Harriman, and Tennessee senator Estes Kefauver, none, in his opinion, had the "competency to run the office of the President."[16]

Eisenhower had said repeatedly that only a national or international crisis would compel him to run for a second term. By February 1956, no such emergency offered the president his expressed rationale to seek reelection. And yet Eisenhower appeared increasingly interested in serving another four years as president. Why? The most plausible explanation was that he had concluded, after considering all possible candidates, that he was the best man for the job. On February 29, he called a special press conference. "If the Republican National Convention asks me to run," he told reporters, "my answer will be positive, that is, affirmative."[17]

FOR HIS FIRST two judicial terms as chief justice, Earl Warren had approached his new duties cautiously, seeking legal advice from his new colleagues while exercising his exceptional political skill with grace and confidence. The leaders of the two ideological wings of the court, Justices Black and Frankfurter, appreciated Warren's obvious leadership skills and were sensitive to the fact that he did not bring to the court expertise in constitutional law or, indeed, any field of appellate practice. While Warren and Black established an immediate rapport, the new chief justice was especially receptive to the ardent attention paid to him by Frankfurter, the former Harvard professor who had assiduously tutored two generations of law students, judges, and politicians.

Frankfurter provided Warren with steady doses of legal scholarship leavened by dollops of flattery. He was also generous in his gestures of friendship, offering to lend Warren one of his law clerks and to help raise money for a bust of the former governor in the California State House in Sacramento. During the court's deliberations in the school desegregation cases, Frankfurter's influence on Warren was particularly noticeable and their personal relations close. By Warren's third term as chief justice, however, Frankfurter's influence began to wane and their friendship frayed.

Frankfurter viewed Warren, as he did all new court appointees, as a potential recruit to his philosophy of judicial restraint and, during their first two terms together, he appeared successful. But Frankfurter perceived Warren's caution and affability as signs that he was also malleable, a fatal miscalculation. Warren was cautious but, as he had demonstrated as governor of California, he was also a proud man of independence and decisiveness. With Frankfurter's relentless attention, Warren began to feel patronized and manipulated, and he resented it.

Frankfurter made the further mistake of courting Warren's law clerks, taking them and clerks from other chambers to lunch frequently. Professor Jerome Cohen, who was Warren's clerk for the 1955 court term, fondly remembered the lively lunches and personal attention he received from Frankfurter, who treated him like a member of his family. In Warren's chambers, Cohen recalled, "It was all business."[18] Warren never invited him to lunch or to meet his family. When Cohen told the chief justice that he had accepted Frankfurter's offer of a clerkship for the 1956 court term, Warren was livid. He forbid Cohen to speak to Frankfurter for the remainder of the term.

It was clear to Cohen during his year as Warren's clerk that the chief justice was much more influenced by Justice Black than by Frankfurter. Black, the leader of the liberal wing of the court, had been a highly unorthodox choice as FDR's first appointee to the court in

1937. He grew up in the dusty hill country of northern Alabama, the son of a struggling shopkeeper. Largely self-educated, he studied law for two years at the University of Alabama and graduated at the top of his small class. He made his reputation as a superb trial lawyer in Birmingham before successfully running for the Senate in 1926. In his two terms in the Senate, Black's record was unwaveringly that of a liberal populist, and he proved to be one of the most avid supporters of FDR's New Deal. He was also one of the Senate's true intellectuals, reading voraciously in the fields of American history, philosophy, and political theory. On the court, Black was joined by William O. Douglas, the rough-hewed westerner, former Yale Law School professor and chairman of the Securities and Exchange Commission, in staunchly defending civil rights and liberties and regularly opposing Frankfurter's judicial restraint.

In style, Black was "soothing," Cohen recalled, while Frankfurter was "irritating."[19] Black's growing influence on Warren, beyond style, subtly began to pull the chief justice toward Black's expansive interpretation of the Constitution's protection of civil rights and liberties. That impression was backed by a study of voting patterns during the 1955 term by political scientist Clyde Jacobs. In contrast to Warren's first two terms on the court, when he had taken "a center position, perhaps facing slightly in the conservative direction on matters of civil liberties," Jacobs wrote that Warren most often voted with the liberals, Black and Douglas, during the 1955 term.[20]

In the justices' conferences during his third term on the court, Warren became more outspoken, demonstrating a willingness to stake out strong positions at the outset of the brethren's discussions. He stated his views vigorously and unequivocally in a case argued during the term that became one of the most important criminal procedure decisions of the entire Warren Court era. The defendant in the case had been convicted in an Illinois courtroom of armed robbery. He filed a motion for a free transcript of the trial record, arguing that he was indigent and could not receive adequate appellate review without the transcript. His motion was denied.

At the justices' conference in the case on December 9, 1955, Warren pointed out that Illinois had provided for full appellate review in such a case. Since another defendant with money could pay for a trial transcript, he concluded that the state had violated the defendant's rights to due process and equal protection of the law. "We cannot have one rule for the rich and one for the poor," Warren declared.[21] He assigned the majority opinion to Black, who wrote in *Griffin v. Illinois* that "in criminal trials, a state can no more discriminate on account of poverty than on account of religion, race or color."[22] *Griffin* was the first of a series of historic Warren Court decisions that insisted that an indigent defendant not be disadvantaged in the criminal process.

In the first of two sedition cases, Warren supported the civil liberties claim of Harry Slochower, a tenured associate professor at Brooklyn College, who had lost his job after invoking his Fifth Amendment privilege against self-incrimination in testimony before a Senate committee investigating domestic subversion. Slochower had answered all questions about his professional life after 1941 but invoked the Fifth Amendment and refused to answer questions about his Communist Party membership during 1940 and 1941. Under a New York anticorruption law, a municipal employee who refused to answer questions relating to his duties was deemed to have quit and therefore was automatically terminated.

At the justices' conference in *Slochower v. Board of Education*, Warren said that he thought that the New York law placed an unwarranted constitutional burden on the defendant.[23] "The premise in the plea is one of guilt and this is violative of the Constitution," he declared.[24] Warren cast the decisive fifth vote supporting Slochower's civil liberties claim and assigned the majority opinion to Justice Clark.

Warren again demonstrated decisiveness in leading the discussion in the most controversial case of the term, *Pennsylvania v. Nelson*, which dealt with the appeal of Steve Nelson, an acknowledged Communist leader in western Pennsylvania who had been convicted of violating the state's sedition law.[25] The state law was similar to a federal statute that made it unlawful to knowingly advocate the overthrow of the U.S. government by force and violence. The Pennsylvania Supreme Court had reversed Nelson's conviction on the ground that the federal statute, the Smith Act, proscribed the same conduct and, therefore, superseded the state law.

Warren began the conference discussion by stating that, as he saw it, the case was reduced to one issue: "Has the U.S. superseded this state act?"[26] He said he thought it had, and that the state supreme court was correct in overturning the conviction. In his view, there would be "no loss to the U.S. if these [state] acts are stricken." He voted to affirm the state supreme court decision, assigning himself the court's opinion that would effectively invalidate the sedition laws of forty-two states. Despite the incendiary result, Warren's opinion in *Nelson* was a dry discussion of the technical doctrine of preemption, holding that the federal sedition statute superseded and nullified state laws enacted with the same legislative purpose.

With his vote in *Griffin v. Illinois*, Warren broke his proprosecution pattern that dated back to his days as Alameda County district attorney and continued into his first two terms on the Supreme Court. His votes in *Slowchower v. Board of Education* and *Pennsylvania v. Nelson* were even more striking departures from his past. In both cases, Warren, an outspoken anti-Communist for decades, supported the civil liberties claims of two suspected subversives, one the leader of a branch of the American Communist Party.

DESPITE THE COURT'S decision in *Brown II*, not a single public school was desegregated in the eight states of the Deep South in 1955. At the same time, racial tensions intensified throughout the southern states. In Mississippi, the most reactionary southern state, the existing white power structure moved quickly to defy the law. White Citizens Councils, often made up of the most respected local citizens, formed to stop any attempt to integrate the public schools. African Americans who signed petitions asking local school boards to implement the *Brown* decision suddenly lost their jobs. Those who had registered to vote were turned away at voting booths. The number of African Americans on voting rolls in the state decreased from 22,000 to 8,000 during the year.

Racial tension turned to violence. Emmett Till, a fourteen-year-old black boy from Chicago visiting relatives in Tallahatchie, Mississippi, was savagely murdered after reports circulated in the local white community that he had made inappropriate advances toward a white woman in a grocery store. A month later an all-white jury acquitted the two white defendants, who never took the witness stand. For a fee of $4,000, the acquitted men later confessed to William Bradford Huie, a journalist representing *Look* magazine, that they had committed the crime.

No lynching had taken place in Mississippi for five years; in 1955, there were three.

The *Brown II* decision emboldened courageous black activists to assert their civil rights. In Montgomery, Alabama, on the evening of December 1, 1955, a forty-three-year-old black seamstress named Rosa Parks silently defied the city's white power structure as well as its enforced segregation.[27] Mrs. Parks, a leader of her church and the local chapter of the NAACP, paid her fare on a local bus for her ride home. She was tired and took her seat in the first row reserved for blacks. When a white man came aboard, there were no empty seats in the section reserved for whites, so he stood. The bus driver ordered Parks to give her seat to the man and move to the back of the bus. She refused. She was arrested, briefly jailed, and ordered to trial on December 5 on the charge of violating the city's segregation laws.

The next night, fifty leaders of the black community met to discuss the case of Mrs. Parks in the Dexter Avenue Baptist Church, founded by free blacks during Reconstruction. The minister of the church was Dr. Martin Luther King, Jr., twenty-six years old, whose father and maternal grandfather had been church leaders and civil rights activists in King's hometown of Atlanta. Dr. King, who had received his doctorate in theology from Boston University, was named president of the Montgomery Improvement Association, the organization chosen to lead the mass protest against segregation on the city's buses. On the day of Rosa Parks's trial, 90 percent of Montgomery's black population, who ordinarily rode the city's buses, stayed away. That night, at a mass meeting, black leaders asked members of their community to stay off the city's buses until conditions were satisfactory "to all citizens." The Montgomery boycott had begun.

After talks between city officials and black leaders to settle the boycott broke down, the mayor and city commissioners announced that they would join the Citizens Council. King and other black leaders refused to be intimidated, and the boycott continued into 1956. The black community organized a three-hundred-car pool for rides to work. With black riders comprising 65 percent of the city's bus passengers before the boycott, the bus company's gross income plummeted. Even when the company raised fares, it still operated at a loss.

Dr. King led the boycott with confidence, courage, and, most of all, with his eloquence. In his deep, resonant voice, King called for passive resistance, blending a rational appeal to civic duty with the religious fervor of a crusade. The protest was not against a single incident, but over things that "go deep down into the archives of history," he said.[28] "We have known humiliation, we have known abusive language, we have been plunged in the abyss of oppression," he continued. "And we decided to rise up only with the weapon of protest. It is one of the greatest glories of America that we have the right of protest." The protest, he emphasized, is "not war between the white and the Negro but a conflict between justice and injustice." He repeatedly counseled non-violence in the protest over segregation, which he called "the great issue of our age."

During the boycott Montgomery's black citizens were shot and their homes and churches bombed. The city's police officers ignored the violence and arrested the boycotters. King and nearly one hundred other African Americans were indicted and convicted on the charge of conspiracy to conduct an illegal boycott. King paid a fine of $500, but he and the other black leaders achieved their goal later that year. The Supreme Court, in a brief order citing the school segregation decisions, unanimously affirmed a district court order that Montgomery's bus segregation violated the Equal Protection Clause of the Constitution. The Montgomery boycott was not just an important victory in the fight against segregation, but also introduced the nation to Dr. King, the greatest leader of the civil rights movement.

THE POLITICAL LEADERS of the white South remained defiant and continued to denounce the court's *Brown II* decision. In February 1956, a Southern Manifesto was signed by 101 members of Congress, including every member of the old Confederacy except Senator Lyndon Johnson of Texas and Tennessee's Senators Estes Kefauver and Albert Gore. The Manifesto attacked *Brown* as "a clear abuse of judicial power." "The true meaning of the Manifesto," wrote Anthony Lewis of the *New York Times*, "was to make defiance of the Supreme Court and the Constitution socially acceptable in the South—to give resistance to the law the approval of the Southern establishment."[29]

Less than a month after the Southern Manifesto was announced, the court handed down its decisions in *Slochower* and *Pennsylvania v. Nelson* upholding the civil liberties claims of two suspected subversives. *Brown*'s critics in the South received the decisions as unexpected political gifts. The rulings, they charged, were evidence that the Warren Court's radical agenda to trample on the states' rights of white southerners had spread ominously to the protection of Communists. They hinted that integration was a Communist plot.

Southern critics of *Slochower* and *Nelson* were quickly joined by other outraged anti-Communists, including the censored senator from Wisconsin, Joseph McCarthy. Wasn't there just one "pro-Communist" decision after another? asked Mississippi senator James Eastland, chairman of the Senate Internal Security Subcommittee.

"You are so right," replied Senator McCarthy.[30]

Is there any explanation of the decisions, Eastland continued, "except that the majority of the Court is being influenced by some secret, but very powerful Communist or pro-Communist influence?"

"Either incompetence beyond words, Mr. Chairman, I would say, or the type of influence which you mentioned," McCarthy responded.

Does the chief justice follow the Communist line? Eastland asked expectantly.

"Unfortunately, yes, Mr. Chairman," McCarthy replied, "although I do not accuse Earl Warren of being a Communist."

———

WHEN EISENHOWER WAS asked about the Southern Manifesto at a press conference in early March, he reminded reporters that "the people who have this deep emotional reaction on the other side [of *Brown*] were not acting over these past three generations in defiance of the law. They were acting in compliance with the law as interpreted by the Supreme Court [in the *Plessy* decision]."[31] *Brown* had "completely reversed" *Plessy*, he pointed out, "and it is going to take time for them to adjust their thinking and their progress to that." He offered this advice: "If ever there was a time when we must be patient without being complacent, when we must be understanding of other people's deep emotions as well as our own, this is it."

The president hoped that would be his final word on the Manifesto, but reporters pursued the subject at his next press conference, asking how he felt about the southern congressmen's defiance of a Supreme Court order. He noted that no one had used the words "defy the Supreme Court" in the Manifesto and again spoke of the difficulty experienced by white southerners adjusting to *Brown* after *Plessy*.[32] "As far as I am concerned," he concluded, "I am for moderation, but I am for progress; that is exactly what I am for in this."

Later in the month, Eisenhower discussed his approach to desegregation in a letter to the Rev. Billy Graham, writing that progress achieved "through conciliation will be more lasting and stronger than could be obtained through force and conflict."[33] Graham promised to do his part by working with other white southern ministers to preach moderation from their pulpits.

At a cabinet meeting in March, Attorney General Brownell proposed a civil rights bill that called for a bipartisan commission, created by Congress, with the power to subpoena and to investigate alleged civil rights violations, a new assistant attorney general in charge of civil rights in the Justice Department, new laws enforcing voting rights, and strengthening existing civil rights statutes. Eisenhower was initially enthusiastic about Brownell's proposals, hoping that the desegregation issue could be moved out of the courts and into less contentious forums where compromise between the two sides might be reached.

Brownell's civil rights bill faced resistance from southern Democrats in Congress as well as Republican leaders who hoped to crack the solid Democratic South in the 1956 presidential election. At the same time, civil rights activists vigorously pushed for passage of the legislation, applying pressure that Eisenhower resented. They did not appreciate his dilemma, he complained. "[T]hese civil-rights people" did not understand that he could "send in the military" but could not make them operate the schools."[34]

After prolonged debate on Brownell's bill, the House passed a com-

promise civil rights measure. It contained the first two provisions of
the attorney general's bill, creating a bipartisan commission to investigate civil rights violations and a new assistant attorney general in
charge of civil rights in the Justice Department. But the compromise
bill eliminated the provisions for voting rights and federal authority to
enforce civil rights violations. Even the watered-down bill died in the
Senate Judiciary Committee chaired by Mississippi's James Eastland.

AFTER EISENHOWER ANNOUNCED that he would run for a second presidential term, his choice of a running mate became a topic of
avid national interest. For more than a year before his decision, Ike had
conducted a debate with himself and with close friends, questioning
whether, at the age of sixty-six, he would possess the physical and mental strength to serve effectively as president for another term. A worthy
and younger vice president seemed essential, particularly after his heart
attack. Yet the president was remarkably indecisive.

Eisenhower had his eye on Robert Anderson, his secretary of the
navy, whom he had told close friends would make an excellent president. When he broached the subject with Anderson, the Texan
reminded the president that he was a Democrat and, more importantly,
did not want to be president. Ike's obvious choice then was the sitting
vice president, Richard Nixon. Eisenhower always spoke positively of
Nixon in public, most often praising his loyalty and dedication. Privately, he worried that Nixon was too partisan and immature.

The president was asked frequently by reporters if he intended to
keep Nixon on the ticket, and each time he politely demurred. At first,
he said that the delegates to the Republican convention must make
the decision. Later, he met privately with Nixon and, to the vice president's chagrin, advised him to take a cabinet post, perhaps secretary
of commerce or health, education, and welfare, to build his resume
with high-level administrative experience. But, of course, he added,

it was entirely Nixon's decision. Ignoring Eisenhower's advice, Nixon said that he would do whatever the president wanted, including staying on the ticket. At a press conference in late April, Eisenhower, after being reminded that he had said that Nixon should "chart out his own course," replied that he had not received an answer from his vice president. Nixon seized the opening and asked for a meeting with Ike the next day.[35] "I would be honored to continue as vice president under you," he told Eisenhower.[36] The president said he was pleased, and that was how the decision was made.

In June, Eisenhower suffered an ileitis attack, the latest in a series of stomach problems that had plagued him for years. He was rushed to Washington's Walter Reed Hospital to undergo an emergency operation to correct the malfunctioning of the valve opening into his large intestine. The two-hour operation was successful, but his abdominal pain lingered for more than a month. Eisenhower nonetheless insisted that he was prepared to fulfill the major duties of a second presidential term, should he be reelected. But he conceded that his fall campaign schedule would necessarily have to be severely limited. There would be no barnstorming on the scale of his 1952 campaign, when he traveled more than 50,000 miles by train and airplane. He expected to run on his record, pointing to his administration's accomplishments in a series of major addresses.

———

IN PUBLIC, EISENHOWER remained tight-lipped about the court's *Brown II* decision throughout the spring and early summer. In private, however, he expressed both annoyance and anxiety. In a telephone conversation with Oveta Culp Hobby, Secretary of Health, Education, and Welfare, he objected to any reference to *Brown* as a "Republican" decision. He pointed out that Chief Justice Warren "actually did not affect the decision a bit."[37]

When he later discussed the court's decision with his young speech writer, Emmett John Hughes, his annoyance had turned to anger. "I am convinced that the Supreme Court decision set back progress in the South at least fifteen years," he told Hughes.[38] "The fellow who tries to tell me you can do these things by force is just plain nuts." He added, "No matter how much law we have, we have a job in education, in getting people to understand what are the issues here involved." The president also complained that *Brown* had deprived him of the friendship of southern leaders like South Carolina's James Byrnes. "We [he and Byrnes] used to be pretty good friends," he told Hughes. "Now I've not heard from him, not at all, in the past 18 months—all because of bitterness on this thing."

In August, shortly before the Republican convention, Eisenhower called Attorney General Brownell to object to the proposed wording in the party's platform that referred to the court's decision. It stated that the Eisenhower administration and the Republican Party supported the Supreme Court's desegregation decision. An irate Eisenhower reminded Brownell that in the attorney general's brief before the court he had appeared as a lawyer, not as a member of the Eisenhower administration. He said that he had always denied that his administration took a stand on the issue. He insisted that the word "concur" be struck in the party platform's reference to the court's decision and instructed Brownell to make his position clear to Republican leaders.[39] If they did not come around to his point of view, the president said, he would refuse to attend the convention. The final version of the platform complied with Eisenhower's directive, stating only that the party "accepts" the court's decision.

Republican delegates at the party's convention in San Francisco's Cow Palace nominated Eisenhower by acclamation for a second presidential term and Richard Nixon again to be his running mate.

AFTER THE CONVENTION, Eisenhower took a brief vacation on California's Monterey Peninsula, accompanied by his favorite companions, the Gang. At the Casa Munras Hotel, they played golf and bridge for four days. On the return plane trip to Washington, the president and his friends played another eight and half hours of bridge without interruption. When Eisenhower returned to the White House, he was suntanned, relaxed, and eager to get back to work.

He had hardly settled into a routine when he was informed of mob violence in Clinton, Tennessee, and Mansfield, Texas, where school officials had attempted to carry out court-ordered desegregation. At a press conference on September 5 he was asked if the federal government had a role in helping local communities meet the problem of desegregating schools without violence. It is a local problem, he replied.[40] "And let us remember this," he added, "under the law the federal government cannot . . . move into a state until the state is not able to handle the matter."

A week later in a pre–press conference briefing, the president was more candid about the problem of enforcing desegregation in a predominantly white, hostile community. He noted that the governor of Mississippi had vowed to ignore any federal court decision to desegregate his state's public schools. Eventually, Eisenhower said, "a district court is going to cite someone for contempt and then we are going to be up against it."[41] He suggested that "even the so-called great liberals are going to have to take a second look at the whole thing."

At the same meeting, Eisenhower was briefed on the Supreme Court's ruling earlier that week that had upheld the constitutionality of the Montgomery bus boycott. He again expressed anxiety about aggressive measures to force desegregation. On some of these issues, he said, "he was more of a 'states righter' than the Supreme Court."[42] He feared that "by some steps the country is going to get into trouble, and the problems of the Negroes set back, not advanced."

During the fall campaign, Eisenhower did not discuss the *Brown II* decision beyond noting that the court had devised a method to "eventually" desegregate the public schools.[43] On the general topic of desegregation, he reiterated his support for equal rights for all Americans, called for understanding and tolerance among all races, and expressed pride in his policies that ended segregation in the District of Columbia and on military bases.

The Democratic standard bearer, former Illinois governor Adlai Stevenson, could not afford to raise the issue of the president's reticence on *Brown II*, since his best hope for victory required that he not alienate his party's base in the Democratic South. He told an audience in Little Rock, Arkansas, that he agreed with the court's decision but quickly acknowledged "that some of you feel strongly to the contrary."[44] What was more important than their disagreement, he said, was that "we accept . . . that decision as law-abiding citizens," a position strikingly similar to Eisenhower's.

WHILE EISENHOWER CONSPICUOUSLY kept his distance from *Brown II*, he quietly filled vacancies on the federal courts with judicial moderates who were likely to support the Supreme Court's school desegregation rulings. His second appointment to the court, John Marshall Harlan II, joined the unanimous court opinion in *Brown II*. The president continued to accept the recommendations of Attorney General Brownell to appoint moderates to the lower federal courts covering the Deep South. He appointed Judges Elbert Tuttle of Georgia, John Brown of Nebraska, and John Minor Wisdom of Louisiana to the U.S. Court of Appeals, Fifth Circuit, sitting in New Orleans. All three appointees would consistently uphold the constitutional claims of minorities, backed by the Supreme Court's desegregation decisions. The president also appointed Judge Frank M. Johnson, Jr., to a federal district court in Alabama. It was Johnson who issued the court order striking down segregated seating on Montgomery's buses after Rosa Parks refused to give up her seat to a white man, inspiring the city-wide bus boycott.

In September 1956, Eisenhower was given the opportunity to make his third appointment to the Supreme Court after Associate Justice Sherman Minton announced his retirement. Having appointed two Republicans to the court, the president told Attorney General Brownell that he was interested in appointing "a very good Catholic, even a conservative Democrat" to demonstrate that his judicial choices were nonpartisan. He continued to insist that he would not appoint anyone over the age of sixty-four. And he wanted someone with judicial experience, a qualification that Eisenhower had added after appointing Chief Justice Warren, a subtle but unmistakable sign that he was not pleased with Warren's judicial opinions.

Deputy Attorney General William Rogers told Brownell that he had been impressed by a recent address on court reform by Judge William J. Brennan, Jr., a member of the New Jersey Supreme Court. Brownell spoke to the presiding judge on Brennan's court, Chief Judge Arthur Vanderbilt, who said that Brennan, a Democrat and a Catholic, was an exceptionally well-qualified candidate for the nation's highest court. Brownell read all of Brennan's opinions and found them well reasoned and well written. The New Jersey judge's opinions could not be categorized as conservative, as Eisenhower had suggested, but Brownell nonetheless recommended Brennan to the president.

Although Eisenhower's primary motivation in accepting Brownell's recommendation may have been to show that his appointments to the Supreme Court were above partisan politics, it surely did not escape the president's attention that appointing a Democrat and an Irish-Catholic from the voter-rich industrial Northeast was also a shrewd political decision during his presidential campaign. Neither Eisenhower nor Brownell could have known that the Brennan appointment would be critical to the Warren Court's judicial revolution in civil rights and liberties that had begun with *Brown*.

Brennan, fifty years old, met reporters after Eisenhower announced his court appointment and, with charm and good humor, analogized his appointment to the mule entered in the Kentucky Derby. "I don't expect to distinguish myself," he said, "but I do expect to benefit from the association."[45]

Brennan was altogether too modest in his self-assessment. The story of his rise to an eminent place in constitutional history began in the city of Newark, New Jersey, where William J. Brennan, Sr., an Irish immigrant, and his wife, Agnes, raised four sons and four daughters. Brennan Senior stoked the boiler in a factory, heaved coal in the Ballantine brewery, and later became a labor leader and elected local official. Bill Junior contributed to the family's meager income by making change for passengers waiting for trolley cars and delivering milk in a horse-drawn wagon. There was no time, nor reason, for self-pity since the Brennans' neighbors were much worse off. "I saw all kinds of suffering," he remembered, "people had to struggle."[46] Those early memories inspired a lifelong philosophy—the need for government's protection of the worth and dignity of every human being.

A combination of brains, irrepressible personality, and sheer energy propelled Brennan through a varied and uniformly successful professional career. An honors graduate of the Wharton School at the University of Pennsylvania, Brennan finished in the top 10 percent of his class at the Harvard Law School, then returned to Newark where he joined one of the state's most prestigious law firms as a trial lawyer specializing in labor law.

During World War II he took a leave of absence from his law firm to enlist in the armed forces, becoming a manpower troubleshooter in the War Department to negotiate labor settlements in critical defense industries. To the trained eye, Brennan's skill during the war offered a blueprint for his later success on the court. He impressed a War Department colleague as "the friendly Irish type . . . very convivial, easygoing. A great storyteller."[47] But the jaunty charm did more than entertain. Without threat or bluster, Brennan got things done, his way. "He was a diplomat," a colleague recalled. "People liked to do what he wanted them to do." By war's end, Brennan had achieved the rank of colonel and had been awarded the Legion of Merit.

After the war, Brennan returned to his Newark law firm but soon accepted an appointment to the state trial court. He was elevated to the appellate court three years later, and then to the New Jersey Supreme Court where his proposals for court reform received national attention. He was a registered Democrat but was not active in state politics. Members of the New Jersey bar said that, in contrast to Chief Justice Warren, he would bring to the court a calm, moderating voice.

The accolades that Brennan received after the appointment underscored the nonpartisanship sought by Eisenhower. Trial lawyers applauded the appointment because Brennan's experience as a trial lawyer assured them that he, like them, knew "all the ins and outs of litigation" and had developed "a sixth sense that gets at the truth."[48] Conservative political commentator Arthur Krock of the *New York Times* praised Brennan's extensive experience as a trial lawyer and judge, concluding that his appointment "is also proof of democracy when a Supreme Court Justice is representative of what America can, with honor and industry, achieve without birthright of social and economic privilege."[49]

———

EISENHOWER SET AN exceedingly high bar for his reelection: he would be satisfied with nothing less than a sweeping victory in November. Such a mandate was necessary, he believed, to complete the reformation of the Republican Party in his moderate image as well as to give him the necessary leverage to work with a Congress he expected to be controlled by Democrats. He had a further incentive—to defeat the Democratic ticket of Governor Stevenson and Senator Estes Kefauver, which he rated as "the sorriest and weakest pair that ever aspired to the highest office in the land."[50]

He conducted his reelection campaign on the twin themes of peace and prosperity. When Stevenson called for a nuclear test–ban treaty, the president contemptuously dismissed the proposal as a "theatrical national gesture."[51] After Stevenson devoted a major nationally televised campaign speech to his test-ban proposal, Eisenhower replied in a speech in Portland, Oregon, that the American people had to choose between "hard sense and experience versus pie-in-the-sky promises and wishful thinking."[52] A day later, in Los Angeles, he belittled those who "tell us that peace can be guarded—and our nation secure—by a strange new formula."[53]

Although Stevenson's advisers had warned him against challenging the president on national security issues, his test-ban proposal appeared to be gaining traction among voters. But an unsolicited endorsement of his idea from the Soviet Union's premier, Nicolai Bulganin, quickly put a halt to that hopeful development. After Bulganin wrote a letter to Eisenhower supporting Stevenson's idea, the president responded in a scathing letter rejecting the proposal and giving the Soviet leader a pointed piece of advice to keep out of the United States' internal political affairs.[54]

————

THROUGHOUT THE CAMPAIGN, foreign policy issues dominated Eisenhower's time and effort, and the president's discussions took place primarily behind closed doors at the White House. In July, Egypt's nationalistic leader, Gamal Abdel Nasser, had made good on his threat to take over the operation of the Suez Canal from a private company controlled by British and French directors and stockholders. Great Britain and France angrily challenged Nasser's action, since both nations were largely dependent on the free flow of oil from the Middle East through the canal. Prime Minister Anthony Eden of Great Britain declared that Nasser's action justified military intervention, should negotiations fail, and looked hopefully to his nation's longtime ally, the United States, for support.

Eisenhower urged caution and reconciliation among all parties to the controversy. He distrusted Nasser but could find no legal reason to deny the Egyptian leader control of the canal, which was fully within Egypt's territory. Eisenhower worried, moreover, that the spectacle of two colonial powers once again imposing their will on a weak Third World country would be condemned by nations around the world. It would also deliver to the Soviet Union a huge Cold War propaganda bonanza in its efforts to win converts to communism in Africa, South America, and Asia.

In September, British and French troops mobilized on the eastern Mediterranean islands of Cypress and Malta and in Libya. The French alone gathered 80,000 troops and two hundred warships. In mid-October, Eisenhower received further disturbing intelligence from the CIA's U-2 spy planes that Israel was mobilizing troops and that sixty French Mystère jets were observed on Israeli airfields. The president was incensed by the latest news, since the major buildup of military aircraft in Israel was a clear violation of the 1950 Tripartite Declaration signed by the United States, Great Britain, and France committing the three nations to a status quo in arms and borders in the Middle East. He was also angered by the virtual blackout of communications between the U.S. and Great Britain and France, especially since American intelligence had picked up heavy radio traffic between Britain and France. In fact, Great Britain, France, and Israel had secretly planned to retake the canal by force in late October.

In the midst of the Suez crisis, anti-Soviet political eruptions occurred in Poland and Hungary. Riots in Poland swept out of power the Soviet-dominated government, replaced by a government headed by Wladyslav Gomulka, who had earlier been dismissed by the Soviets. Gomulka declared that the Polish people would defend themselves with all means in their desire for democratization. The Poles' successful defiance of the Soviets inspired a similar rebellion in Hungary where Imre Nagy was installed as premier a year after the Soviets had deposed him. While riots continued in the streets, Nagy promised Hungarians democracy and improved living standards. The Hungarian experiment in democracy was short-lived. Two hundred thousand Soviet troops, supported by four thousand tanks, converged on Budapest. Nagy fled to the Yugoslavian embassy, and another puppet government beholden to Moscow was quickly installed.

Eisenhower issued a statement deploring the Soviet intervention in Hungary, but rejected urgent requests from the CIA to provide air-dropped arms and supplies to the freedom fighters. Hungary was surrounded by Communist and neutral states and shared a common border with the Soviet Union. Realistically, the president concluded, the U.S. could not mount an effective challenge to Soviet hegemony in the region and might risk escalation of the crisis into nuclear war.

On October 29, the president left the White House for a political trip to Miami, Jacksonville, and Richmond. In midafternoon, while Eisenhower's plane, the *Columbine*, was en route between Florida and Virginia, Israeli troops poured over the Egyptian border into Sinai, driving toward the Suez Canal. Eisenhower made his speech in Richmond, then hastily returned to Washington in the early evening to meet in the Oval Office with Secretary of State Dulles and other senior foreign policy advisers. Although Eisenhower and Dulles still were not aware of Britain and France's plan to take the Suez Canal by force, they concluded that their dependence on Middle Eastern oil made their intervention inevitable.

Ike felt the strongest emotional ties to his old World War II allies, Britain and France, attachments that they counted on to defuse any bad feelings that might arise from their clandestine plot to retake the canal. Britain and France also calculated that Eisenhower would not want to become embroiled in a controversy with the U.S.'s most dependable allies on the eve of a presidential election. Similarly, the Israeli government considered that any reaction by Eisenhower to its invasion of Sinai would be mitigated by the strong pro-Israel sentiment in the United States, particularly among American Jews, which could affect the outcome of the election.

All of those calculations badly misread the mood and determination of the American president. Eisenhower felt betrayed by his allies and had no intention of standing passively aside while their forces converged on the Suez Canal. He ordered Dulles to send a telegram to the Israeli government. "Foster, you tell them, Goddamnit, that we're going to the United Nations, we're going to do everything that there is so we can stop this thing."[55] When Dulles suggested that the British and French expected American support in the crisis, Ike reminded him that the U.S., under the Tripartite Declaration, was obligated to support any victim of aggression in the Middle East. "What would they think if we were to go in to aid Egypt to fulfill our pledge?" he asked angrily.[56] "Nothing justifies double-crossing us. I don't care whether I'm re-elected or not. We must make good on our word; otherwise, we are a nation without honor."

Early the next morning, October 30, Eisenhower instructed Henry Cabot Lodge, the U.S. ambassador to the United Nations, to introduce a motion in the Security Council calling for an immediate cease-fire and the withdrawal of Israeli forces. Great Britain and France vetoed the motion, their first in the history of the organization. Lodge was told to appeal the cease-fire resolution to the U.N. General Assembly.

That same day, Britain and France, as planned, issued ultimatums to Egypt and Israel to stop fighting, withdraw from the canal, and permit Anglo-French occupation of the canal zone. Israel immediately announced its willingness to comply with the ultimatum, but the Egyptians ignored it. Twelve hours later, British and French planes began attacks on targets in Cairo, Port Said, and Alexandria. Nasser responded by sinking a 320-foot freighter loaded with cement at the narrowest point of the canal, effectively blocking maritime traffic.

On November 1, Eisenhower's speech writer, Emmet John Hughes, drafted a speech for the president to deliver in a nationally televised address from Philadelphia's Convention Hall, his final formal speech of the campaign. The speech was done "entirely on a crash basis," wrote the president's secretary, Ann Whitman, and "for the record, the last page was typed ten minutes before the broadcast began."[57] In his address, Eisenhower drew a clear line between U.S. policy in the Middle East and that of her most reliable allies, Britain, France, and Israel. "We cannot and will not condone armed aggression—no matter who the attacker, and no matter who the victim. We cannot—in the world, any more than in our own nation—subscribe to one law for the weak, another law for the strong; one law for those opposing us, another for those allied with us.... There can be only one law or there will be no peace."[58]

Later that night, the U.N. General Assembly approved the U.S. cease-fire resolution 64–5, with only Australia and New Zealand joining Britain, France, and Israel in voting no.

Undeterred, Israeli troops continued their attack across the Sinai, while British and French planes bombarded Egyptian targets. On November 5, British and French paratroopers landed around Port Said on the Suez Canal. At the same time, an armada of two hundred British and French ships, including five aircraft carriers, six battleships, and a dozen cruisers, arrived off the Egyptian coast, followed by the amphibious landing of commandos. By noon most of Port Said, at the mouth of the Suez Canal, was under the control of British and French forces.

"You are not going to get a cease-fire by saying everybody please stop," Eisenhower told Dulles.[59] In addition to his formal call for a cessation of hostilities, the president exerted economic pressure on Britain, ordering the Treasury Department to reduce British access to dollar accounts in the U.S. With the value of the pound falling, British deputy prime minister Rab Butler made an urgent call to Secretary of the Treasury Humphrey asking for an emergency loan during the crisis. The U.S. was prepared to give Britain a $1.5 billion loan with deferred interest payments, Humphrey replied, as soon as Britain accepted a cease-fire and withdrew its troops. Eisenhower also shelved plans to provide Western Europe with oil, if supplies from the Middle East were cut off. Irate British motorists, meanwhile, queued in long lines at petrol stations while tens of thousands of demonstrators crowded into Trafalgar Square to protest what the *Manchester Guardian* derisively referred to as "Eden's War."[60]

Just when it seemed that the Suez crisis could not get worse, Soviet Premier Bulganin sent messages to Britain, France, and Israel warning that the Middle East conflict could escalate "into a third World War," vowing to "crush the aggressor and reestablish peace in [the Middle East] by using force."[61] He also sent a letter to Eisenhower suggesting that the U.S. and the Soviet Union join forces to impose order in the region.

Eisenhower was wary but not intimidated by Bulganin's threat of nuclear war. "Those boys are both furious and scared," he told a meeting of senior officials.[62] "Just as with Hitler, that makes for the most dangerous possible state of mind. And we better be damn sure that every intelligence point and every outpost of our armed forces is absolutely right on their toes," he continued. "If those fellows start something, we may have to hit them—and, if necessary, with *everything* in the bucket."

The president, though alert to the potentially catastrophic consequences of a clash with the Soviet Union, appeared fully in control, even relaxed, during the crisis. Instead of responding directly to Bulganin, he issued a White House press release stating that it was "unthinkable" for the U.S. to join forces with the Soviet Union in the Middle East.[63] He warned that the U.S. would oppose any military force to enter the Middle East except under a United Nations mandate. Without a direct threat to the Soviet Union, Eisenhower's message to the Soviets was unequivocal: Stay out of the Middle East.

Although the president remained outwardly calm, the stress of the crisis took its toll on his health. On Monday, November 5, he called in Dr. Snyder, who found Eisenhower's blood pressure elevated and his heartbeat irregular "with an average of 8 skips per minute."[64] After lying down, he complained of a headache and again called Snyder, who gave him Serpatilin, a mood stabilizer. After dinner, he made a final campaign speech to a crowd in Boston via closed-circuit television from the White House library. Shortly after 1 a.m, he drank a tall glass of scotch and water and went to bed.

The next day, Americans went to the polls to elect a president. Ike and Mamie voted early, then returned to the White House. Shortly after noon, Britain's Prime Minister Eden announced that his nation was ready to accept a cease-fire. When he heard the news, Eisenhower immediately placed a call to Eden. "Anthony," said Ike, "I can't tell you how pleased we are that you found it possible to accept the cease-fire."[65] The president pressed Eden to withdraw British troops from Suez within the week, a demand that the British prime minister reluctantly agreed to. France and Israel followed Britain's lead, and the crisis was over.

Eisenhower had said that his policy during the Suez crisis would not be affected by political concerns, and his decisive action underscored his resolve. But historically Americans have rallied around their commander in chief in a time of crisis, and they did so again in the 1956 presidential election. They gave Eisenhower the mandate he had sought, returning him to office by the largest presidential majority since FDR's landslide victory over Kansas governor Landon in 1936. He carried forty-one of the forty-eight states and won ten million more votes than Stevenson, double the margin of victory against his same opponent in 1952.

Chapter Ten

RED
MONDAY

PRESIDENT EISENHOWER'S ONLY CONVERSATION WITH Judge William J. Brennan, Jr., of the New Jersey Supreme Court before Brennan's appointment to the U.S. Supreme Court in late September 1956 lasted just twenty minutes and took place in the Oval Office the day before the official announcement of the nomination. In their brief conversation, Eisenhower asked Brennan about his army service during World War II which, according to Brennan, "apparently did not hurt me at all in Eisenhower's eyes."[1] The president did not ask Brennan a single question about his legal philosophy or his judicial opinions.

After the official White House announcement of his nomination, Brennan was driven to the Supreme Court by Attorney General Brownell and Deputy Attorney General William Rogers where he was greeted with the warm handshake of Chief Justice Warren. Warren had arranged for the four men to have lunch at the University Club, on Sixteenth Street, just a short drive from the court. The luncheon conversation was light and convivial, cut short by Brennan, who had to catch an afternoon train at Washington's Union Station so that he could return to New Jersey in time to attend a small dinner party for a few neighbors and friends at the Brennans' modest home in Rumson.

The party had been planned by Marjorie Brennan before she or her husband knew of his court appointment.

When Brennan returned to Washington to take his seat on the court for the 1956 term, he was escorted by Warren to the justices' third-floor lounge to meet his new judicial colleagues. Once the two men had entered the dimly lit room, the chief justice turned on the light switch to reveal seven associate justices of the Supreme Court munching sandwiches while intently watching the decisive seventh game of the World Series between the Brooklyn Dodgers and the New York Yankees. Warren introduced Brennan to each justice, then one of Brennan's new colleagues snapped, "Put out the lights."[2] After the game was over, won by the Yankees, Justice Harlan invited Brennan downstairs to his chambers.

"Do you smoke?" asked Harlan.

"Yes," Brennan replied hesitantly.

"Oh thank God," Harlan said. "I've been dying, dying around here—nobody smokes."

And that was Brennan's bizarre introduction to his brethren on the Supreme Court, his institutional home for the next thirty-four years, where he would establish one of the most important constitutional legacies of the modern judicial era.

———

ALTHOUGH BRENNAN WAS sworn in to take his place on the court six days after his first meeting with his new colleagues, his was an interim appointment subject to Senate confirmation. The confirmation appeared to be a mere formality until Senator Joseph McCarthy announced that he would oppose the nomination, labeling Brennan "supremely unfit."[3] McCarthy based his conclusion on two speeches delivered by Brennan questioning the anti-Communist hysteria in the country stoked, in no small measure, by the Wisconsin senator. Brennan's speeches contained the "same gobbleygook found in the Communist Daily Worker," McCarthy charged, accusing the nominee of "hiding behind his robes to conduct a guerrilla warfare against congressional committees."[4]

"Do you approve of congressional investigations of the Communist conspiracy?" McCarthy asked.[5]

"Not only do I approve, Senator," Brennan replied calmly, "but personally I cannot think of a more vital function of the Congress than the investigative function of its committees, and I can't think of a more important or vital objective of any committee investigation than that of rooting out subversives in government."

For two hours McCarthy grilled Brennan, circling back again and again to Brennan's speeches that, in his opinion, exposed the judge's Communist sympathies. But despite McCarthy's best efforts to intimidate the nominee, he could only elicit from Brennan the admission that "[t]here was a general atmosphere that bothered me, and I think a lot of other Americans . . . a general feeling of hysteria that I felt was very unfortunate."[6]

Brennan was confirmed by a voice vote on the Senate floor, with only McCarthy shouting "No."*

If McCarthy's demise as a political force in the country was complete by the court's 1956 term, McCarthyism was not. The widespread and often reckless efforts by federal and state governments to rid the country of Communist influence was reflected in the justices' docket that term, which was replete with constitutional challenges by those accused of disloyalty. There were twelve cases involving government efforts to punish suspected Communists during the term. But unlike the record of previous Warren Court terms, the justices decided against the government in all twelve cases. Warren and Brennan joined the

---

* On the same day, the Senate also confirmed Eisenhower's fourth appointment to the court, Charles Whittaker, a Missouri corporate lawyer whom the president had previously appointed to both a federal district court and a court of appeals, to replace Justice Reed.

court's opinion in each of those decisions. The chief justice's confidence in his new colleague was shown in his assignment to Brennan of the court's opinion in one of the most controversial of these cases, *Jencks v. United States.*[7]

Clinton Jencks was president of a local chapter of the International Union of Mine, Mill & Smelter Workers, an organization accused of being "Communist-dominated." Under the regulations of the federal Taft-Hartley law, he was required to file an affidavit with the National Labor Relations Board swearing that he was not a Communist. Two government witnesses, both Communist Party members paid by the FBI to make reports on Communist activities, testified that Jencks was a Communist and had lied under oath. At Jencks's trial, his lawyer asked the two government informers what they had told the FBI about Jencks. Each witness said that he could not recall his conversations with the FBI. Jencks's attorney then requested that the FBI files in the case be turned over to the judge for inspection and, after his inspection, that the judge give relevant information to the defense counsel for use in his cross-examination of the witnesses. The judge denied the motion, and Jencks was convicted of perjury for signing a false non-Communist affidavit with the NLRB. Jencks appealed, arguing that the trial judge had erred in denying his lawyer's motion to direct the government to produce the FBI reports for the judge's inspection.

By the time that the Jencks appeal reached the Supreme Court, one of the paid FBI informers admitted that he had lied in his testimony at the Jencks trial. Undaunted, the government argued in its appeal that the informer's admission that he had lied under oath was the perjured testimony, not his original accusation against Jencks.*

At the first of four conferences in which the *Jencks* case was dis-

---

* The FBI informer who had confessed to lying and fabricating information began serving a five-year prison sentence in the same month that the court announced its *Jencks* decision.

cussed, Chief Justice Warren declared that Jencks had been denied a fair trial and his conviction should be reversed. But Warren went further than Jencks's attorney in his appeal, asserting that the defendant was entitled to examine the reports of the FBI informers directly, without the review of the trial judge "particularly when he [Jencks] says he has no recollection of anything in those reports."[8] Brennan agreed with Warren. "[T]he statements should be made available to the parties," he said. "I don't like this examination by the judge only."

Every justice agreed with Warren and Brennan that Jencks's conviction should be reversed, but there was disagreement over the issue of whether the reports should be turned over to Jencks, or screened by the trial judge, who would give the defendant only those portions relevant to his lawyer's cross-examination. Justice Clark, who had served as attorney general under President Truman and was a close friend and admirer of FBI director J. Edgar Hoover, was outspoken in his objection to handing the FBI files over directly to the defendant.

Brennan, an experienced trial lawyer and judge, asked how a defense attorney could effectively cross-examine a potentially perjuring witness without having the relevant information about the witness's prior statements to the FBI. He concluded that the defense attorney, rather than the judge, would be in a better position to know if the FBI files contradicted the witness's testimony. Brennan gave the government a choice: it could open its files to the defense or dismiss the prosecution. But the government could not have it both ways. "[J]ustice requires no less," Brennan wrote in his opinion for the court.[9]

As expected, Justice Clark wrote an impassioned dissent, charging that the court had opened "a veritable Pandora's box of troubles" for the government in its efforts to protect national security.[10] He called for immediate action by Congress to repair the damage. Otherwise, he warned, "intelligence agencies of our Government engaged in law enforcement may as well close up shop, for the Court has opened their files to the criminal and thus afforded him a Roman holiday for rummaging through confidential information as well as vital national secrets."

Reaction to the court's *Jencks* decision was immediate and overwhelmingly negative. The justices were depicted in one political cartoon digging an escape route for Communist prisoners. Attorney General Brownell declared that *Jencks* had created "an emergency in law enforcement" and proposed legislation to curb its effect.[11] FBI director Hoover vowed not to prosecute suspected subversives rather than open up the agency's files to defense attorneys. Within days, members of Congress had heeded Justice Clark's call to action, introducing eleven separate bills to reverse the decision.

Shortly after the *Jencks* decision was announced, the *Wall Street Journal* reported that "[l]iberal leanings show up more and more in Eisenhower's Supreme Court. Warren lines up closely with Black and Douglas on the liberal side. Brennan promises to make it a foursome."[12] The president who had made the liberal wing of the court "a foursome" with his appointments of Warren and Brennan was not pleased. At a White House stag dinner Eisenhower confided to guests that he had "never been as mad in his life" as he was at the *Jencks* decision.[13]

On June 17, 1957, just two weeks after the *Jencks* decision was announced, the court handed down four more decisions upholding the civil liberties claims of suspected subversives. Two of the court's decisions condemned the freewheeling investigative tactics of government committees hunting subversives. A third decision overturned the dismissal of a high-ranking State Department official accused of Communist sympathies. The fourth decision reversed the convictions of more than a dozen West Coast leaders of the American Communist Party for lack of evidence of incitement to overthrow the American government by force.

Chief Justice Warren assigned himself the court's opinions in the two cases challenging the authority of government committees investigating witnesses suspected of disloyalty. In the first case, *Watkins v. United States*, John Watkins, an organizer for the United Automobile Workers, had freely discussed his support for Communist causes before the House Un-American Activities Committee. But he refused to answer questions about his associates who were no longer members of the Communist Party. When pressed, Watkins told the committee that he did not believe it had "the right to undertake the public exposure of persons because of their past activities." He was convicted of contempt for refusing to answer "pertinent" questions.

At the justices' conference discussion of *Watkins*, Warren set what he considered to be the constitutional parameters for a congressional investigation. The committee could not "expose for the purpose of exposure" but "must show why a witness's testimony is relevant to its investigation."[14] He then outlined what would become the foundation of his opinion: a broad limitation on congressional power into private affairs and a narrow interpretation of questions that were "pertinent" to a committee's investigation. The court majority then voted to reverse Watkins's conviction for contempt. Only Justice Clark dissented, defending the committee's broad authority to gather information on national security.

Both Frankfurter and Harlan urged Warren to write a narrow opinion that would concentrate on Watkins's case alone. As a HUAC witness, they contended, Watkins was entitled to know the relevance of the questions he was required to answer. In Warren's final draft, however, he went beyond the narrow confines of the case to express his revulsion at government-sponsored witch-hunts, for which the HUAC investigations were notorious. "No inquiry is an end in itself; it must be related to, and in furtherance of, a legitimate task of the Congress," he wrote.[15] "Investigations conducted solely for the personal aggrandizement of the investigator or to 'punish' those investigated are indefensible."

Warren's second opinion for the court dealt with the case of Paul

Sweezy, a classical Marxist economist, who had refused to answer questions from the New Hampshire attorney general.[16] The attorney general had been authorized by the state legislature to act as a one-man investigating committee into subversive activities in the state. He interrogated Sweezy about a lecture he had delivered at the University of New Hampshire as well as his activities in support of the Progressive Party during the 1948 presidential campaign. Sweezy, like Watkins, was found guilty of contempt for refusing to answer all of the state attorney general's questions in his far-reaching probe into the professor's professional life and activities. And again, Warren, writing for the court, after reversing Sweezy's conviction as a violation of his due-process rights, went beyond the narrow holding to condemn the attorney general's investigation in sweeping terms as an invasion of the defendant's academic freedom and political expression.

Frankfurter had sent Warren a barrage of written suggestions to tone down and constrict his *Watkins* opinion, with limited success, and made similar efforts to influence Warren's opinion in *Sweezy*. In Frankfurter's insistence on judicial restraint, he was joined by Justice Harlan, who was assigned the other two civil liberties opinions announced on June 17. In each of his opinions, Harlan demonstrated his skill as a legal surgeon, systematically cutting away at the myriad facts and relevant law until he had located the essential principle at stake.

In overturning the dismissal of John Stewart Service, a career foreign service officer who had been found guilty of disloyalty by the State Department's Loyalty Board, Harlan concluded that the State Department had not followed the explicit rules for dismissal laid out by its internal procedures.[17] And in *Yates v. United States*, in which the court reversed the convictions of fourteen second-tier American Communist leaders, Harlan distinguished the defendants' beliefs and abstract advocacy to overthrow the government from actual "incitement," defined as speech that incites illegal action.[18] Finding no evidence of "incitement," as required by the Smith Act, Harlan concluded that the defendants were protected by the First Amendment's guarantee of freedom of expression.

The *New York Times*, in an editorial published the day after the four decisions were announced, declared that "the Supreme Court has shown itself by far the most courageous of our three branches of Government in standing up for basic principles."[19] But the conservative *Chicago Tribune* was appalled. "The boys in the Kremlin may wonder why they need a fifth column in the United States so long as the Supreme Court is determined to be so helpful."[20]

The court decisions provoked a political backlash in Congress led by an alarmed coterie of anti-Communist senators. "If the Court had erred only once or twice in these decisions involving the greatest threat to human freedom, reasonable men could find excuses for it," exclaimed Senator William Jenner of Indiana.[21] "But what shall we say for this parade of decisions that have come down from our highest bench on Red Monday after Red Monday?" Senator Strom Thurmond of South Carolina suggested that all justices who had supported the "pro-Communist" rulings be impeached. Senator James Eastland of Mississippi proposed a constitutional amendment that would require all of the justices to be reconfirmed by the Senate every four years. In the end, Congress settled for much less than a wholesale dismantling of the court, passing legislation, informally known as the "Jencks Act," that modestly limited portions of FBI files that could be disclosed directly to defense counsel.

Overlooked in Congress's anti-Communist frenzy was the fact that the so-called pro-Communist rulings drew the votes of justices across the ideological spectrum, from the liberal wing anchored by Justices Black and Douglas to the most devoted proponents of judicial restraint, Justices Frankfurter and Harlan. In their condemnation of all of the court's decisions, congressional critics did not distinguish Warren's broad, blistering lectures to HUAC and to New Hampshire's attorney general for trampling on civil liberties in *Watkins* and *Sweezy* from Harlan's technical dissection of the facts and law in his *Service* and *Yates* opinions.

But leading newspapers and national magazines understood the difference and sensed that a new liberal bloc was forming among the justices. The *Wall Street Journal* had alerted its readers after the *Jencks* decision, and *Time* and *Life* magazines arrived at similar conclusions at the end of the court's term. *Time* dubbed the liberal wing "B.B.D. & W," a play on the initials of a leading New York advertising firm.[22] *Life* declared that Brennan, as much as Black, Douglas, and Warren, "has made possible the liberal domination of the Warren Court."[23]

At the end of the judicial term, *Time* devoted its cover story to the Warren Court and began with a favorite story of the chief justice about three workmen constructing a building. Asked to describe their work, the first workman answered, "I am following my trade."[24] The second said, "I am making a living." But the third replied, "I am building a temple." The lesson of the story for the chief justice was that "the law is a temple and the Supreme Court a builder." With the groundbreaking decisions of the court's term, *Time* concluded, "the blueprints were ready, the mortar was flying, and the marble blocks were moving toward a new look in U.S. legal architecture."

The enlarged liberal wing of the court was a cause of increasing concern to Justice Frankfurter. In another sign of his growing disenchantment with the chief justice, Frankfurter deplored Warren's opinions, like *Watkins* and *Sweezy*, that appealed to broad concepts of fairness and justice, untethered, in his mind, to the specific legal issues before the court. He expressed disgust that the chief, and now Brennan, had become dependable allies of the court's leading liberals, Black and Douglas, and began to refer to them derisively as "the Framers."[25] His close friend and frequent correspondent, Judge Learned Hand of the

U.S. Court of Appeals for the Second Circuit, nicknamed them the "Jesus Quartet."[26]

PRESIDENT EISENHOWER, whose criticism of the *Jencks* decision at a White House stag dinner had been leaked to the press, was reported to be "furious" over a number of the court's rulings.[27] The embarrassed president felt compelled to write a letter to Chief Justice Warren denying the reports. "I have no doubt that in private conversation someone did hear me express amazement about one decision," he wrote Warren, "but I have never even hinted at a feeling such as anger."[28] The letter left the chief justice to ponder the difference between the president's "amazement about one decision" (presumably *Jencks*) and his denial of "a feeling such as anger." Eisenhower's qualified expression of regret to Warren fell considerably short of support for the court's decisions.

At the president's press conference on June 26, 1957, reporters pursued the widely circulated story of Eisenhower's criticism of the court's decisions. The president conceded that "[p]ossibly in their latest series of decisions there are some that each of us has very great trouble understanding."*[29] He nonetheless dutifully called on the nation to respect the court, which he said was "one of the great stabilizing influences of this country."

Warren did not respond to the president's letter for three weeks. When he did respond, he assured Eisenhower that he was not upset by reports in the press of the president's criticism of the court's decisions.

---

* Ironically, Eisenhower in his pre–press conference briefing had expressed support for the court's *Watkins* decision. "He believes the Supreme Court is absolutely right in saying that congressional investigations have gone much farther than necessary for enacting legislation," the president's secretary, Ann Whitman, wrote. At his press conference, however, Eisenhower did not mention *Watkins* or any other court decision. (AW notes, pre–press conference briefing, June 19, 1957, DDEP.)

Many stories in the press were inaccurate or wrong, he noted, as they both knew. The best thing to do, Warren wrote, was to ignore those stories that were "unfounded," leaving the impression that, perhaps, reports of Eisenhower's displeasure with the court's decisions were accurate.[30]

In his memoirs, Warren left no doubt that he believed reports of Eisenhower's anger over the court's so-called Communists rulings, recalling a conversation on the subject between the two men that occurred in 1965 when both men were aboard Air Force One, at President Lyndon Johnson's invitation, to attend the funeral of Sir Winston Churchill in London. Warren wrote that Eisenhower told him that "he had been disappointed in Justice Brennan and me; that he had mistakenly thought we were 'moderate' when he appointed us, but eventually had concluded otherwise."[31] Warren replied that he had always considered himself a moderate, and asked Eisenhower what decisions he was referring to.

"He said, 'Oh, those Communist cases.'"

"What Communist cases?" Warren asked.

"All of them," Eisenhower replied.

Warren asked Eisenhower if he had read the opinions. "He said he had not, but he knew what was in them," Warren wrote. "I then suggested that he must have some particular case in mind, and he said, 'The Communists in California.'" Warren assumed that Eisenhower's reference was to the *Yates* decision, which, he wrote, "involved some garden variety Communists of no great importance." Warren informed Eisenhower that the opinion was written by another of his appointees, Justice Harlan, whom the former president had praised earlier in their conversation on Air Force One as a "moderate."[32] Eisenhower said it made no difference who wrote the opinion.

Warren then explained to Eisenhower "that in the judging process we were obliged to judge Communists by the same rules that we applied to all others. He refused to accept this statement, and I asked him:

"What would you do with Communists in America?"

"I would kill the S.O.B.s," he said.

Warren assumed the remark "was merely petulant rather than definitive," so he replied, "Perhaps that could be done in the army, but it could not be done through civilian courts."

Warren appreciated the opportunity his conversation with the former president had given him to distinguish "moderation" in the political process from that in the judicial process. He conceded that progress in politics was made by compromise. "The opposite is true so far as the judicial process was concerned," he wrote, especially at the Supreme Court. "[T]he basic ingredient of decision is principle, and it should not be compromised and parceled out a little in one case, a little more in another, until eventually someone receives the full benefit."

Warren's recollection of his conversation with Eisenhower appears in the first chapter of his memoirs, an indication of the importance that the former chief justice assigned to the episode. It depicts the former president as hopelessly naïve in his understanding of the court's work, a characterization that is both unflattering and unfair. Though Ike often reminded reporters that he was not a lawyer, he was hardly ignorant of the court's role. His appointment of Warren to the court demonstrated that he possessed a keen understanding of the qualities of leadership he sought in a chief justice, qualities that most court historians have concluded that Warren demonstrated admirably. When pressed, Eisenhower could also parse the language of a legal document, as he did in revising the Justice Department's *Brown II* brief. And while expressing disappointment in Warren's and Brennan's opinions, Eisenhower said that he appreciated the "moderation" of Justice Harlan, suggesting that Harlan's judicial restraint more accurately reflected his concept of judicial decision-making than the chief justice's.

However accurate Warren's memory of his conversation with the former president, his simmering resentment of Eisenhower's failure to support some of the Warren Court's most controversial civil liberties decisions is clear. The president not only privately disapproved of many of the court's "Communist" rulings, but his Justice Department pushed successfully for the passage of legislation that served as a mild rebuke to the court's *Jencks* decision.

The Warren-Eisenhower conversation on Air Force One, in addition to underscoring the chief justice's resentment of Eisenhower's criticism of the court's "Red Monday" decisions, served as an accurate description of Warren's evolving approach to vital constitutional issues. No longer the cautious jurist of his early judicial terms, the chief justice increasingly conceived of the court's role as the nation's fearless defender of individual rights. As he told Eisenhower, the court could not parcel out justice in technical, mincing decisions, but must act on principle alone, eschewing compromise or regard for political consequence.

ON JANUARY 10, 1957, President Eisenhower reported in his State of the Union address that the nation was moving closer to fair and equal treatment for all American citizens, regardless of race or color, "but unhappily much remains to be done."[33] He then reintroduced Attorney General Brownell's civil rights bill that had failed to pass during the previous congressional session, enumerating the four main provisions of the bill: the appointment of a bipartisan civil rights commission, creation of a civil rights division in the Justice Department, authority for the attorney general to seek judicial enforcement of civil rights violations, and the protection of voting rights.

Eisenhower considered the entire bill a model of moderation, a common-sense approach to an intractable problem. He wanted to replace heated rhetoric with incremental, pragmatic solutions. To the president, it was simply a matter of respecting the rule of law. Without law, he often said, there would be chaos.

But leaders in the white South viewed the proposed legislation through a radically different prism, raising the specter of a second Reconstruction era in which the federal government imposed its will on a brooding, defiant Confederacy. Their first line of defense was resistance to *Brown* by "all available legal means," as the Southern Manifesto had declared a year earlier.[34] Southern leaders had proved adept at erecting multiple legal obstacles to delay or halt integration in their public schools. In 1957, three years after *Brown*, public school desegregation in the Deep South remained an empty promise.

While lawyers for the southern states fought the *Brown II* mandate in the courts, die-hard segregationists' resistance turned to violence. Four black churches in Montgomery, Alabama, were bombed the night before Eisenhower's's State of the Union address. Eisenhower had inexplicably failed to mention the "rising tide of hate-inspired violence," complained Roy Wilkins, the head of the NAACP, in a telegram to the president.[35] A day after Eisenhower's State of the Union, Dr. Martin Luther King, Jr., informed the president that African Americans had been beaten or stoned in Tennessee, Alabama, and Florida.

Eisenhower had deftly managed the Middle East crisis, forcing America's closest allies, Great Britain, France, and Israel, to retreat from Suez. Less than three months after that diplomatic triumph, he faced a comparably daunting challenge at home: to persuade Congress to pass the first federal civil rights bill in eighty-two years. But unlike the Suez crisis, when Eisenhower decisively wielded his executive authority, the president found himself tenuously holding the middle ground, pressed by stubborn white segregationists on one side and impatient black leaders on the other. The halting, often frustratingly slow progress of the administration's civil rights bill through Congress demonstrated the difficulty of Eisenhower's task.

————

THROUGHOUT THE WINTER and spring of 1957, Eisenhower felt intense pressure from both sides of the civil rights divide. Dr. King urged the president to use "the weight of your great office to point out to the people of the South the moral nature of the problem."[36] After Eisenhower refused Dr. King's invitation to go to the South to demonstrate his support for civil rights, the black minister announced that he would lead a prayer vigil in the nation's capital. "If you cannot come south to relieve our harassed people," he wrote Eisenhower, "we shall have to lead our people to you in the capital."[37]

King kept his word. On May 17, 1957, the third anniversary of the court's *Brown* decision, he led a "Prayer Pilgrimage for Freedom" on the national mall culminating at the Lincoln Memorial, where tens of thousands of African Americans gathered to hear the young minister, in his earliest address to a national audience, denounce the persistence of segregation in schools, suppression of voting rights, and the culture of racial violence that continued to plague the nation.

The administration's bill, meanwhile, was fiercely attacked by segregationists in hearings before the House Judiciary Committee. One hostile witness accused the administration of producing a "Soviet type Gestapo."[38] A member of the committee, Congressman Henderson Lanham of Georgia, struck the same theme, comparing the bill to the tyrannical reign of the late Soviet dictator, Joseph Stalin.

The president studiously hewed to his middle course. He told reporters that there was nothing in the civil rights bill "that is inimical to the interests of anyone."[39] The legislation, he said, was intended "to preserve rights without arousing passions and without disturbing the rights of anybody else." It was, he concluded, "a very decent and very needful piece of legislation."

Eisenhower's soothing words in public and quiet lobbying of Republican leaders in Congress succeeded, at least in the House of Representatives. On June 18, the House decisively passed the bill with all four sections intact.

Success in the Senate was a wholly different challenge. The problem for the president was complicated by the power and political ambition of the Senate majority leader, Lyndon B. Johnson of Texas.

Johnson, forty-eight years old, had grown up in the impoverished hill country of central Texas. As a tall, skinny teenager, he worked on road gangs, cleared cedar on neighboring farms, and picked cotton in the blazing Texas summer heat. But even though he grew up in poverty, he possessed a preternatural confidence that he would one day rise to national prominence and power. "I'm going to be President of the United States one day," he predicted.[40]

At the age of thirty, Johnson was elected to the House of Representatives and immediately became an ardent supporter of FDR's New Deal. The young legislator, who impressed the president with his enthusiasm, energy, and loyalty, was offered the directorship of the New Deal's Rural Electrification Administration. He turned it down, determined to pursue his political ambitions. In 1948 he ran for the Senate in a contest in which he was given little chance of victory. He won the Democratic primary (tantamount to election in Texas) by just eighty-seven votes, amid charges and countercharges of ballot-stuffing, earning the sobriquet "Landslide Lyndon." Once in the Senate, Johnson became a consummate deal maker, successfully cajoling and intimidating colleagues into voting for the bills that he wanted passed. He was elected majority leader in 1955.

In 1957, Johnson was the most powerful man in Congress and a leading Democratic candidate for the presidency in 1960. The civil rights bill posed both an opportunity and a danger for him. To be a viable presidential candidate in 1960, Johnson knew that he needed to expand his political base beyond the South. The civil rights bill appeared to present him with the perfect opportunity to burnish his image in the North and West. But if the bill was opposed by his southern Democratic colleagues, they not only could doom the legislation but withhold their vital support from him at the party's convention in 1960.

On June 15, Johnson told the president in a telephone conversation that "[t]he Senate is going to fight on the civil rights issue," adding that "tempers were flaring already and would be worse."[41] He advised Eisenhower to postpone debate on the civil rights bill, so that he could pass a number of appropriations bills "necessary for the running of the government." Anticipating the fight over the civil rights bill, he said, "You can let us fight July and August and, if necessary, into September."

Eisenhower was unhappy with Johnson's advice to delay the legislation, pleading with the majority leader that the administration's bill "was the mildest civil rights bill possible."[42] He stressed that he had lived in the South and "had no lack of sympathy for the southern position." He was "a little struck back on his heels when he found the terrific uproar that was created by the bill."

As if to reinforce his sympathy for "the southern position," Eisenhower delivered a speech to the Governors Conference in Williamsburg, Virginia, nine days later in which he assured his audience that he believed deeply in states' rights. He added the hopeful corollary that he considered it idle to "champion states rights without upholding states responsibilities as well."[43]

Eisenhower had been forewarned by Johnson that there was trouble ahead for the civil rights legislation, and it did not take long for the president to realize that the majority leader, as usual, had a firm grip on the pulse of the Senate. On July 2, Senator Richard Russell of Georgia, the tall, patrician leader of the southern delegation, rose to speak in opposition to the legislation. In his quarter century in the Senate, Russell, fifty-nine years old, had never lost a civil rights fight. He was so revered as a legislative strategist that he had been called the South's greatest general since Robert E. Lee.

Russell denounced the legislation as "a cunning device" that would place the "whole might of the federal government, including the armed forces if necessary, to force a commingling of white and Negro children."[44] The attorney general, he charged, had designed the legislation "to destroy the system of separation of the races in the Southern States at the point of a bayonet." Should anyone have missed his implicit historical analogy, he compared the Senate bill to "the bayonet rule of Reconstruction days." Russell, who had enjoyed a cordial relationship with the president, doubted that "the full implications of the bill have ever been explained to President Eisenhower."

Eisenhower was shaken by Russell's speech, especially the senator's suggestion that he did not fully understand the provisions of the administration's bill. He commented in a pre–press conference briefing the next day that he had assumed the bill's language "provided for the A.G. to use troops only in the event of restriction on voting."[45] But section 3 of the original civil rights bill explicitly authorized the attorney general to seek a court order to enforce federally guaranteed civil rights, which included the court's ruling to desegregate the South's public schools. Eisenhower recalled that "that was not the way the Attorney General explained it to him."

At his press conference on the day after Russell's speech, Eisenhower was asked by the *New York Times's* James Reston to comment on the Georgia senator's charge that the civil rights bill was a "cunning device" to force, by bayonet if necessary, the integration of black and white students in the South's public schools. In response, Eisenhower repeated his view that the bill was "a very moderate move."[46] But he appeared befuddled when asked if he intended to concentrate exclusively on the voting-rights provision of the bill. "I was reading part of that bill this morning," he said, "and there were certain phrases I didn't completely understand. So, before I make any more remarks on that, I would want to talk to the Attorney General and see exactly what they do mean."

Eisenhower called Attorney General Brownell shortly after the press conference to ask for clarification of the bill's coverage, reiterating his concern over the wide scope of the legislation. He told Brownell that he was most interested in protecting voting rights, expressing dismay that only 7,000 African Americans voted out of a population of 900,000 in Mississippi. But he stressed that he did not want a bill "that scares people to death."[47]

Eisenhower's confession of ignorance of one of the main provisions of the civil rights bill was astounding. He had endorsed every provision of the legislation in his State of the Union address. Even if he had not taken the time to carefully examine the administration's bill, it is inconceivable that Attorney General Brownell, a meticulous lawyer, would have failed to explain to his only client, the president of the United States, the ramifications of the civil rights bill, including the AG's authority to seek judicial relief for violations of the court's *Brown* decision. Brownell, one of president's most trusted advisers, was held in such high regard by Eisenhower during the battle over the civil rights legislation in 1957 that he still hoped to appoint him to the Supreme Court.*

In his numerous press conferences as president, Eisenhower had perfected the art of dodging reporters' pointed questions on politically sensitive subjects, often by obfuscation or, at times, outright dissembling. However credible his expression of puzzlement over the civil rights bill's broad scope, his admission effectively provided him

---

* Eisenhower, in a diary entry dated February 5, 1957, wrote that he told Brownell "that if he had any ambition to go on the Court, that we should appoint him immediately to the vacancy now existing on the appellate court in New York and then, when and if another vacancy occurred on the Supreme Court, I could appoint him to it." Brownell later told the president that he preferred to return to private law practice after serving as AG. (DDE diary, February 5, 1957, DDEP.)

with political cover, and flexibility, in his preparation for what now appeared to be a nasty fight in the Senate over the legislation.

Republican legislative leaders who met with Eisenhower and Brownell at the White House on July 9 advised the president and his attorney general that a compromise would be necessary to pass the administration's civil rights bill. Senator Everett Dirksen of Illinois quoted Senator Russell's description of the controversial section 3 of the bill as a "Force Act."[48]

Brownell responded by noting that the administration did not need that provision to enforce existing federal laws with troops, if necessary. Congressman Charles Halleck of Indiana asked Brownell how important the third section of the bill was. He replied that the provision extended civil rights protections beyond the right to vote.

At this point in the discussion, Eisenhower came to the defense of section 3 of the bill. He said that "the only new thing in the picture was the Supreme Court's decision, and the Administration wanted to make certain that federal court orders are not flouted."[49] He stressed that he had a constitutional duty "to support the Courts." In response, the party's congressional leaders reiterated that compromise on the bill was inevitable. Still, Eisenhower refused to abandon section 3. He conceded only that he would consider clarifying language, "but there were four essential points that must be kept in."

Despite his vocal support for all four sections of the bill, Eisenhower was already laying the groundwork for a compromise. He met with Senator Russell the next day to discuss the bill.* In their fifty-five-minute meeting, Senator Russell was "emotional about the matter," according to the notes of Ann Whitman.[50] In response, the president conceded that he would be open to clarifying amendments to the bill.

---

* For months, Eisenhower had ignored numerous requests by black leaders, including the NAACP's Roy Wilkins and Dr. King, to meet with him during the debate over the civil rights legislation.

The meeting, Whitman wrote, restored "some measure of friendship between the Senator and the President."

Eisenhower was aware that Whitman did not share his sympathy for the southern position. "He [Eisenhower] always says, 'I have lived in the South, remember,'" she wrote.[51] "I do think he is adamant on the fact that the right to vote must be protected," she added.

Eisenhower was, indeed, adamant on the protection of the right to vote. He was also acutely aware of the official subterfuges applied in the South to discriminate against blacks. At one meeting with legislative leaders to discuss the bill, he repeated a story that he had heard about a bright, young, white Mississippi law student who had failed the state bar examination twice. The young man's father met with the examining officials and asked if he might see the questions that had been asked of his son. Quickly perusing the questions, he exclaimed, "For goodness sake, you gave him the Negro examination!"[52]

On July 16, in another meeting with Republican legislative leaders, the president continued to defend the entire bill, including the controversial section 3. "[T]he intent is simply that the orders of the federal courts will be supported," he said. The provision, he noted, did no more than support the court's mandate that school integration proceed "with all deliberate speed."[53] But then Eisenhower gave the legislators the opening that they had waited for. He said, "[I]f we got simply the voting rights, that would not be a hollow victory," adding that clarification of section 3 "would not be harmful."

Later that day, the Senate voted to take up the civil rights bill. At his press conference that followed the vote, Eisenhower applauded the Senate action and reaffirmed his support for section 3, which he said was "a reasonable program of assistance in efforts to protect other constitutional rights of our citizens."[54] He did not rule out compromise on the language of the bill, but emphasized that all four sections of the legislation should be approved by the Senate—"each one of which is consistent with simple justice and equality afforded to every citizen under the Constitution of the United States."

But almost in the next breath, the president invited compromise on the substance of the bill. He expressed a preference for protecting black Americans' right to vote (section 4) rather than their right to attend public schools with whites, which would be enforced by section 3. He said, "If in every locality every person . . . is permitted to vote, he has got the means of getting what he wants in democratic government, and that is the one on which I place the greatest emphasis." He was then asked if he would veto a bill that did not include the attorney general's authority to go to court to enforce school integration. While not answering the question directly, he indicated his willingness to jettison the third section of the bill if that was necessary to preserve the guarantee of the right to vote. In an unmistakable reference to the problem of forcing public school integration in the South, he said, "I personally believe if you try to go too far too fast in laws in this delicate field that has involved the emotions of so many millions of Americans, you are making a mistake."

Merriman Smith, the White House correspondent for United Press International, asked the president if he believed he had the authority to use military force to enforce school integration in the South. He had that authority, Eisenhower replied, but "I can't imagine any set of circumstances that would ever induce me to send federal troops into a federal court and into any area to enforce the order of a federal court, because I believe that common sense of America will never require it." And he added, "I would never believe that it would be a wise thing to do in this country."

Privately, Eisenhower continued to express concern over the effect of the court's *Brown* decision on the South. "I think that no other single event has as disturbed the domestic scene in many years as did the Supreme Court's decision on 1954 in the school segregation case," he wrote Swede Hazlett.[55] Noting that the decision had put heavier responsibilities on the federal government, he observed, "[w]hen emotions are deeply stirred, logic and reason must operate gradually and with consideration for human feeling or we will have a resultant disaster rather than human advancement." He understood the reaction of the white South, which had accepted the court's judgment between 1896 (*Plessy*) and 1954 (*Brown*) that segregation was "both legal and ethical." After fifty-eight years of court-sanctioned separation of the races, he continued, "the plan of the Supreme Court to accomplish integration gradually and sensibly seems to me to provide the only possible answer if we are to consider on the one hand the customs and fears of a great section of our population, and on the other the binding effect that Supreme Court decisions must have on all of us if our form of government is to survive and prosper."

In a private meeting with Eisenhower, Senate majority leader Johnson told the president bluntly that he had the votes to defeat the bill if the president refused to cut section 3 from the legislation. Eisenhower, without consulting Brownell, caved in to Johnson's ultimatum.[56] He concluded that it was a necessary price to pay to salvage the other provisions of the legislation. After the president's capitulation, the Senate formally voted to eliminate section 3 from the bill.

Brownell was disappointed. He had been prepared to push for the passage of section 3 on the Senate floor. Even if it had been defeated, he doubted that Johnson controlled enough votes in the Senate to kill the whole bill. With the president's strong support, Brownell was confident that, even if section 3 was defeated, the remaining sections of the bill would have passed.

SOUTHERN LEADERS IN the Senate, emboldened by the president's concession, pressed their advantage. No longer satisfied with the elimination of section 3, they demanded an amendment to section 4, the voting rights section, that would have required a jury trial for anyone charged with contempt of court in a civil law suit for interfering with an individual's right to vote. No one could fail to see that the motive behind the amendment was to undermine the protection of the right to vote for black Americans. In the South, jury rolls were almost exclusively comprised of whites. No white defendant, therefore, was likely to be found guilty by a white jury of violating the voting rights of black voters.

Ninety-eight legal experts, including the deans of fourteen of the nation's leading law schools, publicly opposed the jury trial amendment. "While we fully support trial by jury in its proper sphere," their statement said, "we fear that its unnecessary injection into this legislation will only hamper and delay the Department of Justice and the courts in carrying out their constitutional duty to protect voting ... rights of citizens."[57]

Eisenhower vigorously opposed the amendment, recognizing it for what it was: a ruse to undercut the guarantee of the right to vote. When his old friend, former South Carolina governor Byrnes, wrote him in support of the jury trial amendment, Ike responded angrily. In his rebuttal to Byrnes, he was no longer the confused president of his recent press conference who confessed that he did not fully understand his administration's bill. "[W]hat you are really objecting to is giving of authority to the Attorney General to institute civil actions," he wrote.[58] The legislation "was conceived under the theory that the whole public has an interest in protection of the right [to vote]." The attorney general should be given the authority to enforce this public right by civil action, he continued, just as he already had authority to enforce it by criminal prosecution.

The public interest in the protection of voting rights, the president wrote Byrnes, "is at least as great as the public interest in the maintenance of minimum wages, or in the truthfulness of financial and other statements in connection with security sales, or in the shipment in interstate commerce of contraband oil."[59] To Eisenhower, "the right to vote is more important in our way of life than are the regulations cited above." He then pointed to the anomaly, urged by Byrnes and other southern politicians, that would have required a jury trial only in this one area of federal civil litigation. "I don't see how we can provide a jury trial in this legislation and leave the rest of the great body of federal law covered by the rule of no jury trial," he wrote.

Before closing his letter to Byrnes, Eisenhower challenged the assertion of the former governor that his opposition to the jury trial amendment created doubts among the president's southern friends as to his loyalty to the South. "Many of my dearest friends are in that region," Ike wrote.[60] "I spent a not inconsiderable part of my lifetime in the South or the Border states, and moreover this question of assuring the civil rights to all citizens does *not* apply exclusively to the southern states."

When the jury trial amendment came up for a vote in the Senate, Republican minority leader Knowland shouted to his colleagues, "Support President Dwight D. Eisenhower!"[61] But on August 1, twelve members of the president's party joined thirty-nine Democrats to pass the amendment.

Eisenhower was livid. "We've taken political defeats in [the] past four years, but this one is the worst," he told his cabinet.[62] In a statement issued later that day, the president said that the Senate vote was "bitterly disappointing" and that the amendment would weaken the entire federal judicial system and "make largely ineffective the basic purpose of the bill—that of protecting promptly and effectively every American in his right to vote."[63] His bitterness over the defeat was echoed in his letter to his close friend Bob Woodruff, in which he complained that "the country took an awful beating."[64]

After the administration's defeat on the jury trial amendment, Eisenhower listened to the suggestions from Republican legislative leaders for his next move. Representative Joseph Martin, Jr., of Massachusetts, the House minority leader, recommended that the entire bill be dropped and resubmitted in 1958. Senator Knowland told the president that the Senate would not pass a civil rights bill without a jury trial amendment and said that the administration must pursue "the art of the possible."[65]

Eisenhower brooded silently, then raged at the southern senators "who can bamboozle [the] entire Senate," the liberal Democrats who had abandoned their principles to win votes in the 1958 elections, and, most of all, Lyndon Johnson, whom he derisively referred to as the "great leader" who had torpedoed any hope of effective civil rights legislation.[66] Later, at a pre–press conference, he observed with biting sarcasm that a "lot of people seem to be working to protect the right of the man who might interfere with another's voting right, rather than protecting [the] right of the citizen to vote."[67]

Should the president veto the legislation? Or should he seek a better bill than the one currently being considered by a joint committee of the House and Senate? On August 16, White House counsel Gerald Morgan offered Eisenhower a compromise on the jury trial amendment. A federal judge, Morgan suggested, could try a defendant for contempt without a jury trial so long as the penalty for conviction was no more than a $300 fine or ninety days in jail. It was a legislative palliative that did not provide a strong enforcement mechanism to punish those guilty of interfering with the right to vote. But it was better than completely abandoning the effort to produce a viable civil rights bill.

Eisenhower began to negotiate a compromise in public. At his press conference on August 21, he complained that the bill with the jury trial amendment was not strong enough. "I can't conceive of anything worse than making the basic right of so many millions of our citizens just a part of political snarling as to who is to blame for this and who is to get credit for that."[68]

Lyndon Johnson, however, most assuredly wanted credit for passing a civil rights bill. Failure would have been a notable blemish on his résumé as a presidential aspirant. He called Eisenhower two days after his press conference to report that he thought he could find the votes for "a compromise on the civil rights bill of $300 and 45 days."[69] Johnson's reference was to the penalty limit for civil contempt of court for violating an individual's voting rights before a jury trial would be required. He asked the president "to see quietly if his boys would agree to that."

The president told Johnson that he needed ten minutes to consult with Republican congressional leaders, Martin in the House and Knowland in the Senate. He reached them by telephone at the Capitol, and both agreed to the terms. Eisenhower called Johnson back and said they had a deal. He later wrote Martin that it was "a great victory."[70] Final passage of the Civil Rights Act of 1957 came less than a week later.

EISENHOWER'S "MIDDLE WAY" had produced a historic civil rights law, the first since Reconstruction. But it was a mere shell of the legislation that the president had championed in his State of the Union address. His negotiating position, from the beginning, was compromised by his sympathy for "the southern position," especially when it clashed with the bill's section empowering the attorney general to enforce the *Brown II* mandate in court. His lack of firm conviction, displayed in his rambling, often confusing press conference explanations, was a sign of weakness fully exploited by the bill's southern opponents. And even on the provision he strongly supported, voting rights, he was outmaneuvered, settling for an emasculated version of the original bill that held little promise of meaningful protection.*

* By the end of 1958, in the eight southern states in which official statistics were available, not only had the number of registered black voters not risen, it had actually fallen. Those statistics, compiled by the Southern Regional Council, did not include Mississippi and Alabama, two of the most recalcitrant states in the Deep South.

Eisenhower listed the Civil Rights Act of 1957 with his other major accomplishments in the civil rights field, including desegregating the military, naval yards in the South, and public facilities in the District of Columbia. But a comprehensive civil rights bill, one that placed the full power of the federal government behind the Constitution's guarantee of equal rights for black Americans, would, in the end, require the aggressive advocacy of a future president, Lyndon B. Johnson.

Chapter Eleven

LITTLE
ROCK

IN THE MID–NINETEEN FIFTIES, THE STATE OF ARKANSAS was heralded as a precursor of the New South, bustling and progressive, a generation removed from its image as a cultural backwater dominated by rubes and racists. The state university's law and medical schools had been integrated for a decade without the need of a court order. Arkansas governor Orval E. Faubus, considered a moderate on race relations, had said when *Brown II* was handed down in 1955 that the state's citizens should rely "upon the good will that exists between the races—the good will that has long made Arkansas a model for other Southern states in all matters affecting the relationship between the races."[1]

Leaders of the moderate white establishment in Little Rock, the state capital, planned carefully for the integration of the city's public schools. The Little Rock Board of Education submitted a plan to the federal district court in 1955 to comply with the *Brown II* mandate. It called for the gradual integration of the city's public schools, beginning with the high schools. After the court approved the city's plan, nine black teenagers, raised in middle-class families and chosen for their academic excellence and strength of character, prepared to enter

Central High School in the fall of 1957 as the first step in the implementation of the city's plan.

As the first day of the 1957 school year approached, the habitually garrulous Governor Faubus became guarded and unavailable to school officials. The exasperated school superintendent, Virgil Blossum, finally asked Faubus, "Governor, just what are you going to do in regard to the Little Rock integration plan?"[2] Faubus paused, then answered, "When you tell me what the federals are going to do, I will tell you what I am going to do."

The governor's enigmatic reply suggested that he expected the federal government to relieve him of any leadership role in integrating the Little Rock public schools. What had happened to the moderate governor who held up his state as a model of good will and cooperation in race relations?

No doubt Faubus had begun to feel political pressure from the state legislature, which had passed a flurry of bills to keep the state's public schools segregated. At the same time, the governor's publicly proclaimed moderation was being pilloried by segregationist leaders in the Deep South. Senator James Eastland of Mississippi, for example, singled out Faubus as one of the "weak-kneed politicians in the state capitals" who were promoting the "damnable doctrine of gradualism."[3] Shortly before Little Rock's Central High School was scheduled to admit its first black students, the racist governor of Georgia, Marvin Griffin, and the head of the Citizens Council, Roy Harris, paid a visit to Faubus.

Faubus's overriding consideration in dealing with integration of Little Rock's public schools was his political future. He planned to run for a third two-year term in 1958, aware that the state's voters had been stingy in extending gubernatorial tenure beyond four years. He knew that he would face a right-wing opponent, Jim Johnson, who was an outspoken defender of segregation. Should Faubus be defeated, his job prospects were not bright. He was not a lawyer who could return to a profitable practice. Nor did he have a prosperous family business to run once he left the governor's mansion.

The forty-seven-year-old governor was born in a two-room shack near Greasy Creek in the desolate hill country of northwestern Arkansas. He was one of seven children of Sam Faubus, a poor farmer who raised corn and light grain and railed against Wall Street and the oppression of capitalism. Orval's middle name was Eugene, honoring his father's hero, the Socialist presidential candidate Eugene V. Debs. At eighteen, Orval, with only an eighth grade education, passed an examination for a state teaching certificate and began teaching school five miles from his home in the town of Pinnacle. While teaching, he earned a high school diploma. In the summers, he rode trains as a hobo, following the strawberry harvest north to Michigan or heading west to pick apples and cut timber. He became active in local politics before joining the army in World War II, rising to the rank of major in army intelligence. After the war, he returned to Arkansas, entered politics full time, and became the state highway commissioner with the reputation as the most liberal member of the administration of moderate governor Sid McMath.

In 1954, Faubus successfully ran for governor as a populist, promising more roads, schools, and prosperity to rural Arkansas. He was reelected two years later, barely mentioning the issue of race in his campaign. On the stump and off, Faubus affected an easy, country charm that belied his calculating intelligence. He was like an Airedale dog, said Harry Ashmore, the editor of the *Arkansas Gazette*, a lot smarter than he looked.

ON LABOR DAY, September 2, 1957, Governor Faubus announced in a radio address that he had ordered soldiers from the Arkansas National Guard to report for duty at Little Rock's Central High School the next day to maintain law and order. He cited reports of increased gun sales and mobs of racist vigilantes converging on the high school for the first day of school. His avowed purpose was to keep all students safe, but his true intention was to prevent the nine black students from entering Central High School. The next day, 270 bayonet-wielding guardsmen ringed the high school. On the advice of the school board, the nine black students scheduled to register at the high school stayed home. The board then sought further instructions from U. S. District Judge Ronald Davies, who had issued the original order to desegregate the high school.

The developing crisis in Little Rock was President Eisenhower's worst post-*Brown* nightmare. He had studiously avoided taking sides on the issue of school integration beyond calling for all parties to respect the rule of law. But he had also made it clear in his public statements as well as in his private correspondence that he sympathized with southern whites who had become accustomed to Supreme Court decisions before 1954 that had ruled separation of the races in public schools was constitutional.

At his pre–press conference on Tuesday, September 3, Eisenhower expressed frustration with "these people who believe you are going to reform the human heart by law."[4] In his press conference later that day, Eisenhower was asked if he planned to take any action to resolve the crisis in Little Rock. He had no plans for federal intervention, he said, suggesting that it was neither legally possible nor politically desirable for the executive branch of the federal government to step in at that time.* He urged restraint on all parties involved, adding his familiar refrain that "[y]ou cannot change people's hearts merely by laws."[5]

In a vague, garbled endorsement of *Brown*, Eisenhower told reporters that the court's opinion had "pointed to the emotional difficulties

---

* The lawsuit to integrate Little Rock's public schools had been brought by black parents against the city's school board officials as defendants. Since the federal government was not a party to the lawsuit, it could only participate by filing a brief as an *amicus curiae*, or friend of the court.

that would be encountered by a Negro, even if given . . . equal but sep-arate schools and I think probably their reasoning was correct, at least I have no quarrel with it."[6] But he tacked on an unfortunate observation that "there are very strong emotions on the other side, people that see a picture of mongrelization of the race, they call it." He concluded that "we are going to whip this thing in the long run by Americans being true to themselves and not merely by law."

Eisenhower then engaged in a typical ploy to divert attention from the Oval Office on a politically volatile issue. He said that he had referred the issue to the attorney general's office and "they are going to find out exactly what has happened and discuss this with the Fed-eral Judge."[7] In fact, for months prior to the Little Rock crisis, Attor-ney General Brownell had been involved with his staff in developing contingency plans to deal with such a crisis. He was fully versed in the legal precedents available to the president to act should local and state officials violate the Constitution as interpreted by the Supreme Court. Contrary to Eisenhower's professed ignorance, he had already authorized the attorney general to issue a public warning to Governor Faubus should he disobey federal law.

On the day of the president's press conference, Judge Davies renewed his original order that the school board proceed with its plan to inte-grate Central High School. He also ordered the Justice Department to investigate Governor Faubus's claim that the imminent threat to the public order justified his attempts to stop integration of the high school.

Attorney General Brownell immediately took a tougher stand against Faubus than the president had done at his press conference. He announced that he had dispatched FBI agents and staff from the U.S. attorney's and marshal's offices on a fact-finding mission to deter-mine the validity of Faubus's claim as well as the exact instruction the governor had given to the National Guard. Should Faubus continue his defiance of the federal judge's order, Brownell said, he could be cited for contempt of court and prosecuted for a federal crime. "The president could use federal troops or National Guard units of any state to enforce the court order," Brownell warned, and said that he had prepared a detailed legal rationale for military intervention and would be in constant communication with the president, who would make the decision.[8]

On Wednesday morning, September 4, Daisy Bates, the leader of the Little Rock NAACP, had arranged for the black students scheduled to register at Central High School to be accompanied by a group of black and white ministers and escorted to the school by a police car. As they approached the school, a crowd of four hundred white men and women jeered, booed, and shouted racial epithets at the black students. "Go home, niggers," they yelled, and chanted, "Two, four, six, eight, we ain't gonna integrate!"[9] When the beleaguered students reached the school entrance, they were turned away by a captain of the National Guard who said that he was acting under the orders of Governor Faubus. What are your orders? one of the guardsman was asked. "Keep the niggers out!" he replied.[10]

Once the crowd realized that the National Guard troops were on their side, they became bolder and more menacing in their threats. The students quickly retreated.

One of the black students, fifteen-year-old Elizabeth Eckford, had not received the message from the NAACP's Bates to assemble with the other black students that morning. Elizabeth, just five feet tall and dressed in a neatly ironed black-and-white dress, approached the school alone. "Here she comes!" the crowd screamed.[11] "Here comes one of the niggers!" When Elizabeth saw the National Guard troops, she felt that she would be protected and continued to walk toward the school. But one of the troopers raised his bayonet and blocked her entrance. She stepped back, then tried again, but two more soldiers stopped her.

"Lynch her! Lynch her!" someone yelled.[12] "Go home, you bastard of a black bitch!" yelled another. Elizabeth, terrified and unsteady, retreated, hemmed in on all sides by the angry crowd. She looked down the street and saw a bench by a bus stop about one hundred yards away. Slowly, tentatively, she walked to the bench. When she reached it, an elderly white woman came over and put a comforting arm around the shaken teenager. Despite howls from the crowd, the two were able to board a bus and leave the harrowing scene.

ON THE MORNING of Elizabeth Eckford's narrow escape, President Eisenhower and his wife, Mamie, left the White House and flew to Newport, Rhode Island, to begin a long-anticipated vacation. Ike was exhausted from the fight over the civil rights bill and looked forward to many rounds of golf at Newport Country Club and marathon bridge games with his closest friends, members of the Gang who were joining him in Newport. The president and first lady landed in the late morning at Quonset Point Naval Station, festooned with flags and patriotic bunting, and were greeted by Rhode Island governor Dennis Roberts before boarding the presidential yacht for a ten-mile cruise across Narragansett Bay.

Later that day, Governor Faubus held a press conference in his office in Little Rock and said that he would not permit black students to enter white schools in the city. He insisted that he was not flouting the federal judge's integration order, but acting to preserve the peace and to prevent bloodshed.

Little Rock mayor Woodrow Wilson Mann immediately condemned Faubus's action. The governor had called out the National Guard, the mayor declared, to "put down trouble where none existed."[13] His order, the mayor continued, came "without request from those of us who are directly responsible for the preservation of peace and order." The only effect of the governor's action, Mann said, "is to create tensions where none existed." If any "racial trouble" does develop, he declared, "the blame rests squarely on the doorstep of the governor's mansion."

That night Faubus sent a telegram to President Eisenhower asking him to stop the "unwarranted interference of federal agents in this area."[14] He vowed not to cooperate with the federal agents then investigating his use of troops to block integration of Central High School. He said that he had reason to believe that the agents had tapped the telephone in his executive mansion and he had been "reliably informed" that federal authorities planned to take him into custody by force. "The situation in Little Rock and Arkansas grows more explosive by the hour," he told the president.

On his first full day of vacation, Eisenhower was confronted with Faubus's telegram informing him that the governor would not cooperate with federal authorities in Little Rock. In the telegram, Faubus also attempted to establish a rapport with Eisenhower by telling him that he "was one of the soldiers of your command in World War II" and noting approvingly that "many expressions of fairness and understanding have come from you regarding the problems of the South."[15] He made a further effort to ingratiate himself with Eisenhower and justify his action in Little Rock by stating that "you—as a military man—know that the commander must have the authority and the discretion to take the necessary steps warranted by the situation with which he must deal."

Faubus's military analogy depicting his role as "commander" in Little Rock elicited a curt response from the former Supreme Commander of Allied Forces during World War II. Eisenhower informed the Arkansas governor in a telegram that he would uphold the federal Constitution "by every legal means at my command."[16] The president's response was interpreted in the press as the strongest stand he had yet taken in support of the Supreme Court's *Brown* decision. Eisenhower also denied Faubus's charges that federal officials were planning to imprison him or had "tapped" his telephone. He pointedly advised the governor that the National Guard was uniformed, armed, and partly paid from funds provided by the federal government.

The situation remained tense for the next week. Faubus responded to the president's telegram with a promise to cooperate "in upholding the constitution of Arkansas and the nation."[17] His response suggested ominously that his loyalty to his state's constitution took precedence over that owed the U.S. Constitution.

On Saturday, September 7, Judge Davies denied the request of the Little Rock School Board to vacate his order to proceed with the integration of Central High School. Eisenhower flew back to Washington the same day to confer with Brownell, who was adamant that Faubus must obey the court order.

On Monday, September 9, Judge Davies requested that the attorney general participate in the Little Rock lawsuit. The next day Brownell, acting as a friend of the court, applied for a temporary injunction to halt Faubus's action in deploying National Guard troops at Central High School to prevent integration. Judge Davies set September 20 as the date for Faubus to appear in his courtroom to defend his action in defiance of the federal court order.

Meanwhile, Congressman Brooks Hays of Arkansas, convinced that Faubus was looking for a way out of the crisis, attempted to set up a meeting between Faubus and Eisenhower to break the impasse. Hays, considered a moderate on civil rights, chose his friend Sherman Adams, the president's chief of staff, as his liaison with the Eisenhower administration. During their secret talks, Adams avoided discussing the proposed meeting with Brownell who, he knew, would oppose it. To Brownell, nothing could be accomplished by such a meeting. Faubus must obey the law as laid down by Judge Davies. Period.

But Eisenhower did not think the solution was so straightforward. He expressed frustration with the widespread perception in the country that the president "has a right to walk in and say 'disperse—we are going to have negroes in the high school.' . . . That is not so."[18] He said that the administration must "take into consideration the seething in the South." He told Brownell that he did not want his administration to be perceived as taking sides in the controversy, emphasizing that it was not a party to the federal suit, but appearing only as a friend of the court. He also said that he wanted to assure Faubus that the federal government would not interfere with the legitimate responsibilities of the governor to preserve order.

Eisenhower told Adams that if Faubus "honestly wanted to talk with him, he would see him any time, any place."[19] He asked Brownell to meet with Adams to compose a telegram for Faubus to send to the president requesting a meeting. The president insisted that the governor pledge to "obey all proper orders of our courts."

Adams called Hays with the president's instructions, and Hays conveyed them to Faubus. By Wednesday afternoon, September 11, Hays had read a draft of Faubus's proposed telegram to Adams, who accepted it on behalf of the president. But when the actual telegram was delivered to Eisenhower shortly after he began an afternoon round of golf at the Newport Country Club, Faubus had made a troubling change in the agreed-upon wording of the telegram. He pledged to comply with the order of Judge Davies "consistent with my responsibilities under the Constitution of the United States, *and that of Arkansas.*" (Italics added.)[20] Faubus's sly revision left open the possibility that he could defy Judge Davies's order if it did not comport with his interpretation of his responsibilities under the Arkansas constitution.

Faubus's latest evasion confirmed Brownell's view that the Arkansas governor's primary interest was winning a third gubernatorial term, which meant that he would not allow black students to integrate Central High School.

By the time Eisenhower read Faubus's telegram, Brownell had received a four-hundred-page report from the FBI that found no evidence supporting Faubus's contention that violent agitators were advancing on Little Rock. Eisenhower then realized that Faubus was more intent on preserving his political career than obeying the *Brown II* mandate and Judge Davies's order. He nonetheless agreed to meet with Faubus in his vacation office at Newport on Saturday morning, September 14, as a last-ditch effort to avoid a military confrontation in Little Rock.

––––––––––

EISENHOWER AND FAUBUS met alone for twenty minutes in a tiny office on the grounds of the naval base at Newport on Saturday morning. After their private meeting, they were joined in a larger office by Attorney General Brownell, Sherman Adams, Congressman Hays, and the president's White House counsel, Gerald Morgan. The president summarized his private conversation with Faubus, then turned to Brownell to ask if the federal court order could be postponed for a few weeks. Brownell's response was immediate and decisive. "No, that's impossible," he replied.[21] "It isn't legally possible." The governor must obey the court's order. Faubus, according to Adams, listened "in inscrutable silence."[22]

Afterward, Eisenhower and Faubus, both smiling, posed for photographers. The president later issued a statement praising Faubus for his "constructive and cooperative attitude" and said that the Arkansas governor had agreed to respect the federal court order to desegregate Central High School in Little Rock.[23] "I am sure it is the desire of the Governor not only to observe the supreme law of the land but to use the influence of his office in orderly progress of the plans which are already the subject of the order of the Court."

Faubus's statement had a subtly different tone and emphasis. He agreed with Eisenhower that their meeting had been "constructive," but said that the discussion had focused on "the problem of compliance" with the court order to desegregate the high school.[24] While pledging to fulfill his duties under the federal constitution, he said that he must "harmonize" his actions with his responsibilities under the Arkansas constitution. In implementing the federal court order, he asked that "the complexities of integration be patiently understood by all those in Federal authority."

Despite Eisenhower's optimistic public statement following his meeting with Faubus, Ann Whitman did not think her boss was pleased. "I got the impression that the meeting had not gone as well as had been hoped, that the Federal government would have to be as tough as possible in the situation," she wrote in her diary.[25] "I gather, too, that Governor Faubus has seized this opportunity and stirred the whole thing up for his own political advantage, a feeling that is, I believe, borne out by the FBI report."

Eisenhower's and Faubus's later recollections of their confidential meeting sharply differed. The president said that Faubus had stressed that he was a World War II veteran and a law-abiding citizen who recognized that the federal law was supreme. Eisenhower appeared sympathetic, suggesting that Faubus "go home and not necessarily withdraw his National Guard troops but just change their orders," so that Faubus would tell the Guard "to continue to preserve the order but to allow the Negro children to attend Central High School."[26] If the governor cooperated in this way, the president promised that the Justice Department would go before Judge Davies on September 20 to request that Faubus not be charged with contempt of court.

Eisenhower urged Faubus to avoid "a trial of strength" between the president and a governor where the federal government had assumed jurisdiction supported by a decision of the U.S. Supreme Court. "[T]here could be only one outcome—that is, the State would lose, and I did not want to see any governor humiliated," he told Faubus. Eisenhower thought that Faubus appreciated his candor and "would return to Arkansas "to act within a matter of hours to revoke his orders to the Guard to prevent re-entry of the Negro children into the school."[27]

In Faubus's recollection of his meeting with the president, Eisenhower assumed a condescending air of authority. "[A]t first he was going to tell me off," he wrote, "like a general tells a lieutenant."[28] The president insisted, according to Faubus, that the crisis was going to be solved his way. But Eisenhower did not appreciate the legal complexities of the situation, Faubus recalled, and appeared impatient to return to the golf course.

AFTER FAUBUS RETURNED to Little Rock, he refused to revoke his orders to the National Guard to block the nine black students' entrance to Central High School, as Eisenhower had hoped and expected. Instead, the governor held steadfastly to the position that he had taken before he and the president met at Newport. "Violence is still a possibility," he told ABC reporter Mike Wallace, in a television interview the day after his Newport meeting with Eisenhower.[29] But what if Faubus ordered a small coterie of guardsmen to escort the black students into the high school? Wallace asked. Wouldn't that resolve the crisis? No, the governor replied, "[b]ecause the best way to prevent the violence was to remove the cause," implying that the black students were the problem.

"Well, you were right, Herb," an angry Eisenhower told Brownell after learning of Faubus's continued defiance.[30] "He did just what you said he'd do—he double-crossed me."

As Faubus's scheduled appearance in Judge Davies's courtroom on September 20 approached, the president's White House staff became increasingly apprehensive that the governor would defy the federal court order. Chief of Staff Adams, in a telephone conversation with an aide, concluded that "Governor Faubus is not going to carry out the order of the Court but is going to engage in some legal maneuvering to try to block and frustrate the order of the court."[31] When Eisenhower was told of Faubus's continued intransigence, he considered issuing a public statement condemning the governor. But both Adams and

Brownell advised him to say nothing until Faubus's scheduled court appearance.

On the morning of September 20, Faubus's attorneys appeared before Judge Davies and formally requested that he recuse himself since, they asserted, he was biased against the governor. When the judge rejected their motion and issued an injunction against Faubus to prevent him from blocking the integration of Central High School, the governor's attorneys walked out in protest.

Faubus announced that he would appeal Judge Davies's injunction. He also ordered National Guard troops to withdraw from the high school when school opened on Monday and asked the parents of the black students to keep their children home. He then said that he was leaving the state to attend a conference of southern governors in Sea Island, Georgia.

Brownell informed Eisenhower of the latest developments in the crisis, advised him that he must act, and again raised the possibility of sending army troops to Little Rock. Eisenhower responded that he was "loath to use troops," fearing that the resistance shown by Faubus would spread throughout the South and lead to violence.[32] He had no doubt of his authority to use troops to enforce a federal court order "to see that the children are protected." But he questioned the wisdom of such a drastic action. Suppose the children are taken to school, and the governor closes it? he asked. That could lead to similar actions by governors throughout the South, effectively abolishing the public school system—a possibility that Eisenhower had feared since the court announced the *Brown* decision.

Early Saturday morning, September 21, Eisenhower issued a statement offering a hopeful interpretation of Faubus's latest actions. He said that the governor's order to withdraw National Guard troops from the high school was "a necessary step in the right direction."[33] He was confident that the citizens of Little Rock and other areas of the state "will welcome this opportunity to demonstrate that in their city and their state proper orders of a United States Court will be executed promptly and without disorder."

For the remainder of the weekend, the president was determined to enjoy his vacation. He played golf and bridge with members of the Gang. And on Sunday night he put on his chef's hat and apron and cooked steaks for his friends and Mamie.

By early Monday morning, September 23, Eisenhower's prediction of a peaceful resolution to the crisis in Little Rock lay in shards outside Central High School. A mob of more than one thousand angry white protesters, including members of the Citizens Council, the Ku Klux Klan, and Jimmy Karam, the state athletic commissioner and close associate of Governor Faubus, howled their outrage. They attacked two black reporters, knocking them down and beating them. "Kill them, kill them," one person screamed. When the mob learned that while they assaulted the two reporters, the black students had quietly entered through a side entrance to the school, they shouted, "Lynch the niggers."[34] On orders of Little Rock's Mayor Mann, local police removed the students three hours after they had entered the school.

THE PRESSURE BUILT INEXORABLY. The White House had received alarming cables from around the world that the Little Rock crisis was a propaganda disaster for the United States. In the Egyptian press the Little Rock crisis was seen as another example of a colonial power oppressing a racial minority. In Great Britain, the U.S.'s closest ally, a leading newspaper condemned Governor Faubus's actions as "bigoted and packed with the prejudices of the South," concluding that the crisis "would be a joke if it was not so tragic."[35] In France, the press questioned why the U.S. president appeared helpless to resolve the crisis.

Most troubling to Eisenhower, Radio Moscow accused the United States of hypocrisy in promoting democracy and human rights abroad while tolerating racism and violence at home.

On the afternoon of September 23, following the latest eruption of violence outside Central High School, Eisenhower issued a blunt statement: "The federal law . . . cannot be flouted with impunity by any individual or any mob of extremists. I will use the full power of the United States including whatever force may be necessary to prevent any obstruction of the law and to carry out the orders of the Federal Court."[36] He followed the statement with a proclamation setting forth his authority to use troops to enforce federal law.

Early the next morning, Eisenhower received a panicked telegram from Mayor Mann:

> THE IMMEDIATE NEED FOR FEDERAL TROOPS IS URGENT.
> THE MOB IS MUCH LARGER IN NUMBERS AT 8 AM THAN
> AT ANY TIME YESTERDAY. PEOPLE ARE CONVERGING ON
> THE SCENE FROM ALL DIRECTIONS. MOB IS ARMED AND
> ENGAGING IN FISTICUFFS AND OTHER ACTS OF VIOLENCE.
> SITUATION IS OUT OF CONTROL AND THE POLICE CANNOT
> DISPERSE THE MOB.[37]

Faced with the threat of civil insurrection, Eisenhower had no choice but to use force to restore law and order. The president and Brownell were in constant telephone contact that morning discussing the president's military options. The attorney general told the president that General Maxwell Taylor, U.S. Army Chief of Staff, had advised him to use troops from the National Guard, rather than the army. Eisenhower worried that deputizing National Guard troops from Little Rock would pit "brother against brother" and suggested using National Guard troops from other locations in Arkansas.[38] He also revised the wording of a statement sent by Brownell for the president's approval that began, "The law has been defied."[39] The president preferred an opening phrase expressing sympathy for the law-abiding citizens of the South.

Eisenhower was sensitive to the fact that he had remained at his vacation retreat in Rhode Island, playing golf and bridge, while the crisis in Little Rock simmered and finally exploded in violence. "The White House office is wherever the President may happen to be," he wrote his old friend, General Alfred Gruenther, the former Army Chief of Staff, who had urged him to return to Washington.[40] "To rush back to Washington every time an incident of a serious character arose would be a confession that a change of scenery is truly a 'vacation' for the president and is not merely a change of his working locale," he insisted. He did not want "to exaggerate the significance of the admittedly serious situation in Arkansas."

Shortly after noon on Tuesday, September 24, Eisenhower called Brownell to say that he had changed his mind: he would dispatch U.S. Army troops to Little Rock, supported by Arkansas National Guard troops called into federal service. At 12:15 p.m. he gave the order to General Taylor. Within hours, five hundred paratroopers from the 101st Airborne Division had flown to Little Rock; another five hundred troops were there by nightfall.

Eisenhower decided to fly to Washington to deliver an address to the nation that evening. Speaking from the White House, he told a radio and television audience that he had acted to prevent "mob rule" and "anarchy."[41] He emphasized that the federal troops were there to enforce a court order, not integration. He said that the violent defiance of a federal court order in Little Rock had done grave harm to "the prestige and influence, and indeed to the safety, of our nation and the world." The Soviet Union, he said, was "gloating over this incident and using it everywhere to misrepresent our whole nation." He called on the people of Arkansas and the South to "preserve and respect the law even when they disagree with it" and appealed to the protesters in Little Rock to return to "normal habits of peace and order" and help remove "a blot upon the fair name and high honor of our nation."

Eisenhower's decision to deploy U.S. soldiers to put down civil unrest, which he had considered unthinkable only two months earlier, was the first time that an American president had used federal troops to compel equal treatment of black Americans in the South since Reconstruction.

The reaction from southern leaders was predictable and vehement. Senator Richard Russell of Georgia sent Eisenhower a telegram comparing the soldiers in Little Rock to "Hitler's storm troopers."[42] Former South Carolina governor James Byrnes declared, "The President has given the world the impression that civil war exists and the United Sates Government has declared war on Arkansas."[43] Senator James Eastland of Mississippi accused the president of "an attempt to destroy the social order of the South."[44] Senator Olin Johnston of South Carolina asserted, "If I were a governor and he came in, I'd give him a fight such as he's never been in before."[45] Governor Faubus, after returning to Little Rock from the southern governors conference, proclaimed in a television address, "We are now an occupied territory."[46]

At 9:25 a.m. on Wednesday morning, September 25, the nine black students, accompanied by a guard of thirty soldiers, walked up the steps of the main entrance to Central High School. Outside, the crowd of 1,500 white protesters was dispersed by troops of the 101st Airborne Division. "Heil Hitler," shouted one passerby at the soldiers of the famed division that had fought valiantly against the Nazis in World War II.[47] Another yelled, "All you need now is a Russian flag."

Inside the school, twenty-four paratroopers patrolled the halls, while the black students sat in their first classes with whites. Eight of the nine black students endured racial taunts throughout the school year. The ninth, Minnie Jean Brown, was expelled after a white student called her a "nigger bitch," and she responded with "white trash."[48]

EISENHOWER SAID LITTLE publicly about the Little Rock situation.[48] But he was eager to remove the federal troops as soon as possible and, again, was frustrated by the machinations of Governor Faubus. Shortly after his return to Washington at the end of September, the president conferred with four moderate governors from southern and border states (Frank Clement of Tennessee, LeRoy Collins of Florida, Luther Hodges of North Carolina, and Theodore McKeldin of Maryland) and agreed to a drafted statement for Faubus's signature. It read: "I now declare that I will assume full responsibility for the maintenance of law and order and that the orders of the Federal Court will not be obstructed."[49]

But the wily Faubus was not eager to be pinned down. He knew that his defiant stance was extremely popular with Arkansas voters, virtually guaranteeing him another gubernatorial term. After receiving the draft statement approved by Eisenhower, he inserted qualifying language that began with the precondition, "Upon withdrawal of federal troops."[50] He added a phrase at the end, "by me," which relieved him of the obligation to prevent the obstruction of the federal court order by others. Faubus's revisions were quickly rejected by Eisenhower.

Despite Faubus's continued resistance, Eisenhower was confident enough that peace and stability had been restored that in mid-October he ordered the withdrawal of half of the army troops and kept 1,800 National Guard troops under federal control, releasing the rest to Arkansas. By October 23, the nine black students entered Central High without military protection. Three weeks later, the National Guard assumed control of security around the high school. The remaining federal troops were withdrawn from Little Rock the day before Thanksgiving, and the National Guard troops left at the end of the school year in late May 1958.

But as one crisis subsided, another arose. The Soviet Union announced in early October that it had launched a satellite named Sputnik I into space. Suddenly, the Cold War had taken an unpredictable and unsettling turn.

THE DECISION TO send federal troops to Little Rock, Eisenhower insisted, was motivated by his duty to uphold the rule of law. He made no effort to defend the *Brown* decision on constitutional or moral grounds. Chief Justice Warren was dismayed by Eisenhower's reticence. Even after the president sent troops to Little Rock, Warren noted, "there was no direct appeal from the White House to obey the mandate of the Supreme Court."[51]

In his private correspondence, Eisenhower insisted that his action had nothing to do with the merits of the *Brown* decision. "My biggest problem has been to make people see, particularly in the south, that my main interest is not in the integration or segregation question," he wrote Swede Hazlett.[52] "My opinion as to the wisdom of the decision or the timeliness of the Supreme Court's decision has nothing to do with the case. The point is that specific orders of our courts, taken in accordance with the terms of the Constitution as interpreted by the Supreme Court, must be upheld."

He made the same point to Senator John Stennis of Mississippi, who had criticized his action. "[A]s to the mission of Federal soldiers in Little Rock, I emphasize that they are there not to enforce or to advance any governmental policy respecting integration, desegregation or segregation," he wrote.[53] "They are there, simply, because the normal processes of law have been frustrated." And to Governor Price Daniel of Texas, who had compared his use of troops to those sent to the South during Reconstruction, he wrote that the governor had totally missed the purpose of the mission of the federal soldiers in Little Rock. "They are not there to force desegregation," he wrote. "They are there to support our Federal Court system."[54]

Eisenhower bristled at criticism from leading southern politicians. "I must say that I completely fail to comprehend your comparison of our troops to Hitler's Storm Troopers," he wrote Senator Russell.[55] "In one case military power was used to further the ambitions and purposes of a ruthless dictator; in the other to preserve the institutions of free government." To Senator Stennis, he wrote that "[t]he alternative to supporting the law" in Little Rock "is to acquiesce in anarchy, mob rule, and incipient rebellion. Such unthinkable consequence would be quite as disastrous for the South as for any other region. Ultimately, of course, such a course would destroy the Nation."[56]

Although the president expended considerable effort explaining his action to southern leaders, he did not expect them to publicly support him. For this reason, he considered a proposed meeting with southern governors to be an exercise in futility. "There is no question that many political leaders in the south now realize that some beginning toward accommodation should be undertaken," he wrote Ralph McGill, the moderate editor of the *Atlanta Constitution*, "but they are prisoners of their own prior statements and pronouncements."[57]

If Eisenhower did not expect to persuade leading southern politicians, such as Byrnes, Russell, and Stennis, to support his moderate approach to civil rights, why did he devote so much time to corresponding and meeting with them? One reason was that he respected them and valued their friendship. After *Brown II*, he complained that the decision had destroyed his warm relationship with Byrnes. At the height of the controversy over the 1957 Civil Rights Act, he met at length with Senator Russell, the chief strategist opposing the bill, and appeared relieved that their friendship remained intact. He wrote long, candid letters to all three men, explaining his positions on civil rights, more to placate than to persuade them.

IN CONTRAST TO his solicitous treatment of prominent southern leaders, Eisenhower's interaction with black leaders was notably constrained. Despite many requests, he adamantly refused to meet with two of the most prominent black leaders, Dr. Martin Luther King, Jr., and the NAACP's Roy Wilkins.* His refusal was a source of great

---

* Although Eisenhower did not meet with Dr. King, Vice President Nixon not only met with King but encouraged the president to do so; Nixon thought Eisenhower would like the civil rights leader. (Maxwell Rabb to Sherman Adams, September 27, 1957, DDEP.)

frustration to Frederick Morrow, a special assistant to the president and the first black assistant ever to work in the White House. Morrow, forty-six, a former field secretary for the NAACP and a Republican, had served Eisenhower during the 1952 campaign as a liaison with the black community.

On the campaign trail, Morrow recalled that he had a wrenching personal conversation with Eisenhower about segregation of the military during World War II. Morrow told Eisenhower that he had served in World War II in a segregated unit, and that he and his fellow black soldiers resented the forced separation when the war was ostensibly being fought for democratic ideals.[58] He questioned a statement that Eisenhower had made shortly before the final victory over Japan that the Allies' top priority should be to win the war, and that it was no time for social experimentation. Eisenhower acknowledged his statement and noted with regret that his field commanders, almost all from the South, had convinced him to oppose integrating the armed forces. Upon learning that Morrow's father and grandfather were ministers, Eisenhower asked his forgiveness. He then confessed that he had been guilty of racial prejudice in the early years of his military career when he was in charge of a poorly trained and educated black unit of the Illinois National Guard that did not perform well for him. He told Morrow that he was working to overcome his early prejudices. Morrow concluded that Eisenhower was a good and decent man.

After Eisenhower's election in 1952, Morrow had expected to receive a job offer from the new administration, but he had to wait three years. In 1955, he was assigned to a small office in the Executive Office Building and immediately suffered daily indignities. He was isolated from other members of the administration and given little encouragement. No other staff aides would eat with him, and none of the young women in the secretarial pool wanted to work with him. To make matters worse, he was virtually ignored by the administration. Despite his repeated requests, his boss, Maxwell Rabb, the White House assistant for minority affairs, refused to send him to Montgomery in 1956 to show the administration's support for the bus boycott. That same year, Rabb expressed his disappointment to Morrow about the continued loyalty of black Americans to the Democratic Party despite Eisenhower's civil rights record. He reprimanded Morrow for his failure to make blacks appreciate Eisenhower's accomplishments.[59] Blacks were too aggressive in their demands, Rabb said, inviting a white backlash.

After Rabb resigned in April 1958, Morrow was given his responsibilities and was asked to complete arrangements for the president's address to the National Negro Publishers Association in Washington on May 12. Morrow attempted to prepare the president for a speech before a black audience, suggesting that he avoid such references as "you people."[60] In his prepared remarks, Eisenhower stressed that all Americans must respect equal rights under the law. But he also admonished his audience that law alone could not solve the problems of race "because they are buried in the human heart."[61] He then set aside his prepared text, removed his glasses, and implored American blacks to practice "patience and forbearance." With those words, Morrow wished that he were invisible and could slip unnoticed out of the auditorium.

Thurgood Marshall and Roy Wilkins were outraged by the president's call for patience. Patience? Almost a century after the war that ended slavery? Ninety years after passage of the Constitution's Equal Protection Clause? And after *Brown*?

"Oh, no! Not again!" thought Jackie Robinson, the legendary black baseball star, who was in Eisenhower's audience.[62] Afterward, he wrote the president that black Americans had been "the most patient of all people," and could not wait for "the hearts of men to change." He admonished Eisenhower, "You unwittingly crush the spirit of freedom in Negroes by constantly urging forbearance and give hope to those pro-segregation leaders like Governor Faubus who would take from us even those freedoms we now enjoy."

In a letter to Robinson drafted by Morrow, Eisenhower wrote, "I am firmly on record as believing that every citizen—of every race and creed—deserves to enjoy equal rights and liberties, for there can be no such citizen in a democracy as a half-free citizen."[63]

Robinson responded respectfully but, nonetheless, persisted in challenging the president to aggressively act to eliminate racial discrimination. Too many black Americans believe "that you favor patience alone rather than patience backed up when necessary with law enforcement," he wrote.[64] He urged Eisenhower to meet with black leaders to exchange views on pressing civil rights issues.

Shortly before the exchange of letters between Robinson and Eisenhower, Dr. King sent a telegram to the president, renewing his long-standing request for a meeting between the president and black leaders, citing the continued violence against blacks in the South and the prospect that many public schools would close in September rather than follow federal orders to desegregate.[65] Finally, after more than two years of failed efforts by King and other black leaders, the president agreed to a meeting.

It was held at the White House on the morning of June 23, 1958, hosted by Eisenhower and attended by King, Roy Wilkins, A. Philip Randolph, founder of the Leadership Conference on Civil Rights, Lester Granger, executive secretary of the National Urban League, Frederick Morrow, Attorney General William Rogers, who had replaced Brownell in October when Brownell returned to private practice, and Rocco Siciliano, the president's special assistant for personnel management. In advance of the meeting, the black leaders had submitted a lengthy statement on the plight of black Americans who still did not enjoy equal protection of the law, followed by detailed recommendations to achieve that goal. The statement praised Eisenhower's action in Little Rock and his role in passing the first civil rights bill since Reconstruction. But it also informed the president that black Americans were frustrated and angry and faulted the Eisenhower administration for the slow pace of progress. "We cannot combat pneumonia by prescribing an occasional tablet of aspirin and a goblet of goodwill," the statement concluded.[66]

Randolph, who was the spokesman for the group, commended Eisenhower for his courage, integrity, and action in Little Rock. He then summarized the black leaders' recommendations, which included a new civil rights law authorizing the Justice Department to enforce the *Brown II* mandate (section 3 of the civil rights bill that had been eliminated before passage of the 1957 legislation), a Justice Department investigation of the bombings in the South, and a White House conference on the enforcement of school desegregation. Such actions, King added, would help "mobilize the emotions of the spirit which, in turn, would aid in the fight for abolishment of segregation."[67]

The National Urban League's Granger then injected a somber, disquieting observation. He could not recall another period when black Americans were more bitter over the lack of progress, he told the president, and he saw signs that their bitterness was "congealing."[68] Attempting to explain African Americans' reaction to Eisenhower's plea for patience, he said that they had believed that progress was being made when "suddenly it appears stopped."

Eisenhower was perturbed by Granger's message of dissatisfaction with his administration's progress on civil rights.[69] He told Granger and the other black leaders that he was extremely dismayed to hear that after five and a half years of effort and action in this field they were saying that the bitterness of blacks was at its height. He wondered if more action would produce only more bitterness.

Granger quickly assured the president that the anger expressed was not directed at him but at the communities in the South that were resisting racial progress. The meeting ended cordially but without any commitment from Eisenhower to act upon the group's recommendations.

The day after the meeting, Siciliano wrote a memo to Eisenhower reporting that "the Negro leaders were more than enthusiastic about their reception with the president and appreciated the intense and sympathetic attention given them."[70] He concluded, "I am convinced that this meeting was an unqualified success—even if success in this area is built on sand."

———

BY 1958, the relationship between Chief Justice Warren and Associate Justice Brennan had blossomed into an unusually warm friendship, built on mutual respect and animated by their avid shared interests in family, politics, and sports. The large, relaxed chief justice and his small (5'8"), sprightly, Irish-Catholic companion became a familiar sight at Washington Redskins' football games, happily ensconced in the owner's box of prominent Washington attorney Edward Bennett Williams. Off the court, the two justices exhibited the gregariousness of natural politicians, eager to shake hands with old friends and new acquaintances. At the court, they formed an unusually close judicial alliance in which Brennan increasingly translated Warren's broad notions of fairness and justice into opinions expanding civil rights and liberties.

Brennan served the chief justice in a role similar to that of an earlier Warren confidant and adviser, William Sweigert, when Warren was governor of California. Brennan and Sweigert, both more than a decade younger than Warren, were honest, liberal, and loyal. And they exhibited a talent for reducing Warren's sometimes vague abstractions into concrete liberal public policy positions. Sweigert, for example, had converted Warren's emotional reaction to the lack of state-financed health care into a viable legislative initiative. More than a decade later,

Brennan articulated the chief justice's commitment to individual liberties in judicial opinions that frequently became the law of the land.

While the chief justice's friendship with Brennan deepened over the years, his relationship with Justice Frankfurter, initially so close and productive, became increasingly rancorous, eventually leading to overt hostility between the two men. The breaking point came in September 1958, after the justices heard arguments in a case that originated in Little Rock during the crisis over the integration of Central High School.

Although troops maintained order around the high school throughout the 1957–58 school year, segregationists in Little Rock, from Governor Faubus down, continued their fight against the implementation of the *Brown II* decree. The city's school board, convinced that violence was probable without troops, requested that a federal district court judge postpone the integration plan for two and a half years because of the "unfavorable community attitude." The board received a sympathetic hearing from Judge Harry J. Lemley who, on June 27, 1958, granted its request, citing "chaos, bedlam and turmoil" in and around Central High School, concluding that the tension was "intolerable."[71]

Lemley's decision posed the constitutional question that the U.S. Supreme Court was ultimately asked to answer: Should the *Brown II* mandate give way when faced with community resistance?

On August 18, 1958, the U.S. Court of Appeals for the Eighth Circuit reversed Judge Lemley's ruling in the case of *Cooper v. Aaron* but stayed its order pending Supreme Court review.* Chief Justice Warren, after consulting with other justices by telephone, announced that the court would hold a special session for oral arguments in the case on August 28, just a week before the Little Rock public schools were scheduled to open.

Eisenhower issued a public statement two days after the appellate decision in which he reiterated his support for the decisions of the fed-

---

* *Cooper v. Aaron*, 358 U.S. 1 (1958). Cooper was the chairman of the Little Rock School Board; Aaron was one of the black students.

eral courts. But a week later, he appeared to be less vigilant, at least in defending the *Brown II* decision, when he suggested at a press conference that "slower" movement toward racial integration in the schools would more readily lead to full acceptance of the court's mandate.[72] His equivocation was reflected earlier in the month at a pre–press conference briefing when he expressed anger "about the refusal of the North to see how deeply the people of the South feel on the subject of integration."[73] He reminded those at the meeting that "it was not his responsibility to keep order anywhere, but only to see that the orders of a federal judge were carried out."

The president also warned Attorney General Rogers, who had drafted a speech in August on the progress of school desegregation for the president's review, against making predictions on the permanence of *Brown*. There should be no expectation of complete success in five or ten years, he said. It might take "30 or 40 years in reaching the ideal."[74]

Governor Faubus, meanwhile, ratcheted up tensions in advance of the arguments at the Supreme Court. In July, he had won an overwhelming victory in the Democratic primary (assuring his election in November), pledging to fight any federal court order to desegregate the state's public schools. On August 26, he convened a special session of the state legislature requesting new laws granting him authority to resist the Supreme Court should it rule in favor of immediate desegregation. The legislators responded by introducing bills allowing Faubus to close public schools if integration was ordered and to transfer state funds to private, segregated schools.

On the morning of August 28, only minutes into his oral argument before the court in the case of *Cooper v. Aaron*, Richard C. Butler, attorney for the Little Rock School Board, uncovered the raw anger of Chief Justice Warren. Warren reacted furiously to a statement by Butler "that if the governor of any state says that a United States Supreme Court decision is not the law of the land, the people of that state . . . have a doubt in their mind and a right to have a doubt."[75]

"I have never heard such an argument made in a court of justice before," Warren shouted at the attorney, "and I have tried many a case through many a year. I never heard a lawyer say that the statement of a governor as to what was legal or illegal should control the action of any court."

Butler, known for his calm courtroom demeanor, was visibly shaken by the chief's attack. His plea for time "to work in a period of peace and harmony rather than turmoil and strife" did not satisfy the chief justice.

"Can we defer a program of this kind because elements in a community will commit violence to prevent it from going into effect?" asked an impatient Warren.

"Mr. Chief Justice," Butler said, "you have been governor of a great state."

Warren interrupted, "But I have never tried to resolve any legal problem of this kind as governor of my state. I thought that that was a matter for the courts, and I abided by the decision of the courts."

At the end of the special session, the court asked for additional arguments on September 11. On that same day, the Arkansas legislature passed the bills requested by Faubus granting the governor authority to close public schools facing integration and to transfer public school funds to private segregated schools. But the Little Rock School Board, acting on the advice of Attorney Butler, refused to immediately bow to the pressure from the governor and legislature and postponed the opening of the Little Rock Schools for two weeks.

To Justice Frankfurter, the Little Rock School Board, and particularly its attorney, represented the best hope for the South to obey the rule of law laid down by the court in *Brown*. With its postponement of the opening of the city's public schools, the board, it seemed to Frankfurter, "showed a good deal of courage to stand up against Faubus and Company."[76] He thought the court could help the board as well as the larger cause of desegregation in the South by publicly recognizing the effort of moderates like Butler. With this in mind, Frankfurter suggested to Warren that he acknowledge the board's "courageous" action just before Attorney Butler addressed the court for his second oral argument on September 11. "My own view has long been that the ultimate hope for the peaceful solution of the basic problem largely depends on winning the support of lawyers of the South for the overriding issue of obedience to the Court's decision," he wrote Warren.[77] "Therefore, I think we should encourage every manifestation of fine conduct by a lawyer like Butler."

Warren flatly rejected Frankfurter's suggestion. He had no intention of praising the lawyer who had maintained that the obstruction of the court's desegregation mandate by "Faubus and Company" could be tolerated.

When Frankfurter learned that Warren had rejected his suggestion, he was disappointed and predictably condescending toward the colleague who had not taken his advice. "Of course Faubus has been guilty of trickery, but the trickery was as much against the School Board as against us," Frankfurter wrote Justice Harlan.[78] "And in any event the fight is not between the Supreme Court and Faubus, though apparently this is the way it lay in the C.J.'s mind. I am afraid his attitude towards the kind of problems that confront us are more like that of a fighting politician than that of judicial statesman."

Four years after *Brown*, Frankfurter's view of Warren had been transformed. No longer did the chief possess "the breadth of outlook" that Frankfurter had found so appealing earlier. He had become, in Frankfurter's mind, a rather simple-minded, moralistic politician who was incapable of understanding the subtle nuances of constitutional decision-making. Frankfurter found disturbing reinforcement for his revised opinion of the chief justice in the fact that Warren voted regularly with Justices Black, Douglas, and Brennan to expand constitutionally protected individual rights.

For his part, Warren suspected Frankfurter of attempting to subvert his authority on the court. He made it a policy in his chambers that his clerks were forbidden to speak to Frankfurter's clerks or to Frankfurter.

At the oral argument on September 11, Warren resumed his attack on the state of Arkansas's attempts to obstruct the orderly process of desegregation laid down in *Brown II*. Wasn't it a fact, asked an agitated chief justice, that the state had passed laws to frustrate the rights of black students? And if Arkansas, whether represented by the governor or the legislature or the Little Rock School Board, was frustrating the rights of these students, the chief had no doubt that the state was violating the U.S. Constitution.

Following oral argument, Warren called the justices into conference and declared that they should reaffirm the Court of Appeals ruling; there could be no delay by the state of Arkansas in implementing the mandate of *Brown II*. No one disagreed with the chief justice. "We knew the kind of opinion we wanted," Justice Brennan recalled.[79] "I remember Justice Harlan saying that this was the biggest crisis in Court history, since we were told that governors and others courts were not bound by our decision."

Warren asked Justices Frankfurter and Harlan to write a brief, unsigned order supporting the appellate court ruling, and Justice Brennan was given the more difficult assignment of drafting the opinion explaining the reasoning of the court. Before Brennan could begin a first draft, Governor Faubus signed into law the bills passed at the special session of the state legislature opposing *Brown II* and declared that he was closing the Little Rock public schools.

Aware of the importance of a prompt court response, Brennan worked quickly, circulating an eighteen-page draft opinion only six days after the chief had given him the assignment.[80] In the draft Brennan first laid out in factual detail the background of the case. His conclusion, however, was never in doubt. On behalf of the court, he declared that it was the duty of the judiciary, and ultimately the U.S.

Supreme Court, to serve as the final interpreter of the Constitution. *Brown II* must be obeyed.

At the conference in which the justices discussed the Brennan draft, Frankfurter proposed that each justice sign the opinion as a further sign of the court's unanimity, especially since there had been several new appointments to the court since *Brown* was decided.* "I do not recall this ever having been done before," Warren later wrote.[81] "However, in light of the intense controversy over the issue and the great notoriety given Governor Faubus's obstructive conduct in the case, we thought well of the suggestion, and it was done."

Brennan returned to his chambers to rework his draft, incorporating some suggestions made by his colleagues, rejecting others. Six days and three additional drafts later, Brennan circulated his opinion to his colleagues, including a new opening paragraph written by Justice Black, which suffused the document with dramatic urgency. It began: "As this case reaches us it involves questions of the highest importance to the maintenance of our federal system of government. It squarely presents a claim by the Governor and Legislature of a State that there is no duty on state officials to obey federal orders resting on this Court's deliberate and considered interpretation of the United States Constitution.... We have concluded that these contentions call for clear answers here and now."[82]

Frankfurter responded to the final Brennan draft enthusiastically. "Dear Bill," he wrote in the margin of the draft.[83] "You have now made me content. Yours FF." His contentment was short-lived. After agreeing to sign the court opinion, freshly redrafted by Brennan, Frankfurter shocked his colleagues by announcing in conference that he would file a concurring opinion. The brethren were incredulous. Frankfurter, after all, had introduced the idea of a unanimous opinion in the case, signed individually by the justices. In fact, he had been the

---

* Since the court's decision in *Brown I*, Harlan, Brennan, and Charles Whittaker had joined the court, replacing, respectively, Justices Jackson, Minton, and Reed.

primary force behind the drive for unanimity in the school desegregation cases dating back to the early nineteen fifties. And now it was the same Felix Frankfurter who willingly was breaking the tradition of unanimity in the school desegregation decisions that he, more than any other justice, had established.

Frankfurter's explanation of his puzzling course seemed feeble to all but the justice himself. He wanted to send a special message to the lawyers and law professors of the South, he later wrote, because that was "an audience which I was in a peculiarly qualified position to address in view of my rather extensive association, by virtue of my twenty-five years at the Harvard Law School, with a good many Southern lawyers and law professors."[84]

Chief Justice Warren recalled that Frankfurter's action "caused quite a sensation" among the brethren.[85] Brennan remembered the episode more pointedly. "Felix was a pariah around here for days," he said.[86]

Warren was outraged, as were Brennan and Black, who drafted an opinion disassociating themselves from the Frankfurter concurrence and reiterating their support for the court's opinion. Only a last minute tongue-in-cheek admonishment by Justice Harlan "that it is always a mistake to make a mountain out of a molehill" defused the volatile situation.[87] Frankfurter filed his concurrence, but Brennan and Black withdrew their separate opinion.

Brennan's anger and frustration were vented in the margins of a circulated draft of Frankfurter's concurrence.[88] Frankfurter had written that "only the constructive use of time will achieve what an advanced civilization demands and the Constitution confirms." Amid his own exclamation points and question marks, Brennan scribbled, "Isn't this bound to be confusing to judges faced for the first time with applications against school boards? As an interpretation by the [an] author of the basic *Aaron* opinion, won't it be read as allowing them to take hostility into account?"

Frankfurter's estrangement from most of his colleagues was temporary. But Chief Justice Warren was permanently alienated. The close working relationship between Warren and Frankfurter, apparent early in the chief's tenure, had gradually become precarious as the overbearing Frankfurter personality began to grate on the proud Warren. The two men split irrevocably with Frankfurter's concurrence in *Cooper v. Aaron.*[89]

Throughout his life, Warren had broken ties with those whom he felt had betrayed or humiliated him. Once on his personal enemies' list, there could be no reprieve. In the chief's mind, Frankfurter's concurrence was a blatant attempt to undermine Warren's authority on the court. It was an act of treachery, and unforgivable.

———————

WARREN'S RELATIONSHIP WITH Eisenhower, as with Frankfurter, which was so promising upon his appointment as chief justice, had seriously deteriorated by 1958. The rupture between the president and the chief justice had begun with *Brown I* and was exacerbated by the massive resistance in the South to *Brown II*'s desegregation mandate. The Little Rock crisis tested the president's resolve. His response, and later that of the chief justice, underscored how differently the two men conceived of their roles in confronting the nation's race problems.

The president, always the pragmatist, dealt with the Little Rock crisis cautiously, even when confronted with Governor Faubus's defiance. He expected to persuade the Arkansas governor to retreat from his extreme position, despite Attorney General Brownell's warning that it was a lost cause. He sent federal troops to Little Rock as a last resort and only after it was obvious that Faubus had no interest in a face-saving compromise.

When Warren was governor of California, he too approached his state's problems as a pragmatist who sought bipartisan agreement. In his early terms as chief justice, he continued to encourage compromise, assuming the role of conciliator between the two ideological wings of the court. But later he embraced a different role—that of the principled leader of the liberal wing of the court. As he demonstrated during the oral argument in *Cooper v. Aaron*, he aggressively seized the moral high ground, pressing the attorney for the Little Rock School Board not only to adhere to the rule of law, but to defend the civil rights of the nine brave black teenagers who had enrolled at Central High School.

Chapter Twelve

THE EGALITARIAN REVOLUTION

DIATRIBES AGAINST THE WARREN COURT MULTIPLIED IN the mid–nineteen fifties. The first attacks were launched by segregationists in the Deep South enraged by the court's *Brown* decision. Anti-Communist zealots, led by Senator William Jenner of Indiana, soon joined the court's southern critics, charging that the court was dangerously soft on communism. But in the summer of 1957, the court was denounced by an unexpected critic, the American Bar Association, and Chief Justice Warren was publicly humiliated by the assault.

No hint of the impending controversy was known to the chief justice when he accepted an invitation by the ABA to lead the delegation of the organized bar in a joint meeting of American and British lawyers and judges in London that summer. Warren and his wife had planned a month's vacation on the British Isles, but the chief justice reluctantly revised his plans so that he could attend the London meeting.

Shortly before he was due to attend the meeting, Warren threatened to cancel his appearance when he heard that Vice President Nixon might be invited. Warren informed the ABA that if Nixon attended, he would not. He said that the presence of Nixon, who was expected to seek the Republican nomination for the presidency in 1960, would turn the convention into a political event, detracting from its legal purpose. Speculation in the press suggested another motive: the chief justice's loathing of the vice president that dated back to the 1952 Republican convention when Nixon worked behind the scenes in the California delegation to undermine Warren's candidacy in an effort to support the party's eventual nominee, General Eisenhower.

"If you let that fellow [Nixon] in, count me out," Warren told the ABA president, David Maxwell.[1] The ABA did not extend an invitation to the vice president.

On the first morning of the London conference, the ABA's Special Committee on Communism filed a report that Warren later termed "a publicity blockbuster."[2] Its title, "Communist Tactics, Strategy and Objectives," was highly misleading, since the report said little about Communist tactics or strategy but, instead, attacked the Warren Court's "pro-Communist" decisions. The report listed fifteen court decisions that, it charged, supported the Communist cause. It concluded that the court was leaning too far in support of "theoretical individual rights" that risked rendering the nation "incapable of carrying out the first law of mankind—the right of self preservation."[3] The committee recommended legislation that, if enacted, would have effectively reversed the court decisions criticized in the report.

"BAR ASSOCIATION TOLD HIGH COURT WEAKENS SECURITY AGAINST REDS" was the banner headline in the Paris edition of the *New York Herald Tribune* followed by subheadings, "New Laws to Protect U.S. Asked" and "Delegates Accept Committee View."[4] Warren was appalled that the committee's report dominated press coverage of an ABA meeting that he had understood to be a good-will mission celebrating the unity of the United States and Great Britain in preserving freedom under law. After the committee's report became the focus of the convention, Warren was badgered by reporters to reply to the attack on the court. He declined.

But the chief justice did not forget his public humiliation. "I was more or less a pariah," he recalled.[5] He felt the sting of "several snide articles" that he believed were designed to embarrass him and to show that he was a discredit to the American bar. No official of the ABA came to the defense of the court. Warren later accused the ABA of willfully besmirching the court to gain publicity for what was, in his view, an otherwise "rather unproductive convention." "[C]an you imagine the uproar," he asked, "if the same things had been said about the President, the Vice President, the Speaker of the House, or some prominent senator?"[6]

After the convention, Warren and his wife spent a month traveling around Ireland, Scotland, and England, returning home in late August on the S.S. *United States*. On the return voyage, Warren, still furious over his treatment at the convention, reappraised his association with the organization. He then wrote a letter of resignation to the ABA president, citing as the main reason for his decision the attack on the court at the London meeting. Referring to the widely publicized criticism of the court at the convention, he wrote: "It conveyed the thought to the world that in the unanimous opinion of the American Bar, the Supreme Court of the United States is advancing the cause of Communism, is unworthy of its heritage, and therefore, must be thwarted by the other Branches of the Government."[7]

IN 1958, the attacks on the court spread beyond the South, the Senate, and the ABA to prominent members of the state and federal judiciary. A report of the Conference of State Chief Justices condemned the Warren Court for its tendency "to adopt the role of policy-maker without proper judicial restraint."[8] Judge Learned Hand, the venerated emeritus jurist on the U.S. Court of Appeals for the Second Circuit, was even blunter in his criticism. In his Holmes Lectures at the Harvard Law School, Hand criticized the court's judicial activism, complaining that it had become a "third legislative chamber," substituting its judgment for that of the elected representatives.[9] "For myself it would be most irksome to be ruled by a bevy of Platonic guardians," Hand said, in a thinly veiled reference to the court's liberals, "even if I knew how to choose them, which I assuredly do not."

In February 1958, the same month as the Holmes Lectures, Senator Jenner and the chairman of the Senate Judiciary Committee, Mississippi's James Eastland, arranged for a public hearing before the Senate Internal Security Subcommittee, inviting a succession of witnesses to flail away at the court's "pro-Communist" decisions. "The choice we face in this country today is judicial limitation or judicial tyranny," warned subcommittee member Senator Strom Thurmond of South Carolina.[10]

Jenner then reintroduced legislation that targeted more than a dozen Warren Court decisions that he claimed threatened the internal security of the nation. His bill, if passed, would have crippled the *Watkins* decision, in which the court had insisted that questions from the House Un-American Activities Committee and other congressional committees be "pertinent" to the committee's investigative purpose. Under Jenner's bill, the presiding officer of the congressional committee, not the court, was given the statutory authority to judge what was a "pertinent" question to a witness. The bill also protected state sedition laws from federal preemption, a measure that would have nullified Warren's majority opinion in *Pennsylvania v. Nelson*. And it undercut the court's *Yates* decision that had overturned the convictions of West Coast leaders of the American Communist Party because there had been no showing of "incitement" by the defendants. Under the proposed legislation, it would be a crime to advocate the overthrow of the government "without regard to the immediate probable effect of such action."[11]

Jenner's legislation, combined with other bills introduced in Congress to curtail the court's appellate jurisdiction, posed the greatest danger to the court's independence since President Franklin Roosevelt's "court-packing" plan in 1937.[12] Under FDR's plan, the president could appoint a new justice for every sitting justice over the age of seventy who did not retire. Roosevelt was aware that six of the sitting justices exceeded his proposed age limit. If passed, the proposed legislation could have increased the court's membership to fifteen. A new court majority, bolstered by six Roosevelt appointees, would almost certainly have reversed decisions by a conservative majority on the court that had declared key New Deal legislation unconstitutional. FDR disguised his power grab as a reform measure to relieve the over-worked septuagenarian justices, but nobody was fooled. Though Roosevelt had won a landslide victory for reelection in 1936, his attempt to undermine the independence of the court was rejected by a majority of the American voters (according to Gallup polls) and the Senate.

Congress's anti-court bills, like FDR's court-packing plan, produced shivers of alarm among defenders of the court's independence, even those who had publicly criticized the decisions of the Warren Court. The American Bar Association's House of Delegates passed a resolution opposing Congress's efforts to limit the court's appellate jurisdiction. Judge Hand, soon after his blistering critique of the Warren Court, said that any statute removing the court's appellate jurisdiction "would be detrimental to the best interests of the United States."[13]

Attorney General William Rogers described the Jenner bill as a "retaliatory measure" that "threatens the independence of the judiciary."[14] His boss, President Eisenhower, was characteristically more circumspect. While the legislation was pending, he asked Rogers to explain some of the controversial Warren Court decisions, including *Pennsylvania v. Nelson*. He also sought Rogers's guidance on the purpose of the Jenner bill. He asked, "Who determines when the Court is 'legislating?'" and "Can Congress limit the Court's function?"[15]

Publicly, however, the president said very little about the Jenner bill or other anti-court bills introduced in Congress. In his only explicit reference to the legislation, he displayed his talent for willful obfuscation when he said: "I do believe most emphatically in the separation of powers . . . but on the other hand, when we get down to this, just law interfering with the constitutional rights and powers and authority of the judiciary, I think that that will have to take a lot of studying, and by very fine lawyers, before I could see the justification of any law."[16]

The Jenner bill (cosponsored with conservative Senator John Butler of Maryland) was voted favorably out of Senator Eastland's judiciary committee. But Majority Leader Lyndon Johnson kept the bill and two other anti-court measures off the floor of the Senate until mid-August, when he hoped to bury the legislation in end-of-session confusion. Johnson was opposed on principle to what he referred to as the "Court-ripper" bills.[17] He also wanted to woo northern liberals in the Senate, who he hoped would support his presidential bid in 1960.

But the anti-court bills were backed by a formidable coalition of southern Democrats and northern conservatives of both parties. It did not help the majority leader's cause that the senators were tired and querulous when the final bill (the first two had been tabled by narrow votes) was brought to the floor late one evening in mid-August. Old passions were stirred by debate over the court's controversial decisions. It looked as if the proponents of the bill had the votes to pass the final anti-court legislation. Suddenly Johnson made a motion to adjourn and demanded a roll call.[18] As the roll call began, Johnson stood at his desk, clipboard in hand, with a long sheet of paper attached. When a vote was cast against him, the majority leader made a show of writing down the name of the senator. The next day, after a night of the famous Johnson "treatment" of wavering colleagues, the motion to table the bill passed by a single vote.

In his memoirs, Warren wrote that "[s]ome of this (anti-Court) legislation, evoking as it did the atmosphere of Cold War hysteria, came dangerously close to passing."[19]

EVEN THOUGH THE anti-court measures failed, thanks primarily to adroit maneuvering by Johnson, Congress had sent the Warren Court a stern warning: either trim your judicial decisions on politically explosive issues or risk more legislative challenges to your independence.

Chief Justice Warren refused to be intimidated. While Congress was threatening to curb the court's authority, Warren asserted the court's power to limit Congress's authority. Two cases, decided in March 1958, dramatically illustrated Warren's willingness to challenge Congress. The decisions were handed down at precisely the time that Congress was churning out bills to limit the court's appellate jurisdiction. In both cases, *Trop v. Dulles*[20] and *Perez v. Brownell*,[21] the constitutional issue raised was whether Congress, under the Nationality Act of 1940, could strip a U.S. citizen of his citizenship. Trop was expatriated after his conviction by court-martial for desertion in time of war. Perez lost his citizenship for voting in a foreign election.

The court split on the cases, invalidating Trop's expatriation but sustaining Perez's. Warren, writing for the court in *Trop* and in dissent in *Perez*, insisted that citizenship was a fundamental right shielded from encroachment by congressional statute. The scope of Warren's theory of citizenship was breathtakingly expansive. In *Trop*, he advanced the novel theory that expatriation was "cruel and unusual punishment" under the Eighth Amendment. "The basic concept underlying the Eighth Amendment is nothing less than the dignity of man," he wrote.[22] "The amendment must draw its meaning from the evolving standards of decency that mark the progress of a maturing society." Since the judiciary had a "duty of implementing the constitutional safeguards that protect individual rights" and citizenship was a fundamental right, he concluded, Congress's statutory restrictions conflicted with the Constitution. The court, therefore, "had no choice but to enforce the paramount commands of the Constitution."

The problem with Warren's analysis was that he could not point to specific language in the Constitution to back his claim of a "fundamental right" to citizenship. He did not explain, moreover, why Congress was powerless under its constitutional authority to impose rational limits on citizenship.

Both *Trop* and *Perez* presented Justice Frankfurter with a splendid opportunity to expound on his philosophy of judicial restraint. In both cases, he wrote (for the court in *Perez* and dissenting in *Trop*) that Congress had acted reasonably and within its authority under its foreign affairs and war powers.

Frankfurter had laid the foundation for his opinions during the previous term after the court first heard arguments in the cases (they were reargued in October 1957). He wrote a letter to Justice Harlan, posing the critical question: "Who is to judge" on denationalization?[23] "Is it the Court or Congress?" The court must "put on the sackcloth and ashes of deferring humility" he wrote, unless it could be shown that Congress had acted arbitrarily. His opinions in *Perez* and *Trop* followed that reasoning. To sustain the congressional statutes in the denationalization cases, he concluded, was to "respect the actions" of the elected branches.[24] The court's "awesome power" to invalidate congressional statutes, he wrote, "is bounded only by our prudence" and "must be exercised with the utmost restraint."

Frankfurter's opinions were delivered one month after his longtime friend and confidant, Judge Hand, had given the Holmes Lectures at Harvard, admonishing the justices to resist the temptation to act as "Platonic guardians." Frankfurter, like Hand, counseled the justices in the strongest terms to avoid substituting their judgment for that of the elected representatives.

Warren and Frankfurter took the opportunity in the expatriation cases to lecture each other on the proper role of the court. For Frankfurter, prudence was the watchword, especially when Congress threatened to retaliate against what the agitated legislators considered the court's excesses. The chief justice countered that the court had no choice. If the Constitution required a principled result, "prudence" had no place in the court's deliberations.

———

JUSTICE HAROLD BURTON suffered from Parkinson's disease that had become progressively worse during the 1957 court term. His doctor advised him to retire at the end of the term. Burton, who had been appointed by President Truman in 1945, informed Warren on April 30, 1958, that he planned to end his judicial tenure shortly after his seventieth birthday in late June.

On July 17, Burton, accompanied by Attorney General Rogers, met with President Eisenhower at the White House to formally submit his notice of retirement. The conversation was devoted primarily to the question of Burton's successor. The president spoke candidly of his dissatisfaction with two of his appointees, Warren and Brennan. He advised his attorney general to be "most careful" in selecting a candidate for his fifth appointment to the court.[25] He said that he had chosen Warren for his experience as governor of California as well as his years of law practice as Alameda County's district attorney and the state's attorney general. To replace Burton, Eisenhower stressed that he wanted someone with judicial experience and "a conservative attitude."

The only man Rogers recommended appeared to meet the president's qualifications. He was Potter Stewart, forty-three years old, who had been appointed by Eisenhower to the U.S. Court of Appeals for the Sixth Circuit in 1954. Stewart was raised in Cincinnati, a solidly Republican city where the Taft family (conservative Chief Justice William Howard Taft and his son, Robert) served as Republican saints-in-residence. The Stewarts, middle-class, well established, and Republican, fit in perfectly and, in fact, were both friends and admirers of the Tafts. As a small boy, Potter was called "little Jimmy" by Chief Justice Taft.[26] The chief justice was referring to Potter's father, James

Garfield Stewart, who was active in the Republican Party and elected mayor of Cincinnati several times before his appointment to the Ohio Supreme Court.

High achievement came early and easily to Stewart. At Yale, he edited the *Yale Daily News,* was chosen as his class orator, and graduated Phi Beta Kappa. After spending a year abroad at Cambridge University on the prestigious Henry Fellowship, he returned to Yale Law School, where he served on the law journal and graduated with honors. He joined an elite Wall Street law firm but left the practice to serve in the navy during World War II as a deck officer on oil tankers in the Atlantic. After the war, he returned to corporate law practice in New York, then moved back to Cincinnati to join a law firm in his hometown. He was elected to two terms on the city council but always knew that law, not politics, was his preferred profession.

After Eisenhower appointed him to the federal appeals court, the handsome, plainspoken Stewart built a reputation for fairness and judicial craftsmanship. He refused to be categorized ideologically. When asked to describe his judicial philosophy, he responded simply, "I like to be thought of as a lawyer."[27]

At the injudicious hour of 6:45 a.m. on an early October day in 1958, Stewart, weary and bedraggled from an overnight train trip, walked into Washington's Union Station, where he was greeted by Chief Justice Warren. Later, Stewart fondly remembered the chief's small act of kindness.[28]

Warren was not the only justice to pay special attention to the court's newest member. Stewart remembered that both Black and Frankfurter courted him. "Felix was more obvious about it," he recalled. "Felix was so unsubtle and obvious that it was counterproductive. He was the scholar who knew everything about everything."[29]

But just as Warren had welcomed Frankfurter's attention when he first arrived at the court, so too did Stewart listen appreciatively to the former Harvard professor. Frankfurter's philosophy of judicial restraint appealed to Stewart. He was, by temperament, a careful, cautious jurist.

Early in the 1958 court term, Frankfurter sensed that he had found a new ally. "I shall only say about the new man Stewart that on the meager showing to date, I should be much surprised if he does not turn out to be a judge," he wrote Judge Learned Hand.[30] "I entertain a further hope about him," he added. "I do not believe that he will convince himself that the mere fact that he sits on this bench calls for arrogant confidence in his own wisdom and learning."

Stewart fulfilled Frankfurter's expectations that term, tilting the majority narrowly, but decisively, away from the chief justice in two closely watched cases. He cast the fifth vote in *Uphaus v. Wyman*,[31] which undercut the court's decision the previous term in *Sweezy v. New Hampshire*. In *Sweezy*, Warren had written the opinion for the court that upheld the civil liberties claim of a professor at the University of New Hampshire suspected of subversive activity.

Uphaus, like *Sweezy*, involved an investigation by New Hampshire attorney general Louis Wyman, authorized by the state legislature, into suspected subversive activities in the state. Uphaus, the executive director of World Fellowship, Inc., ran a discussion program on political, economic, and social themes at a summer camp. Wyman suspected Uphaus and some of the speakers at the camp of being associated with "Communist front" movements. Uphaus, like Sweezy, was willing to discuss his own activities but would not discuss his associates. He refused to provide the names of those who attended the summer camp and was convicted of contempt for refusing to comply with a subpoena directing him to do so. He claimed, as had Sweezy, that the state's investigation exceeded its authority and violated his First Amendment rights.

Frankfurter had concurred in *Sweezy* but voted with Clark, Harlan, Stewart, and Whittaker to uphold Uphaus's conviction. Warren and the three other liberals (Black, Brennan, and Douglas) dissented. In upholding the state's conviction in *Uphaus*, Frankfurter was undoubtedly mindful of the need for judicial restraint in the face of congressional threats against the court. He explained his position to Justice Brennan, who wrote a dissent for the four liberals: "I cannot find it within what I deem my allowable scope of judicial review to conclude the Legislature of New Hampshire must first prove that an enterprise that is in effect run as an inn is a communist affiliation before it can make the inquiry now before us."[32]

Frankfurter, as the senior justice in the majority, assigned the court opinion to Justice Clark, who aggressively defended New Hampshire's wide-ranging authority to root out subversives. Clark facilely distinguished *Sweezy*'s successful academic-freedom defense from *Uphaus*'s "since World Fellowship was neither a university nor a political party."[33] The state had reason to be concerned if anyone attending the camp "posed a serious threat to the security of the State," he wrote, especially since many of the speakers at the camp were affiliated with groups on the U.S. Attorney General's list of suspected subversives. The governmental interest in self-preservation," he concluded, "is sufficiently compelling to subordinate the interest in association privacy."

Brennan's dissent contended that there was ample room for accommodation between the state's legitimate interest in self-preservation and an individual's constitutional rights. He concluded that the investigation of Uphaus had no "discernible" legislative purpose beyond "exposure for exposure's sake," precisely the point made by Warren in his opinion for the court the previous term in another controversial decision, *Watkins v. U.S.*

In a second court decision that term, *Barenblatt v. U.S.*,[34] the same narrow majority undercut *Watkins*, the decision that curtailed Congress's broad legislative investigatory power. The lower court in *Barenblatt* had affirmed the conviction of Lloyd Barenblatt, an instructor in psychology at Vassar College, for contempt of Congress for refusal to answer questions about his attendance at a Communist Party meeting when he was a graduate student at the University of Michigan. Barenblatt based his refusal to answer questions from a HUAC subcommittee on the court's decision in *Watkins*. Chief Justice Warren's opinion for the court in *Watkins* had scolded congressional committees for asking questions that were not "pertinent" to their legislative purpose. Barenblatt, invoking his First Amendment rights, said that the committee had not demonstrated that its questions were "pertinent" to its investigation.

At the justices' conference discussing *Barenblatt,* Warren said that he had no doubt the case was governed by *Watkins*, concluding that the pertinence issue was decisive. He maintained that Barenblatt had "sufficiently raised the question that there be pointed out to him the pertinence and, not having it, *Watkins* requires reversal."[35]

Again, Justice Stewart joined the majority to affirm the lower-court decision upholding Barenblatt's conviction. Frankfurter assigned the majority opinion to Harlan, who backtracked from the court's *Watkins* decision without overruling it. He contended that the judiciary lacked authority to inquire into legislative motives and, therefore, could not rule that the "true objective" of the HUAC hearing was "exposure for exposure's sake."[36] He repeated Clark's truism in *Uphaus* that the government had a legitimate interest in the "right of self preservation" but did not explain how meetings that Barenblatt may have attended as a graduate student threatened the national security. On balance, Harlan concluded that Barenblatt's constitutional interests were subordinated to those of the government.

Nothing in the majority opinions in *Uphaus* or *Barenblatt* suggested that the justices were reacting to Congress's counterattack against the court. But there was little doubt that the newly formed majority had rediscovered the passive virtues of judicial restraint.

———

ON SEPTEMBER 12, 1958, two hours after the U.S. Supreme Court had denied the Little Rock School Board's appeal in *Cooper v. Aaron* to delay desegregating Central High School, President Eisenhower publicly endorsed the court's decision, appealing "to the sense of civic responsibility that animates the vast majority of our citizenry to avoid defiance of the Court's orders."[37] He called on state and local officials to maintain peace so that "lawless elements will not be able by force and violence" to deny schoolchildren their constitutional rights.

Governor Faubus's political agenda did not include a duty to obey the court's order or heed the president's plea. His defiant stand against the desegregation of Central High School was extremely popular with the state's white voters. It led to his landslide victory in the Democratic primary during the summer, assuring his election to a coveted third term as governor in November. After the court ordered immediate desegregation of the high school, Faubus closed all of the Little Rock public high schools for the academic year.

As a result of Faubus's action, the city's white students attended state-financed segregated private schools, took correspondence courses, moved to other school districts, or gave up school altogether. Most of the city's black students enrolled in segregated county public schools just outside Little Rock.

On September 24, the first anniversary of Eisenhower's order to send troops to Little Rock, the president released a public statement in which he expressed his deep regret at the closing of the public schools (in Virginia as well as Arkansas) that "could be disastrous" to the schoolchildren and the nation.[38] He implored the nation to "constantly strive to achieve the ideal of equality." The school closing tactic, he said, "represents a material setback not only in that progress, but in what we have come to regard as a fundamental human right—the right to a public education."

Eisenhower found a prominent, and rare, ally in the Deep South during the tumult over school desegregation. He was Ralph McGill, the respected editor of the *Atlanta Constitution*, who anticipated that leaders like Faubus would be willing "to pay the tragic price of closing their schools."[39] In an editorial column entitled "The President as Professor," McGill expressed admiration for Eisenhower's determination to tell the people of the South the truth—that they have "an obligation to suppress unlawful forces that frustrate the preservation of individual rights as determined by a court decree."

McGill sent a copy of his column to Eisenhower, accompanied by a letter in which he lamented the lack of progressive leadership among the Deep South's politicians who refused, at least in public, to accept the inevitability of public school desegregation. "As a Southerner, I am, of course, grieved at the outright and outrageous defiance and the unwillingness to make even a token start," he wrote, contrasting that defiance with the willingness of moderate leaders in other southern and border states to make a good faith effort to begin the process of desegregation.[40] McGill then shared a conversation that he had with Senator Albert Gore of Tennessee, who lamented that the recalcitrance of politicians in the Deep South would lead to a diminution of the region's political power. "I am sure he is right," McGill wrote, "and it saddens me to think that the Deep South blinds itself, not merely to what is happening in the rest of the South but to the great historical forces which are at work."

Eisenhower responded promptly to McGill's letter and column, which, he wrote, reflected his own concerns and convictions. He then candidly shared his frustration over resistance in the Deep South: "The entire situation distresses me profoundly, as I know it does you and all other leaders of American thought. There doesn't seem to be any solution in sight—for the simple reason that not even the principles of political and economic equality will be accepted in some of our states. Any start, any degree of progress toward practicing this kind of equality, even though many years might be required to reach fruition, would, in my opinion, reverse this situation. Lacking such a start, I rather agree with you that there will be a decline in the influence that the Deep South has traditionally exercised. All of us, collectively, seem to lack the wisdom we should have to deal adequately with the entire problem."[41]

McGill personified the thoughtful southern moderate who Eisenhower had hoped would lead the region to gradually accept the *Brown* decision. Chief Justice Warren also envisioned that moderates like McGill would lead the South to comply with the *Brown II* mandate. Warren described McGill as "a great American in every sense of the word."[42]

McGill was born February 5, 1898, near Soddy-Daisy, Tennessee, and attended Vanderbilt University in Nashville, but was suspended his senior year for writing an article in the student newspaper critical of the school's administration. After serving in the Marine Corps during World War I, he pursued a career in journalism, first as a sports writer for the *Nashville Banner* and later for the *Atlanta Constitution*. But the ambitious McGill wanted to write serious articles about politics and international affairs and got his first break in 1933 when he talked his editor into sending him to cover the Cuban revolution; he landed an exclusive interview with dictator Gerardo Machado days before he fled. His second break came in 1938 when he received a fellowship to study and write from Europe. From Vienna, his front-page accounts of the Nazis' seizure of the country earned him a promotion to editor of the newspaper's editorial page when he returned to Atlanta. In 1942, he was promoted to editor in chief of the newspaper.

McGill's editorials in the nineteen forties and early fifties (before *Brown*) courageously portrayed the South's failure to live up the "separate but equal" ruling of *Plessy v. Ferguson*. Without advocating integration, he described the deplorable conditions of Georgia's black schools, comparing their meager budgets for books and buildings with the flush budgets for white schools. In a 1953 column that presaged the *Brown* ruling, he predicted that the court would outlaw segregation and that "somebody, especially those who have a duty so to do, ought to be talking about it calmly and informatively."[43] His commentary enraged implacable segregationists, who sent him threatening letters, burned crosses at night on his front lawn, fired bullets into the windows of his home, and left crude bombs in his mailbox. After *Brown*, McGill continued to be vilified by segregationists as he pleaded for the Deep South to accept the court's mandate.

In 1958, McGill was convinced that the court's decision in *Cooper v. Aaron,* declaring that *Brown* must be obeyed, "was enormously helpful in that it restores the image of inevitability" of the court's school desegregation decision. That sense of inevitability, he observed in a letter to Eisenhower's press secretary, Jim Hagerty, had been undermined by declarations of governors, senators and Citizens Council groups in the Deep South that the court had acted unconstitutionally and, therefore, the *Brown II* mandate was illegal and not binding.[44]

McGill wrote his letter to Hagerty shortly after Faubus and Virginia governor J. Lindsay Almond had closed public schools in their states, and he encouraged Hagerty to share it with "the Boss." He told Hagerty that he and others in the Deep South "have known all along that schools would have to be closed before there could be any hope of acceptance of the [*Brown*] decision. I am sure the President and the Attorney General understand that while this is tragic and painful, there simply is no other way out of it, and any appeasement of it would be disastrous in the long run." McGill emphasized that he and other like-minded southern editors he had talked to believed it "vital that this image of inevitability be scrupulously maintained."

"It is quite possible that your statement that the schools must be closed for a period before there is hope of acceptance of the decision is a correct one," Eisenhower wrote McGill after his letter to Hagerty had been shown to him.[45] The president suggested that "the students themselves will eventually resolve the issue, merely by their desire to have the educational processes resumed, despite the objections they may have to the conditions under which it may proceed." He remarked on the curious phenomenon that extracurricular activities such as a public school's football team or band "seem to become more important levers in urging the reopening of the schools than does educational opportunity. The children will likely be helpful in bringing pressures upon parents, school boards, and local authorities for the reopening of the schools."

Eisenhower closed his letter to McGill on an optimistic note, "heartened by the shrinking perimeter of the areas where prejudices of this kind run so deep." Although the Deep South was in the midst of another traumatic period in its troubled history of civil rights, he concluded, "there must, somewhere, be the common sense and the good will on the part of all to bring about a solution."

ON THE ISSUE of civil rights, a survey of black voters taken shortly before the 1958 midterm congressional elections showed that they were unhappy with both parties. Asked how he planned to vote, a black automobile mechanic in Cleveland replied, "You really want to know how I'd like to vote? I'd like to vote for the whole United States Supreme Court, that's how I'd like to vote. When it comes to this integration and civil rights stuff, neither party is worth a damn."[46] The auto mechanic's response reflected a deep malaise among black voters. They faulted the Democrats for failing to quell the rebellion of the party's southern congressional delegation against *Brown*. But they were no more impressed by President Eisenhower, who was perceived as lackadaisical in his support for the court's desegregation mandate.

The midterm election demonstrated once again that the president's national popularity could not be transferred to his party's congressional candidates. The Democrats gained thirteen seats in the Senate, building a commanding majority, 64–34. The Republicans suffered a comparable shellacking in the House, where they lost forty-seven seats, resulting in a 283–153 advantage for the Democrats.

At his first press conference after the election, Eisenhower spoke at length, and passionately, about the need to balance the federal budget.[47] He lamented that his denunciation of the "spender wing of the Democratic Party" had no apparent effect at the ballot box. He nonetheless pledged to do everything in his power during the last two years of his presidential term to curb excessive spending by the federal government. In his budget fight, he vowed to enlist "the conservative Democrats, the newspapers, every kind of person that has got the brains to see what is happening to this country with our loose handling of our fiscal affairs."

"When I'm in a fight," he told Republican congressional leaders in an early strategy session to produce a balanced budget, "I want every rock, pebble, club, gun, or whatever I can get."[48] And he meant it. He threatened to veto any budget-busting legislation. If Congress overrode his veto, he would propose new taxes to cover the increase in spending. He also lobbied for a balanced budget in his press conferences, in hundreds of letters to powerful businessmen, and in meetings with executives of the Chamber of Commerce and the National Association of Manufacturers.

His campaign was successful, with critical support from conservative Democrats from the South. For the fiscal year 1960, the budget was not only balanced, but showed a large surplus.

Eisenhower's vigor in pushing relentlessly for a balanced budget stood in stark contrast to his approach to civil rights legislation. In January 1959, he proposed new legislation to strengthen the provisions of the Civil Rights Act of 1957. But his advocacy, while sincere, lacked the fire and determination of his fight for a balanced budget. In his budgetary fight, he did not hesitate to oppose what he termed "the spender wing of the Democratic Party." Conservative Democrats from the South were not similarly condemned for their opposition to any meaningful civil rights legislation.

Reporters provided the president with numerous opportunities to give powerful voice to his opposition to racial discrimination. At a press conference on January 21, 1959, he was advised by William McGaffin of the *Chicago Daily News* that "many persons feel you could exert a strong moral backing for desegregation if you said that you personally favored it [the *Brown* decision]. If you favor it, sir, why have you not said so; if you are opposed to it, could you tell us why?"[49]

Eisenhower gave his standard answer. "I do not believe it is the function or indeed it is desirable for a President to express his approval or disapproval of a Supreme Court decision. His job, for which he takes an oath, is to execute the laws."[50]

The following week, Merriman Smith of United Press International told the president that there was a widely circulated report "that Chief Justice Warren has communicated to friends his feeling that your stand on school desegregation is too indecisive," and that he was "pained by what was described as your failure to take forceful action."[51]

Eisenhower repeated his earlier statement that he would not comment on a Supreme Court decision, but added, "I have regarded the Chief Justice as my personal friend for years" and that he knew of "no personal rift" between them.[52]

EISENHOWER'S PROPOSED CIVIL RIGHTS legislation, drafted by Attorney General Rogers in January 1959, extended the term of the Civil Rights Commission and provided greater safeguards to protect the vote, including the appointment of federal referees to investigate any interference with the right to vote and criminal penalties for obstructing federal orders protecting the vote. It also included protection of the process of desegregating public schools, imposing criminal penalties for obstructing the admission of students to desegregated schools, and resurrecting section 3 of the original 1957 bill that had authorized the attorney general to sue in federal court anyone who denied the equal protection of the laws. And it made it a crime to cross state lines to bomb schools or religious institutions. In

1958 alone, there had been fifty bombings of schools, churches, and synagogues.

Senate majority leader Lyndon Johnson, who hoped to succeed Eisenhower as president, sponsored his own, less ambitious, civil rights bill. In addition to extending the life of the Civil Rights Commission, Johnson's version empowered the attorney general to subpoena witnesses and voting records to investigate charges of voter discrimination, and made it a federal crime to transport explosives across state lines for the purpose of damaging religious, educational, or civic buildings.

Although Eisenhower did not trust Johnson, he knew that he needed the majority leader's support if the administration's bill was to have any chance of success. When the two men met at the White House in early February, the president agreed to eliminate section 3 of the 1957 bill, as he had done two years earlier under pressure from the southern delegation. Shortly after the meeting, the administration's bill was sent to Congress.[53]

In a letter to Ralph McGill, Eisenhower expressed confidence that his proposed legislation would become law. "The legislative program I have placed before the Congress is a modest, but I believe, effective one. Its enactment should be accomplished quickly. One of the finest results that I would anticipate would be a wider acceptance of the philosophy of progress through moderation. This might inspire extremists on both sides to gravitate a bit more toward the center line, which is the only path along which progress in great human affairs can be achieved."[54]

In the same letter, the president elaborated on his moderate approach to progress in the field of civil rights. "As you know, the reason that I so earnestly support moderation on the race question is because I believe two things. The first of these is that until America has achieved reality in the concept of individual dignity and equality before the law, we will not have become completely worthy of our limitless opportunities. The second thing is that I believe that coercive law is, by itself, powerless to bring about complete compliance with its own terms when in any extensive region the great mass of public opinion is in bitter opposition. This generalization was true under the carpet-bagging government of the South, under the Prohibition Amendment and the Volstead Act,[*] and it is still largely true with the four states you name in the deep South.[†]

"But the second fact," he continued, "does not excuse us from using every kind of legitimate influence to bring about enlightenment through education, persuasion, leadership, and, indeed, example. Of course, we cannot overlook the need for law, where law is clearly necessary and useful."

While the administration's bill was pending in Congress, Eisenhower did not help his cause by his flaccid public statements in support of civil rights. He remained curiously detached in his language, as if reading from a dull civics textbook. He was asked by a reporter in early May, days before the fifth anniversary of *Brown,* to comment on the nation's response to the court decision. He replied, "I believe that the United States as a government, if it is going to be true to its own founding documents, does have the job of working toward that time when there is not discrimination made on such inconsequential reason as race, color, or religion."[55] But even then he added the qualifying statement that "the real answer here is in the heart of the individual."

This was the president who had written McGill only three months earlier of the importance of "persuasion, leadership, and, indeed, example" in making progress in the field of civil rights.

The administration's bill languished in the Senate for most of the summer. Finally, in August, the southern delegation in the Senate, led by Senator Russell, threatened a filibuster against the bill that would have extended into September, embarrassing the president during a

---

[*] The statute enacted to carry out the intent of the Prohibition amendment (the Eighteenth).

[†] McGill had listed Alabama, Georgia, Mississippi, and South Carolina as the states most resistant to federal laws prohibiting racial discrimination.

scheduled visit to the United States by Soviet premier Nikita Khrushchev. Johnson did not oppose the filibuster. The only provision of the administration's civil rights bill that passed in 1959 was the extension of the term of the Civil Rights Commission, a provision also supported by the majority leader.

The next year, Eisenhower tried again, sending Congress the administration's civil rights bill with the provisions from the previous year intact. This time, he received critical assistance from Johnson, who wanted desperately to pass a modest civil rights bill in advance of the Democratic convention. The majority leader needed Senator Russell's cooperation to avoid a southern filibuster.[56] Russell, who supported Johnson's presidential candidacy, tacitly approved of a bill that concentrated on voting rights with what he considered ineffective provisions to register black voters. In the spring of 1960, southerners did not filibuster, allowing Congress to pass a civil rights bill that focused on voting rights. It required voting officials to retain and protect state voting records and authorized federal district court judges to appoint referees when there was a pattern of discrimination. It also authorized the FBI to investigate bombings of schools or houses of worship where there was evidence that the perpetrators had crossed state lines and made it a federal crime to obstruct a court order by threats or force.

The *New York Times* gave Johnson major credit for passage of the legislation and reported that his campaign for the Democratic presidential nomination "is expected to benefit from the result."[57]

Eisenhower praised the provisions that dealt with "the key constitutional right of every American, the right to vote without discrimination on account of race or color."[58] Although he regretted that Congress had eliminated the provisions of the administration's original bill that protected public school desegregation, he nonetheless, called the legislation a "historic step forward in the field of civil rights."

The significance of the Civil Rights Act of 1960, like the legislation three years earlier, was primarily symbolic. It was tangible proof that, after more than eighty years of inaction, Congress was capable of passing a second civil rights bill. But its immediate impact in protecting African Americans' voting rights in the Deep South was minimal. Significant progress in black voter registration in the region would only be realized after the passage of the Voting Rights Act of 1965.

———

IF EISENHOWER COULD have run for a third presidential term, he might have been tempted. Although he had complained since 1956 that the presidency was too physically and intellectually demanding for a man of his age, he never identified a successor who, in his judgment, possessed the necessary leadership qualities. Richard Nixon was the most obvious choice, and the vice president, as Ike and everyone else in the Republican Party knew, considered himself to be the heir apparent. But Eisenhower never fully warmed to Nixon, who, the president observed, had few close friends and, unlike Ike, appeared painfully ill at ease when not performing the formal duties of his office. The president also worried that Nixon was too partisan and would not be able to attract conservative Democrats and independents to support Eisenhower's middle-of-the-road policies.

When Republicans met in Chicago in late July, it was a foregone conclusion that Nixon would be the party's presidential nominee. Still, Eisenhower did not embrace him. In the president's address to the delegates, he devoted his entire speech to the accomplishments of his administration and never once mentioned Nixon by name.[59]

After Nixon formally accepted his party's nomination for the presidency, Eisenhower appeared to diminish the luster of his candidacy every time he spoke to the press. On August 10, he was asked if he would give Nixon more responsibilities now that he was his party's presidential nominee. No, Ike replied, he alone would continue to make all decisions. And while he would consult others, if a decision had to be made, "I'm going to decide it according to my judgment."[60]

Two weeks later, journalist Sarah McClendon asked the president to tell the press some of the big decisions that Nixon had participated in. An irritated Eisenhower replied, "I don't see why people can't understand this: No one can make a decision except me."[61]

The final squelch came later in the same press conference after Charles Mohr of *Time* magazine attempted to give the president an opportunity to say something reassuring about the vice president. "We understand that the power of the decision is entirely yours, Mr. President," said Mohr. "I just wondered if you could give us an example of a major idea of his [Nixon's] that you had adopted in that role, as the decider and final —" Eisenhower cut him off. "If you give me a week," he said, "I might think of one. I don't remember."[62]

Eisenhower realized that he had made a terrible mistake. When he returned to the Oval Office, he called Nixon to apologize. But the damage had been done, and Democrats gleefully repeated the president's press conference remarks.

By this time, the president fully supported Nixon's candidacy, in part, because he feared the alternative—the Democratic candidate, John F. Kennedy, the forty-three-year-old U.S. senator from Massachusetts. Eisenhower resented Kennedy's Cold War rhetoric, including his false charge that the United States suffered from "a missile gap" with the Soviet Union, and that the president placed a higher priority on a balanced budget and the consumer price index than national defense. Kennedy promised to "get America moving again," insisting that the nation must make a choice between "the public interest and private comfort."[63] Every campaign speech by Kennedy seemed to be a repudiation of the policies that Eisenhower had steadfastly advocated during his eight years in the White House.

A highlight of the campaign came in the first presidential debate between Nixon and Kennedy. Eisenhower had advised Nixon to reject the invitation to debate Kennedy, arguing that Nixon was much better known than the Massachusetts senator and should not give Kennedy free public exposure. Nixon rejected Ike's advice, confident that he was a superior debater. He never overcame his indelible televised image that night, perspiring profusely while listening nervously to the handsome, self-assured Kennedy at the podium.

When Eisenhower began to actively campaign for Nixon, he talked more about the fine record of his administration than Nixon's qualifications to lead the country. He boasted of the booming domestic economy—gross national product and personal income had increased by almost 50 percent over the eight years of his presidency, individual savings were up more than a third, college enrollment was at an all-time high, and 9 million new homes had been built. The Eisenhower years, as the president proudly pointed out with facts and figures, were undeniably a time of domestic prosperity, especially for the burgeoning white middle class.

Kennedy, more than Nixon, made civil rights a campaign issue. He said that the president "must exert the great moral and educational force of his office to bring about equal access to public facilities—from churches to lunch counters—and to support the right of every American to stand up for his rights—even if that means sitting down for them."*[64] He added, "If the President does not himself wage the struggle for equal rights—if he stands above the battle—then the battle will inevitably be lost." No one could mistake his meaning: he promised a proactive, vigorous fight for civil rights, in contrast to Eisenhower's perceived detachment.

Meanwhile, Nixon appeared to equivocate, at least during one uncomfortable speech that he delivered in Jackson, Mississippi. "It would not be appropriate for me to come before an audience like this and talk one way in the South and another way in the North."[65] He

---

* The reference to "lunch counters" was to sit-in protests by young black students at lunch counters that began on February 1, 1960, when four freshmen from North Carolina A&T College in Greensboro sat down at a segregated Woolworth's lunch counter, a protest that spread within weeks to sit-ins in nine southern states.

did not say what his convictions were on civil rights issues, admitting only that the issues were "complex" and were a problem in the North as well as the South.

An incident involving the civil rights leader Dr. Martin Luther King, Jr., may well have cost Nixon the election. At the height of the campaign, King was jailed by a Georgia judge, ostensibly for violating probation for a trivial traffic charge, after he participated in a sit-in protest in Atlanta. It was a cause célèbre in the national press. Nixon said nothing.

Officials in the Justice Department prepared a statement for President Eisenhower to issue on the King controversy. It read: "It seems to me fundamentally unjust that a man who has peacefully attempted to establish his right to equal treatment free from racial discrimination should be imprisoned on an unrelated charge, in itself insignificant. I have asked the Attorney General to take all proper steps to join with Dr. Martin Luther King in an appropriate application for his release."[66]

Eisenhower refused to issue the statement, unwilling even to appear to play politics with the situation. Nixon may not have been informed of the statement. He did not, in any case, issue his own statement.

While Nixon and Eisenhower maintained a public silence on the King controversy, Kennedy and his advisers moved quickly to fill the void. At the urging of Kennedy's brother-in-law, Sargent Shriver, Kennedy called King's wife to express his concern.

"He [Kennedy] wanted me to know he was thinking about us, and he would do all he could to help," Coretta King said.[67] "I told him I appreciated it and hoped he would help."

Kennedy's brother, Robert, who was his campaign manager, called the judge in the case and asked whether there was any reason Dr. King could not be released on bail. There was none, and he was released.

In the last week of the campaign Kennedy supporters printed 2 million copies of a pamphlet headed *"No Comment" Nixon Versus a Candidate with a Heart, Senator Kennedy*.[68] In Chicago alone 250,000 copies of the pamphlet were handed out in the last days before the election. Kennedy carried the state of Illinois by some 8,000 votes.

Nixon lost the popular vote by less than 113,000 votes out of more than 68 million votes cast. Kennedy carried twenty-three states with 303 electoral votes; Nixon won twenty-six states with 219 electoral votes. With a shift of only 4,500 votes in Illinois and 28,000 in Texas, Nixon would have been elected president.

A dejected Eisenhower blamed Nixon's defeat on "a couple of phone calls" by the Kennedys.[69] He bitterly complained about black voters' ingratitude for his civil rights policies. "We have made civil rights a main part of our effort these past eight years but have lost Negro support instead of increasing it," he said.[70] Negroes, he added, "just do not give a damn."

THE WARREN COURT was not an issue in the 1960 presidential election. It had not ruffled southern sensibilities over a civil rights decision since *Cooper v. Aaron* in 1958. And though the justices had felt the intense heat of congressional outrage and threat after their "Red Monday" decisions in 1957 and 1958, a narrow majority, led by Justice Frankfurter, had lowered the heat and diminished the threat in 1959 by finding virtually every challenged congressional statute reasonable and, therefore, constitutional.

The justices maintained strict public neutrality during the presidential campaign in 1960. But in private, only a year before the election, Chief Justice Warren did not hide his antipathy toward the presumptive candidate of the Republican Party, Richard Nixon. "You are a liar!"[71] Warren yelled at Earl Mazo, the author of a recently published favorable biography of the vice president. His outburst occurred at a crowded cocktail party in the nation's capital. He told Mazo that the book was a "dishonest account" written in order to promote Nixon's presidential candidacy. For more than twenty minutes, Warren lashed out at Mazo, his lacerating criticism so intense at times that onlookers feared that the chief justice might resort to physical violence.

Warren offered a milder version of the incident in his memoirs published in 1977. According to Warren, Mazo had asked the chief justice if he liked his book. Warren replied that he had not read it, but had read a review that recounted Mazo's claim that Warren had tried to stop Nixon's political career because of his campaign tactics against Helen Gahagan Douglas for the Senate in 1950. "I told him it was an old political canard which had been bruited around in some political circles for years but was not true," Warren wrote.[72] He said that a journalist friend of Mazo, Clark Mollenhoff, a reporter for the *Des Moines Register*, had rushed out and filed an article in which Warren called Mazo "a damned liar." Warren denied it. "I was taught better manners than that, and I am quite sure that never at a public affair during my half century of public service have I called a man a damned liar whether he was present or not."

Professor Bernard Schwartz, a Warren biographer, spoke to Mollenhoff, who stood by his published account of the incident. One of Warren's law clerks also confirmed Mollenhoff's account, recalling that the chief justice had said that Mazo's book was "nothing but a whitewash of Nixon" and, further, that "there were a lot of things I would have liked to have told the son of a bitch, but I didn't think I could do it."[73]

IN THE EARLY NINETEEN SIXTIES, while public school segregation in the Deep South remained stubbornly in place, the Warren Court studiously avoided additional decisions to fortify the *Brown II* mandate. At the same time, the justices provided critical legal protection for a new generation of civil rights protesters, the black students sitting in at segregated lunch counters throughout the South.

In 1961, the court handed down the first of a series of decisions providing protection for the protesters. In *Garner v. Louisiana*, the first sit-in case to be argued before the court, John Garner and other black college students had taken seats at a segregated Baton Rouge lunch counter and were asked to leave.[74] When they refused, they were arrested and charged with breach of the peace. Their convictions were affirmed by the Louisiana Supreme Court. On appeal, the defendants argued that their conduct at the lunch counter did not breach the peace, a position corroborated by the arresting officer who had testified at the trial that the students sat politely in their seats. Chief Justice Warren wrote the opinion for the court reversing the convictions, concluding that there was no evidence that the defendants' peaceful conduct could be considered a crime under state law.

The pace of the court's decisions prohibiting racial discrimination quickened after President Kennedy filled two court vacancies. In March 1962, Justice Charles Whittaker, Eisenhower's fourth appointee, retired from the court after a short, unhappy five-year tenure. The pressures of the court's work had plagued Whittaker since his appointment and, finally, jeopardized his health.

Shortly after Whittaker's retirement, Justice Frankfurter suffered the first of two strokes and was forced to retire from the court that he had revered for a professional lifetime. The former Harvard Law professor was an indefatigable advocate for his judicial positions. His advocacy in judicial conference, Justice Stewart noted wryly, often lasted fifty minutes, exactly the time of a law school lecture.[75] To his colleagues who did not agree with him, Frankfurter could be maddeningly condescending. But as the leading proponent for judicial restraint on the modern court, his place in its history was secure.

President Kennedy's two appointees dramatically changed the justices' internal dynamic, tipping the court majority toward the emerging activism of the chief justice. To replace Whittaker, Kennedy chose Byron White, who had served with the president in the navy during World War II and managed his presidential campaign for the Midwest region. White achieved superhero status on the football field, first as an all-American halfback at the University of Colorado and later as the leading rusher for the Pittsburgh Steelers of the National Football League. He was equally accomplished in the classroom, graduating Phi Beta Kappa, winning a Rhodes scholarship, and serving on the Yale Law Journal.

After clerking for Chief Justice Fred Vinson, White returned to Colorado to practice law. In 1961, he joined the new administration as deputy attorney general under Robert Kennedy. At the Justice Department, he was known for his calm, analytical approach to even the most volatile problem. He demonstrated his calm demeanor as well as his toughness when he flew to Montgomery, Alabama, to protect the legal rights of "freedom riders," whose efforts to integrate interstate buses in the South faced the imminent threat of violence.

On the court, White regularly voted with the liberal majority in civil rights cases, but abandoned that majority in many civil liberties cases, especially when the court expanded the rights of criminal defendants.

Kennedy's second appointee, Arthur J. Goldberg, a highly successful labor lawyer from Chicago and an intellectual leader of the national labor movement, served as secretary of labor in the new president's cabinet. After his court appointment, Goldberg told his wife that he intended to be an activist justice and quickly made good on his promise. He became a dependable fifth vote for the court's liberals in both civil rights and civil liberties cases. In the three years that Goldberg served on the court, he voted with the chief justice between 85 and 89 percent of the time. After he resigned in 1965 to serve as U.S. ambassador to the United Nations, his successor, Abe Fortas (appointed by President Lyndon Johnson), agreed with Warren between 83 and 92 percent of the time.

After several years of inactivity, the justices returned to the issue of school desegregation, showing marked impatience with states resisting the *Brown* mandate. In 1964, the court revisited one of the original cases argued in *Brown* from Prince Edward County, Virginia, and discovered that there were no African Americans in the county's public schools with whites, because there were no public schools. Like the rest of the state, Prince Edward County in rural south central Virginia had closed its public schools, replacing them with private schools for whites only, as part of the massive resistance called for by the senior senator from Virginia, Harry Byrd.

Justice Black wrote the opinion for the court, declaring that "the time for mere 'deliberate speed' has run out."[76] The federal courts had a duty to see that black Americans received a public education. If necessary to prevent further racial discrimination, Black said that county supervisors must exercise their power to levy taxes to raise funds adequate to reopen, operate, and maintain public schools without racial discrimination.

Four years later, in the last major school desegregation ruling by the Warren Court, the justices rejected a belated and hastily drawn up plan to desegregate the two schools in New Kent County, Virginia, an effort primarily inspired by the threat of loss of federal funds. The county's "freedom of choice" plan did not substantially change the racial makeup of the two schools. No whites elected to go to the black school. Approximately 85 percent of blacks remained in the black schools. A unanimous court, speaking through Justice Brennan, wrote that *Brown II* called for the affirmative duty to eliminate racial discrimination in the public schools "root and branch."[77] School officials were required to "fashion steps which promise realistically to convert promptly to a system without a 'white' school and a 'Negro' school, but just schools."

The Warren Court of the nineteen sixties was equally vigilant in protecting the voting rights of African Americans in the South, providing strong constitutional support for the Voting Rights Act of 1965. The state of South Carolina challenged the statute, arguing that Congress could not single out one region, the South, and, therefore, had exceeded its constitutional authority under the general terms of the Fifteenth Amendment.* Chief Justice Warren's opinion for the court indignantly dismissed South Carolina's argument. He noted that congressional hearings showed that the legislation was aimed at the South because that was the region where the "insidious and pervasive evil" of racial discrimination in voting was most persistent.[78] That discrimination, he continued, had been perpetuated "through unremitting and ingenious defiance of the Constitution." Since earlier attempts to remedy the evil had been unsuccessful, he concluded, the broad remedies provided for in the legislation, rather than case-by-case adjudication, were sensible, necessary, and constitutional.

CHIEF JUSTICE WARREN will always be identified with *Brown* and subsequent decisions by the Warren Court that aimed to eliminate official racial discrimination. But the boldness of Warren's rulings expanding individual liberty were as important in two other constitutional areas that the court addressed in the nineteen sixties. The first dealt with the pervasive problem of unequal voter representation caused by malapportioned state and congressional district plans. The United States had changed from a nation of farmers in the nineteenth century to one of city dwellers in the twentieth. In 1885 only one-third of the nation's population lived in cities; by 1960 it was two-thirds. Yet the makeup of almost every state legislature in the mid-twentieth century promoted the illusion that the United States was still a frontier country with predominantly rural voters and rural values. Since the legislatures refused to redistrict according to population shifts, the rural votes counted for two, five, even ten times those of city dwellers.

In 1962, when the Warren Court listened to arguments challeng-

---

* The amendment protects the right of citizens to vote regardless of race or color and gives Congress the power to enforce the right by appropriate legislation.

ing the malapportionment of the Tennessee legislature, which had last been redistricted in 1901, the justices faced an institutional problem as well as a constitutional issue. Justice Frankfurter had long warned the court to avoid "the political thicket" of redistricting.[79] After all, the appropriate political institution, the state legislature, could readily remedy the problem by redistricting. The court majority ignored Frankfurter's advice, and ruled that malapportionment was not a "political question" off limits to the justices. It was, instead, a violation of the Equal Protection Clause of the Fourteenth Amendment.[80]

Two years later, Chief Justice Warren wrote the constitutional sequel, deciding that the Alabama legislature, which, like Tennessee, had last redistricted itself at the turn of the century, violated the Equal Protection Clause. At the oral argument, the chief justice had impatiently asked the state's attorney, "How long can we wait?"[81] Warren clearly was not contemplating an "all deliberate speed" formula to correct the constitutional deficiency. In his court opinion, after observing that "people, not land or trees or pastures, vote," he concluded that population alone was the single criterion for redistricting.[82] Warren spoke with the moral certitude of his judgment in *Brown*. Malapportionment, like racial discrimination, undermined American democracy. It also offended the chief justice's notion of fairness, a bedrock principle that pervaded his most outspoken opinions. He later rated the court's reapportionment decisions more important than *Brown*.

The chief justice exerted enormous influence in a third constitutional field, criminal procedure, in pursuit of the Warren Court's vision of a more just society. What became known as the court's egalitarian revolution began with the insistence that black Americans be accorded first-class citizenship. In the nineteen sixties, the justices protected another of society's outcasts, the poor criminal defendant. The court ruled that a poor drifter named Clarence Earl Gideon was entitled to an attorney after his arrest for breaking and entering the Bay Harbor Poolroom in Panama City, Florida.[83] The justices also ruled in favor of Dolree Mapp, whose Cleveland apartment had been ransacked by police without a warrant, establishing the "exclusionary rule" in state criminal trials that prohibited the introduction of evidence that had been obtained illegally.[84]

Warren wrote the majority opinion in *Miranda v. Arizona*, the most controversial Warren Court decision expanding the rights of criminal defendants.[85] In his opinion, he reviewed with revulsion a police manual's procedures to induce confessions from criminal defendants. "When normal procedures fail to produce the needed result, the police may resort to deceptive stratagems such as giving false legal advice," he wrote. The whole purpose was to "persuade, trick or cajole [the defendant] out of exercising his constitutional rights." When he discussed the facts of the case of Ernesto Miranda, who had confessed and been convicted of kidnapping and rape, Warren expressed outrage at the lack of constitutional safeguards to protect the defendant from a coerced confession. As a result, Warren, for the court majority, issued what became known as the "Miranda warnings," obligating police in every state to inform a criminal suspect in custody that he had the right to remain silent, that anything he said could be used against him, and that he was entitled to a lawyer, even if he could not afford to pay for one.

The reaction from police departments across the country was apoplectic. "You might as well burn the books on the science of police interrogation," said a Houston police officer.[86] *Miranda* was another "shackle that the Supreme Court gives us from time to time in the handling of criminal cases," complained a Nevada police chief. He added, "Some day they may give us an equal chance with the criminals."

ON SATURDAY, JUNE 1, 1968, the chief justice was having lunch with one of his law clerks in a small restaurant on Pennsylvania Avenue near the court. Their discussion turned to politics and the Democratic primary to be held in California the following Tuesday. Warren noted newspaper reports of the enormous crowds that had lined Senator Robert Kennedy's route from the airport to downtown Los Angeles. "I can remember when I was at the peak of popularity running for Governor following the same route from the airport and seeing no one on the streets," he said.[87] He then predicted that Senator Kennedy would win the California primary, and that victory would lead to his party's nomination and the presidency.

Three days later, Kennedy was assassinated, leaving the Democratic Party in disarray. The leading Republican candidate, Richard Nixon, instantly became the odds-on favorite to be elected the next president of the United States.

In the wake of the shocking turn of events, Warren, seventy-seven years old, decided that he must resign so that President Johnson could appoint his successor rather than leave that historic choice to his long-time nemesis, Richard Nixon. He asked Justice Fortas, who had long been Johnson's confidant, to call the president to arrange a meeting. When Warren met the president on June 13, he told Johnson that he felt he should retire because of his age, and that he hoped the president would appoint as his successor a man who shared his views on national issues.[88] The president asked Warren his opinion of the possible appointment of Fortas as his successor, and Warren responded positively.

After his meeting with the president, Warren wrote two retirement letters, one giving his age as the reason for his retirement, the other advising the president of his "intention to retire as Chief Justice of the United States effective at your pleasure."[89] After Warren's plan to retire was made public, the president announced that he would nominate Justice Fortas to succeed Warren as chief justice.

By this time, the chief justice had attracted more than his share of enemies, led by southern segregationists. It was a common sight in the South of the sixties to see "IMPEACH EARL WARREN" billboards dotting the landscape. Conservative Republicans had never forgiven Warren for his broad opinions condemning the tactics of the House Un-American Activities Committee and other government investigative committees in their pursuit of suspected Communists. Communism was no longer perceived as an existential threat to the nation in the sixties, but conservatives in both parties found other reasons to resent the leader of the liberal court. Exhibit A was Warren's opinion in *Miranda,* which, they believed, virtually guaranteed that the nation's streets would be overrun by criminals freed under the court's ruling.

The Fortas nomination became enmeshed in controversy almost immediately. It was not just southern Democrats and conservative Republicans who objected. Moderate Republicans in Congress thought it unseemly for a lame-duck president to appoint the next chief justice. So did prominent Republican governors, like Ronald Reagan of California, who complained that Warren had no "right to choose which president he thinks should dominate for the next twenty years at the Supreme Court."[90] The Republican presidential candidate, Richard Nixon, suggested that Warren should serve only through the fall of the 1968 court term, leaving the appointment of his successor to the next president.

In his testimony before the Senate Judiciary Committee, Fortas fielded a barrage of hostile questions about reports (later verified) that he remained a close adviser to President Johnson on a host of political issues, including U.S. military strategy in the unpopular war in Vietnam. The questioning then turned to the liberal decisions of the Warren Court in which Justice Fortas and his colleagues were accused of increasing the crime rate in America, among a multitude of judicial sins. Shortly after the hearings, Fortas's fate was sealed when it was reported in the press that he had been paid $15,000 to teach a nine-week seminar during the summer at American University, almost half his judicial salary of $39,000. After Democrats failed to break Senate

Republicans' filibuster against the nomination, Fortas asked the president to withdraw his name.

As if the news of Fortas's failed nomination was not bad enough for Warren, Nixon made the Warren Court a prime target in his presidential campaign. He deplored the controversial court criminal procedure rulings that "have had the effect of seriously hamstringing the peace forces in our society and strengthening the criminal forces."[91] From the point of view of "the criminal forces," Nixon went on, "the cumulative impact of these decisions has been to set free patently guilty individuals on the basis of legal technicalities. The tragic lesson of guilty men walking free from hundreds of courtrooms across the country has not been lost on the criminal community."

Several studies showed that *Miranda* and other controversial Warren Court rulings expanding criminal defendants' constitutional rights did not hamstring police. There appeared to be no significant change in the arrest rate, confessions, or convictions of criminal defendants as a result of the decisions.[92] But that was beside the point in the presidential campaign. Nixon had become the "law and order" candidate and tapped into the fears of what he called "the silent majority." In November 1968, he was narrowly elected president of the United States.

ON JUNE 23, 1969, in a brief ceremony in the ornate chambers of the U.S. Supreme Court, the fourteenth Chief Justice of the United States, Earl Warren, administered the oath of office to his successor, Warren E. Burger, a conservative federal appeals court judge and outspoken critic of the Warren Court's criminal procedure decisions. President Nixon, dressed in a cutaway coat and striped trousers, proudly witnessed the ceremony that officially installed his first court appointee as chief justice. The president chose the occasion to deliver a speech, the first given by a president to the court in the nation's history. He spoke of the court as a dual symbol of continuity and change in the nation and praised Chief Justice Warren as "the example of dignity, the example of integrity, the example of fairness."[93]

Warren responded by defending his judicial record and that of the Supreme Court under his leadership. "We have no constituency," he said. "We serve no majority. We serve no minority. We serve only the public interest as we see it, guided only by the Constitution and our own consciences."[94]

EPILOGUE

BEFORE HIS INAUGURATION IN 1953, EISENHOWER HAD refused President Truman's invitation to have coffee at the White House.[1] He was still angry over Truman's attacks on him during the 1952 presidential campaign. Eight years later, Ike had similar reasons to snub his successor, Senator John F. Kennedy. During the 1960 presidential campaign, Kennedy had relentlessly criticized Eisenhower, portraying the president as an out-of-touch chief executive who allowed the United States to lose ground to the Soviet Union in the Cold War while fretting over a balanced budget. But in January 1961, Eisenhower chose not to return to the chilly resentment he had exhibited toward Truman. The day before Kennedy's inauguration, Eisenhower called the president-elect to tell him that hot coffee would be waiting for him when he arrived at the White House the next morning.[2]

Eisenhower may have been motivated by more than a display of elementary courtesy toward his successor. Only three days before Kennedy's inauguration, Eisenhower, in his farewell address, demonstrated that he still had important advice to communicate to the American people. In that address, perhaps the most memorable of his presidency, he warned of the impending danger of a "military-industrial complex" that threatened both the stability and progress of America's constitutional democracy.[3] Once out of office, Eisenhower stood ready to advise the confident but callow young president.

Less than three months after his inauguration, Kennedy faced the first crisis of his presidency: the invasion of Cuba by some 1,400 Cuban exiles who had been trained by the CIA in Guatemala. The operation was an abject failure. Deprived of vital air support or reinforcements, the paramilitary force that landed on the southern coast of Cuba in an area known as the Bay of Pigs was easy prey for the troops of the Cuban revolutionary leader, Fidel Castro. Every member of the insurgency was either killed or captured.

Shortly after the debacle, Kennedy invited Eisenhower to join him at Camp David for consultation. Kennedy met Eisenhower when his helicopter landed at the secluded presidential retreat in the dense woods of Maryland.* The two men went immediately to a cottage on the premises where Kennedy outlined in detail the plan for the invasion and confessed that the operation had been "a complete failure."[4] Later, when they strolled around the grounds, Eisenhower asked questions about the tactical planning for the invasion and wondered aloud why the new president had not fully discussed the pros and cons of the operation with the National Security Council before approving the invasion. He also asked why the invading force had not been supported by American air power. Kennedy replied that he had wanted to conceal the United States' role in the invasion, a possibility that Eisenhower deemed highly dubious. "There is only one thing to do when you get into this kind of thing: make sure it succeeds," he told Kennedy.[5]

As to future policy, Eisenhower advised Kennedy that he should support every effort by the Organization of American States to repel communism in the Western Hemisphere. But he cautioned that he did not

---

* The retreat was originally named Shangri-La by President Franklin Roosevelt but renamed by Eisenhower to honor his father and his grandson.

believe the American people would approve direct military intervention by U.S. forces "except under provocations against us so clear and so serious that everybody would understand the need for the move."[6]

Such a provocation occurred in mid-October 1962, after the president was sent photographs taken by a U-2 spy plane flying over Cuba that showed intermediate-range-missile sites being built that could reach any part of the United States. Kennedy called Eisenhower on October 22, informing him hours before his scheduled televised address to the nation that the U.S. possessed irrefutable evidence of Soviet missiles in Cuba, and that he would demand their removal. He also told Eisenhower that he would impose a naval quarantine around the island until the Soviet Union agreed to dismantle the missile sites and guaranteed that no further missiles would be shipped to Cuba.

In his telephone conversation with Eisenhower, Kennedy predicted that the Soviet Union would threaten nuclear war if the U.S. invaded Cuba. He asked, "And what's your judgment as to the chances they'll fire these things off if we invade Cuba?"[7]

"Oh, I don't believe they will," Eisenhower replied. But, he added, "I'd want to keep my people very alert."[8]

Soviet premier Nikita Khrushchev responded furiously to Kennedy's announcement of a naval blockade of Cuba. "You, Mr. President, are not declaring a quarantine, but rather are setting forth an ultimatum and threatening that if we do not give in to your demands you will use force.... You are no longer appealing to reason, but wish to intimidate us."[9]

For the next week, tensions mounted while secret negotiations between the two superpowers proceeded. Kennedy called Eisenhower on Sunday morning, October 28, to report on his conversations with Khrushchev.[10] The president told Eisenhower that the Soviets agreed to dismantle all missile sites in Cuba if the United States would guarantee that it would not invade the island. Kennedy said that he considered the proposed agreement acceptable, and Eisenhower concurred.[11]

The crisis was over. Ike, who had been extremely critical of Kennedy's foreign policy, conceded that the president had performed well under intense pressure.

―――――――

IN THE LATE AFTERNOON of January 20, 1961, shortly after Kennedy's inauguration, Dwight and Mamie Eisenhower were driven to their farm outside the town of Gettysburg, Pennsylvania, in the 1955 Chrysler Imperial that Mamie had bought for Ike on his sixth-fifth birthday.[12] The Eisenhowers had purchased the 190-acre farm and two-story brick farmhouse on the property in 1950 when Ike was president of Columbia University. It was the first home that the couple had owned during their thirty-four-year marriage.

Mamie had inspected the property first and fallen in love with it. Ike needed no arm-twisting to buy it. It was adjacent to the Gettysburg battlefield, an ideal location for a serious student of military history like Ike, who was steeped in the strategies and details of the bloody fight that led to the Union's critical Civil War victory. The property had the further attraction of its location in rural Pennsylvania where Ike's ancestors had settled and farmed after immigrating from Germany in the eighteenth century.

It was a working farm, overseen by Eisenhower's old military friend, retired Brigadier General Arthur Nevins. Ike raised hay, corn, oats, barley, soybeans, and sorghum, as well as prize Angus cattle.

In 1955, largely with profits from Ike's best-selling memoirs, *Crusade in Europe*, the Eisenhowers renovated the house, transforming it into a rural mansion suitable for the needs and pleasures of the nation's president and first lady and their guests. It contained fifteen rooms, eight baths, and a glassed-in sun porch, and was furnished with elegant gifts that the Eisenhowers had received from heads of state and millionaire admirers.

For Ike, there was a putting green and a skeet-and-trap-shoot range shielded by rows of trees planted by his old friend and neighbor, Pete

Jones. The Eisenhowers purchased an additional five acres adjacent to their property that included an abandoned schoolhouse, which they remodeled to provide a home for their son, John, his wife, Barbara, and their four children, whom both Ike and Mamie doted on, especially during their retirement.

Ike indulged his love of oil painting, bridge, and his ritual steak barbeques cooked for friends and family on a specially built patio. But most weekdays, he kept to a familiar daily regiment. He rose early, usually by 6 a.m., read the daily newspapers while eating breakfast, and was in his office, provided by the president of Gettysburg College, by 7:30. He spent the morning working on his presidential memoirs, returned to the farm for lunch, took an early afternoon nap, then either returned to his office or headed for the golf course. He was home by 5 p.m., showered, dressed, and had a scotch before joining Mamie for dinner served on trays in front of their television set. After dinner, he played bridge with friends, watched a movie (his favorite: the 1951 inspirational baseball fantasy, *Angels in the Outfield*) or read, usually history, biography, or popular westerns. He was in bed by 10 p.m.

Beginning in the late fall of 1961, Ike and Mamie spent the winter months in Southern California. A Texas oil baron, Robert McCulloch, had constructed a house for their exclusive use on the eleventh fairway of the Eldorado Country Club in the Coachella Valley, between the towns of Palm Desert and Indian Wells. Ike enjoyed the dry desert heat and desolate beauty of the landscape as well as the exclusive gated community populated by the rich and powerful. Whereas tourists constantly drove past the Eisenhowers' Gettysburg farm hoping to catch a glimpse of the former president, the Eldorado Country Club was strictly private, so that Ike was free to play golf and work on his memoirs without distraction.

WRITING THE TWO-VOLUME memoirs of his White House years proved to be an onerous task for Eisenhower that took almost four years to complete. In contrast to his wartime memoirs, which he had dictated in only a hundred days, writing his presidential memoirs was a committee effort. His son, John, and his secretary, Rusty Brown, began the process of collecting and organizing documents. They were later joined by William Ewald, Jr., a former speech writer for the president, and Samuel Vaughan, a senior editor at Doubleday, the publisher of the memoirs. Eisenhower then edited the drafts.

The final product had the trappings of an official government document, dry and comprehensive, but too often devoid of Eisenhower's candid observations. Unlike his wartime memoirs, it often appeared defensive and self-serving, as demonstrated by his discussion of the controversy during his 1952 presidential campaign when he eliminated a paragraph from a speech in Milwaukee defending General George Marshall, who had been charged with disloyalty by Joseph McCarthy.[13]

Eisenhower did not want to mention McCarthy at all, but Vaughan said that he was obligated to recount his relationship with the Wisconsin senator. Ike agreed, but did not want to discuss the Milwaukee speech. Both Vaughan and Ewald insisted that he must do so and should admit his mistake in eliminating the paragraph defending Marshall. He refused. Instead, in the first volume of his memoirs, *Mandate of Change*, he blamed his staff and Wisconsin governor Walter Kohler for insisting on the deletion, and denied that he had "capitulated" to the McCarthyites.

His discussion of Chief Justice Warren's opinion in *Brown v. Board of Education* was cursory and similarly unrevealing. He discounted Warren's role in the controversial opinion, because he did not believe that "he [Warren] could possibly have exercised the amount of influence ascribed to him over this group of men [the Associate Justices]." As to the decision itself, he wrote, "I have questioned many eminent lawyers on the soundness of this decision, and without exception, they have expressed the opinion that it conformed to the Constitution of the United States." For the first time, he publicly admitted that "the judgment of the Court was right."[14]

He returned to *Brown* in the second volume of his presidential memoirs, *Waging Peace*, defending his refusal to publicly endorse the decision. "[T]o indulge in a practice of approving or criticizing Court decisions could tend to lower the dignity of government, and would, in the long run, be hurtful," he wrote.[15]

Nowhere in either volume of his presidential memoirs did Eisenhower criticize Chief Justice Warren, his opinion in *Brown*, or later Warren Court decisions. But in informal conversations, particularly after his retirement, he was more candid about his opinion of the chief justice and some of the more controversial Warren Court opinions, including *Brown*. According to his biographer Stephen E. Ambrose, the former president told friends in numerous private conversations that his biggest mistake as president was appointing "that dumb son of a bitch Earl Warren."[16] The veracity of that quotation has been questioned by Eisenhower's attorney general, Herbert Brownell, as well as later Eisenhower biographers.[17]

This author asked Eisenhower's grandson, David Eisenhower, who wrote a biography of his grandfather in retirement, if he could have been quoted correctly by Ambrose. "Maybe," he replied, and suggested that the former president would most likely have made such a statement to his southern friends in private conversations to deflect criticism of Warren's opinion in *Brown*.[18] A variation of the Ambrose quote was contained in Warren's memoirs. Eisenhower "was widely quoted as having said that his appointment of me as Chief Justice 'was the biggest damn fool thing I ever did,'" Warren wrote.[19] Warren's memoirs were published posthumously in 1977, seven years before Ambrose's publication with the controversial quotation. Reports of Eisenhower's regret in appointing Warren, expressed in harsh, outspoken terms by the former president, obviously had circulated widely for many years before it appeared in Ambrose's biography.

In conversations with his close friend Lucius Clay, Eisenhower spoke frankly of his regret in appointing Warren to the court. Eisenhower suspected that Warren's true ambition was to be president, said Clay, and that he had compensated for his frustrated political hopes by expanding the power of the court well beyond its traditional and appropriate limits.[20]

Eisenhower was critical of a number of Warren Court decisions, including *Brown*, according to his grandson.[21] He questioned Warren's reliance on sociological data as the basis for *Brown*, which he thought made it more of a political opinion than a judicial decree. He also criticized later groundbreaking Warren Court decisions, such as the reapportionment ruling, *Baker v. Carr*, for what he considered the discovery of new "inherent" rights not enumerated in the Constitution.

"Eisenhower was concerned about judicial activism as inappropriate, not just in the desegregation decision but later with school prayer, reapportionment and criminal procedure decisions," his grandson said.* He thought that "these were good ideas gone amuck."[22]

DURING A PARTICULARLY frustrating legislative fight with Senate Republicans, Senator John F. Kennedy grumbled in exasperation, "The Republicans, how can you hope for anything from them? They nominated Dewey and Nixon when they could have had Earl Warren."[23] After Warren administered the presidential oath to Kennedy on the cold, blustery day of his inauguration, the new president noticed with both concern and admiration that the sixty-nine-year-old chief justice remained on the reviewing stand while others scurried to shelter from the piercing winds. Soon afterward, Kennedy dropped in unan-

---

* In 1962, the Warren Court ruled in *Engel v. Vitale* that the New York Regents' Prayer recited in the state's public schools was a violation of the First Amendment's prohibition against the establishment of religion. (*Engel v. Vitale*, 370 U.S. 421 [1962].)

nounced at a surprise party given by Warren's clerks to celebrate the chief justice's seventieth birthday.

Although Warren had initially harbored doubts about Kennedy's youth and inexperience, he soon came to admire him. Kennedy's vision of civil rights closely aligned with Warren's. "In an age which insistently and properly demands that government secure the weak from needless dread and needless misery, the catalogue of civil rights is never closed," the new president declared.[24] "[B]oth [Warren and Kennedy] had a vision," recalled Warren's son, Robert, "not so much a political vision as they had a vision of what life should be for Americans in regard to human rights."[25]

Toward the end of the justices' Friday morning conference on November 22, 1963, Associate Justice Arthur Goldberg, as the court's junior member, answered the knock at the door. He took a typed note from Warren's executive secretary, Margaret McHugh, informing the justices of the report that "the President has been shot while riding in a motorcade in Dallas, Texas."[26] Warren quickly adjourned the conference and rushed back to his chambers to listen alone to the radio bulletins, until Kennedy was pronounced dead in the emergency room at Dallas's Parkland Hospital shortly after 1:00 p.m. (CST).

Warren delivered an emotional eulogy two days later in front of Kennedy's flag-draped casket resting in the Capitol rotunda: "We are saddened; we are stunned; we are perplexed. John Fitzgerald Kennedy, a great and good President, the friend of all men of good will, a believer in the dignity and equality of all human beings, a fighter for justice and apostle of peace, has been snatched from our midst by the bullet of an assassin. What moved some misguided wretch to do this horrible act may never be known to us, but we do know that such acts are commonly stimulated by forces of hatred and malevolence, such as are today eating their way into the bloodstream of American life."*[27]

---

* Warren was the target of such hatred from right-wing groups in the early sixties. A speaker at the National Indignation Convention in Dallas complained that the

A despondent Warren returned to work the following week. "It was like losing one of my own sons," he recalled.[28] "You know, he was just a little older than my oldest boy."

On Friday, November 29, Solicitor General Archibald Cox and Acting Attorney General Nicholas Katzenbach made a telephone call to Warren requesting an immediate appointment. At the meeting Cox and Katzenbach told Warren that they had been sent by President Lyndon Johnson, who wanted the chief justice to serve as chairman of a commission to investigate and report on the Kennedy assassination.

Warren turned Cox and Katzenbach down. He told them that he and his judicial colleagues had often discussed extra-court activities by justices in the past, which had been perceived as political and a serious distraction from the work of the court. Associate Justice Owen Roberts regretted that he agreed to lead an investigation of the Pearl Harbor attack on December 7, 1941, which only led to further investigations. After World War II, Associate Justice Robert Jackson served as a prosecutor at the Nuremberg war crimes trials, which stirred public controversy and resentment from his colleagues.

President Johnson refused to take no for an answer from Warren. Ninety minutes after Warren had declined Cox and Katzenbach's invitation to lead the commission, the president called the chief justice and asked him to come to the White House that afternoon. When the two men met in the Oval Office, Johnson told Warren that rumors of foreign involvement in the assassination had created a dangerous international situation that could lead to war. He then appealed to Warren's deep sense of patriotism. "You were a soldier in World War I," he reminded Warren, "but there was nothing you could do in that uniform comparable to what you can do for your country in this hour of trouble."[29]

---

chairman of the meeting had been too soft on the chief justice: "All he wants to do is impeach Warren—I'm for hanging him." (Schlesinger, Arthur M., Jr., *A Thousand Days: John F. Kennedy in the White House* [1965], p. 753.)

"Mr. President, if the situation is that serious, my personal views do not count. I will do it."[30] By Johnson's account, the chief justice left his office in tears.[31]

———

THE WARREN COMMISSION was composed of six members in addition to Warren, carefully selected by the president so that there could be no suggestion of partisanship: Senators Richard Russell (D-Ga.) and John Sherman Cooper (R-Ky.); Congressmen Hale Boggs (D-La.) and Gerald Ford (R-Mich.); and two former directors of the Central Intelligence Agency, Allen Dulles and John McCloy. The committee unanimously approved J. Lee Rankin, a Republican who had served as solicitor general in the Eisenhower administration, to be general counsel.

Warren arrived before 9 a.m. for each meeting of the commission, then went to the court to preside over a calendar filled with important cases, including those challenging malapportioned legislatures and the lack of constitutional safeguards for defendants in state criminal court trials. At 2:30 p.m., Warren returned to the commission meeting and sat well into the evening.

Despite the burden of his court responsibilities, Warren was clearly in charge of the commission's work. One of the staff attorneys, Professor Norman Redlich of the New York University Law School, characterized Warren's approach to the investigation as "tough but fair." At first, the toughness came as a surprise to Redlich: "[Y]ou just don't expect it. Then you start to respect it. He lets you know his reasons. He has a mind that grasps facts, organizes them, and weighs them quickly. After a while we all recognized that the Chief Justice was running a tight ship and that he wasn't an easy man to argue with."[32]

For ten months, the staff sifted through materials contained in approximately 25,000 interviews conducted by the FBI and 1,550 by the Secret Service, along with the testimony of its own 552 witnesses in an atmosphere described by Redlich as "a pressure cooker."[33] Toward the end of the investigation, when the pressure to produce the final report was extreme, Warren sometimes broke the tension by changing the subject to baseball, rhapsodizing about the grace of San Francisco Giants center fielder Willie Mays catching a fly ball or the speed of the fastball of Los Angeles Dodgers pitcher Sandy Koufax.

There were disagreements over procedures and details, but, according to General Counsel Rankin, never over the contents or conclusions of the report. That final 888-page report, which Warren insisted must be unanimous, concluded that Lee Harvey Oswald had fired the shots that killed President Kennedy. It was greeted with widespread acclaim. The *New York Herald Tribune* called the report "clear, detailed, conscientious" and concluded that it proved "that no conspiracy, no calculated perversion of justice, no hidden forces, were involved."[34] *Time* magazine said the report was "amazing in detail, remarkable in its judicious caution and restraint, yet utterly convincing in its major conclusions."[35] Both the London *Times* and the *Times of India* used the same phrase—"dispelled all doubt"—in describing the report's conclusions.[36]

That effusive praise proved transitory. A cottage industry of conspiracy theories soon followed in an endless profusion of books and magazine articles questioning the credibility of the commission's report. Although no author has disproved the commission's basic conclusion, questions have persisted about whether Oswald acted alone. One member of the commission, Senator Russell, refused to sign the final report until a categorical statement that there was no conspiracy was taken out. In 1979, a report of the Select Committee on Assassinations of the House of Representatives concluded that there was "a high probability that two gunmen fired at President John F. Kennedy" and that the president "was probably assassinated as a result of a conspiracy."[37] But it also reported that the unknown second gunman missed Kennedy and that, as the Warren Commission had concluded, the two bullets that struck the president were fired by Oswald.

Despite the sustained criticism of the commission's report, Warren never wavered in his belief that it was accurate and conclusive. "If I were still a District Attorney and the Oswald case came into my jurisdiction, given the same evidence, I could have gotten a conviction in two days and never heard about the case again."[38]

ON MARCH 18, 1966, the day before his seventy-fifth birthday, Warren scheduled his first press conference in five years. Looking fit and smiling broadly, the chief justice walked briskly into the study adjoining the court's conference room and shook hands with the reporters before taking his seat behind a long, narrow table.

He anticipated the first question: Did he have any plans to retire?

"I have not given serious thought to that at the present time," he replied.[39]

The next evening, Warren and his wife, Nina, planned to attend a small dinner party to celebrate the chief justice's birthday hosted by the Warrens' eldest daughter, Virginia, and her husband, John Daly. The Dalys had asked Warren if they could invite President Johnson. No, said Warren, the president was too busy but would feel obligated to come, and such obligations would mean he would never have an evening to himself.

Warren was dressing for the party when the phone rang. It was the White House informing him that the president was on his way to the Warrens' apartment. Johnson arrived and presented Warren with a copy of Samuel Eliot Morrison's *The Oxford History of the American People* and a photograph inscribed to "the greatest Chief Justice of them all."[40] He then noted that the Warrens were dressed in evening clothes and commented mischievously that it looked like they were dining out. An embarrassed Warren explained that he and his wife were attending a small birthday party, and that his daughter and her husband had wanted to invite the president, but he had overruled them. At the door, after congratulating Warren, Johnson said, "And next time, you let your daughter and her husband pick their own guests."[41]

When Warren retired from the court more than three years later, it was not under circumstances of his choosing. He had hoped that President Johnson, who had expressed such admiration for him, could have appointed his successor. But Johnson's nomination of Associate Justice Abe Fortas had been an unmitigated disaster, leading to Fortas's withdrawal of his nomination under pressure and ultimately his resignation from the court.

To Warren, California remained "home, the place I love," but he and his wife nonetheless chose to remain in their apartment at the Sheraton-Park Hotel in Washington, D.C. after his retirement.[42] Warren was seventy-eight years old and his wife, Nina, seventy-six, not the time in their lives to go house-hunting on the West Coast. Besides, they were comfortable in their apartment and had lived in D.C. for sixteen years.

Warren also had professional reasons to stay in Washington. He wanted to participate in the public conversation on important national issues, including civil rights and liberties. What better place to do so than in the nation's capital? He could work on his memoirs in an office provided for him at the court. While still on the court, he had told his biographer, John Weaver, that he had no interest in writing his memoirs. "It's all in there," he said, pointing to the bound volumes of the *U.S. Reports*, which contained all of the judicial opinions he had written as chief justice.[43] But later he changed his mind. A lucrative publishing contract, he concluded, would assure his wife of a comfortable old age.

Weekday mornings during his retirement Warren was driven to his office at the court and, assisted by a law clerk, worked on his memoirs. He found the task to be drudgery. Warren was not a particularly reflective man. He did not keep a diary and was not in the habit of writing long letters revealing his innermost thoughts. The memoirs, not surprisingly, appeared to be a dutiful effort to cover the highlights of his extraordinary public career. They contained few insights into his professional or personal life. They did, however, allow him to settle a few scores, notably criticizing President Eisenhower for what Warren considered Eisenhower's misunderstanding of the court's proper role in defending civil rights and liberties and, specifically, the president's failure to support the court's *Brown* decision.

Professor G. Edward White, who was Warren's clerk for the 1971 court term and worked on his memoirs, recalled his concern that Warren had placed his conversation with Eisenhower depicting the former president as woefully uninformed on the role of the Supreme Court in the memoirs' introduction.[44] "Are you sure you want to put that conversation with the former president at the beginning of your memoirs?" White asked. "Yes, I do," Warren replied emphatically.

White, who spoke to previous clerks in preparing his critically acclaimed biography of Warren, said that he and the other clerks found Warren to be a formidable boss. "He was outwardly genial, but somewhat detached and demanding in a gentle kind of way. He would read the clerks' drafts of opinions out loud, correcting line by line, sentence by sentence. After he had corrected the draft, he would read it again and express his satisfaction. He was indifferent as to who had written the first draft. The clerk's work was largely rejected. The process was excruciating."

White was never invited to lunch with Warren or to meet his family. Despite the arms-length relationship, he expressed great respect for Warren as a judicial leader: "On the surface, he appeared to be a regular fellow interested in chit-chat, a politician type, not particularly interested in ideas. That was not an accurate description of who he was. He was, in fact, very smart and had the ability to go to the jugular in an argument. He was quite formidable on constitutional issues. My impression was that he was pretty indifferent to the form of legal reasoning, the source of the arguments, the precedents. He put a high priority on policy, not the intricacies of constitutional doctrine. His highest priority was the right result."

"As Chief Justice, he was very good at marshaling his colleagues to a common task," White said. "On opinions like *Brown*, he argued from shame, and he was very good at it. To him, *Brown* was a simple case— would the court adopt the white supremacists' ideology?"

Warren's relationship with his successor, Chief Justice Warren Burger, began well enough, with Burger asking Warren for a signed photograph to hang in his office and inviting the Warrens to join him and his wife for dinner at the Supreme Court. But that cordiality quickly faded, in large part because Warren profoundly disagreed with the conservative Burger's judicial philosophy. "Warren was absolutely convinced that Chief Justice Burger and President Nixon were on a mission to reverse the major Warren Court criminal procedure decisions," White recalled. "He considered Burger and Nixon 'law and order' types. He was certain that the Burger Court was going to overrule *Miranda* and other major criminal procedure decisions."*

When a panel appointed by Burger recommended a National Court of Appeals to relieve the Supreme Court's caseload, Warren lashed out at the recommendation. He was convinced that the proposed appellate

---

* Nixon vowed during the 1968 presidential campaign to appoint justices who were "strict constructionists," a political phrase commonly understood to mean conservative judges. He appointed four justices in his first term: Burger, Harry Blackmun, William Rehnquist, and Lewis Powell, Jr. But despite Warren's fears, the Burger Court did not overrule *Miranda, Mapp,* and other major Warren criminal-procedure decisions.

court "threatened to shut the door of the Supreme Court to the poor, the friendless, the little man."[45] He spoke out against the recommendation at every opportunity. It was never adopted.

Warren also attacked President Nixon. At the fiftieth anniversary of the American Civil Liberties Union, he condemned Nixon's 1968 presidential campaign as "merely an exercise in the rhetoric of accusation and recrimination throughout the nation."[46] In 1973, he addressed the unfolding scandal known as Watergate, which involved the burglary of the Democratic National Committee headquarters and subsequent cover-up by the president and his top aides. He told an audience at the National Press Club that it was "the great tragedy of our time" and "cancerous to the body politic."[47]

The following year, Warren's health began to fail. He gave his last speech at Atlanta's Morehouse College, where he received an honorary degree on May 21, 1974. "We are only partway up the mountain we have assayed to climb," he told the black graduates.[48] "We must not falter in the face of recalcitrance born of race prejudice."

Two days after returning to Washington, Warren suffered a heart attack and was taken to Georgetown University Hospital, where he remained for more than a week. Still weak, he returned to his apartment where he intently followed legal developments in the Watergate scandal. Federal District Court Judge John Sirica had issued a subpoena to President Nixon requiring him to produce taped conversations in the White House in which the burglary and cover-up were discussed by the president with his aides. Invoking executive privilege, Nixon refused to release the tapes. The constitutional issue of the scope of the president's executive privilege was then before the Supreme Court.

On July 8, after Warren had again entered the hospital, Watergate was the subject of a conversation between him and former justice Arthur Goldberg. Warren said, "No man, not even a king, can put himself above the law. I am confident the Court will do its duty and so will the nation."[49] The next day Justices Brennan and Douglas visited Warren and informed him that the justices had voted unanimously to compel the president to obey Judge Sirica's order to release the tapes. Warren approved. "If Nixon is not forced to turn over tapes of his conversations with the ring of men who were conversing on their violations of the law," he whispered, "then liberty will soon be dead in this nation."[50]

That evening, Earl Warren, the nation's fourteenth chief justice, died.

On August 5, President Nixon agreed to comply with the court's decision. Four days later, he resigned his office.

In 1961, a poll of historians rated President Eisenhower as twenty-eighth on the list of presidents in order of greatness, near the bottom of the "average" category. The poll was conducted by Harvard historian Arthur Schlesinger, Sr. His son, Arthur Schlesinger, Jr., was then a White House assistant to President Kennedy, who had been a vocal critic of his predecessor. Eisenhower could, therefore, be pardoned for questioning the objectivity of the poll. He was, nonetheless, wounded by his low rating. According to his son John, Ike concluded that his low rating was due to the lack of a war during his presidency and his refusal to be stampeded into sweeping social reform amid the first rumblings of the civil rights revolution.[51]

Eisenhower's health deteriorated in 1965, after he suffered a near fatal heart attack. He lost weight and was less energetic, but nonetheless continued to enjoy golf. On April 20, 1968, he was playing a round on the Seven Lakes Country Club course in Southern California when he quit after nine holes, complaining of chest pains. He was diagnosed by doctors as suffering a mild heart attack but failed to respond to treatment. After four weeks, he was flown to Washington and placed in the presidential suite at Walter Reed Hospital. He remained hospitalized for the next ten months.

From his sickbed, he strongly endorsed Richard Nixon for president in a short televised speech to the delegates at the Republican convention in Miami in August 1968. The month after Nixon's election, he and Mamie happily listened to the audio of the marriage of their grandson, David, to President-elect Nixon's daughter, Julie. On March 27, 1969, Eisenhower instructed his son John to remove him from the life support system to which he was attached. At 12:35 p.m. the next day Eisenhower, the nation's thirty-fourth president, died surrounded by his family.

Almost fifty years after his death, the assessment of Eisenhower's presidency has markedly improved, placing him in the top echelon of the nation's chief executives. Eisenhower biographer Jean Edward Smith, in his book published in 2012, rated him as the second-greatest president of the twentieth century, behind only FDR.[52] Other recent biographers have offered comparably admiring appraisals.

Once Eisenhower's papers could be studied at his presidential library in Abilene, Kansas, scholars realized that he was neither a passive nor a dithering president, as he sometimes appeared in press conferences. To the contrary, he was an extremely intelligent, able, and calculating chief executive who cast a cold, sober eye on what was possible to accomplish in his complicated job. "He didn't want to win the Nobel Prize," said his grandson. "He just wanted to get the job done."[53]

Eisenhower's first priority was always to keep the peace during the dangerous days of the Cold War. And for the eight years of his presidency, he was successful, despite periodic threats from the Soviet Union and Communist China to disrupt the world order. Only six months into his first term he had used subtle threats and diplomacy to bring North Korea and Communist China back to the negotiating table to end the Korean War. In 1956, when the Soviet Union threatened nuclear war if America's allies, Great Britain, France, and Israel, did not withdraw from Egypt, Ike's tough stance backed down both the Soviets and our allies.

In his defense of civil liberties, his record was less impressive. He never confronted Senator Joseph McCarthy, who ran roughshod over the constitutional liberties of many loyal Americans. Ike always maintained that he was depriving McCarthy of publicity that was crucial to his power. But while he waited for McCarthy's recklessness to bring him down, many American lives were ruined. Later, when Chief Justice Warren led a court majority in upholding the constitutional liberties of suspected subversives, Ike was publicly silent and privately critical.

On the paramount civil rights issue of his presidency, the desegregation of the public schools in the South, Eisenhower temporized. He repeatedly said that the Supreme Court's decision in *Brown v. Board of Education* was the law of the land and should be obeyed. But his statements were often followed by the caveat that the law could not change people's hearts or minds. Such mixed messages only encouraged white southerners to resist, and resist they did.

During his presidency, historians and civil rights activist alike were disappointed in his seemingly languid response to the early tremors of the civil rights revolution. The question continues to be asked: Why didn't Eisenhower forcefully put the prestige of his office behind *Brown*, particularly in his second term, after he had won reelection in a landslide? There is no definitive answer, but several reasons are suggested by his private correspondence, comments at his pre–press conference briefings, and his public statements. He appeared to be genuinely conflicted in his support of the *Brown* mandate, unlike his forthright opposition to discrimination in voting and economic rights. His ambivalence may have been based in part on a residual racism, rooted in his segregated upbringing and his career in the segregated military. In addition, he made no secret of his sympathy for his white friends in the South who were asked to abruptly adjust to a historic change in both custom and law. Finally, he did not want to encourage violent resistance in the South and thought his muted response to *Brown* would prove more effective than a strong public stand against segregation.

Eisenhower's overall civil rights record was more impressive than his many critics at the time acknowledged. His "middle way," ineffective in the eyes of detractors like Chief Justice Warren, produced tangible and far-reaching results. In areas where he could wield federal power without fear of southern defiance, he did so decisively. Without fanfare or violence, he desegregated the military, Veterans Administration hospitals, naval yards, and schools on military bases in the South, and the public schools and restaurants in the District of Columbia. He strongly endorsed equal political rights for black Americans, pushing aggressively for voting rights provisions in the Civil Rights Acts of 1957 and 1960, and proudly signed both statutes, the first civil rights legislation since Reconstruction.

Although Eisenhower did not use his bully pulpit to support *Brown,* his actions certainly did. He sent federal troops to Little Rock to uphold the law and protect the black students integrating Central High School. And, perhaps most importantly, he appointed federal judges at every level who steadfastly stood behind the historic school desegregation ruling.

EARL WARREN IS CONSIDERED by most constitutional historians to be one of the greatest chief justices in American history. His high place is remarkable since he lacked the obvious attributes of other chief justices in that lofty category. No one could mistake a Warren opinion for that of the magisterial Chief Justice John Marshall, whose brilliance was evident on virtually every page of his seminal opinions. Nor did Warren possess the sophisticated command of constitutional law exhibited by Chief Justices Charles Evans Hughes. How, then, could historians place Warren in such distinguished company?

One of Warren's most important contributions to the nation as Chief Justice of the United States was symbolic. He was the very personification of honesty, decency, and fairness. His mere presence on the U.S. Supreme Court was a reassuring sign to ordinary Americans that justice would be done. His persistent inquiry of lawyers—"But is it fair?"—was not easily evaded. And that elemental sense of fairness pervaded his opinions: outlawing public school segregation in *Brown;* upholding the rights of witnesses bullied by congressional investigative committees; assuring city dwellers that their votes would count equally with those living in rural areas; and expanding constitutional protections for poor criminal defendants.

The key to Warren's leadership on the court was first revealed in the justices' conference discussion on *Brown* in December 1953, when his moral condemnation of the official practice of racial segregation could not be ignored by his colleagues, most of whom had a firmer grasp of constitutional doctrine than the new chief justice. His stated premise—that forced racial segregation in the public schools was both unconstitutional and wrong—ultimately carried the day. And when it was time to bring all nine justices together for a unanimous opinion, no one could have performed the task with more grace and political acumen than Warren.

Brown was just the first of many historic Warren Court decisions expanding civil rights and liberties. How did Warren, the moderate politician in California, become the renowned liberal activist chief justice? Warren himself may have provided the best explanation in his conversation with Eisenhower on Air Force One in 1965 that he recounted in his memoirs. He told the former president that politicians were expected to compromise to get results. But the standard for judges, especially those on the U.S. Supreme Court, was principle, not expedience. As a new member of the court, his caution was not unusual. But as he became more confident in his leadership role, he pushed aggressively for an expansion of civil rights and liberties, based on his broad reading of the Constitution.

Many of Warren's critics, including Eisenhower, considered his most controversial opinions inappropriately activist. Undoubtedly, those opinions broke new judicial ground, but that did not mean that they were outside the constitutional canon. *Brown* jolted the status quo. But who would now argue that Warren was wrong to declare that the law separating public school students by race violated the Equal Protection Clause? His defense of the civil liberties of suspected subversives occurred during the age of McCarthyism more than fifty years ago, but the core issue, protecting individual rights in a time of national anxiety, resonates during the Trump presidency. His majority opinion calling for redistricting of a malapportioned state legislature is today settled precedent. And while his *Miranda* opinion for the court expanding the rights of poor criminal defendants was denounced by conservative judges and politicians alike, that decision is still the law fifty years later.

Warren offered this defense of his opinions: "I have heard a great many people say to me, 'Well, I agree with your opinions on these civil rights, all right, but don't you think you are going too fast?' Of course, the answer to that is 'We haven't anything to say about how fast we go.' We go with the cases that come to us, and when they come to us with a question of human liberties involved in them, we either hear them and decide them, or we let them go and sweep them under the rug, only to leave them for future generations."[54]

What Chief Justice Warren lacked in subtlety and institutional humility, he compensated for with a broad vision of the Constitution's protections. With bold judicial thrusts, he expanded civil rights and liberties regardless of an individual's race or class. Americans accepted the most important decisions of the Warren Court because, deep down, they knew those decisions were right. The Chief Justice told them so.

ACKNOWLEDGMENTS

This book began with the enthusiastic support of my superb agent, Esther Newberg. I have been privileged to have had Esther's wise counsel for more than thirty years. At Liveright, I was fortunate to have my manuscript carefully edited by Will Menaker and Katie Henderson Adams and was assisted at every stage of the publishing process by Gina Iaquinta.

The professional staff at three institutions were essential to the completion of this book. The librarians at New York Law School under the capable leadership of Camille Broussard responded efficiently to my seemingly endless requests. Bill Mills, my longtime library liaison, supervised the project with his usual competence and good humor. The research staff at the Manuscript Division of the Library of Congress dealt with my research needs, as with my previous books, with high professionalism. At the Eisenhower Library in Abilene, Kansas, the entire staff was courteous and helpful. The archivists served as both guides and experts on that superb collection. In particular, I would like to thank Kevin Bailey, Mary Burtzloff, and Kathy Struss for their advice and assistance. In addition, Franz Jantzen and Fred Schilling in the Office of the Curator at the Supreme Court of the United States were extremely helpful in the selection of photos for the book.

Dean Anthony Crowell at New York Law School supported my research needs throughout the project. Professor Michelle Zierler supervised the selection of my outstanding research assistants. Those researchers were Stephanie Drotar, Alina Slabodkina, Lacey Garner, Abbey Gauger, Sarah Close, and Andrew Weisberg. All did superb work in responding to my numerous requests.

I was fortunate to call upon three outstanding scholars to read the manuscript and offer critical commentary, although, of course, I alone am responsible for the published work. They are: David A. Nichols, an authority on the Eisenhower presidency; Edward Purcell, Jr., Joseph Solomon Distinguished Professor of Law, New York Law School; and G. Edward White, David and Mary Harrison Distinguished Professor of Law, University of Virginia School of Law. As with my previous books, my greatest debt is to my family, Sara and Keith More, Lauren and Tom Irwin, David and Lara Simon, and their wonderful children (my grandchildren: Justin and Ryan More; Lindsay and Natalie Irwin; Aaron, Audrey, and Ethan Simon) who provided joy and love during the long process of writing this book. Keith More and David Simon also served as my savvy computer experts, coming to my rescue more times than I can count. Finally, my thanks to Marcia, my life's companion, who, besides offering her love and support, read the manuscript with a keen editor's eye and a poet's heart.

NOTES

The bibliography on Eisenhower and Warren is immense and too great to reproduce here. I have limited the source notes to primary source materials and the basic secondary works that I have used. Eisenhower's private papers and public speeches, statements, and transcribed press conferences are available in his presidential library at Abilene, Kansas. Eisenhower wrote four volumes of autobiography: *Crusade in Europe* (1949); *Mandate for Change, 1953–1956: The White House Years* (1963), *Waging Peace, 1956–1961: The White House Years* (1965), and *At Ease: Stories I Tell My Friends* (1967). Warren's papers as chief justice are available at the Library of Congress. His memoirs, *The Memoirs of Earl Warren*, were published in 1977.

The source notes are, for the most part, self-explanatory. I have used acronyms to identify frequently cited sources. U.S. Supreme Court decisions follow legal methods of citation: *Brown v. Board of Education,* 347 U.S. 483 (1954) means that the Supreme Court decided the case in 1954 and the decision begins at page 483 of volume 347 of the *U.S. Reports.*

Abbreviations Used

DDEAE, Eisenhower, Dwight D., *At Ease: Stories I Tell My Friends*
DDECE, Eisenhower, Dwight D., *Crusade in Europe*

DDEMC, Eisenhower, Dwight D., *Mandate for Change*

DDEWP, Eisenhower, Dwight D., *Waging Peace*

DDEP, Papers of Dwight D. Eisenhower, Eisenhower Library, Abilene, Kansas

EWM, Warren, Earl, *The Memoirs of Earl Warren*

EWP, Papers of Chief Justice Earl Warren, Library of Congress

FFPLC, Papers of Justice Felix Frankfurter, Library of Congress

FFPHLS, Papers of Justice Felix Frankfurter, Harvard Law School

HBP, Papers of Justice Harold H. Burton, Library of Congress

WBP, Papers of Justice William J. Brennan, Jr., Library of Congress

EPIGRAPHS

1. Dwight D. Eisenhower to Brigadier General Bradford G. Chynoweth, July 20, 1954, DDEP.
2. EWM, p. 6.
3. Ambrose, Stephen E., *Eisenhower*, Vol. 2, *The President* (1984), p. 190.

PROLOGUE

1. DDE press conference, September 30, 1953, DDEP.
2. EWM, p. 291.
3. Ibid.
4. *Brown v. Board of Education* [*Brown I*], 347 U.S. 483 (1954).
5. *Brown v. Board of Education* [*Brown II*], 349 U.S. 294 (1955).
6. EWM, p. 5.

Chapter One MAN OF THE WEST

1. *Time*, January 31, 1944.
2. Ibid.
3. EWM, p. 14.
4. Ibid., p. 22.
5. Newton, Jim, *Justice for All: Earl Warren and the Nation He Made* (2006), p. 22.
6. Ibid., p. 25.
7. EWM, p. 36.

8. Ibid., p. 42.

9. Ibid., p. 43.

10. Ibid., p. 44.

11. Ibid., p. 57.

12. Ibid., p. 61.

13. *Oakland Tribune*, September 20, 1931.

14. EWM, p. 86.

15. *San Francisco Examiner*, August 29, 1936.

16. *San Francisco Chronicle*, September 1, 1936.

17. *San Francisco Examiner*, November 28, 1941.

18. EWM, p. 126.

19. White, G. Edward, *Earl Warren: A Public Life* (1982), p. 64.

20. Ibid.

21. Ibid., p. 66.

22. Weaver, John D. *Warren: The Man, the Court, the Era* (1968), p. 105.

23. Ibid., p. 109.

24. White, p. 73.

25. Ibid., p. 78.

26. Newton, p. 157.

27. Ibid., p. 167.

28. EWM, p. 192.

29. Ibid., p. 194.

30. Warren's address, *Vital Speeches of the Day*, July 15, 1944, pp. 538–42.

31. *Los Angeles Times*, October 15, 1944.

32. Ibid., November 4, 1944.

Chapter Two SUPREME COMMANDER

1. D'Este, Carlo, *Eisenhower: A Soldier's Life* (2002), p. 467.

2. DDECE, p. 250.

3. Atkinson, Rick, *The Guns at Last Light: The War in Western Europe, 1944–1945* (2013), p. 36.

4. Eisenhower, David, *Eisenhower: At War, 1943–1945* (1986), p. 252.

5. DDECE, p. 252.

6. DDEAE, p. 76.

7. *New York Times*, July 19, 2014.

8. DDEAE, p. 41.

9. Ibid.

10. DDEAE, p. 8.

11. Holt, Daniel D., and James W. Leyerzapf, eds., *Eisenhower: The Prewar Diaries and Selected Papers, 1905–1941* (1998), p. 243; see also Ferrell, Robert H., *The Eisenhower Diaries* (1981).

12. Holt and Leyerzapf, p. 249.

13. Ibid., pp. 254, 256.

14. Ibid., p. 411.

15. Ibid., p. 491.

16. Lyon, Peter, *Eisenhower: Portrait of a Hero* (1974), pp. 82, 83.

17. DDECE, p. 18.

18. Ibid., p. 22.

19. Ibid.

20. Smith, Jean Edward, *Eisenhower in War and Peace* (2012), p. 239.

21. Atkinson, Rick, *An Army at Dawn: The War in North Africa, 1942–1943* (2002), p. 198.

22. Ibid., p. 199.

23. *Life*, February 22, 1943.

24. DDE to ME, March 2, 1943, Eisenhower, John S. D., ed., *Letters to Mamie* (1978), pp. 104–5.

25. DDECE, p. 157.

26. Ibid., p. 148.

27. Smith, p. 282.

28. DDE to GP, August 17, 1943, DDEP.

29. DDECE, p. 253.

30. Atkinson, *The Guns at Last Light*, p. 124.

31. Ambrose, Stephen E., Vol. 1, *Eisenhower: Soldier, General of the Army, President-Elect, 1890–1952* (1983), p. 318.

32. Ibid., p. 323.

33. Smith, p. 366.

34. DDECE, p. 279.

35. Smith, p. 380.

36. D'Este, p. 576.

37. Atkinson, *The Guns at Last Light*, p. 227.

38. Smith, p. 399.

39. DDECE, pp. 354, 355.

40. Nichols, David A., *A Matter of Justice: Eisenhower and the Beginning of the Civil Rights Revolution* (2007), p. 10.

41. Ambrose, Stephen E., *Eisenhower: Soldier and President* (1990), p. 174.

Chapter Three "LOYALTY COMES FIRST"

1. *New York Times*, January 7, 1947.

2. *Los Angeles Times*, October 19, 1947.

3. *Boston Globe*, February 15, 1947.

4. *New York Herald Tribune*, July 22, 1947.

5. Ibid., December 15, 1947.

6. *Los Angeles Sentinel,* November 6, 1947.

7. *Chicago Defender,* October 9, 1948.

8. *Time,* April 12, 1948.

9. *Washington Post,* May 30, 1948.

10. DDEAE, p. 390.

11. *New York Times,* June 22, 1945.

12. DDECE, p. 444.

13. Ibid., p. 443.

14. *New York Times,* August 15, 1945.

15. DDE to LF, January 22, 1948, DDEP.

16. Senate Armed Services Committee hearing, April 3, 1948; committee transcript, pp. 995–98.

17. Ibid.

18. Ibid.

19. Ibid.

20. *Amsterdam News,* April 17, 1948.

21. Ibid., April 11, 1948.

22. DDE to WW, July 4, 1944, DDEP.

23. *New York Herald Tribune,* May 13, 1948.

24. O'Dwyer statement, undated, DDEP.

25. DDE to RT, September 10, 1948, DDEP.

26. *New York Times Magazine,* April 18, 1948.

27. *Time,* June 21, 1948.

28. Ibid., September 27, 1948.

29. Ibid.

30. White, G. Edward, *Earl Warren: A Public Life* (1982), p. 135.

31. *Los Angeles Times,* November 5, 1948.

32. DDEAE, p. 341.

33. McCullough, David, *Truman* (1992), p. 633.

34. DDE to JR, July 8, 1948, DDEP.

35. Smith, Jean Edward, *Eisenhower in War and Peace* (2012), p. 474.

36. Ibid., p. 475.

37. *New York Times,* October 13, 1948.

38. Roberts interview, September 29, 1968, Columbia Oral History Collection.

39. Gardner, David P., *The California Oath Controversy* (1967), p. 25. See also Stewart, George R., *The Year of the Oath: The Fight for Academic Freedom at the University of California* (1971).

40. Gardner, p. 14.

41. Ibid., p. 61.

42. Ibid., p. 82.

43. *San Francisco Chronicle,* February 25, 1950.

44. Gardner, p. 125.

45. Ibid., p. 145.

46. Ibid., p. 158.
47. *Oakland Tribune*, October 4, 1950.
48. Gardner, p. 220.
49. EWM, p. 218.
50. DDE to PJ, March 18, 1950, DDEP.
51. Freeman, I. H., "Eisenhower of Columbia," *New York Times Magazine,* November 7, 1948.
52. For Eisenhower's early tenure at Columbia, see, generally, Jacobs, Travis B., *Eisenhower at Columbia* (2001); also Freeman, *New York Times Magazine*, November 7, 1948.
53. DDEAE, p. 356.
54. DDE to HST, November 18, 1948, DDEP.
55. DDE to JF, November 4, 1948, DDEP.
56. Frank, Jeffrey, *Ike and Dick: Portrait of a Strange Political Marriage* (2013), p. 19.
57. *Washington Post*, October 19, 1950.
58. DDE diary, October 13, 1950, DDEP.
59. *New York Times*, October 15, 1950.
60. EWM, p. 249.

Chapter Four EYES ON THE WHITE HOUSE

1. DDEAE, p. 361.
2. Ibid., p. 371.
3. Ibid., p. 372.
4. Ibid.
5. Ambrose, Stephen E., *Eisenhower*, Vol. 1, *Soldier, General of the Army, President-Elect* (1983), p. 505.
6. Ibid., p. 502.
7. DDE address, June 6, 1951, DDEP.
8. WC to DDE, July 5, 1951, DDEP; see also DDEAE, p. 376.
9. DDEAE, p. 373.
10. DDEMC, p. 18.
11. *New York Herald Tribune*, October 25, 1951.
12. WR to DDE, October 26, 1951, DDEP.
13. DDE to WR, October 31, 1951, DDEP.
14. Halberstam, David, *The Fifties* (1993), p. 209.
15. Ambrose, *Eisenhower* 1, p. 516; see also Smith, Jean Edward, *Lucius D. Clay: An American Life* (1990), p. 588.
16. LC to DDE, September 29, 1951, DDEP.
17. DDE to LC, October 3, 1951, DDEP.
18. Smith, p. 586.
19. McCullough, David, *Truman* (1992), p. 888.
20. Ibid.

21. *New York Times*, January 7, 1952.

22. Ibid., January 8, 1952.

23. Ibid., January 11, 1952.

24. Ibid., February 8, 1952.

25. DDE to LC, February 9, 1952, DDEP.

26. Cochran interview, DDEP.

27. *Washington Post*, October 19, 1950.

28. Newton, Jim, *Justice for All: Earl Warren and the Nation He Made* (2006), p. 231.

29. Cray, Ed, *Chief Justice: A Biography of Earl Warren* (1997), p. 209.

30. *Los Angeles Times*, August 31, 1950.

31. Cray, p. 209.

32. Katcher, Leo, *Earl Warren: A Political Biography* (1967), pp. 255, 256.

33. *Los Angeles Times*, May 28, 1950.

34. Ibid., September 13, 1950.

35. Ibid., November 4, 1950.

36. Katcher, p. 262.

37. Korda, Michael, *Ike: An American Hero* (2007), p. 648.

38. Katcher, p. 261.

39. *New York Times*, November 15, 1951.

40. Ibid.

41. Ibid.

42. Newton, p. 240.

43. *Boston Sun*, February 13, 1951.

44. *Chicago Defender*, October 20, 1951.

45. *Baltimore Sun*, April 21, 1952.

46. *Pittsburgh Courier*, April 19, 1952.

47. DDE to LC, May 20, 1952, DDEP.

48. EWM, p. 253.

49. Newton, p. 245.

50. Smith, Jean Edward, *Eisenhower in War and Peace* (2012), p. 522; see also Smith, Richard Norton, *Thomas E. Dewey and His Times* (1982), p. 584.

51. EWM, p. 251.

52. HST to DDE, April 6, 1952, DDEP.

53. Lyon, Peter, *Eisenhower: Portrait of the Hero* (1974), p. 439.

54. *New York Times*, June 6, 1952.

55. EWM, p. 252.

56 Ibid., p. 250.

57. *New York Times*, July 10, 1952.

58. Smith, *Eisenhower in War and Peace*, p. 520.

59. DDE address, July 11, 1952, DDEP.

60. DDEMC, p. 50.

61. Smith, *Eisenhower in War and Peace*, p. 527.

62. *New York Herald Tribune*, August 22, 1952.

63. DDEMC, p. 55.

64. *New York Times*, September 3, 1952.

65. Ibid.

66. Ibid., September 4, 1952.

67. Ibid.

68. *New York Times*, September 9, 1952.

69. *New York Times*, October 26, 1952.

70. Ibid., September 10, 1952.

71. Parmet, Herbert S., *Eisenhower and the American Crusades* (1972), p. 128.

72. Hughes, Emmet John, *The Ordeal of Power: A Political Memoir of the Eisenhower Years* (1963), p. 41.

73. Ibid., p. 42.

74. *New York Times*, October 4, 1952.

75. *Los Angeles Times*, October 28, 1952.

76. *New York Herald Tribune*, September 19, 1952.

77. Lyon, p. 496.

78. *Los Angeles Times*, September 20, 1952.

79. Frank, Jeffrey, *Ike and Dick: Portrait of a Strange Political Marriage* (2013), p. 47; see also Gelman, Irwin F., *The President and the Apprentice: Eisenhower and Nixon, 1952–1961* (2015), pp. 39, 40.

80. Frank, p. 47.

81. *New York Times*, September 24, 1952.

82. EWM, p. 260.

83. Ibid.

Chapter Five "To My Mind, He Is a Statesman"

1. For background on the five lawsuits in *Brown v. Board of Education*, see generally, Kluger, Richard, *Simple Justice: The History of Brown v. Board of Education and Black America's Struggle for Equality* (1975); Schwartz, Bernard, *Super Chief: Earl Warren and His Supreme Court—A Judicial Biography* (1983), pp. 72–127.

2. *Time*, December 22, 1952.

3. *New York Times*, February 7, 1952.

4. Ibid., September 30, 1952.

5. *Vital Speeches of the Day*, October 15, 1952.

6. *Norfolk Journal and Guide*, October 4, 1952.

7. Oral arguments in *Brown*, Friedman, Leon, ed., *Argument: The Oral Argument Before the Supreme Court in Brown v Board of Education of Topeka, 1952–1955* (1969).

8. Urofsky, Melvin I., "Among the Most Humane Moments in All Our History": Brown v. Bd. of Education in Historical Perspective, in *Black, White and Brown: The Landmark School Desegregation Case in Retrospect*, Cushman, Clare, and Melvin I. Urofsky, eds., (2004), p. 21.

9. *Los Angeles Times*, December 16, 1952.

10. *Boston Globe*, December 17, 1952.

11. DDE State of the Union, February 2, 1953, DDEP.

12. *Washington Post*, March 11, 1953.

13. DDE press conference, March 19, 1953, DDEP.

14. *New York Times*, March 26, 1953.

15. *Washington Post*, March 27, 1953.

16. *District of Columbia v. John R. Thompson, Inc.*, 346 U.S. 100 (1953).

17. *Atlanta World*, June 11, 1953.

18. *New York Herald Tribune*, June 12, 1953.

19. For Eisenhower's civil rights initiatives, see generally, Nichols, David A., *A Matter of Justice: Eisenhower and the Beginning of the Civil Rights Revolution* (2007).

20. Frankfurter memo, May 27, 1953, FFPLC.

21. DDE to JB, August 14, 1953, DDEP.

22. DDE diary, July 24, 1953, DDEP.

23. Ibid.

24. Ibid.

25. Ibid.

26. DDE to JB, August 14, 1953, DDEP.

27. Ibid.

28. JB to DDE, August 27, 1953, DDEP.

29. DDE to RN, August 15, 1953, DDEP.

30. JB to DDE, August 27, 1953, DDEP.

31. DDE to RN, September 4, l953, DDEP.

32. DDE to files, August, 19, 1953, DDEP.

33. Ibid.

34. Kluger, p. 659.

35. EWM, p. 260.

36. DDEMC, p. 228.

37. DDE to ME, September 11, 1953, DDEP.

38. YBS to DDE, September 11, 1953, DDEP.

39. DDE to YBS, September 14, 1953, DDEP.

40. EE to DDE, September 16, 1953, DDEP.

41. DDE to EE, September 22, 1953, DDEP.

42. EWM, p. 270.

43. Brownell, Herbert, *Advising Ike: The Memoirs of Attorney General Herbert Brownell* (1993), pp. 167, 168.

44. Nichols, p. 57.

45. DDE press conference, September 30, 1953, DDEP.

46. EE to DDE, September 28, 1953, DDEP.

47. DDE to EE, October 1, 1953, DDEP.

48. DDE diary, October 8, 1953, DDEP.

49. Ibid.

50. *New York Times*, October 6, 1953.

51. HB to sons, Hugo Jr. and Sterling, October 15, 1953, Black Papers, Library of Congress.

52. Notes on DDE phone calls, November 16, 1953, DDEP.

53. *Washington Post*, November 15, 1953.

54. *Chicago Tribune*, November 28, 1953.

55. *Baltimore Sun*, November 28, 1953.

56. DDE to JB, December 1, 1953, DDEP.

57. Ibid.

58. *Brown*, December 7–9, 1953, see Friedman, *supra*, note 7.

59. Conference notes, December 12, 1953, HBP.

60. Ibid.

61. Ibid.

62. Ibid.

63. Ibid.

64. Ibid.

65. Ibid.

Chapter Six A LIST OF 205 COMMUNISTS

1. DDEMC, p. 95.

2. Halberstam, David, *The Fifties* (1993), p. 69.

3. Goldman, Eric F., *The Crucial Decade: America, 1945–1955* (1956), p. 174.

4. Halberstam, p. 85.

5. Ibid., p. 86.

6. Ibid., p. 113.

7. Goldman, p. 204.

8. Ibid.

9. Ibid., p. 208.

10. Ibid., p. 199.

11. *New York Times*, December 15, 1952.

12. DDE diary, June 30, 1950, DDEP.

13. Thomas, Evan, *Ike's Bluff: President Eisenhower's Secret Battle to Save the World* (2012), p. 71.

14. Ibid.

15. Ibid., p. 72.

16. DDEMC, p. 181.

17. DDE press conference, April 2, 1953, DDEP.

18. Ambrose, Stephen E., *Eisenhower*, Vol. 2, *The President* (1984), p. 97.

19. Ibid.

20. Eisenhower address, July 27, 1953, DDEP.

21. Korda, Michael, *Ike: An American Hero* (2007), p. 678.

22. Goldman, p. 137.

23. Ibid.

24. Ibid., p. 138.

25. Spillane, Mickey, *One Lonely Night* (1951), p. 208.

26. Goldman, p. 101.

27. DDE diary, April 1, 1953, DDEP.

28. Ambrose, *Eisenhower* 2, p. 59.

29. Smith, Jean Edward, *Eisenhower in War and Peace* (2012), p. 586.

30. DDE press conference, March 26, 1953, DDEP.

31. DDE diary, April 1, 1953, DDEP.

32. *New York Times*, February 27, 1953.

33. DDE press conference, February 25, 1953, DDEP.

34. DDE speech at Dartmouth, June 14, 1953, DDEP.

35. DDE press conference, June 17, 1953, DDEP.

36. *St. Petersburg Times*, June 18, 1953.

37. Eisenhower statement, June 19, 1953, DDEP.

38. Newton, Jim, *Eisenhower: The White House Years* (2011), p. 96.

39. Ambrose, *Eisenhower* 2, p. 83.

40. DDE to CM, June 10, 1953, DDEP.

41. DDE to JE, June 16, 1953, DDEP.

42. DDE to HB, November 4, 1953, DDEP.

43. Ibid.

44. Greenstein, Fred I., *The Hidden-Hand Presidency: Eisenhower as Leader* (1982), p. 184.

45. Halberstam, p. 54.

46. Smith, p. 591.

47. Ibid.

48. Greenstein, p. 200.

49. DDE press conference, March 24, 1954, DDEP.

50. *Smith,* p. 593.

51. Ibid.

52. *New York Times,* June 10, 1954.

53. Newton, p. 153.

54. DDE to PH, March 9, 1954, DDEP.

Chapter Seven "THIS IS A DAY THAT WILL LIVE IN GLORY"

1. *Plessy v. Ferguson*, 163 U.S. 537 (1896).

2. FF to EW, undated, EWP.

3. FF memo, January 15, 1954, FFPLC.

4. Conference notes, January 16, 1954, FFPHLS.

5. Ibid.
6. Ibid.
7. EWM, p. 291.
8. DDE to JWD, January 18, 1954, DDEP.
9. EWM, p. 291.
10. DDE diary, July 24, 1953, DDEP.
11. Ewald, William B., Jr., *Eisenhower the President: Crucial Days* (1981), pp. 81, 82.
12. Brownell, Herbert, *Advising Ike: The Memoirs of Attorney General Herbert Brownell* (1993), p. 174.
13. Ewald, p. 82.
14. Kluger, Richard, *Simple Justice: The History of Brown v. Board of Education and Black America's Struggle for Equality* (1975), p. 693.
15. Ibid., p. 694.
16. *Missouri ex rel. Gaines v. Canada*, 305 U.S. 337 (1938).
17. *Sweatt v. Painter*, 339 U.S. 629 (1950).
18. *McLaurin v. Oklahoma State Regents* 339 U.S. 637 (1950).
19. *New York Times*, March 4, 1954.
20. *Irvine v. California*, 347 U.S. 128 (1954).
21. *Barsky v. Board of Regents*, 347 U.S. 442 (1954).
22. Slater, Jack, *Ebony*, May 1974.
23. *Brown v. Board of Education* I, 347 U.S. 483 (1954).
24. *Bolling v. Sharpe*, 347 U.S. 497 (1954).
25. Kluger, p. 702.
26. Ibid.
27. Ibid., p. 701.
28. *New York Times*, May 18, 1954.
29. Ibid.
30. Kluger, p. 712.
31. EWM, p. 286.
32. *Time*, May 18, 1954.
33. *New York Times*, May 18, 1954.
34. *Los Angeles Times*, May 18, 1954.
35. Ibid.
36. Kluger, p. 713.
37. Lomax, Louis, *The Negro Revolt* (1962), pp. 73, 74.
38. DDE press conference, May 19, 1954, DDEP.
39. Nichols, David A., *A Matter of Justice: Eisenhower and the Beginning of the Civil Rights Revolution* (2007), p. 67.
40. DDE to SH, October 23, 1954, DDEP
41. DDEMC, p. 230.
42. EWM, p. 289.
43. Ibid., p. 5.

Chapter Eight "With All Deliberate Speed"

1. EW to FF, August 6, 1954, FFPLC.

2. FF to EW, August 17, 1954, FFPLC.

3. *New York Times*, September 26, 1954.

4. Kluger, Richard, *Simple Justice: The History of Brown v. Board of Education and Black America's Struggle for Equality* (1975), p. 713.

5. EW to FF, September 27, 1954, FFPLC.

6. *Plessy v. Ferguson*, 163 U.S. 537 (1896).

7. Kramer, Victor H., "President Eisenhower's Handwritten Changes in the Brief in the School Segregation Cases: Minding the Whys and Wherefores," 9 *Minnesota Law Review* 223 (1992), p. 225.

8. DDE to SH, October 23, 1954, DDEP.

9. DDE to EE, November 8, 1954, DDEP.

10. Kramer, p. 228.

11. Ibid., p. 229.

12. *New York Times*, November 25, 1954.

13. Kramer, p. 231.

14. Kluger, p. 725.

15. Nichols, David A., *A Matter of Justice: Eisenhower and the Beginning of the Civil Rights Revolution* (2007), p. 70.

16. *New York Times*, November 16, 1954.

17. Kluger, p. 726.

18. Ibid., p. 727.

19. *New York Times*, January 12, 1955.

20. DDE to WR, March 23, 1954, DDEP

21. DDE to BGC, July 13, 1954, DDEP.

22. DDE to BGC, July 20, 1954, DDEP.

23. DDE diary, February 7, 1953, DDEP.

24. DDE to TD, October 8, 1954, DDEP.

25. DDE diary, November 20, 1954, DDEP.

26. Ibid.

27. DDE to SH, December 8, 1954, DDEP.

28. DDE diary, January 10, 1955, DDEP.

29. *Irvine v. California*, 347 U.S. 128 (1954).

30. *Peters v. Hobby*, 349 U.S. 331 (1955).

31. DDE to JMH, April 6, 1955, DDEP.

32. Kluger, p. 733.

33. Rearguments in *Brown*, April 11–14, 1955, see Friedman, Leon, editor, *Argument: The Oral Argument Before the Supreme Court in Brown v. Board of Education of Topeka, 1952–1955* (1969).

34. Kluger, pp. 733–35.

35. Frankfurter memorandum, April 14, 1955, FFPLC.

36. Conference notes, April 16, 1955, FFPHLS, HBP.

37. Kluger, p. 740.

38. Conference notes, April 16, 1955, FFPHLS, HBP.

39. Ibid.

40. Ibid.

41. Ibid.

42. Warren opinion, *Brown II, Brown v. Board of Education*, 349 U.S. 294 (1955).

43. *Virginia v. West Virginia*, 222 U.S. 17 (1911).

44. Powe, Lucas A., Jr., *The Warren Court and American Politics* (2000), p. 58.

45. *New York Times*, June 1, 1955.

46. *Miami Herald*, June 1, 1955.

47. *Louisville Courier Journal*, June 1, 1955.

48. *Raleigh News and Observer*, June 1, 1955.

49. Kluger, p. 750.

50. Ibid.

51. DDE diary, May 31, 1955, DDEP.

52. *New York Times*, June 1, 1955.

53. Ibid., June 4, 1955.

54. DDE to SH, June 4, 1955, DDEP.

55. AW notes, pre–press briefing, June 8, 1955, DDEP.

56. DDE press conference, June 8, 1955, DDEP.

57. Leuchtenburg, William E., *A Troubled Feast: American Society Since 1945* (1973), p. 93.

58. Brownell, Herbert, Jr., *Advising Ike: The Memoirs of Attorney General Herbert Brownell* (1993), p. 197.

59. HB interview, November 15, 1985, Washington University Libraries, St. Louis, Mo.

60. *New York Times*, August 29, 1955.

Chapter Nine DOUBLE-CROSSING IKE

1. DDE to SH, June 4, 1955, DDEP.

2. *New York Times*, June 30, 1955.

3. DDE to SH, June 4, 1955, DDEP.

4. Eisenhower statement at Geneva, July 21, 1955, DDEP.

5. Smith, Jean Edward, *Eisenhower in War and Peace* (2012), p. 670.

6. DDE to ME, September 12, 1955, DDEP.

7. *New York Times*, November 12, 1955.

8. Ibid., November 10, 1955.

9. Warren statement, April 15, 1955, EWP.

10. FF to EW, April 15, 1955, EWP.

11. *New York Times*, November 10, 1955.

12. Nichols, David A., *A Matter of Justice: Eisenhower and the Beginning of the Civil Rights Revolution* (2007), p. 119.

13. DDE press conference, January 25, 1956, DDEP.

14. DDE diary, January 30, 1956, DDEP.

15. Author's interview with Jerome Cohen, New York City, March 8, 2016.

16. Ambrose, *Eisenhower* 2, p. 281.

17. DDE press conference, February 29, 1956, DDEP.

18. Author's interview with Cohen, March 8, 2016.

19. Ibid.

20. Jacobs, Clyde, "The Warren Court—After Three Terms," 10 *Western Policy Quarterly* (1956), p. 942.

21. Conference notes, December 9, 1955, HBP.

22. *Griffin v. Illinois*, 351 U.S. 12 (1956).

23. Conference notes, October 21, 1955, HBP.

24. *Slochower v. Board of Education*, 350 U.S. 551 (1956).

25. *Pennsylvania v. Nelson*, 350 U.S. 497 (1956).

26. Conference notes, November 18, 1955, HBP.

27. Branch, Taylor, *Parting the Waters: America in the King Years*, 1954–63 (1988), pp. 128, 129.

28. Lewis, Anthony, *Portrait of a Decade: The Second American Revolution* (1964), 74.

29. *New York Times*, March 11, 1956.

30. Powe, Lucas A., Jr., *The Warren Court and American Politics* (2000) p. 86.

31. DDE press conference, March 14, 1956, DDEP.

32. DDE press conference, March 21, 1956..

33. DDE to BG, March 22, 1956, DDEP.

34. Ambrose, *Eisenhower* 2, p. 327.

35. DDE press conference, April 25, 1956, DDEP.

36. Ambrose, *Eisenhower* 2, p. 321; see also Gelman, Irwin F., *The President and the Apprentice: Eisenhower and Nixon 1952–1961* (2015), pp. 302–8.

37. Notes on DDE phone calls, August 19, 1956, DDEP.

38. Hughes, Emmet John, *The Ordeal of Power: A Political Memoir of the Eisenhower Years* (1963), p. 201.

39. Notes on DDE phone calls, August 19, 1956, DDEP.

40. DDE press conference, September 5, 1956, DDEP.

41. AW pre–press conference notes, September 11, 1956, DDEP.

42. Ibid.

43. DDE television broadcast, October 12, 1956, DDEP.

44. *Time*, October 8, 1956.

45. *New Yorker*, March 12, 1990.

46. Ibid.

47. *New York Times*, September 30, 1956.

48. Ibid.

49. Ibid.

50. DDE to A. Gruenther, November 2, 1956, DDEP.

51. *New York Times*, September 20, 1956.

52. Ibid., October 19, 1956.

53. *Los Angeles Times*, October 20, 1956.

54. DDE to NB, October 21, 1956, DDEP.

55. Nichols, David A., *Eisenhower 1956: The President's Year of Crisis, Suez and the Brink of War* (2011), p. 203.

56. Ibid., p. 204.

57. AW diary, October 31, 1956, DDEP.

58. DDE speech, November 1, 1956, DDEP.

59. Nichols, *Eisenhower 1956*, p.221.

60. Smith, p. 702.

61. Thomas, Evan, *Ike's Bluff: President Eisenhower's Secret Battle to Save the World* (2012), p. 228.

62. Hughes, p. 223.

63. DDE statement, November 5, 1956, DDEP.

64. Nichols, *Eisenhower 1956*, p. 247.

65. Notes on DDE-AE phone conversation, November 6, 1956, DDEP.

Chapter Ten RED MONDAY

1. Stern, Seth, and Stephen Wermiel, *Justice Brennan: Liberal Champion* (2010), p. 81.

2. Ibid., p. 93.

3. Ibid., p. 114.

4. *New York Times*, February 27, 1957.

5. *Chicago Tribune*, February 27, 1957.

6. Ibid.

7. *Jencks v. U.S.*, 353 U.S. 657 (1957).

8. Conference notes on *Jencks*, October 19, 1956, HBP.

9. *Jencks*.

10. Ibid.

11. Schwartz, Bernard, *Super Chief: Earl Warren and His Supreme Court—A Judicial Biography* (1983), 228.

12. *Wall Street Journal*, June 7, 1957.

13. Katcher, Leo, *Earl Warren: A Political Biography* (1967), p. 364.

14. Conference notes on *Watkins*, March 8, 1957, HBP.

15. *Watkins v. United States*, 354 U.S. 178 (1957).

16. *Sweezy v. New Hampshire*, 354 U.S. 234 (1957).

17. *Service v. Dulles*, 354 U.S. 363 (1957).

18. *Yates v. U.S.*, 354 U.S. 298 (1957).

19. *New York Times*, June 18, 1957.

20. *Chicago Tribune*, June 18, 1957.

21. Simon, James F., *In His Own Image: The Supreme Court in Richard Nixon's America* (1973), p. 34.

22. *Time*, July 1, 1957.

23. *Life*, July 1, 1957.

24. *Time*, July 1, 1957.

25. Stern and Wermiel, p. 128.

26. Ibid.

27. Ann Whitman diary, June 21, 1957, DDEP.

28. DDE to EW, June 21, 1957, DDEP.

29. DDE press conference, June 26, 1957, DDEP.

30. EW to DDE, July 15, 1957, DDEP.

31. EWM, p. 5.

32. Warren-Eisenhower conversation on Air Force One, EWM, pp. 5, 6.

33. DDE State of the Union, January 10, 1957, DDEP.

34. Lewis, Anthony, *Portrait of a Decade: The Second American Revolution* (1964), p. 46.

35. RW to DDE, January 10, 1957, DDEP.

36. MLK to DDE, January 11, 1957, DDEP.

37. MLK to DDE, February 14, 1957, DDEP.

38. *New York Times*, February 8, 1957.

39. DDE press conference, February 6, 1957, DDEP.

40. Caro, Robert A., *The Years of Lyndon Johnson*, Vol. 4, *The Passage of Power* (2012), p. 3.

41. Notes on DDE-LBJ phone conversation, June 15, 1957, DDEP.

42. Ibid.

43. DDE speech at Williamsburg, June 24, 1957, DDEP.

44. Russell speech, July 2, 1957, *Congressional Record-Senate*, pp.10771–75.

45. AW pre–press conference notes, July 3, 1957, DDEP.

46. DDE press conference, July 3, 1957, DDEP.

47. Notes on DDE call to HB, July 3, 1957, DDEP.

48. Notes on legislative meeting, July 9, 1957, DDEP.

49. Ibid.

50. AW diary, July 10, 1957, DDEP.

51. Ibid.

52. Notes on legislative meeting, July 30, 1957, DDEP.

53. Ibid., July 16, 1957, DDEP.

54. DDE press conference, July 16, 1957, DDEP.

55. DDE to SH, July 22, 1957, DDEP.

56. Brownell, Herbert, *Advising Ike: The Memoirs of Attorney General Herbert Brownell* (1993), p. 225.

57. *Washington Post*, July 28, 1957.

58. DDE to JB, July 23, 1957, DDEP.

59. Ibid.

60. Ibid.

61. *New York Times*, August 2, 1957.

62. Notes on cabinet meeting, August 2, 1957, DDEP.

63. DDE press release, August 2, 1957, DDEP.

64. DDE to BW, undated, DDEP.

65. Notes on legislative meeting, August 13, 1957, DDEP.

66. Ibid.

67. AW pre–press conference notes, August 21, 1957, DDEP.

68. DDE press conference, August 21, 1957, DDEP.

69. Notes on phone call, LBJ to DDE, August 23, 1957, DDEP.

70. Notes on DDE phone calls, August 23, 1957, DDEP.

Chapter Eleven LITTLE ROCK

1. Halberstam, David, *The Fifties* (1993), p. 668.

2. Ibid., p. 671.

3. Ibid.

4. Ann Whitman diary, September 3, 1957, DDEP.

5. DDE press conference, September 3, 1957, DDEP.

6. Ibid.

7. Ibid.

8. *New York Times*, September 5, 1957; see also Brownell, Herbert, *Advising Ike: The Memoirs of Attorney General Herbert Brownell* (1993), pp.206, 207.

9. *New York Times*, September 5, 1957.

10. Halberstam, p. 674.

11. Ibid., p. 675.

12. Ibid.

13. *New York Times*, September 5, 1957.

14. OF to DDE, September 4, 1957, DDEP.

15. Ibid.

16. DDE to OF, September 5, 1957, DDEP.

17. Faubus telegram, September 11, 1957, DDEP.

18. Notes on DDE-HB phone call, September 11, 1957, DDEP.

19. Notes on DDE-SA phone call, September 11, 1957, DDEP.

20. Faubus telegram, September 11, 1957, DDEP.

21. Halberstam, p. 686.

22. Adams, Sherman, *Firsthand Report: The Story of the Eisenhower Administration* (1961), p. 351.

23. DDE statement, September 14, 1957, DDEP.

24. OF statement, September 14, 1957, DDEP.

25. AW diary, September 14, 1957, DDEP.

26. DDE notes, October 8, 1957, DDEP.

27. Ibid.

28. Nichols, *A Matter of Justice: Eisenhower and the Beginning of the Civil Rights Revolution* (2007), p. 180.

29. *New York Times*, September 16, 1957.

30. Halberstam, p. 687.

31. Notes on SA phone call, September 19, 1957, DDEP.

32. Notes on DDE-HB phone calls, September 20, 1957, DDEP.

33. DDE statement, September 21, 1957, DDEP.

34. *Washington Post*, September 24, 1957.

35. Newspaper articles, September 12 and 13, 1957, DDEP.

36. DDE statement, September 23, 1957, DDEP.

37. WWM to DDE, September 24, 1957, DDEP.

38. Notes on DDE-HB phone calls, September 24, 1957, DDEP.

39. Eisenhower draft, September 24, 1957, DDEP.

40. DDE to AG, September 24, 1957, DDEP.

41. DDE speech, September 24, 1957, DDEP.

42. RR to DDE, September 26, 1957, DDEP.

43. *New York Times*, September 27, 1957.

44. JE to DDE, September 26, 1957, DDEP.

45. Ambrose, *Eisenhower* 2, p. 420.

46. *New York Times*, September 27, 1957.

47. Ibid., September 26, 1957.

48. Beals, Melba P., *Warriors Don't Cry: A Searing Memoir of the Battle to Integrate Little Rock's Central High* (1994), p. 241.

49. AW notes on DDE pre–press conference briefing, October 9, 1957, DDEP.

50. Adams, pp. 357, 358.

51. EWM, p. 290.

52. DDE to SH, November 18, 1957, DDEP.

53. DDE to JS, October 7, 1957, DDEP.

54. DDE to PD, October 3, 1957, DDEP.

55. DDE to RR, September 29, 1957, DDEP.

56. DDE to JS, October 7, 1957, DDEP.

57. DDE to RM, November 4, 1957, DDEP.

58. Halberstam, p. 425.

59. Halberstam, p, 427.

60. Morrow, E. Frederic, *Forty Years A Guinea Pig* (1980), p. 163.

61. DDE speech, May 12, 1958, DDEP.

62. JR to DDE, May 13, 1958, DDEP.

63. DDE to JR, June 4, 1958, DDEP.

64. JR to DDE, June 10, 1958, DDEP.

65. MLK to DDE, May 29, 1958, DDEP.

66. African-American leaders' statement, June 23, 1958, DDEP.

67. Rocco Siciliano, memo of meeting, June 24, 1958, DDEP.

68. Ibid.

69. Ibid.

70. RS to DDE, June 25, 1958, DDEP.

71. *New York Times*, June 28, 1958.

72. DDE press conference, August 27, 1958, DDEP.

73. AW pre–press conference notes, August 6, 1958, DDEP.

74. DDE memo of phone conversation with WR, August 22, 1958, DDEP.

75. Oral argument in *Cooper v. Aaron*, Kurland, Philip and Gerhard Casper, eds., *Landmark Briefs and Arguments of the Supreme Court of the United States*, Vol. 54 (1975). See also Schwartz, Bernard, *Super Chief, Earl Warren and the Supreme Court—A Judicial Biography* (1983), pp. 289–303; Simon, James F., *The Antagonists: Hugo Black, Felix Frankfurter and Civil Liberties in Modern America* (1989), pp. 227–33.

76. FF to EW, September 11, 1958, FFPLC.

77. Ibid.

78. FF to JMH, September 12, 1958, FFPHLS.

79. Author's interview with Justice William J. Brennan, Jr., Washington, D.C., November 17, 1987.

80. Brennan draft, WBP.

81. EWM, p. 298.

82. Final Brennan draft, WBP.

83. FF to WB, September 29, 1958, WBP.

84. FF to C. Burlingham, November 12, 1958, FFPLC.

85. EWM, p. 298.

86. Author's interview with Justice Brennan, November 17, 1987.

87. Harlan memorandum, October 6, 1958, WBP.

88. Brennan's comments on Frankfurter draft, WBP.

89. *Cooper v. Aaron*, 358 U.S. 1 (1958).

Chapter Twelve THE EGALITARIAN REVOLUTION

1. *Time*, July 13, 1959.

2. EWM, p. 322.

3. Ibid.

4. *New York Herald Tribune*, July 26, 1957.

5. EWM, p. 323.

6. Ibid., p. 325.

7. Ibid., p. 326.

8. Powe, Lucas A., Jr., *The Warren Court and American Politics* (2000), p. 139.

9. Ibid., p. 130.

10. Cray, Ed, *Chief Justice: A Biography of Earl Warren* (1997), p. 350.

11. Powe, p. 131.

12. For FDR's court-packing plan, see generally, Simon, James F., *FDR and Chief Justice Hughes: The President, the Supreme Court, and the Epic Battle Over the New Deal* (2012).

13. Powe, p. 132.

14. Ibid., p. 131.

15. DDE to WR, May 5, 1958, DDEP.

16. DDE press conference, April 23, 1958.

17. Caro, Robert A., *The Years of Lyndon Johnson: Master of the Senate* (2002), p. 1031.

18. Johnson's maneuvers, ibid.

19. EWM, p. 313.

20. *Trop v. Dulles*, 356 U.S. 86 (1958).

21. *Perez v. Brownell*, 356 U.S. 44 (1958).

22. *Trop.*

23. FF to JMH, May 9, 1957, FFPHLS.

24. *Trop.*

25. Notes on DDE-HB meeting, July 17, 1958, HBP.

26. Simon, James F., *In His Own Image: The Supreme Court in Richard Nixon's America* (1973), p. 175.

27. Ibid., p. 176.

28. Stewart's memory of first meeting with Warren, author's interview with Justice Stewart, Washington, D.C., September 23, 1983.

29. Ibid.

30. FF to LH, October 29, 1958, FFPLC.

31. *Uphaus v. Wyman*, 360 U.S. 72 (1959).

32. FF to WJB, January 7, 1959, FFPLC.

33. *Uphaus.*

34. *Barenblatt v. U.S.*, 360 U.S. 109 (1959).

35. Schwartz, Bernard, *Super Chief Earl Warren and His Supreme Court: A Judicial Biography* (1983), p. 326.

36. *Barenblatt.*

37. DDE statement, September 12, 1958, DDEP.

38. DDE statement, September 24, 1958, DDEP.

39. *Atlanta Constitution*, August 21, 1958.

40. RM to DDE, August 21, 1958, DDEP.

41. DDE to RM, September 3, 1958, DDEP.

42. *Washington Post*, February 5, 1969.

43. *New York Times Magazine*, September 21, 1958.

44. RM to JH, September 16, 1958, DDEP.

45. DDE to RM, October 3, 1958, DDEP.

46. *New York Times*, October 17, 1958.

47. DDE press conference after election, November 5, 1958, DDEP.

48. Ambrose, Stephen E., *Eisenhower*, Vol. 2, *The President* (1984), p. 497.

49. DDE press conference, January 21, 1959, DDEP.

50. Ibid.

51. DDE press conference, January 28, 1959, DDEP.

52. Ibid.

53. Eisenhower-Johnson meeting, AW diary, February 3, 1959, DDEP.

54. DDE to RM, February 26, 1959, DDEP.

55. DDE press conference, May 13, 1959, DDEP.

56. Dallek, Robert, *Lone Star Rising: Lyndon Johnson and His Times, 1908-1960* (1991), p. 564; Caro, p. 1034.

57. *New York Times*, April 9, 1960.

58. DDE statement, May 6, 1960, DDEP.

59. Eisenhower's convention speech, July 26, 1960, DDEP.

60. DDE press conference, August 10, 1960, DDEP.

61. DDE press conference, August 24, 1960, DDEP.

62. Ibid.

63. Leuchtenburg, William E., *A Troubled Feast: American Society Since 1945* (1973), pp. 116, 117.

64. Lewis, Anthony, *Portrait of a Decade: The Second American Revolution* (1964), p. 114.

65. Ibid., p. 115

66. Ibid.

67. Branch, Taylor, *Parting the Waters: America in the King Years, 1954–63* (1988), p. 362.

68. Ibid., p. 368.

69. Ibid., p. 374.

70. Nichols, David A., *A Matter of Justice: Eisenhower and the Beginning of the Civil Rights Revolution* (2007), p. 262.

71. Schwartz, p. 336.

72. EWM, p. 344.

73. Schwartz, pp. 337, 338.

74. *Garner v. Louisiana*, 368 U.S. 157 (1961).

75. Author's interview with Justice Stewart, September 23, 1983.

76. *Griffin v. Prince Edward County*, 377 U.S. 218 (1964).

77. *Green v. New Kent County*, 391 U.S. 430 (1968).

78. *South Carolina v. Katzenbach*, 383 U.S. 301 (1966).

79. *Colegrove v. Green*, 328 U.S. 549 (1946).

80. *Baker v. Carr*, 369 U.S. 186 (1962).

81. Powe, p. 246.

82. *Reynolds v. Sims*, 377 U.S. 533 (1964).

83. *Gideon v. Wainwright*, 372 U.S. 335 (1963).

84. *Mapp v. Ohio*, 367 U.S. 643 (1961).

85. *Miranda v. Arizona*, 384 U.S. 436 (1966).

86. Simon, James F., *In His Own Image: The Supreme Court in Richard Nixon's America* (1973), p. 49.

87. Schwartz, p. 680.

88. Ibid., pp. 680, 681.

89. Ibid., p. 681.

90. *New York Times*, June 24, 1968.

91. Simon, p. 7.

92. *Miranda* Studies, *Wall Street Journal*, December 15, 1966; *New York Times*, December 31, 1967.

93. *New York Times*, June 24, 1969.

94. Ibid.

EPILOGUE

1. McCullough, David, *Truman* (1992), p. 921.

2. Baier, Bret, *Three Days in January: Dwight Eisenhower's Final Mission* (2017), p. 243.

3. DDE address, January 17, 1961, DDEP.

4. DDE diary, April 22, 1961, Ibid..

5. Baier, p. 264.

6. DDE diary, April 22, 1961, DDEP.

7. Baier, p. 269.

8. Ibid.

9. Ibid., p. 270.

10. DDE diary, October 29, 1962, DDEP.

11. Baier, p. 272.

12. For Eisenhower's retirement, see generally, Eisenhower, David, with Julie Nixon Eisenhower, *Going Home to Glory: A Memoir of Life with Dwight D. Eisenhower, 1961–1969* (2010).

13. DDEMC, pp. 316–20.; prepublication background, Ambrose, Stephen E., *Eisenhower*, Vol. 2, *The President* (1984), p. 634.

14. DDEMC, pp. 229, 230.

15. DDEWP, p. 150.

16. Ambrose, *Eisenhower* 2, p. 190.

17. For challenge to the Ambrose quote, see Herbert Brownell, *Advising Ike: The Memoirs of Attorney General Herbert Brownell* (1993), p. 173; for criticism of Ambrose's scholarship, especially on Eisenhower and civil rights, see Gelman, Irwin F., *The President and the Apprentice: Eisenhower and Nixon 1952–1961* (2015), pp. 4–6; Rayner, Richard, "Channeling Ike," *New Yorker*, April 26, 2010; Smith, Jean Edward, *Eisenhower in War and Peace* (2012), p. 730.

18. Author's interview with David Eisenhower, Philadelphia, PA, March 2, 2017.

19. EWM, p.5.

20. Eisenhower, David, *Going Home to Glory*, pp. 104, 105.

21. Ibid., pp. 103–5.

22. Author's interview with David Eisenhower, March 2, 2017.

23. Cray, Ed, *Chief Justice: A Biography of Earl Warren* (1997), p. 368.

24. Katcher, Leo, *Earl Warren: A Political Biography* (1967), p. 419.

25. Cray, p. 369.

26. EWM, p. 351.

27. Ibid., pp. 353, 354.

28. Weaver, John D., *Warren: The Man, the Court, the Era* (1968), p. 300.

29. EWM, p. 358.

30. Ibid.

31. Caro, Robert A., *The Years of Lyndon Johnson: The Passage of Power* (2012), p. 446.

32. Katcher, p. 459.

33. Ibid.

34. *New York Herald Tribune*, September 28, 1964.

35. *Time*, October 2, 1964.

36. *New York Times*, September 28, 1964.

37. U.S. Congress House Select Committee on Assassinations, 96th Congress, 1st session, 1979.

38. Katcher, p. 466.

39. *Washington Star*, March 19, 1966.

40. Weaver, p. 336.

41. Ibid.

42. Cray, p. 515.

43. Ibid.

44. Author's telephone interview with G. Edward White, May 11, 2017.

45. Brennan, Associate Justice William J., 88 *Harvard Law Review* 1 (1974), p. 4.

46. *New York Times*, December 9, 1970.

47. Ibid., December 14, 1973.

48. *Washington Post*, May 22, 1974.

49. Pollack, Earl H., *Earl Warren: The Judge Who Changed America* (1979), p. 326.

50. Douglas, William O., *The Court Years, 1939–1975* (1980), p. 238.

51. Eisenhower, *Going Home to Glory*, p. 74.

52. Smith, Jean Edward, *Eisenhower in War and Peace* (2012), p. xii.

53. Author's interview with David Eisenhower, March 2, 2017.

54. Warren speech, 30th Annual Judicial Conference of the District of Columbia, June 2, 1969.

INDEX

About the Author

James F. Simon is dean emeritus at New York Law School. He is the author of nine books on American history, law, and politics. His books have won the American Bar Association's Silver Gavel Award and have twice been named *New York Times* Notable Books. He lives with his wife in West Nyack, New York.